Edward Gelles was born into a distinguished Jewish family in Vienna and came to England in 1938 after the Anschluss. He was educated at Balliol College, Oxford where he studied Chemistry and obtained his doctorate. After years in academic teaching and research, he has devoted his retirement to a study of European history and genealogy. His published books include *An Ancient Lineage* (2006), *Family Connections: Gelles–Horowitz–Chajes* (2008), *Gelles–Shapiro–Friedman* (2009), *Ephemeral & Eternal: Josef Gelles, a brief life* (2010), and *Meeting my Ancestors: Genealogy, Genes, and Heritage* (2011).

THE
Jewish
Journey

A PASSAGE THROUGH
EUROPEAN HISTORY

EDWARD GELLES

I.B. TAURIS

LONDON · NEW YORK

Published in 2016 by
I.B.Tauris & Co. Ltd
London • New York
www.ibtauris.com

ISBN: 978 1 78453 453 0
eISBN: 978 0 85773 978 0

A full CIP record for this book is available from the British Library
A full CIP record is available from the Library of Congress

Library of Congress Catalog Card Number: available

Typeset by Out of House Publishing
Printed and bound by CPI Group (UK) Ltd, Croydon, CR0 4YY

MIX
Paper from
responsible sources
FSC
www.fsc.org   FSC® C013604

*To the memory of my brother Ludwig Gelles, my aunt Rosa Gelles,
my cousins Josef and Giza Gelles, my grandparents
David Mendel Griffel and Chawa Wahl, and many other
relatives who perished during the Second World War*

*Seal of Kalonymos ben Todros of Narbonne c.1300 showing lion rampant
within shield with inscription in Langue d'Oc
(courtesy of Archives Municipales de Narbonne)*

Contents

CONTENTS

CONTENTS

Genealogical charts and tables

Photographs

All photos are from the author's personal collection, except where indicated.

Seal of Kalonymos ben Todros of Narbonne c. 1300
showing lion rampant within shield with inscription in
Langue d'Oc (courtesy of Archives Municipales de Narbonne)   vi

Preface

In this volume I have brought together some of my published articles with hitherto unpublished essays in order to show how a group of families belonging to the bedrock of European Jewry was intricately involved with the millennial history of our continent. In combining biography, traditional genealogy, and a contribution from the rapidly developing field of genetic genealogy, my goal has been to weave emerging patterns into the grand tapestry of European history.

The bias towards rabbis in my selected families necessarily follows from the recognition that more than a few of these rabbis provided leadership that held the Jewish people together through the Middle Ages to modern times, and that in a more secular age, many notable people can trace their ancestry back to these Jewish spiritual leaders. This group left more records of their families and communities on which historians and genealogists can draw. Many of the Ashkenazi families in my study had old Sephardic connections.

By way of introduction, I hold up a *mirror of the past* to my immediate family background and outline the connections to ancient Italy and medieval France and Spain. The following essays start with the Kalonymos of Narbonne and their Carolingian connections, and proceed across the continent of Europe in times of war and peace, golden times of cultural harmony and achievement, long periods of repression and persecution, followed by the Age of Enlightenment, the rise of nationalism and two world wars, the Holocaust, and its aftermath.

A major theme that I return to in several essays is the relationship between Jews and non-Jews through the ages. Jews got on well with the Arian Goths in Septimania (modern Languedoc) and also with the Muslims in Spain and later in the Ottoman Empire. Relations between Jews and Catholics took a turn for the worse at the time of the Crusades. Conversions, under duress or otherwise, as at the time of the Spanish Inquisition or with Jacob Frank's followers in eighteenth-century Poland, waxed and waned with the changing religious and political balance across the continent.

A sub-theme that is taken up in a couple of essays concerns the admixture of a Jewish Davidic strain with early European dynasties, which is still of genealogical interest and was for a long time of some political importance, giving newly established ruling families a claim to legitimacy by descent from the House of David and stimulating discussions of the 'divine right of kings'.

For many hundreds of years until fairly recent times, Jews mostly lived in inward-looking endogamous communities and intermarriage with Christians was suppressed, but unions of Jews and Gentiles have been noted by writers since biblical days and the time of the Roman Empire. Genetic genealogy and anthropology are now promising to give us a measure of these admixtures which are the result of decades, centuries and millennia of migrations over the Asian and European continents.

I have attempted to knit together stories of unions between Jews and Gentiles (Chapters 1, 8, 13, 17) and of migrations across Europe (Chapters 2–5, 11, 12, 16). The pan-European nature of some Jewish families is particularly exemplified in Chapter 12, as is the Jewish contribution to our common European culture in Chapter 15. Pilot studies to reconcile traditional histories of European Jewry with the results of a variety of DNA tests are described in Chapters 21–24.

These milestones of a millennial journey indicate how European Jews acquired a genetic mixture of a substantial European as well as Middle Eastern character and how they have been influenced by European culture and contributed much to it.

Acknowledgements

Many correspondents, whose names appear in the following pages, have provided valuable information including DNA test results. Their contributions are much appreciated, as were discussions with numerous friends.

My particular thanks are due to the Master of Balliol College, Oxford, Sir Drummond Bone, and to Vivian, Lady Bone, for their encouragement and continued interest in my work.

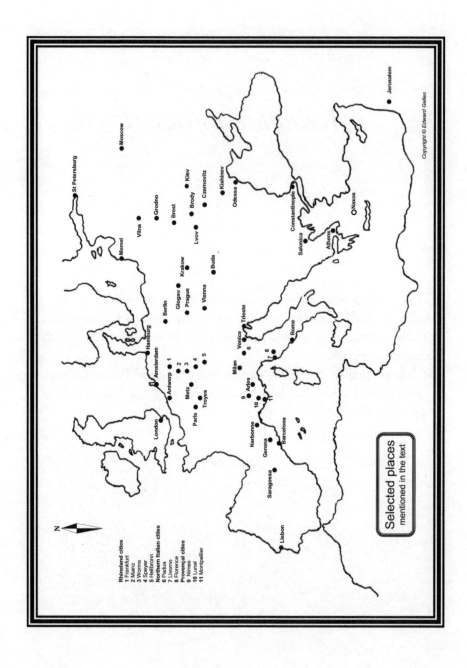

N

Rhineland cities
1 Frankfurt
2 Mainz
3 Worms
4 Speyer
5 Hellbronn
Northern Italian cities
6 Padua
7 Livorno
8 Florence
Provençal cities
9 Nîmes
10 Lunel
11 Montpellier

Selected places
mentioned in the text

Copyright © Edward Gelles

Moscow

St Petersburg

Memel

Vilna

Grodno

Brest

Brody   Kiev

Lvov   Czernowitz

Kishinev

Odessa

Constantinople

Salonica

Athens

Naxos

Jerusalem

Berlin

Glogau   Krakow

Prague

Vienna   Buda

Hamburg

Amsterdam

Antwerp   1

Metz   2
           3

London   5   4

Paris

Troyes

Milan   Venice   Trieste

           6

Arles   7   8
9
10   11

Narbonne   Rome

Gerona

Saragossa   Barcelona

Lisbon

Introduction – A mirror of the past

THIS ESSAY WAS WRITTEN as an introduction to a collection of some of my published and unpublished articles. It could also be regarded as a short account of my ancestral roots or a précis of my *oeuvre*.

The history of European Jewry can be considered in many different ways. For example, as a long journey with milestones going back to a time before the fall of Jerusalem to the Babylonians, to the great Diaspora in Roman times, to our millennial presence in Italy, in the Rhineland, on the Iberian peninsula, in France, and so on, to the great eastward migrations beginning in the period of the Crusades, to Byzantium and the Ottoman Empire, to the Austro-Hungarian Empire, Poland and the Russian Pale and, in the Age of Enlightenment, to a gradual return to the western lands where we had lived in earlier times. The period of nineteenth-century nationalism transmuted the age-old religious prejudices with the accompanying economic jealousies to one of racial intolerance, based on a now discredited pseudo-science that led ultimately to the Holocaust. Throughout this millennial odyssey, Jews had lived at times in amity with their Christian neighbours or indeed with the Muslims in Spain and elsewhere. In those days there was undoubtedly considerable intermarriage and conversion. In later times, segregation in ghettos, active persecutions and temporary or more lasting expulsions led to deeply inward-looking strictly endogamous Jewish communities.

DNA studies, including those of my own family, appear to support historical writings on the incidence of intermarriage in earlier times.

Throughout all these centuries, in the good times of Frankish Septimania, in the golden age of Spanish Jewry, or of sixteenth-century Prague, as well as in a more troubled age, there was cultural as well as economic interaction between Jews and their non-Jewish environment. Jews made great contributions to a pan-European culture and were themselves influenced by it.

The political, social, economic and cultural history of Europe is the backcloth to the tapestry of my own wider ancestral background. This background encompasses a group of ancient families forming the backbone of European Jewry, who produced the rabbis and scholars that have held the Jewish communities together since biblical times, and some of whom could look back to the time of the ancient Jewish kingdoms and to King David.

Regarding the changing interactions between Jews and Christians, much has been written about attitudes of Church and clergy, of merchant class and peasants. My essay deals briefly with the attitudes of kings and princes towards Jews of reputed Davidic descent. The very myth of descent from a divinely anointed king played a significant role at times in early medieval history as giving a legitimacy to rule 'by divine right'. There is a resonance between the boost a Davidic connection is believed to have given the Carolingian royal line in the eighth century and the attitude of the Polish nobility in the sixteenth century towards my ancestor Saul Wahl, whose ancient forebears, biblical learning and cachet of Italian Renaissance culture combined to raise him up in their counsels.

MY FAMILY BACKGROUND

My parents were born in Austrian Galicia. They came from strictly orthodox Jewish families, but brought up their children in the enlightened assimilationist atmosphere of Vienna in the 1920s. My parents still celebrated the Jewish Passover, and went to the synagogue at New Year and on the Day of Atonement, and they also observed *Jahrzeit*[1] as an act of remembrance, but estrangement from their

Photo 1 Edward Gelles in 1959 (middle) and parents in the 1920s:
Regina Griffel with Ludwig and Dr David Gelles

ultra-orthodox parents somehow cut me and my brother off from a full appreciation of our family background.

I was in my first year at one of the best schools in Vienna[2] when our comfortable sheltered world fell apart. When Hitler took over Austria in March 1938 it became apparent, at least to some, what the future held for Austrian Jewry and for Europe. We escaped to England in August of that year, but other members of our family were not so lucky. Some of them vanished without trace in the Holocaust. Those who survived the war were scattered and contacts were lost.

I emerged from World War II and an Oxford education as a British subject with interests centred on the affairs of my new country. I turned my conscious mind away from the horrors of our immediate past. It was nearly half a century later that I embarked on the quest for my ancestral roots.

In a strange way I was not ready for this personal odyssey until I had reached the age of threescore and ten. I had always thought of myself and of my cultural roots as largely European. From the days of my childhood I had been as familiar with Homer and Plutarch, and with chansons de geste, the Nibelungenlied, and Arthurian legends as with the Bible and the legends of the Jews. And my later historical reading added to the essential background for understanding two or three millennia of my ancestral past.

3

Some familiarity with the social customs of Jews in different parts of Europe and at different periods is an essential prerequisite for the study of Jewish genealogy. In particular, an understanding of Jewish names (onomastics) is fascinating in itself and can become an essential adjunct to family research.

My basic genealogical studies are described in several published books and numerous articles that contain full references and an extensive bibliography (p.332).

My paternal rabbinic line

My father, David Isaac Gelles, an advocate and doctor of law of Vienna University, was the second son of Rabbi Nahum Uri Gelles and Esther Weinstein. Nahum Uri was Chief Rabbi of Solotwina in Galicia for 50 years, in succession to his father-in-law, Rabbi Hirsch Leib Weinstein. Nahum Uri's parents were Rabbi David Isaac and Sarah Gelles (Gellis). I am a direct sixth-generation descendant of a scholar of the Brody Klaus, a famous Talmudic study group in a

Photo 2 Edward Gelles and his father Dr David Gelles

4

Photo 3 Dr Max Gellis (1897–1973) (paternal uncle)

Photo 4 Dr Lotte Gelles (1895–1984) (paternal aunt)

city which at that time had the second-largest Jewish community in
Europe (after Amsterdam).

Moses Gelles aka Levush

My ancestor was called Moses Menachem Mendel Levush but he
became known as Moses Gelles after his marriage to a daughter
of a rabbi, S(hmuel) Gelles. This was a not unusual custom in
the early eighteenth century. The name Levush suggests descent
from the sixteenth-century Rabbi Mordecai Jaffe (Yaffe, Yoffe, etc.)
of Prague, who was Chief Rabbi of Grodno, Prague and Posen,
and one of the founders of the Council of the Four Lands (the
semi-autonomous governing body of Polish Jewry), as well as the
author of a major work called *The Levushim* (Rabbinical Robes of
Learning) from which he derived the name of Levush and by which
he is known to posterity. There was a time when it was customary to
call descendants of famous authors by the title of their work.

Moses Gelles of the Brody Klaus had numerous grandsons,
including the younger Moses, who married a granddaughter of
Shmuel Helman, the Chief Rabbi of Mannheim and Metz (d.1764)
and Shmuel Gelles, who married the only daughter of the famous
Chasidic leader, Rabbi Pinchas Shapiro of Koretz (d.1791). I am a
sixth-generation descendant of Rabbi Shmuel Helman of Metz.

Mordecai Jaffe of Prague

My direct paternal line may go back from Moses Levush aka Gelles
to Mordecai Jaffe of Prague, who was perhaps the most distinguished
member of the ancient Jaffe family. They were in medieval Spain
(see, for instance, Pere Bonnin, *Sangre Judía*) before becoming
prominent in northern Italy, notably Bologna, whence they migrated
to Prague and then to points further east. The tombstones of Prague
show Jaffe and Gelles extending to the seventeenth and eighteenth
centuries and there were Gelles–Jaffe marriages in Poland and
Lithuania, including Grodno, where Mordecai Jaffe had been Chief
Rabbi. The latter spent ten years of his life in Venice, where his

6

kinswoman Abigail Jaffe was married to the Chief Rabbi Samuel Judah Katzenellenbogen. My ancestor Saul Wahl, of whom further anon, was a son of that union.

I have a separate connection to Rabbi Mordecai Yaffe via his daughter Bella and Yechiel Michel Epstein and a line of Halpern (Heilprin) rabbis to Rabbi Moshe Heilprin of Berdichev and Solotwina (d.1752). From him and his wife Mindel Katz a Kohanic line descends to Gittel HaKohen Adlersberg and her husband Zalman Berish Rottenberg Margolies of Brodshin and thence to my grandmother Esther Weinstein.

As for the Rabbi S(hmuel) Gelles, who was the father-in-law of Moses Gelles of the Brody Klaus, he might be identified with the Shmuel Gelles, Chief Rabbi of Siemiatycze, who was a descendant of Uri Feivush, the Chief Rabbi of Vilna. The latter went to the Holy Land towards the end of his life. He was made *Nasi* (Head) of the Ashkenazi community in Jerusalem and died there in the 1650s.

Gelles and Polonsky

In a published collection of legends about the founder of the eighteenth-century Chasidic movement there is a tale that Rabbi Israel ben Eliezer, the *Baal Shem Tov* (Master of the Good Name), passed a cemetery in Polonnoye (Volhynia, present-day Ukraine) when he perceived a pillar of fire above a grave. His attendant reported that it was the grave of a Tzaddik (a wholly righteous man) and that his epitaph read 'Moses, the servant of G-d'.[3] This epitaph is quoted in a monograph written by a descendant of Moses Gelles of Brody.[4]

A grandson of this Moses Gelles was Rabbi Shmuel ben Mordecai Gelles, whose progeny were known by the name of Polonsky after the town of Polonnoye. The Baal Shem Tov died in 1760 while Moses Gelles may have died a year or two earlier, possibly while on a visit to his grandson or in-laws. This Chasidic 'miracle' tale may not be unconnected with the fact that the famous Chasidic leader Rabbi Pinchas Shapiro of Koretz gave his only daughter in marriage to the grandson of Moses Gelles.

Isaac ben Abraham Chayes and Judah Loew of Prague

Mordecai Jaffe is not the only sixteenth-century Chief Rabbi of Prague amongst my ancestors. They include Isaac ben Abraham Chayes and his brother-in-law the famous Rabbi Judah Loew, who succeeded Isaac Chayes as Chief Rabbi. Isaac's half-sister Mirel Chayes-Altschuler was Judah Loew's first wife. Their daughter Voegele (Zipporah) married Isaac Katz, of a millennial sacerdotal family. Descent from this couple goes via their son Naftali Katz and Dinah Katzenellenbogen, who was a granddaughter of Saul Wahl, to Katz and Margolioth (Margolies), and so on to a Horowitz line and thence again to my grandmother Esther Weinstein.

Horowitz

The relevant Horowitz line goes back to Pinchas Halevi Ish Horowitz (Prague 1535–Krakow 1618), who was President of the Council of the Four Lands (i.e. the Head of Polish Jewry). He married a sister of Chief Rabbi Moses Isserles of Krakow. Their daughter Hinde became the wife of Rabbi Meir Wahl Katzenellenbogen, eldest son of Saul Wahl. The Halevi Horowitz family took their name from the town of *Horovice* near Prague. They are descended from the medieval Shem Tov Halevi of Gerona, who had connections with the Kalonymos *Nessiim* (Princes) of Narbonne, the Benveniste and others in the Spanish March and the area of the later Languedoc.

History of the Chayes family

The ancient Chayes family came from Portugal and some lived in Provence until a general expulsion of the Jews in the late fourteenth century. Then some of them came to Prague and a branch was called Altschuler after the name of the synagogue they helped to build there, using stones from their Provencal prayer house which they had brought with them. In later centuries the Chayes rabbinical family flourished in Galicia in the city of Brody, which at one time had one of the most important Jewish communities in Europe. The last great rabbi of their line was Zvi Perez Chajes, who was Chief Rabbi of Vienna between the two world wars. A branch of the family in Brody had established itself in Tuscany at the beginning of the nineteenth century. The merchant bank of Berenstein, Chayes & Cie flourished in Florence and they had major trade connections between Livorno and Brody. Guido Chayes was ennobled by the King of Portugal for his services as Vice-Consul in Livorno.

The family produced a world-class chess player in Oscar Chajes of Brody, the composer Julius Chajes, the distinguished Harvard Law professor Abram Chayes, and many other scholars.

Griffel of Nadworna

The Chayes story also connects to the Griffel family. My mother, Regina, was the only daughter of David Mendel Griffel and Chawa Wahl of Nadworna. Her father was the eldest of ten children of Eliezer Griffel and Sarah Matel Chajes while her mother was a daughter of Shulem Wahl and Sarah Safier of Tarnobrzeg.

The Griffel family claimed descent from David Halevi Segal, the seventeenth-century Chief Rabbi of Lwow (the Austrian

Photo 5 Edward Griffel (1904–59) (maternal uncle)

9

Lemberg now called Lviv in the Ukraine). David Halevi Segal was the son-in-law of Joel Sirkes, the Chief Rabbi of Krakow. Eliezer Griffel built up a business empire in timber and oil which gave employment to many members of his clan and to his townsfolk. He was the head of the Jewish community in Nadworna and a follower of the Chasidic rabbis of Otonia of the Hager family with whom the Griffels had a tie by marriage. My great-grandmother Sarah Matel was a daughter of Isaac Chaim and Beile Chajes of the nearby town of Kolomea.

Wahl of Tarnobrzeg

My grandmother, Chawa Wahl, came from the Wahl family of Tarnobrzeg (Dzików) in western Galicia. Her father Shulem's occupation was recorded in a town census as 'capitalist' and his father (my great-great-grandfather) Leiser Wahl and Moshe Hauser were described in an interesting book by the town's mayor, Jan Slomka, as the two richest Jews in the town (*From Serfdom to Self-Government: Memoirs of a Polish Village Mayor 1842–1917*).

Saul Wahl

Our Wahl family tradition, widely accepted by Polish Jewry, was that they were descended from Saul Wahl (1545–1617), who was the son of the Rabbi of Venice, Samuel Judah Katzenellenbogen, and the grandson of Meir Katzenellenbogen, the Chief Rabbi of Padua and founder of the great rabbinical family that came from the eponymous town in Hesse-Nassau. Saul received his education in Padua and went to Poland as a young man to study with his kinsman Rabbi Shlomo Luria. He became leader of the Jewish community in Brest and a highly successful entrepreneur. Through the patronage of Prince Radziwill, whose family was the most powerful in Lithuania, Saul gained the ear of kings and magnates, who called him Wahl, meaning 'the Italian', and in 1587, during the long interregnum leading up to the election of the Swedish Prince Sigismund Vasa to the Polish throne, he is believed to have carried out royal functions as *Rex pro tempore* when an impasse was reached in the electoral process. There is a substantial Jewish literature on his life and times and on his

Photo 6 Zygmunt Griffel (1897–1951) (maternal uncle)

pedigree but very little in the official state papers. They do indicate that the newly elected **King Zygmunt III** favoured him and that he continued to flourish under his rule. Among the many legends that have survived, one suggested that the King had an affair with Saul's daughter Hannele. She was married off to an elderly kinsman, Ephraim Zalman Shor. The potency of this legend, discussed in Chapter 8, may explain why, three centuries later, my mother and her elder brother were named Regina and Zygmunt.[5]

Saul Wahl's epithet became the family name of his descendants. The great Katzenellenbogen clan thus encompassed the Wahl families and later branches such as the Heschel and Babad families (named after Chief Rabbi Abraham Joshua Heschel of Krakow and his grandson Chief Rabbi Isaac Krakower of Brody).

Descendants of Saul Wahl

Saul Wahl's ancestry and his importance in the history of sixteenth-century Poland–Lithuania are matched by the distinction of his progeny, who included scores of rabbis and, in more recent times, the Enlightenment philosopher Moses Mendelssohn, his grandson, the composer Felix Mendelssohn-Bartholdy, Karl Marx, Martin Buber, Isaiah Berlin, Yehudi Menuhin, and many others.

In connection with my maternal grandmother's Wahl ancestry, it might be worth mentioning that the orthodox Chief Rabbi of Nadworna during the time of my great-grandparents was Rabbi Hirsch Leib Wahl, who was knowledgeable about his pedigree (*yichus*) as he revealed in letters to his relatives. He wrote about his descent from Saul Wahl and from the eleventh-century scholar Rabbi Solomon ben Isaac of Troyes, known by the acronym of Rashi. There may well have been a distant connection between my Tarnobrzeg Wahls and Rabbi Wahl of Nadworna (who was a descendant of Rabbi Ezekiel Katzenellenbogen of Hamburg, and incidentally shared with my paternal grandmother a descent from Rabbi Moshe Heilprin of Berdichev and Solotwina and a Kohanic line from Rabbi Shabbatai Katz).

My Wahl of Tarnobrzeg are, however, closely related by blood and marriage to the Wohl family of Krakow, for whose descent from Saul Wahl unpublished evidence is proffered by J. Bunford Samuel in his *Records of the Samuel Family* published in 1912.

The Samuel family and a number of related families of the Anglo–Jewish aristocracy, who established themselves in England in the eighteenth century, share some Katzenellenbogen and Halpern roots with my maternal lineage. We are descended from two children of the great Saul Wahl, namely his eldest son, Meir Wahl Katzenellenbogen, and his daughter, Hannele, and also from branches of the Halpern rabbinical line. Our common ancestors are Rabbi Moses Katzenellenbogen of Chelm, a son of Meir Wahl, and Jacob Shor, the son of Hannele Wahl. I have connections to Rabbi Saul Katzenellenbogen of Pinczow, a son of Moses of Chelm. Rabbi Saul of Pinczow married Yente, a daughter of Jacob Shor. The Samuels may also have connections with another daughter of Jacob Shor who was the wife of Benjamin ben Meir ben Moses of Chelm.

As for the Halperns stemming from Zevulon Eliezer Ashkenazi Heilprin, I have connections with several branches, including one involving my ancestor Chief Rabbi Shmuel Helman of Metz, while the Samuels go back to certain Heilprins who went for some time under the name of *Pulvermacher* (i.e. manufacturers of gunpowder) in Silesia.

In addition to these two children of Saul Wahl, Meir and Hannele, I have another son, (Samuel) Judah Wahl, amongst my forebears. The latter's daughter Dinah Katzenellenbogen married successively two great rabbis, Naftali Katz of Lublin and Abraham Joshua Heschel of Krakow. My ancestral tree encompasses descent through this Katz line (that also goes back to Rabbi Judah Loew of Prague) and from the first marriage of A. J. Heschel, who was a scion of the Katzenellenbogen line. There are also Wahl connections from later marriages between Katzenellenbogen and other ancestral families such as the Chayes.

Other rabbinical connections

The above outline of my family's descent from some of the great rabbis of the sixteenth and later centuries does not cover the larger number of more distantly related lines. The old rabbinical families are so intermarried that some sort of connection is less the exception than the rule. The story of my forebears who lived in eastern Europe in recent centuries should be seen in the context of their millennial migrations, particularly from their ancient homes in Germany to which some returned on the dawning of the Age of Enlightenment.

Davidic descent

A number of the above-mentioned families can trace their lineage back to Rashi (1040–1105). He is of the greatest importance, not only as a scholar and biblical commentator, but in Jewish genealogy as one of the three or four widely accepted links to biblical times and a possible descent from King David. The lineages of Rabbis Judah Loew of Prague and Shlomo Luria of Lublin are also central in discussions of possible Davidic descent, as are descendants of the Exilarchs of Baghdad (heads of the Jewish Community there since the days of the Babylonian captivity).

Rashi to Treves, Shapiro, Luria and Katzenellenbogen

One of my lines of descent from Rashi is via the Treves, Shapiro and Luria families, and thence to Katzenellenbogen and Wahl. The Treves (from Treves or Trier, an imperial city in Roman times) were distinguished rabbis in medieval France. From Mattityahu Treves, who was Chief Rabbi of Paris in the fourteenth century, to the Spira (Shapiro), who were originally from Speyer, and to the old Italian Luria family, we come to Jechiel Luria of Alsace, who was Chief Rabbi of Brest, where he died around 1470. His daughter married Isaac Katzenellenbogen and their son Meir Katzenellenbogen became Chief Rabbi of Padua. The latter's wife was Hannah, the granddaughter of Chief Rabbi Judah Halevi Mintz (from Mainz). Their son, Rabbi Samuel Judah Katzenellenbogen (d.1597), was known as the Rabbi of Venice. As mentioned before, he and Abigail Yaffe were the parents of Saul Wahl.

Rashi was believed to be a descendant of Johanan Ha-Sandelar of the second century AD, a fourth generation from Hillel the Babylonian, who, according to the Talmud, was a descendant of Shepatiah, son of Avital, a wife of King David (c.1040–970 BC).

Kalonymos of Narbonne

The Kalonymos of Narbonne were a branch of one of the most important Jewish families of the Middle Ages. They were *Nessiim* (Princes) of their city from the eighth to the beginning of the fourteenth century. They traced their line back to one Makhir, a descendant of Exilarchs of Davidic lineage, who came from Baghdad. Our ancestor Rashi is descended from the Makhir–Kalonymos line through his mother.

The beginnings of the Kalonymos in Narbonne go back to a time when Saracens, Visigoths and Franks contested the hegemony of Septimania and the Spanish March, and the family's rise is bound up with the fortunes of the Carolingian line from Charles Martel, his son Pepin the Short, and his grandson Charlemagne. These Carolingian connections are the subject of a following essay.

In the first millennium of our era there was intercourse between the upper classes of different ethnic backgrounds. From the time of

*Photo 7a Dr Abraham Low (1891–1954) in World War I
uniform (mother's first cousin)*

Photo 7b Reverse of postcard from Dr Abraham Low to Miss Regina Griffel

the Crusades, religious intolerance led to European Jewry becoming increasingly inward-looking and endogamous.

GENETICS, GENEALOGY AND ANTHROPOLOGY

In the past few years a variety of commercial DNA tests have become available. Some of these tests are already useful tools in backing up genealogical research, but others will have to be refined and the databases will have to grow substantially. These tests are not an easy substitute for old-fashioned traditional research. A substantial knowledge of the genealogical background is usually required before DNA tests can make a significant contribution. Fortunately, I had gained this knowledge through many years of research that went beyond my immediate family to include the families of close and more distant cousins. Since the current DNA tests are aimed at finding matches between individuals on the extant databases I came fairly well prepared to this new and increasingly important field.

The most straightforward test is perhaps the comparison of Y-DNA (which passes along the male line from father to son for hundreds of years subject to infrequent mutations). Y-DNA tests carried out by FamilyTree DNA showed a very close match between myself and Dr Jeffrey Mark Paull, of known Polonsky descent, who had contacted me after reading my first book, published in 2006. The matches of 36/37 and 65/67 markers were the closest on the database for either of us and indicated a common ancestry in the male line roughly ten generations ago. Dr Paull and I are tenth- and sixth-generation descendants, respectively, of Moses Gelles of the Brody Klaus. This was a most gratifying outcome after years of research on the 'paper trail'.

FamilyTree DNA have devised a test for comparing autosomal DNA, which can show up matches irrespective of sex on both sides of a family tree. From these matches their *Family Finder* calculates an approximate generational distance to the nearest common ancestor. While it works well for the closest of cousins, its underlying algorithms do not allow adequately for the substantial inbreeding over hundreds of years that are found in our family circle. Nevertheless, I have achieved worthwhile results in examining the autosomal DNA matches of a small group of first and second cousins and comparing these with results for some more distant relatives. An immediate dividend of this study was an enquiry from David Samuel Nir, whose tests suggested that we were second or third cousins. I was able to send him part of a family chart, published in my first book, which showed the pedigree of his father Dr Yehuda Nir. Our common ancestor is my maternal great-grandfather Eliezer Griffel. Detailed comparisons of DNA segments in the 22 chromosomes indicate the effects of inbreeding which can result, for example, in close paternal cousins also being distant maternal cousins and vice versa.

Autosomal DNA data from the *Family Finder* and from rival test providers called 23andme and Ancestry.com can be uploaded on to GEDmatch, which is a very useful and innovative website. By bringing the results from several test providers together it opens up a larger database. It allows access to X-DNA matches, which may give a different slant to ancestral research. X-DNA is passed from mother to child and from father to daughter but of course not from father to son, so it is usually quite difficult to follow back in time, but matches may throw light not only on close common ancestors but on the distant past. Thus it is not uncommon for two individuals to show scarcely any autosomal DNA match – in other words, indicate little or no consanguinity over the past few centuries – and yet show significant X-DNA matches that may relate to a distant past that is not accessible to autosomal DNA testing. Gedmatch. com also incorporates two of the three or four facilities currently available that allow family researchers access to the fascinating field of genetic anthropology by way of genetic admixture estimates from the autosomal DNA data. The methods of Dienekes Pontikos Dodecad and Davidski Eurogenes relate individual DNA data to their different bio-geographical reference groups. My immediate and distant cousins appear to have a recognisable genetic signature that relates to their distant past in the Middle East and their later presence in Europe. This is very much in line with the results of many studies of Ashkenazi Jews using Y-DNA, mitochondrial DNA and autosomal DNA comparisons that have been carried out over the past 15 years or so. A very useful précis of this work in about 50 pages is to be found on the Khazaria.com website.

This brings us back to the history of the Jewish people. In their 4,000-year odyssey from ancient Persia and Mesopotamia there have been periods of great achievement and also catastrophic times, and each must have left its mark on their genetic admixture in different ways, as did other migrations across Europe, which in our era included the expansion of Islam and the Moorish invasion of Spain, the migrations of the Goths, the rise of the Franks, the adventures of Vikings and Norsemen, and so on.

The final chapter of this volume presents some results of ongoing DNA tests which are part of a study of this admixture process.

In conclusion to this *tour d'horizon* of my work I should like to emphasise that I have tried to place the results of my genealogical research at the service of European history. Most of my material is based on primary documentation. Full references are provided, starting with my first book *An Ancient Lineage*, which also includes a useful bibliography. With so much destroyed or lost, particularly in the upheavals of recent times, there are inevitably genealogical gaps and speculative links based on circumstantial evidence, which new methods, including those of genetic genealogy, will continue to address. These lacunae are always clearly identified. Old legends and family traditions, not necessarily accepted at face value, are part of the warp and weft of any millennial history. Some of these legends are embedded in the great epics of our culture while a few, such as claims to Davidic descent and the doctrine of the divine right of kings, have had a considerable impact on European history.

NOTES

1 Lighting of a candle on the anniversary of a relative's death.
2 Real-Gymnasium1. The eight-year course led to matriculation required for entry to the university.
3 Dan Ben-Amos & Jerome R Mintz (eds), *In Praise of the Baal Shem Tov.* (Schocken Books, New York, 1970). Tale 216.
4 Rachel Sheindel, daughter of Rabbi Pinchas of Koretz, married Rabbi Shmuel, son of Mordecai son of Moses Gelles, one of the scholars of the Brody Klaus, whose epitaph refers to him as 'Moses the Servant of God'. Rabbi Levi Grossman, *Shem U' She'erith.* (Tel Aviv: 1943), p. 92.
5 My mother's Jewish name was Rebecca and my uncle Zygmunt's was Shulem (after his grandfather Shulem Wahl).

Chart 0.1 Descent from Rabbi Mordecai Jaffe of Prague

Rabbi Mordecai Yaffe of Prague "Ha Levush" (died 1612)
|
Bella m Yechiel Michel Epstein (a physician, d. 1632)
|
daughter m   Rabbi Abraham Heilprin of Kowel
|
Rabbi Israel Heilprin of Svierz
|
daughter   m   Rabbi Isaiah Heilprin of Vitkov and Brody
|
Rabbi Moshe Heilprin of Berdichev & Solotwina (d. 1752)
  m Mindel Katz
|
Rudel   m   Rabbi Shmuel Katz
|
Reb Menachem Mendel Katz of Rosilna near Brodshin
|
Rabbi Abraham Katz, Rabbi of Brodshin
|
Reb Gershon Mendel Katz of Brodshin (d. 1841)
|
Gittel Hakohen Adlersberg (d. 1862)
(sister of Rabbi Saul Hakohen Adlersberg, ABD of Brodshin, died 1850)
  m   Zalman Berish Rottenberg (Margolies) of Brodshin
|
Miriam   m   Rabbi Yehuda Ahron Horowitz of Solotwina
|
Gittel   m   Rabbi Hirsch Leib Weinstein of Solotwina (d. 1884)
|
Esther   m   Rabbi Nahum Uri Gelles of Solotwina (d. 1934)

Chart 0.2 Treves–Spira–Luria family nexus

Mattityahu Treves, Chief Rabbi of Paris ca. 1325–1385

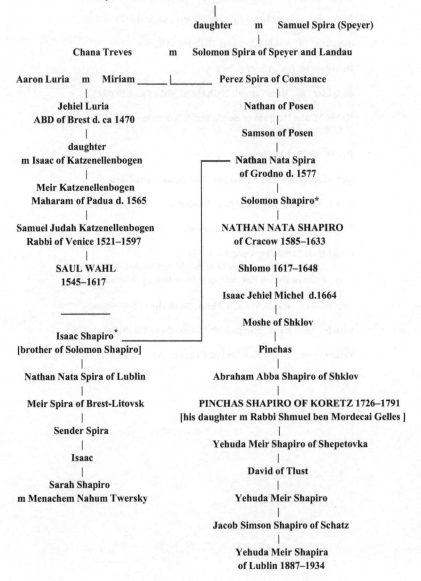

daughter   m   Samuel Spira (Speyer)

Chana Treves   m   Solomon Spira of Speyer and Landau

Aaron Luria   m   Miriam _____|_____   Perez Spira of Constance

Jehiel Luria
ABD of Brest d. ca 1470

Nathan of Posen

Samson of Posen

daughter
m Isaac of Katzenellenbogen

Nathan Nata Spira
of Grodno d. 1577

Meir Katzenellenbogen
Maharam of Padua d. 1565

Solomon Shapiro*

Samuel Judah Katzenellenbogen
Rabbi of Venice 1521–1597

NATHAN NATA SHAPIRO
of Cracow 1585–1633

SAUL WAHL
1545–1617

Shlomo 1617–1648

Isaac Jehiel Michel d.1664

Moshe of Shklov

Isaac Shapiro*
[brother of Solomon Shapiro]

Pinchas

Nathan Nata Spira of Lublin

Abraham Abba Shapiro of Shklov

Meir Spira of Brest-Litovsk

PINCHAS SHAPIRO OF KORETZ 1726–1791
[his daughter m Rabbi Shmuel ben Mordecai Gelles]

Sender Spira

Yehuda Meir Shapiro of Shepetovka

Isaac

David of Tlust

Sarah Shapiro
m Menachem Nahum Twersky

Yehuda Meir Shapiro

Jacob Simson Shapiro of Schatz

Yehuda Meir Shapira
of Lublin 1887–1934

Chart 0.3 Connections between ancient clans

Bezalel ben Chaim LOEW of Worms born ca 1480	Meir KATZENELLENBOGEN of Padua 1483–1565	Josef COLON of Mantua d. ca. 1480	Moses ISSERLES ABD Cracow ca. 1520–1572 m Sprintze Katz
daughter m Zacharya Mendel KLOISNER Hazaken of Posen	Samuel Judah of Venice 1521–97 m. Abigail YAFFE d. 1594	daughter m Abba Mari Delmedigo CHALFAN	Dreisel Isserles, d. 1601 m. Simcha Bonem MEISELS d. Cracow 1624
	Saul WAHL, 1545–1617 m. Deborah Drucker	Eliyahu Menachem Chalfan of Venice d. 1560 m. Fioret, daughter of Kalonymos ben David	daughter m. Itzchak Bonems of Pinsk
Benjamin of Posen d. 1626 *	Meir Wahl Katzenellenbogen * d. 1631 m Hinde, dr of Pinchas HOROWITZ Pres of Four Lands Council	Yechiel Chalfan Kadosh	Simeon Wolf of Vilna & Hamburg
Zacharyah Mendel the prophet		Yitzchak of Vienna	Yente Leah Meisels m Shabbatai KATZ 1621–62
Aryeh Leib FISCHLS ABD Cracow d. 1671	Deborah m Jacob of Lublin	Yechiel ——Chaim Menachem Man	daughter m David Katvan d. 1698
Efraim Fischl of Ludmir d. 1719 Pres of Four Lands Council and Zacharyah Mendel of Betz, d. 1706	Abraham Joshua HESHEL ABD Cracow, d. 1663	Mordecai YOLLIS of Cracow Yisrael Yitzchak of Cracow	two daughters married Nachman ben Simcha Rapaport and Isaac Krakower
dr m Aryeh Leib of Grodno, d. 1729	Yissachar Ber d. 1690 Pres of Four Lands Council	Roza m Isaac Krakower ABD Brody d. 1704 head of BABAD family	grand daughter m Rafael Meisels of Cracow
Nathan Nata ABD Brody, d. 1764 m Dr. of Gershon Vilner of Shklov		Mordecai Yollis Babad of Brody d. 1752	
David Tebele of Lissa d. 1792 whose sisters married			
Isaac CHAJES, head of the Brody community Nachman, son of Chaim HaKohen RAPAPORT, ABD of Lvov			

Chart 0.4 Descent from Katzenellenbogen of Padua and Judah Loew of Prague

Saul ben Samuel Judah Katzenellenbogen aka Saul Wahl 1545–1617   Judah Loew of Prague ca 1525–1609 m Mirel Chayes –Altschuler

Judah Katzenellenbogen   Isaac ben Samson Katz of Prague, d. 1624 m Voegele Loew d. 1629

Abraham Joshua Heschel of Cracow d 1663 m (2) Dinah Katzenellenbogen   Naftali Katz of Lublin d. 1649
m (1) Miriam Lazers

m (1)

Isaac Katz of Stepan m Margolioth

Isaiah Katz of Brody

Naftali Hirsch Katz of Frankfurt & Posen d. 1719

Menachem Meinish Katz

Shprintze m Jacob Ashkenazi-Katzenellenpogen of Posen   Bezalel Katz of Ostrog d. 1717
m Halpern

Meir Horowitz of Tiktin d 1743 m daughter

Abraham of Posen and a daughter m Efraim Fischel of Ludmir d.1719   Isaac Katz of Ostrog d. 1734

Jacob Jokel Horowitz of Brody & Glogau d. 1755

daughter   Jacob of Ludmir d.1730   daughter
m Isaac Dov Ber Margolioth   m Hinde Katzenellenbogen   m Nahum Zausmer   Isaac Horowitz 1715–1767
of Jaslowitz   of Sandomierz   of Brody, Glogau, & Hamburg

Benjamin Bushka of Zamosc   m Reitze–Babad d. 1755 - *BABAD chart*

Jacob of Tlust

Zwi Hirsch Zamosc 1740–1807   Menachem Nahum Zausmer   Beile Horowitz m Menachem Mendel Rubin

Abraham Mordecai Margolies   of Brody, Glogau, & Hamburg
of Ustechko

Chaya m Aryeh Leib Berenstein   m (3) Hinde Fraenkel
of Brody d. 1788   daughter of

Zalman Berish Rottenberg of Brodshin   Isaac Wolf Berenstein   Jacob Jokel Horowitz   Yehuda Ahron Fraenkel
m Gittel Hatkohen Adlersberg   of Bolechow 1772–1832   of Brody

Miriam Rottenberg Margolies   daughter m Menachem Manish Chajes m (1) Efraim Fischel Horowitz   Yehuda Ahron Horowitz
of Brody & Florence d. 1832   of Bolechow ^ Munkacz   of Solotwina to Bukowina 1858

Menachem Manish Chajes
son of Isaac Chajes of Brody

Yehuda Ahron Horowitz
m Miriam Margolies

Leiser Wahl of Tarnobrzeg m **Zlate Roisel** of Nisko	**Isaac Chaim Chajes** of Kolomea m Beile	**Gittel m Hirsch Leib Weinstein** died 1884 **ABD of Solotwina**

Sarah   m   David Isaac Gellis ca 1785–1868 of Glina & Brody

Shulim Wahl m **Sarah Safier**	**Sarah Matel Chajes** m **Eliezer Griffel** of Nadworna	**Esther Weinstein 1861–1907** born in the Bukowina

Nahum Uri Gelles 1852–1934   m   **Esther Weinstein 1861–1907**
born at Narajow and **ABD of Solotwina**

Efraim Fischel Gelles   1879–
Berta (Feige Rivka)   1881–
David Isaac Gelles   1883–
Hirsch Leib   1886–
Rosa
Lotte   1895–
Max Gellis   1897–

Chawa Wahl   m   **David Mendel Griffel**
1877–1941   1875–1941

Regina Griffel   m   **David Isaac Gelles**
1900–1954   of Vienna, 1883–1964

Edward Gelles

Footnotes

Efraim Fischel Gelles, died at a young age – his wife was from the rabbinical Laufer family of Nadworna, his son **Joseph Gelles** was considered for the succession to Rabbi Nahum Uri Gelles, but a kinsman **Yoel Babad** was appointed ABD of Solotwina.

Dr David Isaac Gelles, died 1964 – in his youth he studied at the **Munkacz** Yeshiva – became advocate in Vienna (1916) married **Regina Griffel** (1900–54), daughter of David Mendel Griffel (1875–1941) of Nadworna and Chawa **Wahl** (1877–1941). **Issue: Ludwig Gelles (1922–43)** and **Edward Gelles**

David Mendel Griffel was the eldest son of Eliezer Griffel (1850–1918) of Nadworna and Sarah Matel Chajes (d.1940), daughter of **Isaac Chaim Chajes** of Kolomea (1823–66), descendant of **Isaac Chayes of Brody**, died 1807.

Chart 0.5 Naftali Hirsch Katz of Frankfurt and Posen, Shmuel Helman of Metz, and Gelles of Brody

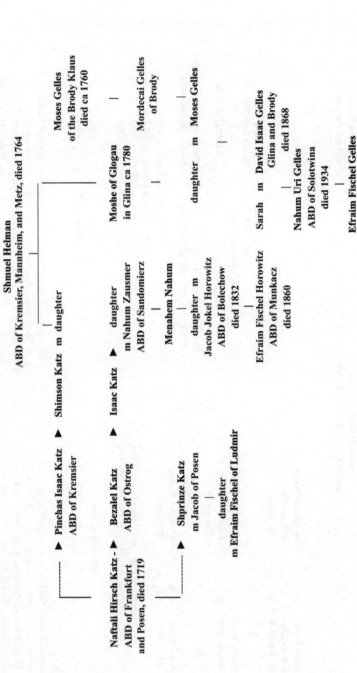

Footnotes

Naftali Hirsch Katz was a member of an ancient and distinguished sacerdotal family (Katz is an acronym of Kohen Zedek = righteous priest). He was a great-grandson of Isaac ben Samson Katz, who married a daughter of Rabbi Judah Loew of Prague. Naftali Hirsch occupied a number of important posts. He was ABD (Av Beth Din, head of the Rabbinical Court) of Frankfurt am Main and of Posen. His children included Shprintze Katz, who married Jacob Ashkenazi-Katzenellenbogen of Posen and whose daughter was the wife of Efraim Fischel of Ludmir, son of Chief Rabbi Aryeh Leib Fischls of Krakow (d.1671) and grandson of Efraim Fischel of Lvov (d.1653), President of the Council of the Four Lands.

Shmuel Helman had a very long and distinguished career that took him from his studies in Prague under Abraham Broda to the Chief Rabbinates of Kremsier, Mannheim and Metz and to a position of pan-European influence. His daughters, Jached, Beila, and Deborah, married respectively Eliezer Katzenellenbogen, ABD of Bamberg and Hagenau, Judah Leib Fraenkel, the son of Chief Rabbi David Mirels-Fraenkel of Berlin, and Isaac Rapaport, son of Israel Ashkenazi, ABD of Offenbach and Hanau.

Shmuel Helman's younger son, Rabbi Uri Feivush, was the father-in-law of Shmuel Landau, a son of the great Chief Rabbi of Prague, Ezekiel Landau (d.1793). Helman's eldest son, Moshe of Glogau, was the father-in-law of Yechiel Michel Segal, ABD of Eisenstadt, and of others including Moses Gelles, grandson of the eponymous scholar of the Brody Klaus (E. Gelles, *An Ancient Lineage*, Vallentine Mitchell, London 2006, chapter 33). Shmuel Helman was already a widower when he studied at Prague in 1709. He was supported by his wealthy father-in-law from Glogau and ultimately married a sister of his late wife (Phineas Katzenellenbogen, Yesh Manhilin, Jerusalem 1984). The marriage of Helman's daughter to Shimson, son of Rabbi Pinchas Isaac ben Naftali Hirsch Katz of Kremsier has now come to light (private communication from Rabbi Dov Weber of New York referring to a Judaica auction catalogue published in 1998). It appears to date from the time of Helman's association with Kremsier in Moravia and this daughter probably came from his first marriage for which documentation has been lacking. A line of descent from Naftali Hirsch's son Bezalel Katz of Ostrog ultimately unites with a Horowitz line descended from Isaiah Katz of Brody, who was a brother of Naftali Hirsch Katz.

Chart 0.6 Chief Rabbis Ezekiel Landau of Prague, Shmuel Helman of Metz, and Isaac Horowitz of Hamburg

Zwi Hirsch Witteles Landau of Apt, died 1714   m   granddaughter of Abraham Joshua Heschel of Cracow

Judah Landau, died 1737

Isaac Landau, died 1768
ABD of Lvov & Cracow

Zvi Joseph Landau
ABD of Greiding

Alexander Sender Landau
of Brody

Zwi Hirsch Horowitz
who was a brother of
Yehuda Ahron Horowitz
of Solotwina & ABD of Mihalaini
from **m (3)**

daughter
m

Isaac Horowitz, died 1767
ABD of Brody, Glogau, and Hamburg

Beile Horowitz
m Menachem Mendel Rubin
died 1803

Jacob Jokel Horowitz
ABD of Bolechow, died 1832

m (1) dr of Menachem Nahum Zausmer
m (3) dr of Yehuda Ahron Fraenkel
from **m (1)**
daughter
who was a sister of
Efraim Fischel Horowitz
ABD of Munkacz, died 1860

m

Esther Weinstein,   *granddaughter of*

m

Shmuel Helman, died 1764
ABD of Mannheim and Metz

Moshe
of Glogau

Uri Feivush
ABD of Lissa etc
died 1771

Ezekiel Landau
ABD of Prague
died 1793

Shmuel Landau
of Prague
died 1834   **m**   Hinde Hillman
died 1835

daughter
m
Moses Gelles
of Brody

David Isaac Gellis
of Glina & Brody
m Sarah (Horowitz ?)

Nahum Uri Gelles
ABD of Solotwina
died 1934

Footnotes

The Rabbis Efraim Fischel Horowitz and his half-brother Yehuda Ahron Horowitz were sons of Rabbi Jacob Jokel Horowitz of Bolechow by his first (Zausmer) and his third (Fraenkel) wife, respectively. As the chart shows, each of these half-brothers had a sibling linked by marriage to Landau descending from Zvi Hirsch Witteles Landau of Apt. Jacob Jokel Horowitz was descended from Isaac Horowitz, the Chief Rabbi of Brody, Glogau and Hamburg, by his wife Reitze Babad, daughter of Jacob Yollis Babad and granddaughter of Isaac Krakower, who was Chief Rabbi of Brody and head of the Babad family. (Isaac Horowitz had three marriages, one being to a granddaughter of Chief Rabbi Isaac Landau of Lvov and Krakow).

The Landaus of Apt (Opatow) were Levites also known as Segal Landau. The Horowitz were an old sprig of the ancient Shem Tov Halevi. Marriages linked these two families over many generations. Zvi Hirsch Witteles Landau was a member of the Council of the Four Lands. He and his brother-in-law Rabbi Gershon Vilner of Shklov were connected by marriage to the Heschel (Katzenellenbogen) line. Gershon Vilner's brother Isaac was the father of Rabbi Shmuel Gelles, ABD of Siemiatycze.

Chief Rabbis Ezekiel Landau of Prague and Shmuel Helman (Hillman) of Metz had connections by blood and marriage. Two of the latter's granddaughters married Ezekiel Landau's son, Shmuel Landau of Prague, and my direct ancestor, Moses Gelles of Brody.

Efraim Fischel Horowitz may be the grandfather of Nahum Uri Gelles (1852–1934), the ABD of Solotwina, whose first son was Rabbi Efraim Fischel Gelles.

Yehuda Ahron Horowitz married Miriam Rottenberg of Brodshin, a daughter of Zalman Berish Rottenberg Margolies and Gittel Hakohen Adlersberg. Miriam's ancestors of the Margolies (Margolioth) rabbinical family had several marriage links with Horowitz. Yehuda Ahron and Miriam appear to be the grandparents of my grandmother Esther, a daughter of Rabbi Hirsch Leib Weinstein (d.1884), who became ABD of Solotwina about the time of removal of Yehuda Ahron Horowitz from Solotwina to Saniawitz in the Bukowina in 1858–9. Esther Weinstein is recorded as born in the Bukowina in 1861. [For the links of my grandparents to these two Horowitz half-brothers see Edward Gelles, *Family Connections, Gelles-Horowitz-Chajes,* Shaker Publishing 2008, Tables 2 and 10. Specific references for the Horowitz–Landau connections in the chart are Meir Wunder, *Meorei Galicia,* Vol. 2, pp. 236 and 340 and Neil Rosenstein, *The Unbroken Chain,* Vol. 2, pp. 738 and 983.]

Chart 0.7 Zundel Ramraz and Gelles – Rokeach cousins

R. Ahron Zelig ben Yehuda Zundel Segal
d. 1731 *scholar of the Brody Klaus*

R. Todros (desc. Abulafia) [1]

R. Moshe R. Zelig's of Brody
d. 1759 *called Ramraz*   m   daughter

R. Yehuda Leib Zundel Ramraz d. 1804 [2]   m   Malka, daughter of R. Yehuda Leib Bick
scholar of the Brody Klaus

Moses Gelles
scholar of the Brody Klaus

R. Michel Levush

R. Yissachar Ber Ramraz of Sokol   Rivka Henya m R. Eleazar Rokeach

R. Mordecai Levush   m   Sarah Bathya, d. 1826

R. Yehuda Zundel
of Sokol

R.Moshe Levush or Gelles [3]
d. 1851

Malka   m   R. Shalom Rokeach [3]
1780–1850   1779–1855
                                    First Belzer Rebbe

R. Liebish Rokeach
of Berdichev

Footnotes

[1] R. Todros was a descendant of R. Todros Abulafia, of the family distinguished as scholars and courtiers in thirteenth- and fourteenth-century Spain. The mystical tradition of Abulafia runs for half a millennium to the Rokeach rabbis of the famous Chasidic dynasty of Belz in Galicia.

[2] R. Yehuda Zundel of Brody may have been married (secondly) to Frieda, daughter of R. Yitzchak of Sokol, who was a descendant of many famous rabbis. Rabbi Yehuda Zundel, like his grandfather, was a scholar of the Brody Klaus, and so were Moses Gelles and Jacob Horowitz. The latter married Sarah, a daughter of R. Todros Zundel Ramraz (nephew of the above Yehuda Leib Zundel). Jacob's son Rabbi Todros Zundel Horowitz (d. 1866) of Brody and Busk, author of *Sharesh Miyakov*, was thus a cousin of one of our Gelles lines.

[3] Some descendants of Moses Gelles of Brody and of the Rokeach Grand Rabbis of Belz share a Zundel Ramraz ancestor. Chaya, a granddaughter of R. Liebish Rokeach of Berdichev, married Israel Brodsky (1823–89).

Sources:

E. Gelles, 'Finding Rabbi Moses Gelles', *Avotaynu*, Vol. 18, No. 1, Spring 2002
Arim Ve'Imahot Be'yisrael, Vol. 6 (Brody), pp. 54, 56, 69–70.
Meir Wunder, *Meorei Galicia* (Institute for the Commemoration of Galician Jewry, Jerusalem 1978), Vol. 4, pp. 844–907 and 967–9
Yitzchak Shlomo Yodlov, *Sefer Yichus Belza*, pp. 25–35 and 311–15
Neil Rosenstein, *The Unbroken Chain: The Katzenellenbogen Family and its Origins* (Avotaynu, 1990), pp. 806–07 and 1103–04 for Brodsky connections.

PART 1

Genealogical threads

Chapter 1

Carolingian connections in the eighth century

Kalonymos of Narbonne

THE INTERACTION of Jews and Christians over the ages was not confined to cultural and economic life but had a genetic dimension, as several chapters of this volume will describe. The first chapter outlines the partly legendary Jewish connections of the Carolingian dynasty dating from the eighth century of our era.

THE CAROLINGIAN BACKGROUND

As Europe slowly emerged from the dark ages that succeeded the fall of the West Roman Empire its new rulers embraced various means to bolster their dynastic pretensions. Some of the legends surrounding the origins and connections of the Merovingian Kings of France appeared to underwrite the legitimacy of their rule, but the Church of Rome ultimately gave its support to the ministers into whose hands effective power had gradually passed.

Clovis, the descendant of Merovech, became king of all the Frankish tribes at the end of the fifth century. By the late seventh century, the so-called Mayor of the Palace Pepin of Heristal was virtual ruler. His grandson Charles Martel was called Duke of the Franks and the latter's son Pepin III (the Short) finally assumed the title of king in 751 when the enfeebled Merovingian Childeric was deposed [1].

Charlemagne, following his father Pepin, became king in 768. In the year 800 he was crowned by Pope Leo III in Rome and assumed the title of Holy Roman Emperor. His son, Louis I (the Pious), was made emperor before his father's death in 814. The power of Charlemagne resurrected the glory of the Roman Empire, and with the blessing of Rome it appeared to receive divine sanction recalling that given to the royal house of King David. It is interesting that Charlemagne was addressed as *my Lord David* by some of his entourage [2].

The Empire in Charlemagne's lifetime embraced the heartland of the continent, namely most of present-day France, Holland, Belgium, Germany, Switzerland, Austria and a large part of Italy, as well as the Spanish and Hungarian Marches. While its constituent parts did not hold together for long, its ethos endured for a thousand years.

JEWS IN NARBONNE

Europe's early Judeo-Christian civilisation was buffeted by struggles between the followers of the Church of Rome and a variety of heretics. Jews and Muslims became part of this complex interplay of dynastic and religious strife. The Saracen conquest of Spain extended into southern France and was halted by Charles Martel at Poitiers in 732.

31

For some time, the province of Septimania, centred on Narbonne, the Toulousin, and the so-called Spanish March, including Gerona and Barcelona, was a cauldron in which Visigoths, Muslims, Jews and Franks formed volatile alliances in their quest for political hegemony. The Jews of Narbonne (who had had a significant presence there since at least the fifth century) were generally on friendly terms with the Arian Goths, but later formed close connections with the Catholic Charles Martel and his successors, sealed with the elevation of Makhir of Narbonne to a princely status [3].

The split between the Ummayads of Spain and the Abbasid Caliphate of Baghdad was exploited by the Franks. The trading links and linguistic skills of Jews from east and west came to the fore in diplomatic exchanges. Descendants of Jewish Exilarchs are reported to have come from Baghdad and married into the Frankish nobility. This process began before the reign of Charlemagne, whose diplomatic contacts with the Caliph Haroun-al-Rashid have been the subject of frequent citations [4].

Aude or Aldana, a daughter of Charlemagne's grandfather, Charles Martel, married Theoderic or Thierry. The latter was mooted to be of a Davidic royal line. Zuckerman's thesis that Thierry could be identified with the above-mentioned Makhir of Narbonne, who was of Davidic descent, has been met with scholarly criticism which is summarised by Nathaniel L. Taylor. The subject continues to arouse much interest [5].

While there is considerable ambiguity regarding names and dates, early chronicles and the weight of age-old tradition do favour the widely held belief that a Jewish strain was added to the Merovingian heritage of the Carolingians in some such manner. Legend has it that Makhir was made ruler of a part of Narbonne and given titles and privileges by Pepin the Short as a reward for Jewish help in the capture of that city in 759.

THE KALONYMOS PRINCES OF NARBONNE

The Jewish princes (*Nessiim*) of Narbonne, who were prominent from the eighth to the fourteenth centuries, traced their line back to Makhir. The famed travel writer Benjamin of Tudela described the exalted position of Makhir's descendants in twelfth-century Narbonne. Members of this line, who held some semi-autonomous powers, were once described as 'client kings' of the Frankish rulers; documents contain designations of *rex Judaeorum* and refer to the ancient family residence as *Cortada Regis Judaeorum* [6].

The Kalonymos family came to the fore in eighth-century Lucca, appeared in Narbonne, and were prominent in Mainz. They produced community leaders, scholars and poets who testified to this Jewish family's importance in the heart of Europe of the Middle Ages. *The Nessiim* of Narbonne were allied by marriage with the Shem Tov Halevi and Benveniste of the Spanish March and Provence, who are the subject of Chapter 2.

Jewish communities in the Languedoc included those at Béziers, Carcassonne, Lodève, Lunel, Mende, Montpellier, Narbonne, Nimes, Pamiers, Pasquière, Saint Gilles and Toulouse. Narbonne and Saint Gilles were particularly important centres of Jewish scholarship [7].

WILLIAM OF GELLONE

William of Gellone, a son of Thierry of Narbonne and his wife Aldana, was variously known as Guilhem or Guillaume d'Orange and Count of Toulouse. He was a cousin and faithful follower of Charlemagne. Deemed to have some Davidic ancestry, he ultimately became a Catholic saint. Dante found him in Paradise next to Godfrey de Bouillon and Robert Guiscard. William was the hero of so many *chansons de geste* that it is difficult to disentangle history from legend, but he is undoubtedly a seminal figure of European genealogy. Charlemagne made him Count of Toulouse in 789 or 790. He frustrated a Saracen incursion into Septimania in 793, captured Barcelona in 801 or 803, and founded monasteries, including that of Gellone (now Saint Guilhem-le-Désert) to which he retired in 806 [8].

His Christian descendants number many royal and noble families, including those of William the Conqueror and of some of his followers, the Dukes of Guise and Lorraine, Habsburg Lorraine and d'Este and many others.

In the days of Charlemagne an ancient Davidic blood connection was clearly valued by the aristocracy. Charlemagne's son, Louis the Pious, who had been a ward of William of Gellone, and members of his family appeared to hold this connection in high esteem [9].

RABBI SOLOMON BEN ISAAC OF TROYES

The most influential Jewish scholar of the following period was Solomon ben Isaac of Troyes in Champagne (1040–1105), who was known by the acronym of Rashi. As a famous sage, biblical commentator and translator he influenced generations of Jews and Christians. Many rabbinical families of later times trace their lineage from him. Rashi was descended on his mother's side from the Makhir–Kalonymos of Narbonne. His ancestry has been the subject of much study and though there are many gaps in his pedigree, he is generally held to be a descendant of King David [10].

Godfrey of Bouillon (1058–1100), whose brother Baldwin became the first of the crusader kings of Jerusalem, and Rashi of Troyes may have had distant ancestral connections and known each other long before their legendary meeting on the eve of the First Crusade. This meeting might be taken as a symbolic watershed in relations between Christians and Jews. The perennial religious acrimony of earlier times was focused more on Christian heresies and schisms. Jews got along quite well with their Christian neighbours. As far as the Carolingian elites were concerned, these were the result of mixing aristocratic families of various origins (cf. Christian Settipani in a recent interview on the internet). Relations between Christians and Jews underwent drastic changes as the second millennium advanced. The Crusades fuelled a religious fanaticism that was initially directed against the infidel in the Holy Land, but also found expression in attacks on Jews, and later in the Albigensian Crusade and in the suppression of the Templars. Economic motives played an important part in all these persecutions.

The great epics produced in this later period celebrated the paladins of Charlemagne's time and their descendants. Their historical inaccuracy can be ascribed to the confusions of time, the conflations of poetic licence and to religiously or politically motivated obfuscation. Chretien de Troyes and Bertrand de Born, for example, had Jewish ancestors, as did many of their Christian heroes. The epics were part of the treasure trove of European literature that added romance and colour to the extant accounts of the biographers, chroniclers and travel writers.

The descendants of Rashi of Troyes included a number of distinguished French rabbis of the Treves family, called after the ancient imperial city of Trier (Treves). The nexus of this family with the Spira family from Speyer and the Lurias from Italy led to Rabbi Jechiel Luria of Alsace, who became Rabbi of Brest-Litovsk, where he died around 1470. From him many rabbinical families are descended. Isaac of Katzenellenbogen from the eponymous town in Hesse-Nassau married one of his daughters, and their son Meir Katzenellenbogen (1482–1565) became a famous Chief Rabbi of Padua. His son Rabbi Samuel Judah Katzenellenbogen (1521–97) was the father of Saul Wahl.[1]

CONCLUSION

The Carolingian links with the preceding dynasty and the fascinating legends of the Merovingian line's Jewish roots are beyond the scope of this essay. Centuries of fact and fable, chronicle and epic, biography and family tradition, throw a sombre light on movements in European history that were of millennial significance. There seems to be an almost ineluctable line of cause and effect from the early days of Christianity and the Jewish Diaspora, to Carolingian relations with Jews and Arabs, the role of Davidic lineage and dynastic rivalries, the changing attitudes of the Church of Rome, the Spanish Reconquista, the motivation and legacy of the Crusades, the Jewish odyssey from the Iberian peninsula to the Russian Pale, to modern nationalism with its persecutions culminating in the Holocaust, the creation of the state of Israel, and the seemingly intractable relations with part of the Islamic world.

Chart 1.1 Legendary Carolingian connections with Jewish princes of Narbonne

CHARLES MARTEL 688-741
son of PEPIN II of Heristal descendant of PEPIN I of Landen
Mayors of the Palace to Merovingian Kings

Bertrada ("Goosefoot") * m PEPIN III (the Short)
King of the Franks 751-68

CHARLEMAGNE 742-814
Holy Roman Emperor 800

Louis the Pious
Emperor 814

Aude / Aldana m Teodoric / Thierry *
Narbonne (Septimania)

Makhir *

Jewish Princes of Narbonne
from 8th century to ca 1306

Kalonymos Line .
Rashi of Troyes
1040-1105

Treves - Spira - Luria
Jechiel Luria of Alsace d. ca 1470

Saul Wahl 1545-1617
son of Samuel Judah Katzenellenbogen
Rabbi of Venice 1521-1597
Saul was a great-great-grandson of Jechiel Luria

William of Gellone 755-812 *
(Guillaume d'Orange)
Count of Toulouse 789 etc

Rollo the Dane, William the Conqueror,
Godfrey of Bouillon, Counts of Anjou
Dukes of Guise and Lorraine
Habsburg Lorraine & Habsburg d'Este

* Davidic descent ?

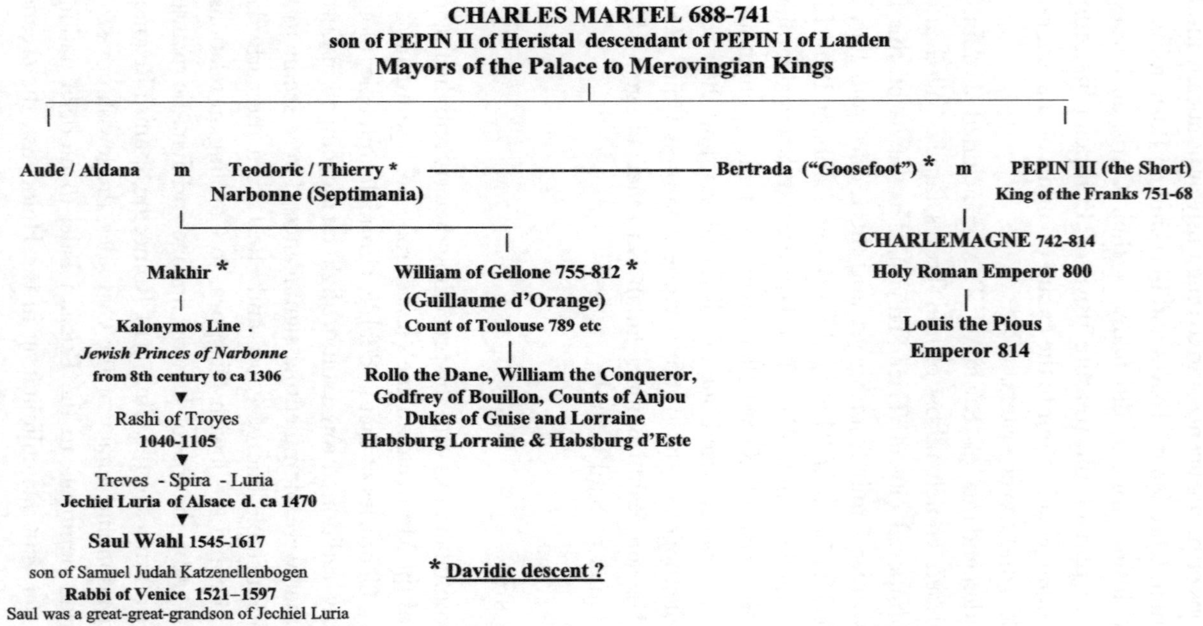

NOTE

1 Whose connections with King Sigismund Vasa III of Poland in the sixteenth century have a curious resonance with the Kalonymos Carolingian connections of the previous millennium. Saul Wahl appears in several chapters of the present volume and particularly in Chapters 7, 8, and 15.

REFERENCES

[1] James Bryce, *The Holy Roman Empire* (London: Macmillan 1961), p. 39:

> *the Holy See, now for the first time invoked as an international or supranational power, pronounced the deposition of the enfeebled Merovingian Childeric, and gave to the royal office of his successor Pipin a sanctity hitherto unknown, adding to the old Frankish election, which consisted of raising the chief on a shield amid the clash of arms, the Roman diadem and the Hebrew rite of anointing.*

[2] Steven Allott (ed.), *Alcuin of York – His Life and Letters* (William Sessions 1974), pp. 83–4.

Vita Caroli Magni Einhard, *The Life of Charlemagne*, translated by Samuel Epes Turner (New York: Harper & Brothers 1880) (in 1960 the University of Michigan Press reprinted this translation, with a copyrighted forward by Sidney Painter).

[3] Abraham ibn Daud, *Sefer HaKabbalah* (written *c.*1161):

> *Then King Charles sent to the King of Baghdad requesting that he dispatch one of his Jews of the seed of royalty of the House of David. He hearkened and sent him one from there, a magnate and sage, Rabbi Makhir by name, and – settled him in Narbonne, the capital city, and planted him there, and gave him a great possession there at the time he captured it from the Ishmaelites [Arabs]. And he [Makhir] took to wife a woman from among the magnates of the town; – and the King made him a nobleman and designed, out of love for [Makhir], good statutes for the benefit of all the Jews dwelling in the city, as is written and sealed in a Latin charter; and the seal of the King therein [bears] his name Carolus; and it is in their possession at the present time. The Prince Makhir became chieftain there. He and his descendants were close [inter-related] with the King and all his descendants.*

There was some confusion in later writings as to whether King Charles referred to Charlemagne or his grandfather (v.i.).

[4] Edward Gibbon, *Decline and Fall of the Roman Empire* (Dent: Everyman Library 1962), Vol. 5, p. 187:

He [Charlemagne] maintained a more equal intercourse with the caliph Haroun-al-Rashid, whose dominion stretched from Africa to India, and accepted from his ambassadors a tent, a water clock, an elephant, and the keys to the Holy Sepulchre.

cf. Heinrich Graetz, *Volkstümliche Geschichte der Juden* (3 vols) (Berlin and Vienna: Benjamin Kurz 1923), Vol. 2, p. 307. The embassy sent by Charlemagne to Haroun-al-Rashid included Isaac, the Jewish interpreter, who returned with the Caliph's gifts.

[5] Arthur J Zuckerman, *A Jewish Princedom in Feudal France 768–900* (Columbia University Press 1972). Zuckerman's thesis that the historical Count Theoderic was one and the same as the Prince Makhir of Narbonne has been rejected by a number of scholars.

Nathaniel L Taylor, 'Saint William, King David, and Makhir', *The American Genealogist*, 72 (1997), pp. 205–23), gives references to other critical assessments of Zuckerman's writings.

[6] Benjamin of Tudela, *Travels (from c.1165 onwards): The Itinerary of Benjamin of Tudela. Travels in the Middle Ages*, translated by Marcus Nathan Adler (Joseph Simon/Pangloss Press 1993):

[from Gerona] a three day's journey takes one to Narbonne which is a city pre-eminent for learning; thence the Thora goes forth to all countries. Sages and great and illustrious men abide here. At their head is R. Kalonymos, the son of the great and illustrious R. Todros of the seed of David, whose pedigree is established. He possesses hereditaments and lands given to him by the ruler of the city of which no man can forcibly dispossess him. Prominent in the community is R. Abraham, head of the Academy, also R. Makhir and R. Judah and many other distinguished scholars. At the present day 300 Jews are there.

Doat collection (Bibliotheque Nationale de France), p. 53ff., and pp. 339–53 records of a Jewish 'king' at Narbonne

Saige, *Histoire des Juifs du Languedoc* (Paris 1881), p. 44 documents the description of the residence of the Makhir descendants in Narbonne as the 'Cortada Regis Judaeorum', the titles of these so-called 'kings' being understood to refer to princes of a fiefdom subservient to the King of the Franks.

Henri Gross, *Gallia Judaica* (Amsterdam: Philo Press 1969) records the early foundation of an important Talmudical school at Narbonne.

[7] *Jewish Encyclopedia* (1906 edition), Article on Languedoc.

[8] Dante Alighieri, *Divine Comedy* (Dent: Everyman Library 1961), p. 374, Paradiso, Canto xviii: 'Last, along the cross, William, and Renard, and Duke Godfrey drew my ken, and Robert Guiscard' – referring to

38

William of Gellone, aka Guillaume d'Orange (cousin of Charlemagne), and Renard his brother-in-law, Godfrey of Bouillon (descendant of the Carolingian line and leader of the First Crusade), and Robert Guiscard (son of Tancred de Hauteville and founder of a Norman dynasty in southern Italy and Sicily).

Wolfram von Eschenbach's *Willehalm* is an epic of the exploits of Guillaume d'Orange written in the second half of the thirteenth century, including the relations of William with Louis the Pious (based on the earlier French epic *Chanson d'Aliscans*).

The French *chanson de geste Aymeri de Narbonne* and the *Gesta Karoli Magni ad Carcassonam et Narbonam* of the same period both refer to Aymeri of Narbonne as the father of William.

[9] Graetz (see [4]), Vol. 2, p. 310 stresses the benevolent attitude towards the Jews of Louis the Pious and of his wife Judith.

Glanville Price (ed.), *William, Count of Orange*, four Old French epics, published in translation (Dent 1975), p. 4.

The Crowning of Louis is one of the poems in the Geste of William of Orange. It describes William placing the crown on the head of Louis while the latter's father Charlemagne looks on:

> *Seeing the crown sitting there on the altar the Count seized it without delay, came up to the youth and set it on his head. 'Receive this fair lord, in the name of the King of Heaven; may he give you the strength to be a just ruler'. When the father saw this he was glad on his son's account. 'Lord William' he said 'accept my hearty thanks.* **It is your lineage that has raised up mine***'.*

If credence is to be given to this poetic rendering, it might indeed be interpreted as referring to Davidic ancestors of William and of Charlemagne's mother.

J. de Pange, *L'Auguste Maison de Lorraine* (Lyons 1966), p. 60 with introduction by Otto von Habsburg (whose ancient titles included Duke of Lorraine and King of Jerusalem) records that a sixteenth-century Duke of Guise was welcomed by cries of 'Hosanna filio David' on entering the town of Joinville in Champagne.

[10] On Rashi's descent from King David:

Neil Rosenstein, 'Rashi's Descent from King David', *Avotaynu*, Vol. 8, No. 3 (1992).

Laurence Tauber, 'The Maternal Descent of Rashi', *Avotaynu*, Vol. 9, No. 2 (1993).

David Einsiedler, 'Descent from King David', *Avotaynu*, Vol. 3, No. 3, (1992) and Vol. 9, No. 2 (1993).

Chapter 2

In the Spanish March and Provence from the tenth century

Benveniste and Shem Tov Halevi

Some Jewish families became prominent as community leaders and royal advisers in the medieval Catholic kingdoms of northern Spain. The connections of the Shem Tov Halevi of Gerona and the Benveniste of Barcelona widened from about the tenth century in Spain and southern France and led some centuries later to descendant branches that are believed to be the forebears of the Epstein and Horowitz families. These Levites took their names from the towns of Eppstein in Germany and Horovice in Bohemia.

The Kalonymos of Narbonne were related to some important Jewish families who from the days of Charlemagne were quite mobile within Frankish Septimania and the so-called Spanish March. In the following centuries these families, including the Benveniste of Barcelona and other cities and the Shem Tov Halevi from Gerona, played important roles, not only as scholars and leaders of Jewish communities but also as physicians, interpreters, financial agents and counsellors to the Count of Barcelona and successive kings of Aragon. The first appended chart outlines some of the family connections. The footnotes to the chart go into some of the complex detail with appropriate references.[1]

From the medieval Shem Tov Halevi, who spread into Provence, sprigs established themselves in German and Bohemian centres and became the distinguished Epstein and Horowitz lineages of later times.

Photo 8 Ramon Berenguer IV, Count of Barcelona and his consort, heiress of Aragon

41

Chart 2.1 Benveniste Nessiim of Barcelona and Shem Tov Halevi of Gerona (descent to Epstein and Horowitz)

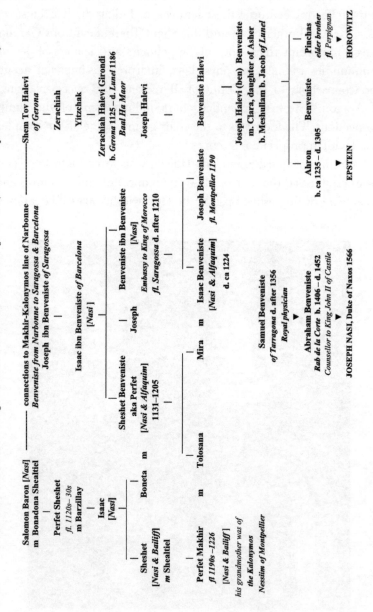

Footnotes

The above chart focuses on Sheshet ben Isaac ben Joseph Benveniste, also called Perfet (Catalan for the Hebrew name Meshullam), his brother Benveniste ibn Benveniste and his nephew Isaac Benveniste. They were Jewish community leaders with the title of *Nasi* and also served Count Ramon Berenguer IV of Barcelona and succeeding kings of Aragon in more than one capacity (*Alfaquim* = counsellor; *Bailiff* = financial administrator). Their connections to other leading Jewish families such as the Shealtiel and Barzillay are indicated on the chart (references: Elka Klein, *Jews, Christian Society, and Royal Power in Medieval Barcelona* (University of Michigan Press 2006); Moshe Shealtiel-Gracian, *Shealtiel* (Academy Chicago Publishers 2005).

A later Benveniste line runs to the family of Joseph Nasi, whose economic and political services to the Ottoman Empire were recognised when he was made Duke of Naxos in 1566 (Cecil Roth, *The House of Nasi: Dona Gracia* (Philadelphia: Jewish Publication Society 1948), p. 13).

According to family traditions, the Epstein and Horowitz families descend respectively from Aharon and his elder brother Pinchas, the sons of Joseph Halevi (ben) Benveniste and his wife Clara, although some believe that a brother of Pinchas and Aharon, named Benveniste, was the progenitor of the Horowitz line (see Meir Wunder, *Meorei Galicia*, Vol. 6 (Jerusalem 2005)), p. 450. Rabbi Aharon de na Clara ben Yosef Halevi of Barcelona in his book *Bedek Habayit* gave his paternal pedigree as follows: *Aharon Halevi b. Yosef b. Benveniste b. Yosef b. Zerachiah b. Shem Tov*. Later scholars had *Zerachiah* as the son of *Yitzchak* son of *Zerachiah* (see Chayim Yosef David Azulai, *Shem Hagedolim* Vol. 1 (Jerusalem 1979), p. 18; Itzhak Epstein, Epstein Research message 112 posted 31 December 2002). So it appears that descent from Zerachiah ben Yitzchak Halevi Girondi to Aharon Halevi proceeded via Zerachiah's son Joseph to a Benveniste (grandfather of Aharon and Pinchas Halevi), and then to their father Joseph Halevi ben Benveniste (see also Henri Gross, *Gallia Judaica*, new edition (Amsterdam: Philo Press 1969), pp. 330ff.).

A Joseph Benveniste is believed to have been the brother of the *Nasi* Isaac Benveniste (see Jewish Encyclopedia article on Benveniste and Neil Rosenstein, 'Ashkenazi rabbinic families', *RAV-SIG online journal*). This Isaac Benveniste, a distinguished leader of Aragonese Jewry, died at a mature age c.1224 and is identified as a son of Benveniste ibn Benveniste (Elka Klein, loc. cit.). Aharon Halevi was born around 1235 to 1240 (H. Gross, loc. cit.) and one of his teachers was his elder brother Pinchas. Their father Joseph might have been born round about 1195–1205 so he could not be a brother of the *Nasi* Isaac ben Benveniste. However, a Joseph Benveniste is recorded as living in Montpellier around 1190. The connections indicated in the chart appear to reconcile most of the details in the above references.

Chart 2.2 Millennial descent from Shem Tov Halevi of Gerona

The Shem Tov Halevi of Gerona and some other leading families, including the Benveniste, moved between Provence and Aragon. The Hebrew name Shem Tov and the Greek Kalonymos meant 'of good name'. They were related to the Kalonymos *Nessiim* of Narbonne.

1 Shem Tov Halevi of Gerona (a leading Talmudic scholar in Provence) (the Ha-Yitzhari family claimed direct descent from Samuel the Prophet)

2 Zerachiah

3 Yitzchak (scholar in Provence)

4 Zerachiah Halevi Girondi 1125–86 (author of *Ha-Maor* and other works)

5 Joseph Halevi

6 Benveniste Halevi

7 Joseph Halevi ben Benveniste m Clara bat Asher ben Meshullam ben Jacob of Lunel (reputedly of Davidic descent)

8 Pinchas Halevi – lived near Perpignan (elder brother of Aharon Halevi, 1235–1305, who gives his descent from Zerachiah Halevi in *Bedek Habayit*)

9 Yitzchak Halevi

10 Joseph Halevi

11–13 (?)

From the Shem Tov Halevi of medieval Spain and Provence a sprig transplanted to Bohemia in the fifteenth century became the Horowitz family, taking their name from the town of Horovice near Prague where they settled before moving to Prague and beyond

14 Moshe Halevi

15 Isaiah ben Moshe Halevi Ish Horowitz *c.*1440–1515 – in Prague 1480

16 Ahron Meshullam Zalman Horowitz 1470–1545 aka *Zalman Munka*

17 Israel Horowitz 1500–72 of Prague

18 Pinchas Halevi Ish Horowitz Prague 1535 – Krakow 1618, President of the Council of the Four Lands – m sister of Rabbi Moses Isserles

19 Jacob Horowitz died in Vienna 1630

20 Joshua Horowitz ABD of Przemysl died 1661

21 Shmuel Schmelke Horowitz ABD of Tarnow died 1694 m granddaughter of Yehoshua Heschel Charif, Chief Rabbi of Krakow (author of *Meginei Shlomo*)

22 Meir Horowitz of Bolechow, Zloszow, and ABD of Tykocin died 1743 m daughter of Menachem Manish Katz, son of Isaiah Katz of Brody (descendants of Judah Loew of Prague)

23 Jacob Jokel Horowitz ABD of Glogau and Brody died 1755

24 Isaac Horowitz ABD of Brody, Glogau, and Hamburg died 1767

(*continued*)

25	Beile Horowitz m Menachem Mendel Rubin ABD of Lesniow etc. died 1803
26	Jacob Jokel Horowitz ABD of Bolechow 1773–1832
27a	Efraim Fischel Horowitz ABD of Munkacz died 1860
27b	Yehuda Ahron Horowitz of Solotwina and ABD of Mihaileni
28a	Sarah (?) m David Isaac Gellis c.1790–1868
28b	Gittel Horowitz m Hirsch Leib Weinstein ABD of Solotwina died 1884
29	Nahum Uri Gelles ABD of Solotwina died 1934 m Esther Weinstein died 1907
30	David Gelles of Vienna 1883–1964 m Regina Griffel 1900–54
31	Edward Gelles 1927–

The second chart indicates the millennial descent from the Shem Tov Halevi through a Horowitz line to the present day.[2]

The great misfortune of the Spanish Inquisition that drove so many Jews from the land in which they had lived since before Roman times was the beginning of a great chapter for the latter-day Benveniste.

From Spain to Portugal, Antwerp, across Europe to Italy, and finally to the Ottoman Empire, this is the story of the House of Mendes and Joseph Nasi, Duke of Naxos and Prince of the Cyclades, as outlined in the following chapter.

NOTES

1   Benveniste was a first name that also became a family name – the prefix *ibn* meaning 'of the tribe of' rather than the Hebrew *ben* meaning 'the son of'.

2   The full name of the Horowitz who came to Horovice near Prague in the fifteenth century is 'Halevi Ish Horowitz', i.e. the Levite, man of Horowitz.

Chapter 3

From Portugal to the Ottoman Empire in the sixteenth century

Joseph Nasi, Duke of Naxos

A T THE END OF the fifteenth century the expulsion of the Jews from Spain and Portugal led to a mass exodus to the Low Countries and to the Ottoman Empire, while other co-religionists submitted to outward conversion. Such was the case with the Benveniste–Nasi family, who moved from Spain to Portugal where they adopted the *converso* name of Mendes. The subsequent pan-European progress of Joseph Nasi in the sixteenth century reflects the upswing in economic conditions following the great voyages of discovery at the beginning of the modern era and relates to the struggle of Catholic powers with the Ottoman Empire.

The Kalonymos *Nessiim* or Princes of Narbonne were related to the Shem Tov Halevi of Gerona and the Benveniste family, whose connections also included Shealtiel, Perfet, Barzillay and Cavaller (see Chapter 1). From the eleventh century, the Benveniste were prominent in Barcelona. Some had the Jewish title of *Nasi*, and also held high office such as *Alfaquim* or chief counsellor. They produced men of learning whose knowledge of medicine and Arabic and talent in the fields of diplomacy and finance were appreciated by their rulers (see Chapter 2).

Three centuries later, in the reign of King John II of Castile, Jewish courtiers included Abraham Benveniste (*c.*1406–52) who was *Rab de la Corte* and the most important adviser to the king beside the Constable Alvaro de Luna. Other Jewish notables were Joseph ibn Shem Tov and Joseph Nasi. It has been suggested that the descendants of this Abraham Benveniste and Joseph Nasi were among those who settled in Portugal after 1492 and continued to live there as nominal Christians when the decree expelling Jews from Portugal came into force in 1497 [1].

Jews who converted or were forced to convert to Christianity, and who frequently continued to practise rabbinical Judaism in secret, were called *marranos*. These *New Christians* or *conversos* came under pressure in Portugal when the Inquisition was established there in 1536.

Amongst these Portuguese *conversos* were Francisco and Diogo Mendes, whose Jewish names were Semah and Meir Benveniste. They married the sisters of the Portuguese king's physician, Dr Miguez, whose Jewish family name of Nasi had been borne as a title by his forebears. One of his sisters was known to her family as Gracia (Hannah) Nasi but she had been baptised as Beatrice de Luna, the name of her grandmother whose husband was a Benveniste and whose grandfather is believed to have been Benveniste Judah de la Cavalleria of Saragossa. The Benveniste–Nasi family continued a policy of endogamy to keep their pedigree and fortune undiluted. Gracia Nasi arranged for her daughter Reyna and her niece Gracia (la Chica) to marry her two Nasi (Miguez) nephews.

The family attained immense wealth through the spice trade with the Indies that had been opened up by the epic voyage of

Chart 3.1 Benveniste–Nasi endogamy (including Joseph Nasi, Duke of Naxos)

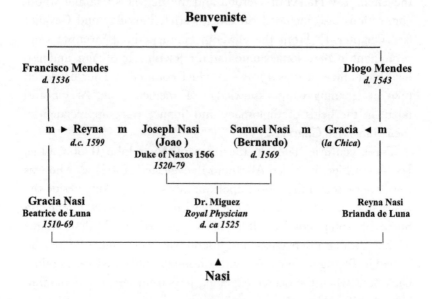

Benveniste
▼

Francisco Mendes	**Diogo Mendes**
d. 1536	*d. 1543*

m ► **Reyna** m	**Joseph Nasi**	**Samuel Nasi** m	**Gracia** ◄ m
d.c. 1599	**(Joao)**	**(Bernardo)**	*(la Chica)*
	Duke of Naxos 1566	*d. 1569*	
	1520-79		

Gracia Nasi	**Dr. Miguez**	**Reyna Nasi**
Beatrice de Luna	*Royal Physician*	Brianda de Luna
1510-69	*d. ca 1525*	

▲
Nasi

Vasco da Gama. With the expansion of their business and the dangers increasingly facing crypto Jews in Portugal, it became politic to transfer to Antwerp, where they had opened a branch in 1512 with the help of their kinsman Rabbi Abraham Benveniste. The Antwerp branch became the base for a trading network that increasingly involved loans and other transactions with a number of European rulers. This in turn required delicate diplomacy in negotiating a course through fluctuations in the balance of power and the influence of the Papacy in Catholic realms. The family had to contend with the ever-present dangers of being accused of secretly adhering to Judaism. The King of France refused to repay a loan after one of the Mendes brothers was accused of 'judaising'. He asserted that 'he had borrowed from a Christian not a Jew'. The Venetians were among those who brought such charges and tried to seize the family fortune. Those who intervened at one time or another on the family's behalf included Henry VIII of England, the King of Portugal and the Ottoman Sultans Suleiman the Magnificent and Selim II. The family later had good relations with the d'Este of Ferrara, the King of Poland, and William of Orange [2,3].

After the death of her husband Francisco in 1536, Dona Gracia settled in Antwerp, and when her brother-in-law Diogo Mendes died in 1543 she became the head and guiding spirit of the family. They had stayed briefly in London and later progressed from Antwerp through France to Italy. They were in Venice for a while, before and shortly after a fruitful sojourn in Ferrara (around 1549–52), where the philosemitic rulers made them welcome [4]. In Venice, family squabbles and accusations were only resolved after international diplomatic ructions that ultimately led Dona Gracia and her closest family to accept the hospitality of the Sultan. They rose to influence and honour in the Ottoman Empire, where they could again openly profess their Jewish faith and continue to extend a helping hand to their imperilled co-religionists. The pan-European trading activities of the House of Mendes were of great benefit to the Ottomans. During the reigns of Suleiman the Magnificent and his successor Selim II, Joseph Nasi played a significant role in European politics, steering Ottoman policy in a direction that was essentially anti-Venetian and anti-French. It was thought that he might come to play a vice-regal role in Cyprus after it was captured in the war with Venice, but his influence waned after the death of Selim in 1574. Dona Gracia lived to see Joseph Nasi – her son-in-law and nephew – become Duke of Naxos and Prince of the Cyclades (see Chart 3.2).

The loss of talent Spain and Portugal suffered through the Inquisition benefited the Ottoman Empire – as in the twentieth century the loss to Germany through Nazi persecution led to economic and intellectual benefits for the Western democracies.

REFERENCES

[1] Cecil Roth, *The House of Nasi: Dona Gracia* (Philadelphia: Jewish Publication Society of America 1948).
[2] Daniel S. Katz, *The Jews in the History of England: The House of Mendes* (Oxford: Clarendon Press 1994) p. 3ff. deals at some length with the Mendes family and its agents in England during the reign of Henry VIII including the King's personal intervention to secure the release of Diogo Mendes when arrested in Antwerp on charges of 'judaising' in 1532.

[3] Heinrich Graetz, *Volkstuemliche Geschichte der Juden* (Berlin & Vienna: Benjamin Harz 1923), Vol. 3, p. 317.

[4] Dolores Sloan, *Ferrara: Spiritual Home for Conversos in the Early Renaissance* (HaLapid: Society for Crypto Judaic Studies 1999) the liberal policy of Alfonso and Ercole d'Este of Ferrara is extolled, as are the philanthropic and charitable activities of Dona Gracia Nasi.

[5] David Abulafia, *The Great Sea* (Penguin 2012), pp. 441–6.

References to more recent studies can be found in articles on the House of Mendes, including: wikipedia.org/wiki/Gracia_Mendes_Nasi, wikipedia.org/wiki/Joseph_Nasi, answers.com/topic/nasi-family.

Chart 3.2 Rulers of the Ottoman Empire: Mehmed II to Murad III

MEHMED II The Conqueror 1432–81	Ruled 1444–6 and from 1451
	Capture of Constantinople 1453
BAYAZED II 1447–1512	Ruled 1481–1512
	Accepted exiled Jews from Italy, Spain and Portugal *Following the epic voyage of Vasco da Gama, the spice trade with the east brought great wealth to the House of Mendes (Nasi) and to Antwerp whence they removed from Portugal. It contributed to the decline of Venice in the eastern Mediterranean and to the rise of Ottoman power*
SELIM I 1465–1520	Ruled 1512–20
	Danubian Acquisitions Conquest of former Caliphates of Damascus, Cairo and Baghdad *Abrogation of the Roman Law of No Return thus enabling Jews to travel freely to the Holy Land*
SULEYMAN I *The Magnificent* 1494–1566	Ruled 1520–66
	Capture of Belgrade 1521 Capture of Rhodes 1522 After the battle of Mohacs in 1526 the Ottomans advanced to the gates of Vienna in 1529 *Dona Gracia Nasi with her son-in-law (and nephew) Joseph Nasi settled in Constantinople 1554* *Tiberias and Safed were granted to Joseph Nasi in 1561, who developed Jewish settlements there*

(continued)

SELIM II 1524–74	Ruled 1566–74
	Joseph Nasi made Duke of Naxos 1566 Peace of Adrianople with the Habsburgs 1568 *Joseph Nasi was involved in negotiations with France. He had diplomatic and business relations with William of Orange and the Low Countries, with Sigismund August II of Poland, and with the Emperor Ferdinand.* *Deaths of Gracia Nasi and of Samuel Nasi 1569* Supremacy of Venice contested and Cyprus captured 1570 The combined forces of Venice, the Papacy, and Spain checked Ottoman power at the great sea battle of Lepanto in 1571 *With the fading influence of Joseph Nasi, the "peace" party of the Grand Vizier Sokolli gained ascendancy and the physician Solomon Ashkenazi was sent to Venice as ambassador to negotiate a peace treaty in 1574*
MURAD III 1546–95	Ruled 1574–95
	Numerous Jewish doctors received official appointments *Death of Joseph Nasi 1579 (his wife Reyna died in 1599)*
MEHMED III 1566–1603	Ruled 1595–1603
	Nathan ben Solomon Ashkenazi acted as foreign policy adviser, Gabriel Buonaventura negotiated with Spain, and Solomon Abenaes (Alvaro Mendez) prepared a treaty with England against Spain

Chapter 4

From Provence to Venice and beyond

Eliyahu Menachem Chalfan

Rabbi Eliyahu Menachem Chalfan, of ancient Provencal descent, died in 1560. He was a member of the Rabbinical Court of Venice and an authority on Jewish law whose opinion was sought by the agents of King Henry VIII of England, who wished to obtain an annulment of his marriage. Chalfan was also a fashionable doctor of medicine, and a master of arts with wide literary interests. In short, he was a noble and learned representative of the Italian Renaissance. The journeys of some of his progeny from Venice, to Prague, Vienna and Berlin is illustrative of the trials and tribulations faced by Jewish families in succeeding centuries.

The three preceding chapters trace the history of some ancient Jewish families. Starting with the Kalonymos of Narbonne in the eighth century, connections are made with the Shem Tov Halevi of Gerona and the Benveniste of Saragossa and Barcelona. These families continued to flourish in the province of Septimania and the so-called Spanish March. In the following centuries they spread more widely in Spain and Provence. Persecution in the last decade of the fourteenth century led many Jews to abandon their Spanish homeland. This was soon followed by a general expulsion of the Jews from Provence.

A hundred years later the Inquisition brought to an end the splendid Jewish civilisation on the Iberian peninsula. Large numbers fled to Holland or the Ottoman Empire and elsewhere, while many others became crypto Jews or *conversos*, outwardly accepting conversion while secretly maintaining their Jewish faith. The odyssey of the Mendes family (Benveniste–Nasi) that took them from Spain to Portugal, and then to Antwerp, France, Italy, and ultimately to the Ottoman Empire, falls into this period.

Descendants of the Shem Tov Halevi living in Provence were among those who found their way to Bohemia in the fifteenth century, where they were known as the Halevi Ish Horowitz (*the Levites, men of Horovice*). The Horowitz became an important and influential family in Prague.

Those who shared their exile from Provence and were connected to them by marriage included the Portuguese Chayot, who also flourished in Prague and later in Poland and beyond under the name of Chayes.

The story of another Provencal family with Iberian antecedents is that of the Chalfan (Halfan, Alfano), who migrated to Italy at this time [1, 2]. The family was linked by marriage to the Delmedigo of Crete who, as their name suggests, were physicians as well as mathematicians, astronomers and rabbinic scholars in Italy and elsewhere. Most noteworthy members of the family were Elijah ben Moses Abba Delmedigo (1460–97) and Joseph Solomon Delmedigo (1591–1655).

The astronomer Abba Mari Delmedigo Chalfan married a daughter of the leading Talmudic scholar in fifteenth-century Italy,

Joseph Colon, the so-called *Maharik of Mantua*. The Trabot family to which he belonged were scholars who had come to Italy from France.

Rabbi Eliyahu Menachem Chalfan (Elia Alfano) of Venice (*c*.1500–60) was a son of this union. He in turn married Fioret, a daughter of the scholar and physician Calo Kalonymos ben David, a descendant of the ancient Kalonymos of Narbonne [3].

Eliyahu (Elijah) Chalfan was not only a prominent physician but a man of letters and member of the Rabbinical Court of Venice, in which capacity he was consulted by the agents of King Henry VIII in pursuit of grounds for the annulment of his marriage to Catherine of Aragon [1, 2, 4]. He was a man of considerable culture, who maintained a friendly correspondence with the poet and satirist Pietro Aretino [5].

One of the lines of descent from Eliyahu Chalfan and Fioret Kalonymos, shown in Chart 4.1, has interesting connections with several important Jewish families. There are links with Yollis of Krakow and with the ancient Katzenellenbogen through the marriage of Roza Yollis with Yissachar Ber, a President of the Council of the Four Lands, who was the son of Chief Rabbi Abraham Joshua Heschel of Krakow, the latter's lineage going back on both his mother's and father's side to the patriarch of the family, Meir Katzenellenbogen, who was known as the *Maharam of Padua*. Yissachar Ber's son Isaac Krakower was Chief Rabbi of Brody and head of a family branch which adopted the name of Babad (Hebrew acronym for sons of the Chief Rabbi). From him a line descends to Berenstein (first Chief Rabbi of Galicia) and Chayes of Brody (family of the later Chief Rabbi of Vienna and of my maternal great-grandmother). Chayes were later linked with Berensteins as merchant bankers in Florence and Livorno (see Chapter 16). From the Yollis connection there are also more distant links to Horowitz, Rapaport, Fischl and Gelles.

Chart 4.2 indicates the movements of four generations from Eliyahu Menachem and Fioret Chalfan from Venice to Prague, Vienna and Krakow [6, 7]. The story of the immediate family line is bounded by the expulsion of Jews from Provence in 1394, successive local difficulties in Venice, Prague and Vienna, and the general expulsion from the latter city in 1670. In due course, some descendants returned to their old homes. Jews were re-admitted to

PETRVS ARRETINVS ACERRIMVS VIRTVTVM AC VITIORVM
DEMOSTRATOR
NON MANVS ARTIFICIS MAGE DIGNVM OS PINGERE NON OS
HOC PINGI POTERAT NOBILIORE MANV
PELLÆVS IVVENIS SI VIVERET HAC VOLO DESTRA
PINGIER HOC TANTVM DICERET ORE CANI

Photo 9 Pietro Aretino

France in the later sixteenth century and included some Halphen of Metz, mooted as having a connection with the Halfon of old.

An appended sketch of a related family descent illustrates the complex intertwining of Chalfan, Horowitz, Fraenkel and other lines. From a Chalfan–Ries connection the sketch shows a line of descent to the composer Giacomo Meyerbeer (1791–1864).

REFERENCES

[1] Cecil Roth, *Venice* (Philadelphia: Jewish Publication Society 1930), p. 77: 'Elijah Menachem Halfon, poet, Talmudist, and physician, the most illustrious member of a distinguished family, who was one of the most fashionable medical practitioners in Venice.'

Ibid., pp. 79 et seq.:

Henry VIII of England had been constrained for political reasons to marry the Infanta Catherine of Aragon, daughter of Ferdinand and Isabella, and widow of his deceased brother Arthur … he desired to have this marriage annulled. The Pope would no doubt have been ready to grant the favour, but for his fear of Catherine's nephew, the Emperor Charles V, who resented the slight put upon his house. Thus little by little there spread the conflagration which was to end in the severance of England from its traditional allegiance to the Roman Church. For Henry's desire there was Biblical authority. In the Book of Leviticus, indeed, marriage between a man and his deceased brother's wife appears to be expressly forbidden. On the other hand in the book of Deuteronomy, it is expressly prescribed in the case of a childless match in order that the dead man's name should be perpetuated.

The problem of interpretation was highly perplexing. The consequence was that the importance of Hebrew tradition for the correct interpretation of Holy Writ was suddenly realised.

[2] Alfred Julius Bruck, *The Bruck Family, Historia Judaica*, Vol. 8 (New York 1946), pp. 159 et seq includes a short outline of the Chalfan family and their connection to the Kalonymos of Narbonne:

Menachem Elia (Eliyahu Menachem Chalfan) whose wife Fioret was the daughter of Calo Kalonymos ben David, was an outstanding physician and Talmudist in Venice. He was one of the Rabbinical authorities from whom Richard Croke, the agent of King Henry VIII, in 1529, obtained a [favourable] rabbinical opinion regarding the King's divorce from Catherine of Aragon. Several letters of this correspondence are preserved in the Public Record Office in London (quoting Paul Rieger, Geschichte der Juden in Rom, Vol. 2 (Berlin 1895)).

[3] M. Steinschneider, *Catalogus librorum Hebraeorum in Bibliotheca Bodleiana* (Berlin 1931) No. 6067 'Kalonymos ben David ex familia Kalonymorum'.

[4] David S. Katz, *The Jews in the History of England* (Oxford: Clarendon Press 1994) pp. 24 et seq. gives a more detailed account of Rabbi Eliyahu Chalfan's involvement in King Henry's efforts to have his marriage annulled.

[5] Correspondence of Elia Alfano with Pietro Aretino (1492–1556)
Extract from a letter, dated Venice, 6 July 1542, addressed to *Esteemed Don Elia Alfano* and signed *Pietro Aretino* (courtesy of Max Ludwig Mayer of London):

… from you who are a Jew all can learn how to be a Christian, for the fear of God and the love for your fellow man are inborn to the kindness of your nature. I have never met a man who equalled you in the love for their relatives. And

anyone who was near you when you secured the health of your mother with the energy of your spirit, the means of your medical science, and with the prayers of your heart, will appreciate how one should look after, support, and cherish one's mother. I should like anyone who has a family to see the tenderness and the purity of the way you honour your wife and bring up your children in the dignity of your customs.

[6] Bernard Wachstein, *Inschriften des alten Jüdenfriedhofes in Wien* (Vienna 1912), p. 60, No. 72.

L.A. Frankl, *Zur Geschichte der Juden in Wien* (Vienna 1853), No. 20 Inscription on the tombstone of Isaac Halfan who died in Vienna, 1617:

here lies a highly regarded youth distinguished for his piety, Isak, son of the famous doctor Elias Halfan, grandson of the doctor Abba Mari Halfan, great-grandson of the most learned Elias Halfan, great-great-grandson of the most learned Abba Mari Halfan.

[7] Guido Kisch, *Die Prager Universität und die Juden* (Mårisch Ostrau 1935), p. 111: Geleitbrief (Passport or Letter of Protection) from Emperor Rudolf II dated 1598 permitting Elias ben Abba Mari Chalfan and his family to settle in Vienna (the original document is in the Staatsarchiv Hanover).

Elias ben Abba Mari Halfan, father of the above-mentioned Isaac Halfan, was a physician, born in Prague in 1561, who moved to Vienna, where he died in 1624 (see second attached chart).

Chart 4.1 Descent from Kalonymos of Narbonne and Delmedigo Chalfan

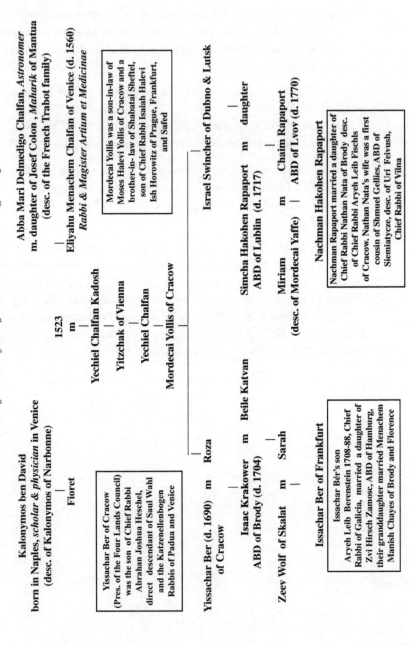

Kalonymos ben David
born in Naples, *scholar & physician* in Venice
(desc. of Kalonymos of Narbonne)

Fioret

Abba Mari Delmedigo Chalfan, *Astronomer*
m. daughter of Josef Colon , *Maharik* of Mantua
(desc. of the French Trabot family)

Eliyahu Menachem Chalfan of Venice (d. 1560)
Rabbi & Magister Artium et Medicinae

1523
m

Yechiel Chalfan Kadosh

Yitzchak of Vienna

Yechiel Chalfan

Mordecai Yollis of Cracow

Mordecai Yollis was a son-in-law of
Moses Halevi Yollis of Cracow and a
brother-in- law of Shabatai Sheftel,
son of Chief Rabbi Isaiah Halevi
Ish Horowitz of Prague, Frankfurt,
and Safed

Yissachar Ber of Cracow
(Pres. of the Four Lands Council)
was the son of Chief Rabbi
Abrahan Joshua Heschel,
direct descendant of Saul Wahl
and the Katzenellenbogen
Rabbis of Padua and Venice

Yissachar Ber (d. 1690)   m   Roza
of Cracow

Israel Swincher of Dubno & Lutsk

Simcha Hakohen Rapaport   m   daughter
ABD of Lublin (d. 1717)

Isaac Krakower   m   Beile Katvan
ABD of Brody (d. 1704)

Miriam   m   Chaim Rapaport
(desc. of Mordecai Yaffe) | ABD of Lvov (d. 1770)

Zeev Wolf of Skalat   m   Sarah

Nachman Hakohen Rapaport

Nachman Rapaport married a daughter of
Chief Rabbi Nathan Nata of Brody desc.
of Chief Rabbi Aryeh Leib Fischls
of Cracow. Nathan Nata's wife was a first
cousin of Shmuel Gellies, ABD of
Siemiatycze, desc. of Uri Feivush,
Chief Rabbi of Vilna

Issachar Ber of Frankfurt

Issachar Bėr's son
Aryeh Leib Berenstein 1708-88, Chief
Rabbi of Galicia, married a daughter of
Zvi Hirsch Zamosc, ABD of Hamburg,
their granddaughter married Menachem
Manish Chayes of Brody and Florence

Chart 4.2 Chalfan from Venice to Prague, Vienna, Krakow and Berlin

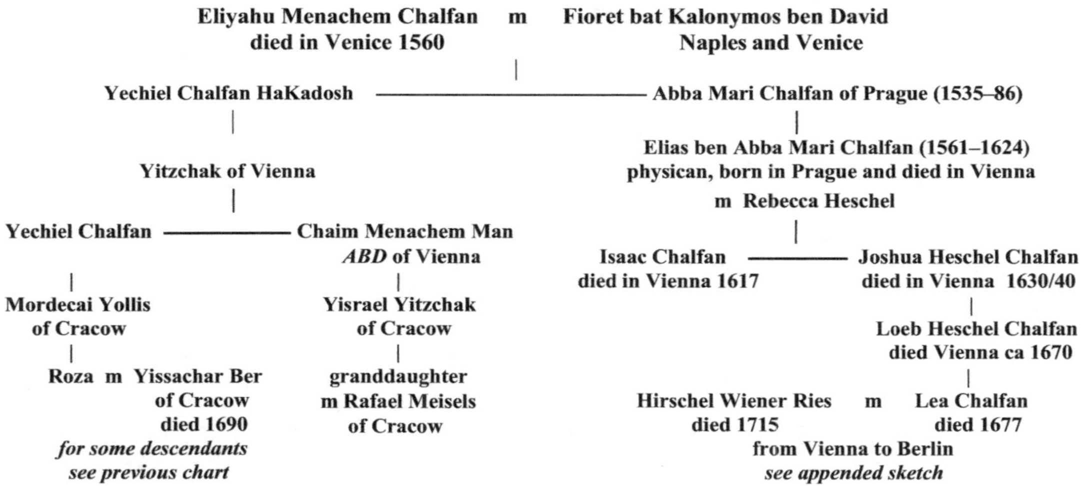

Eliyahu Menachem Chalfan   m   Fioret bat Kalonymos ben David
died in Venice 1560   Naples and Venice

Abba Mari Chalfan of Prague (1535–86)

Elias ben Abba Mari Chalfan (1561–1624)
physican, born in Prague and died in Vienna
m Rebecca Heschel

Joshua Heschel Chalfan
died in Vienna 1630/40

Loeb Heschel Chalfan
died Vienna ca 1670

Isaac Chalfan
died in Vienna 1617

Hirschel Wiener Ries   m   Lea Chalfan
died 1715   died 1677
from Vienna to Berlin
see appended sketch

Yechiel Chalfan HaKadosh

Yitzchak of Vienna

Chaim Menachem Man
ABD of Vienna

Yisrael Yitzchak
of Cracow

granddaughter
m Rafael Meisels
of Cracow

Yechiel Chalfan

Mordecai Yollis
of Cracow

Roza   m   Yissachar Ber
of Cracow
died 1690

*for some descendants
see previous chart*

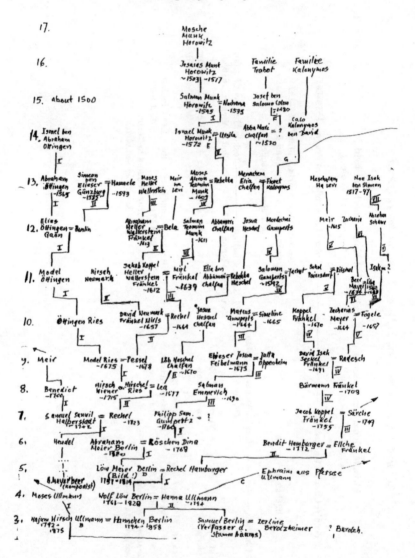

PART 2

Sixteenth to seventeenth centuries

Chapter 5

Bohemia, England and America

David and Chaim Gans of Prague

Dᴀᴠɪᴅ Gans was born in the Rhineland, studied in Frankfurt and Krakow with leading Jewish scholars, and then moved to Prague, where his circle included Rabbi Judah Loew and other Talmudists but also the great scientists and astronomers of the later sixteenth century. He wrote a notable secular history, the *Zemach David*.

His kinsman Chaim Gans (aka Joachim Gaunse) was an accomplished metallurgist who spent fascinating years in Elizabethan England and also travelled to America.

Their distinguished careers exemplified the transition from the learning of the old world to the scientific spirit of the Renaissance.

Most visitors to Prague will have come across the name of David Gans. He is a famous figure in the history of the city and of its Jewish community. Few will have heard of his near kinsman Chaim Gans, whose adventurous life and work is better known to students of the history of science in England and America. The common thread is their background of Talmudical study and their ready engagement with the new ideas of the Renaissance. A few genealogical digressions help to show their sixteenth-century world hovering between old and new philosophies and continents.

Several Jewish families of their name emerged from Germany in the Middle Ages [1]. David Gans was born in the Westphalian town of Lippstadt in 1541 His family developed branches at Leipen and Bischitz in Bohemia.

David was the son of Solomon ben Seligman Gans. His teachers included Eliezer Treves in Frankfurt and Moses Isserles in Krakow. He also studied under Judah Loew in Prague, where he finally settled in 1564. He took an active interest in mathematics, astronomy and geography and also wrote a history, the *Zemach David* [Sprig of David], which transcended the scope of the usual Jewish history and earned the description of *Historia Chronologica Sacra et Profana*. His circle of friends in Prague included the great Rabbi Judah Loew and the astronomers Kepler and Tycho Brahe. David was a true Renaissance scholar in a city which at the time stood at the crossroads between Germany and Italy and the centres of Jewish learning in Poland. He died in Prague in 1613. His tombstone is decorated with the Shield of David, the title of one of his many books, and also with the familiar emblem of a goose. The name of Gans [goose] derived in typical medieval German fashion from a house name and shield. The migration of this family over the centuries from towns in Germany, and specifically from Frankfurt, to Prague, and then to Krakow and beyond, followed a common pattern among Ashkenazi Jews.

David Gans had children and relatives who lived in these cities and further afield. His brother was Joshua Seligman, and his children included Israel Gans of Krakow (d.1619), Joshua Seligman Gans of Bischitz (d. Prague 1638), and a daughter who married Wolf Fleckeles. The eighteenth-century Rabbi Eleazar Fleckeles of Prague was their descendant [2].

David's father-in-law Samuel Rofe [doctor] was credited with devising a cure for syphilis with less-dangerous side effects than the quicksilver treatment then generally employed. His first cousin Nathan Nata Shapiro of Grodno (d.1577) is mentioned in the *Zemach David* [3]. He was the author of several books and reportedly had 'a vast knowledge of the Hebrew language and grammar'. He belonged to the Shapiros who go back to the Spiro son-in-law of Mattityahu Treves, the medieval rabbis of France, and thence to Rashi of Troyes, the biblical scholar and commentator of the eleventh century. Nathan of Grodno was the grandfather of the Rabbi of Krakow of the same name (1585–1633) and the line continued to Rabbi Pinchas Shapiro of Koretz (1721–96) and to Rabbi Yehuda Meir Shapira (1887–1934). The Gelles rabbis of Brody had links of descent, marriage and friendship with the three last-named rabbis [4].

The records of Frankfurt hint at a possible connection of the descendants of Geyle, who died there in 1634 and is identified as a daughter of Rabbi David Gans, with the rabbis bearing the Gelles matronymic in Prague [5–7].

Simon Hock's transcriptions of the Prague tombstones include numerous entries for the Gans family covering the period from 1598 to 1776 [8]. For example, No. 5395 [1634] is for Seligman, son of the pious Rabbi David of Bischitz. A footnote refers to a Rabbi Seligman Gans of Prague and also mentions the name of Chaim Gans, the metallurgist who developed copper mining in England. The Prague burial lists also contain many entries for Gelles from 1632 to 1745, including an entry for 1651 for the honourable Rabbi Mendel, son of Salman Gelles, 'emissary of the Beth Din'. There is no evidence as to possible connections with later bearers of the name in Lithuania and Poland.

Chaim Gans was David's near kinsman, perhaps a nephew [9, 11]. His family background was one in which the traditional Talmudic learning was combined with that of the new science. Interest in Jewish arcane lore such as the Kabbalah, astrology and alchemy remained intense. Chaim's interest in metallurgy was also not unconnected with the proximity of the so-called *Erzgebirge* [ore mountains] at the borders of Bohemia and Saxony, which had long been exploited for its wealth of minerals. Here and in the Austrian Tyrol were the prime areas of European metal production. Following the publication in

1556 of the classic work *De Re Metallica* by Georg Bauer [Agricola], the above-mentioned regions far surpassed the rest of Europe in the sophistication of mining and metallurgy.

Chaim Gans was an expert in his field. He came to England in 1581 and made an outstanding contribution to the development of the mining industry. He took part in an expedition to the New World and appears to have been the first professing Jew to set foot in English-speaking North America. He has been regarded by some as one of the pioneers of the modern scientific method [10–12].

Chaim, known here as Joachim Gaunse, enjoyed the patronage of some of the most important men in Elizabethan England. Sir Francis Walsingham was the principal patron of his work for the Society of the Mines Royal at Keswick in the Lake District. It revolutionised English copper production and was just in time to give English ships the advantage of good bronze cannon to pit against the cast iron guns of the Spanish Armada. Sir Walter Raleigh recruited him for his expedition of 1584–86 which established a base on Roanoke Island, Virginia. The site at which Gans carried out metallurgical tests has been described as 'America's First Science Center' [11]. Fort Raleigh National Historic Site in North Carolina preserves relics of his work. The ship that took Gans and his team of German miners to America was captained by Sir Richard Grenville. When supplies failed, the survivors of the expedition were brought back to England by Sir Francis Drake.

It has been suggested by Lewis S. Feuer that Joachim Gaunse was the model for Joabin, the Jewish innovator of scientific enquiry, in Sir Francis Bacon's *New Atlantis* [12].

Gans introduced procedures for treating minerals and producing copper in which the lengthy and repeated roastings of ores was replaced by a much less time consuming and less costly treatment of the powdered material, alternating with repeated washings by means of which metal sulphates and impurities were gradually removed. The iron and copper sulphates thus extracted were put to use in the dyeing of textiles. Gans further developed his method for smelting ore at Neath near Swansea, and it has been suggested that some Cornish mines were re-opened at his instigation. As the leading 'metal man' of his day it is no wonder that he was sought out to search for minerals and to explore the potential for metal production in America [11].

Chaim appears to have stayed in Bristol and London. He settled in the former city on his return from America. For a few years Gans was near the centre of the great Elizabethan Renaissance. But this was a time for religious as well as scientific revolution. In this great period of transition there were boundless opportunities as well as great dangers. The Elizabethan state in its life and death struggle with Catholic Spain did not tolerate any expressions of religious dissent. Gans was accused of denying the divinity of Christ. As a professing Jew he could not be accused of heresy, but a charge of blasphemy may have been enough to enforce his departure from these shores, and he probably returned to Bohemia, but all trace of him appears to have been lost around 1590 [10,11].

Some Bohemian Jews like David and Chaim, whose minds had been sharpened through Talmudical study over the generations, took readily to the new science and the emerging spirit of empirical enquiry. This family played an interesting role in the process that ultimately led from astrology to modern astronomy and from alchemical lore to modern chemical science.

REFERENCES

[1] Ludwig Herz, *Die Sechshundertjährige Geschichte der Familie Gans 1330–1930*. (London: Wiener Library), Microfiche WLMF 89151 [MFBK503].

[2] Shlomo Berman, *Otzar Israel*, ed., J. Eisenstein. Vol. 3, pp. 233–4 (Menorah Publications 1974).

[3] David Gans, *Zemach David*. (Prague 1592), paragraph 5367 [1507].

[4] Edward Gelles, *Gelles Rabbinical Ancestry*, to be published.

[5] Alexander Dietz, *The Jewish Community of Frankfurt. A Genealogical Study 1349–1849*. (Vanderher Publications 1988), pp. 126, 131–3, 446, 447, 511, 551.

[6] Marcus Horovitz, *Die Inschriften des alten Friedhofs der Israelitischen Gemeinde zu Frankfurt a.M. Kauffman*. (Frankfurt 1901), No. 626.

[7] F.W. Ettlinger, *Ele Toldot*. Manuscript at the Leo Baeck Institute, New York.

[8] Simon Hock, *Die Familien Prags nach Epitaphien des alten Jüdischen Friedhofes*. (Pressburg: Adolf Alkalay 1892).

[9] Cecil Roth, *A History of the Jews in England*. (Oxford 1964), but see entries in the *Jewish Encyclopedia* by I. Abrahams, in the *Encylopedia Judaica* by

C. Roth and Grassl [see Note 11], who places Chaim Gans with the Leipen branch of the family.

[10]State Papers, Domestic, Elizabeth I, London, Vol. 152, item 88, March 1582, Vol. 226, item 40, 1589.

[11]Gary C. Grassl, 'Joachim Gans of Prague: The First Jew in English America', *American Jewish Historical Society Quarterly Publication*, Vol. 86, No. 2. (June 1998) [including extensive references, particularly to Gaunse's metallurgical work and North American expedition].

[12]Lewis S. Feuer, 'Francis Bacon and the Jews. Who was the Jew in the *New Atlantis?*', *Jewish Historical Studies*, Vol. 29 (1982–6), pp. 1–25, and 'The Life and Work of Joachim Gaunse, mining technologist and first recorded Jew in English-speaking North America', *The American Jewish Archives* (Cincinnati 1987), No. 8.

Chapter 6

Golden age for the Jews of Prague

Judah Loew and contemporary rabbis of Prague

THE PERIOD FROM the late sixteenth to the early seventeenth century was a golden one for the Jews of Prague, notwithstanding a background of political and religious controversies. The community had a succession of great rabbis whose influence went far beyond their city. These included the famous Rabbi Judah Loew, his brother-in-law Isaac Chayes, and Mordecai Jaffe – called 'Levush' after the title of his magnum opus. The latter also held senior rabbinical posts in Poland where he was an important community leader. Isaiah Halevi Ish Horowitz, the Chief Rabbi of Frankfurt and Prague, the most renowned of the great Horowitz family, was followed by Yomtov Lipman Heller, who in turn became Chief Rabbi in Vienna, Prague and Krakow.

Judah Loew ben Bezalel of Prague (known as *der Hohe Rabbi Loew* or the *Maharal*) was born in Posen around 1520 (or possibly in Worms) and died in Prague in 1609. He is one of the best known among the important rabbis of post-medieval times. His forebears came from Alsace to Worms, where his uncle Jacob ben Chaim Loew held the imperial title of *Reichsrabbiner* (Chief Rabbi of all German communities in the Empire). The Davidic pedigree of the Loews is believed to rest on descent from Yehudah HaNassi (*c.*135–200) of the House of Hillel, who was descended from King David's son Shepatiah.

Judah Loew first became prominent as *Landesrabbiner* of Moravia (in Nikolsburg) and he attained lasting fame for his wide learning and leadership of the increasingly important Jewish community in Prague. His knowledge of mystical Jewish lore (the *Kabbalah*) is remembered in the popular legend of the *Golem* [1]. His grave and elaborate tombstone and a fine modern statue recall the life of this great rabbi of Prague – a fine city which in the reign of Emperor Rudolf II briefly became the imperial capital. The unprecedented audience granted to Judah Loew by the Emperor in 1592 reflected the reputation the *Maharal* enjoyed in his lifetime [2]. This was a golden period in the life of the Prague community.

Judah Loew's first marriage was to Mirel, a daughter of Rabbi Abraham Chayes of Prague, who was known as Eberel Altschuler. Judah Loew married secondly Perel, the daughter of Shmuel Schmelke Reich [3].

Rabbi Isaac ben Abraham Chayes (Chayot) became Chief Rabbi of Prague. When he retired from this office, his brother-in-law Judah Loew succeeded him.

One of the children of the *Maharal*'s first marriage, to Mirel Chayes-Altschuler, was Voegele. Her union with Isaac ben Samson Katz, scion of a millennial sacerdotal family, gave rise to a number of important lines that are shown on Chart 0.4, in the Introduction.

Shortly after the historic imperial audience, Rabbi Loew moved to Posen, but later returned to Prague, thus changing posts with Rabbi Mordecai Yaffe (1530–1612). The latter in turn became Chief Rabbi of Posen with precedence over all the rabbis of Poland. Mordecai Yaffe was called 'the *Levush*' (after the name of his magnum opus, *The Levushim* or Rabbinical Robes of Learning).

Chart 6.1 Habsburg Emperors, Chief Rabbis of Prague, and antecedents of Judah Loew

Maximilian I	Charles V	Ferdinand I	Maximilian II	Rudolf II	Matthias
1491–1519	1519–1556	1556–1564	1564–1576	1577–1612	1612–1619
				in Prague 1583–	

HOROWITZ Family	Isaac Chayes 1584–
dominate communal appointments	**Judah Loew 1588 ?–**
granted privileges by last two	**Mordecai Yaffe 1592–**
Jagiellonian Kings of Bohemia	**Judah Loew 1597–1609**
	Isaiah Horowitz 1614–21
	Yom Tov Lipman Heller 1627–29

			Bezalel Loew	▶	Judah Loew
Bezalel Loew	▶	**Chaim Loew**	▶	**&**	
		d. Worms 1565	**Jacob Loew**		
			Rabbi of Worms d. 1574		
			Reichsrabbiner		

Davidic descent has been ascribed to a number of Jewish families although none can be said to have an indisputable royal pedigree. Some families claim connections to Babylonian Exilarchs who led the Jewish communities in exile for centuries and were widely believed to be of the House of David. These claimants generally have a Sephardic background. There are also those, thought of as Ashkenazi, who had early Sephardic connections. They include families who were in the Spanish March, in Languedoc and in Provence until persecution set them on eastward journeys to Italy, Bohemia, Austria, Poland and elsewhere.

Such are a sprig of the Shem Tov Halevi, who settled in Bohemia at the close of the fifteenth century, and went by the name of Halevi Ish Horowitz, that is, Levites, men of Horovice (near Prague). The most revered of this family was Rabbi Isaiah ben Abraham Halevi Ish Horowitz (*c.*1568–1627) of Frankfurt, Prague and Safed, who is known as the *Holy Shelah*.

A Provencal branch of the Chayoth (Chayes), who had Portuguese origins, came to Prague at that time and there were marriages between these two families. The famous synagogues built (or rebuilt) by them were called the *Alt-Neu Shul*, from which some of the Chayes derived their epithet of Altschuler followed by the *Pinkas Shul* after Pinkas Horowitz.

Both families later went on to Poland and beyond. Pinchas Halevi Horowitz (1535–1618) became President of the Council of the Four Lands, married a sister of Rabbi Moses Isserles of Krakow, and allied his daughter Hinde to Meir, the son of Saul Wahl.

Saul Wahl's family, the Katzenellenbogen, have a clear descent via a nexus of the Luria, Treivish and Spira families from *Rashi* of Troyes (Solomon ben Isaac of Troyes 1040–1105), who is widely believed to be of Davidic lineage. Rabbi Solomon Luria of Lublin (1510–74) was a kinsman of Saul Wahl. Luria was also related to Judah Loew within the tightly knit group of ancient rabbinical families.

Prague in the sixteenth and early seventeenth centuries was at the crossroads of Jewish migration from west to east. Here many of the historical families such as the Loew, Chayes, Horowitz, Yaffe, Katzenellenbogen, and others mingled and intermarried. Another great rabbi of Prague was Yomtov Lipman Heller, Chief Rabbi of Vienna, Prague and Krakow, though his short tenure in Prague was not until 1627–9. He and his progeny were linked by marriage to the Horowitz and Katzenellenbogen. The tombstones of Prague, indicating some of these manifold connections, include that of Rabbi David Gans (1530–1612), the author of *Zemach David* and pupil of the *Maharal*. Among many better known names, Gelles and G-lles Katz are also to be found there [4].

Members of a priestly family fled in 1391 from persecution in Spain to a safe haven in the Ottoman Empire and settled in Prague after a sojourn in Hungary. Akiba Katz from Gallati was Rabbi of Ofen (Buda) and his daughter Yocheved married Shabbatai Sheftel Horowitz, a son of the first Horowitz of Prague, Isaiah ben Moshe Halevi Ish Horowitz (*c.*1440–1515). Some of the above-mentioned connections are shown on the appended Chart 6.2.

These close connections between the old rabbinical families of Prague continued into later times in Lithuania and Poland, and notably in Galicia.

REFERENCES

[1] The fantastic tale of the *Golem*, a dumb servant fashioned by Rabbi Loew out of clay and brought to life by magical incantation, was a reflection of the awe in which the Rabbi was held by the populace. Nor

was this wonderment confined to the uneducated in an age that still had faith in astrology and alchemy, the philosopher's stone that would turn base metal into gold, and so on. (Heinz Politzer, *Die Goldene Gasse – Jüdische Sagen und Legenden* (Vienna and Jerusalem: R. Löwit 1937)).

[2] At the famous imperial audience of 1592 the *Maharal* was accompanied by his brother Sinai and his son-in-law Isaac Katz (whose family claimed descent from Eli the Priest). The Kabbalah and related matters are believed to have been a principal topic of conversation.

[3] Re: Judah Loew's marriages:

The best known work on the *Maharal's* life is Rabbi Meir Perels, *Megillat Yuchasin Mehral mi'Prag* [German translation in the Jahrbuch der Juedisch-Literarischen Gesellschaft, Frankfurt, Vol. 20, 1929]. From this time-honoured work many people are still under the mistaken impression that Judah Loew had only one marriage, to Perel Reich. David Nachman Rutner, *Beth Ahron Veyisrael*, Vol. 18, No. 2 (Jerusalem), pp. 170–5, refers to a work by Rabbi Yair Chaim Bacharach in a periodical called *Bikurim* published in Vienna in 1865, clearly identifying Judah Loew's first wife as the sister of Rabbi Isaac Chayes, son of Rabbi Abraham Chayes of Prague.

The Maharal married secondly, at the age of 32, Perel, daughter of Shmuel Schmelke Reich, and her descendants were known by the surname of Perels (Rabbi L. Rakow, *Keren Yisrael* (London and Jerusalem 2000), pp. 57–66).

[4] Simon Hock, *Die Familien Prags nach Epitaphien des alten Jüdischen Friedhofes* (Pressburg: Adolf Alkalay 1892).

Chart 6.2 Horowitz Family roots and branches

Generations of Shem Tov Halevi in Barcelona and Gerona

Horowitz in Prague

▶

Isaiah ben Moshe Halevi Horowitz of Provence (ca 1440–1515) also known as *Zalman Horovsky*

Shabatai Sheftel Horowitz (d. 1555 in Prague) ——— **Ahron Meshullam Zalman Horowitz** (1470–1545) aka *Zalman Munka*

Israel Horowitz (1500–1572) **of Prague**

Pinchas Halevi Horowitz (Prague 1535– Cracow 1618)
President of Council of the Four Lands
m sister of Moses Isserles of Cracow
their daughter Hinde m Meir, son of <u>SAUL WAHL</u>

Jacob Horowitz (d.Vienna 1630)
possibly son of Pinchas Halevi Horowitz and father of Joshua Horowitz
(cf MeirWunder, Meorei Galicia, vol 2, 110–111 and 119–120)

Joshua Horowitz (d. 1661)
ABD of Przemysl

Shmuel Shmelke Horowitz (d. 1694)
ABD of Tarnow

Meir Horowitz (d. 1743)
Maharam of Tiktin

Zvi Hirsch Horowitz (d. 1754)
ABD of Czortkow

Yocheved   m   **Shabatai Sheftel Horowitz** (d. 1555 in Prague)
bat Akiba Katz

Avraham Horowitz

Isaiah Halevi Horowitz (1568–1627)
the **"Shelah"** - *Frankfurt, Prague, & Safed*

Shabatai Sheftel Horowitz (ca 1600–60)
m. dr of Moses Halevi Yollis of Cracow

daughter of Menachem Manish Katz   m
son of Isaiah Katz of Brody

Jacob Jokel Horowitz (d. 1755) ——————— **Zvi Hirsch Horowitz** (d. 1754)
ABD of Glogau & Brody

Isaac Horowitz   **Shmuel Shmelke Horowitz** ——— **Pinchas Horowitz**
(1715–1767)   (1726–1778)   (1730–1805)
ABD of Brody, Glogau, & Hamburg   *ABD of Nikolsburg*   *ABD of Frankfurt*

Chapter 7

From Padua and Venice to Poland and Lithuania

Life and times of Saul Wahl

THE UNION OF Poland and the Grand Duchy of Lithuania in 1569 was followed shortly thereafter by the end of the Jagiellonian dynasty. The country became an elective monarchy at a time when it was a burgeoning European power. During the ensuing reigns of the Transylvanian Stefan Bathory and the Swedish Prince Sigismund Vasa the Jewish community attained considerable economic importance. The career of Saul Wahl, a scion of the rabbis of Padua and Venice, who rose to eminence during this period, throws light on relations between the Estates of the Polish–Lithuanian Commonwealth and on wider political changes in eastern Europe.

How could the Italian grandson of a German Jew become king of Poland? It happened in 1587, at least according to Jewish tradition. Poland at that time had an elective kingship. The throne was vacant. The electors were divided. Saul Wahl, a leading financier, was well connected with the biggest magnates in the land and in a position to play an important role during the interregnum. An extraordinary man was in the right place at the right time.

What was so special about the sixteenth century and the condition of the Jews in Europe and in Poland in particular – and who was Saul and where did he come from?

The discovery of the New World in 1492 heralded a period of rapid demographic expansion and Poland became the granary of Europe. At the same time, the Renaissance and the Protestant Reformation brought about a revolution in culture, religious diversity, and political ideas. Last but not least in this extraordinary story is the importance of Padua University, the alma mater of Saul Wahl and some of his later patrons.

THE STATE OF POLAND

Poland flourished under the Jagiellonian kings who were also grand dukes of Lithuania. With Sigismund I (1506–48), the Renaissance came in the person of his queen, Bona Sforza, daughter of the Duke of Milan. Her retinue included Jewish doctors who had studied at the great Italian universities, while Poland's greatest scientist of the age, Nicolas Copernicus, and one of her leading statesmen, Jan Zamoyski, were graduates of both Krakow and Padua.

Jews had been fleeing to Poland from persecution in Germany since before the time of Casimir the Great (1333–70), who ratified and extended an earlier charter of toleration. As elsewhere in Europe, the Jews met religious intolerance from the clergy and marked hostility from townspeople, who felt themselves economically threatened, in contrast to the king and the magnates who benefited from their activities.

The direct Jagiellonian line came to an end shortly after the formal union of the Kingdom of Poland with the Grand Duchy of Lithuania (Lublin 1569). The death of Sigismund II August marked the beginning of the era of elective kingship. In the new 'Republic', political power was vested in the nobility. The election depended on the balance between the great magnates of the land and those of the neighbouring states such as Austria and Sweden. It was an oligarchy with a titular royal head and with a constitution which bore some resemblance to those of the Serene Republic of Venice and the Holy Roman Empire. The Jews benefited from the new system in so far as newly elected kings needed ready funds, which they could supply.

The brief reign of Henri Valois (1573–5) was followed by that of the Transylvanian Prince Stefan Bathory (1576–86), and then the Swedish Prince Sigismund III Vasa and his two sons successively held the Polish crown through a century of expansion, which saw Poland–Lithuania briefly become the most powerful state in eastern Europe. At its widest boundaries, it included White Russia and Ukraine and extended beyond Smolensk and Kiev to the land of the Zaporozhe Cossacks.

In this age, Catholic kings maintained the rights of religious minorities and the privileges accorded to the Jews. An extensive system of Jewish autonomy developed with substantial juridical and fiscal powers, such as the assessment of taxes by the rabbinate and local councils.

Their numbers grew rapidly to over 5 per cent of the population, and they extended their activities from the traditional money-lending to all branches of the economy. They became the favoured agents of the crown and magnates as rent, tax, toll and tithe collectors, and estate managers, which involved running the mills, distilleries, taverns and other enterprises. Inevitably, the resentment of the peasantry was directed against the Jewish agents rather than the absentee landlords.

For a long time, Poland more than held its own against the rising powers of Sweden and Muscovy, the more distant threats of the Tartars and Ottoman Turks, and the ambitions of their Hohenzollern vassals. The deluge came in 1648 with the rebellion of Bogdan Chmielnicki, Ataman of the Dnieper Cossacks, which ultimately led to the transfer of their allegiance to Muscovy and to the loss of Ukraine and much else for Poland. This blow to the Polish state was also a catastrophe for the Jewish communities, which suffered enormous losses in lives and property.

PAN-EUROPEAN CONDITIONS

Conditions were changing elsewhere in Europe. While large numbers of German Jews migrated directly to Poland over a long period, others went to join existing communities in Italy. There the Jews suffered under the religiously inspired intolerance which waxed and waned during the Renaissance, Reformation and Counter-Reformation periods. They were confined to ghettos and severely restricted in the occupations and professions that were open to them. The Church had long forbidden Christians to receive interest, but tolerated or even encouraged Jewish money-lenders, who enjoyed a near monopoly in some countries, though at times they met strong competition from the Lombards.

Jews did not have full civil rights, but their lives and property were generally protected by the secular authorities. The universities gave them access in very limited numbers. Padua was for a long time one of the few schools where they could study medicine.

The mass expulsions from the Iberian peninsula at the end of the fifteenth century were the greatest disaster for Sephardic Jewry, which had flourished in Spain and Portugal for centuries. Many fled to Holland, Italy and Turkey. The Ottomans maintained a hospitable and tolerant attitude for a considerable period. Jews prospered in Constantinople but, after the battle of Lepanto in 1571, the Sultan's power and protection declined. Prominent at that time was Joseph Nasi, who had fled from Portugal to Holland, and later not being made welcome in Venice, accepted an invitation to move to Constantinople. He became the powerful favourite of Sultan Selim and was created Duke of Naxos and Prince of the Cyclades. Salomon Ashkenasi, whose family had come to Italy from Germany, was physician to Sigismund August in Krakow and later to the Grand Vizier in Constantinople. He is reputed to have been influential in the negotiations leading to the election of Henri Valois and later of Stefan Bathory to the Polish throne, and he was sent as ambassador of the Sublime Porte to the Serene Republic of Venice in 1574. His son, Nathan, who also studied medicine at Padua, was Ottoman ambassador to Venice in 1605. These men were favourably placed to conduct discreet diplomatic and financial negotiations by nature of the dispersion and their wide international contacts.

In contrast to the fifteenth-century persecutions in Germany and the Empire, the Reformation ushered in a better time for the Jews there, perhaps because it divided their potential oppressors. The ensuing turbulence, changing alliances, fluctuating fortunes of war, and the expanding need for credit and finance led the Habsburg emperors to adopt a friendlier policy.

Maximilian II allowed the Jews to return to Bohemia, and in 1577 Rudolph II gave them a charter of privileges. One of his agents, Marcus Meisel, was a prototype of the 'Court Jew'. He helped to finance the war against the Ottoman Turks.

THE FAMILY BACKGROUND

Returning to the importance of Padua in this period, noble Poles travelled in Italy and learned Jews went to Poland. That is the background to the career of Saul Wahl, scion of the Katzenellenbogen family, hailing from the town of that name in the German state of Hesse-Nassau.

The name Katzenellenbogen is believed to derive from the Catti, an ancient Frankish tribe. It may refer to their settlement near the bend (elbow) of the Rhine or to another geographical feature in that area known by the Latin name of Cattimelibocus. Descendants of Hugh Capet became counts of Katzenellenbogen in the twelfth century and gradually permitted small numbers of Jews to settle there. A Jewish community was firmly established early in the fourteenth century. Rabbi Isaac of Katzenellenbogen married the daughter of Rabbi Jehiel Luria of Alsace and later moved to Prague, where his son Meir (1482–1565) studied before going on to Padua. There Meir married Hannah, the granddaughter of his teacher Judah Minz. The latter had come to Padua when the Jews were expelled from Mainz in 1461 and he established a Talmudic academy which achieved worldwide fame, attracting students from north of the Alps and as far as the Levant. Meir took over the leadership from Judah's son Abraham in 1541. He is considered the patriarch of the Katzenellenbogen family.

According to the historian Cecil Roth, Rabbi Meir was among the most eminent Talmudic authorities of his day and his opinion was sought from every quarter of Europe in connection with knotty problems of Jewish law. His son, Samuel Judah (1521–97), succeeded him in Padua and subsequently became Chief Rabbi of Venice. His reputation extended to non-Jewish scholars such as Paul Weidner, who dedicated his works to him (Vienna 1562). Like his father, he wrote numerous *responsa* and some of his sermons were published in Venice in 1594. His friend Leone da Modena delivered his funeral oration in 1597. He and his wife Abigail had two daughters and a son, Saul, born in Padua about 1541–5. The family background was thus distinguished for learning, wealth and social position in one of the most flourishing Jewish communities.

FROM ITALY TO POLAND

Saul attended the University of Padua, and around 1560 he set out for Poland to study at the Yeshiva of the *Maharshal* (R. Shlomo Luria) in Brest. There he settled after marrying the daughter of a local rabbi. Brest was fast becoming an important centre for Lithuanian Jewry and he might well have ended his days as the respected rabbi of this distant town. But now there occurred one of those chance events which shape the lives of individuals and nations. The path of the Katzenellenbogens crossed that of the Radziwills, the richest and most powerful nobles in Lithuania, who remained prominent in the councils of Poland for several centuries.

Nicholas Radziwill, who died in 1477, was Marshal of the Court of Lithuania and Palatine of Wilno, the most important person in the country after the Grand Duke. His two great-grandsons, Nicholas 'Rufus' and Nicholas 'the Black', were given the title of Prince of the Holy Roman Empire by Charles V as part of the latter's machinations to prevent the union of Lithuania with Poland. But this was trumped by Sigismund August, who not only confirmed their princely status but granted them the freeholds of their enormous estates of Olyka and Nieswiez, from which they henceforth took their ducal titles. All this was reaffirmed by both king and parliament in Lublin in 1569. The position of the Radziwills in Poland was further strengthened by the king's marriage to Barbara, Prince Rufus's sister.

Nicholas the Black's son, Prince Nicolas Christoph 'the Orphan' (1549–1616), returned to the Catholic faith and undertook a

Photo 10 Prince Nicolaus Christof Radziwill

pilgrimage to Jerusalem, which he recorded in his *Peregrinatio Hierosolymitana*. He also offered to buy up the extant copies of the Protestant 'Radziwill Bible' published by his father, intending to have them destroyed. According to legend, this is the Prince Radziwill who, returning from the Holy Land, found himself short of funds in Italy and appealed to Rabbi Samuel Judah for assistance, which was amply provided. Regaining his domain, he repaid the rabbi's kindness by seeking out his son Saul and taking him under his wing. Not so strange when one considers that they had been contemporaries at Padua! Radziwill and his friends favoured Saul with appointments and eased his advancement to wealth and influence.

There are records that Saul leased breweries at Kandawa (west of Riga) in 1578 and owned ships for this business, and that he acquired similar interests at Wieliczka near Krakow in 1580. In these years King Stefan Bathory leased him the salt pans in the

Grand Duchy, giving him the sole rights to sell their products, and also the salt mine at Wieliczka. Since at one time salt furnished nearly a fifth of the crown revenues, these were major commercial concessions. There are also documents relating to Saul's paying a large sum for the right to farm the Lithuanian taxes for three years and, again, the sum of 150,000 gold florins for the right to collect tolls on bridges and duties on flour and brandy for ten years. In 1589 King Sigismund gave him titles and privileges in a decree granting him 'a place among our royal officials and that he may be assured of our favour we exempt him and his lands for the rest of his life from subordination to the jurisdiction of any court in our lands'. Saul, referred to as 'Servus Regis', the King's Servant, became the king's principal agent in the opening up of commerce in Lithuania and Courland in particular.

From the 1580s onwards, Saul was among the leaders of the Brest community, taking an important part in the Council of the Lands. He interceded in a number of law suits on behalf of Jewish communities, as, for example, in 1592 when the Jews of Brest appealed to the king against the local municipality. In the same year, he persuaded the king to order the courts in Courland to judge disputes with Jews according to Polish, rather than the less favourable Prussian, law. This ruling was extended and confirmed by later kings. Saul was also given credit for the confirmation that disputes between Jews should be subject only to Jewish courts, thus strengthening the autonomy rights of Lithuanian Jewry.

During this time, he brought up a family and united himself with the most prominent Jewish rabbis through the marriages of his children. His son Meir, who later became Rabbi and Head of the Rabbinical Court at Brest, married Heinde, the daughter of Rabbi Pinchas Horowitz, the brother-in-law of the RAM'A, Rabbi Moses Isserles. He built a synagogue, a house of learning and public baths, and made many other benefactions. When the Brest synagogue was demolished in 1842, a plaque was discovered with the following inscription: 'Saul, son of the Chief Rabbi of Padua, built this synagogue in honour of his pious wife Deborah, daughter of (David) Drucker'.

Other information that has come down to us includes references to the gold chain which Saul wore with other decorations and which he bequeathed to the poor, as well as a trust fund of 20,000 Polish gulden, to a seal displaying a lion (rampant) holding in its paw two tablets with a Latin inscription (representing the ten commandments), and to title deeds for property still recorded as extant in the mid nineteenth century.

HISTORICAL RECORDS AND ORAL TRADITION

Saul became an intimate of the Radziwills and other magnates and of King Sigismund, who is supposed to have addressed him as Wahl. As for the adoption of that name, it is in my considered opinion a reference to his coming from Italy (land of the *Walen*). However, another derivation might be from a trade or tavern sign. A closely related family had the name of Shor. This is Hebrew for ox, and the Polish for ox is *wo(h)l*. A similar type of name derivation applies to the Rothschilds. A third possibility is that mentioned by early writers such as his direct eighteenth-century descendant Rabbi Phineas ben Moses Katzenellenbogen. He set down the oral tradition passed from Saul's contemporaries to his father, undoubtedly glamourising the history of the Polish Interregnum of 1587 to create an enduring legend (see also the following Chapter 8).

Rabbi Samuel Judah's son was the great Saul Wahl of blessed memory. All learned in such matters well know that his surname Wahl was given him because he was chosen king of Poland by the unanimous vote of the noble electors of the land. I was told by my father and teacher of blessed memory that the choice fell on him in this wise. Saul Wahl was a favourite with the Polish noblemen and highly esteemed for his shrewdness and ability. The king of Poland had died. Now it was customary for the great nobles of Poland to assemble for the election of a new king on a given day on which it was imperative that a valid decision be reached. When the day came many opinions were found to prevail among the electors, which could not be reconciled. Evening fell and they realised the impossibility of electing a king on the legally appointed day. Loath to transgress their own rules the nobles agreed to make Saul Wahl king for the rest of the day and the following night and thus conform with the letter of the law. And so it was.

In earlier Polish and Lithuanian state documents Saul had been variously referred to as Saul Judicz, i.e. Saul the Jew. These records are scanty. Much was lost or deliberately destroyed in the late seventeenth century and during the eighteenth-century partitions. However, the oral tradition and the weight of anecdotal evidence that Saul carried out royal functions prior to the election of Sigismund III is impressive. For example, Edelmann sent out a circular to the rabbis in 'Ashkenaz' in the mid nineteenth century and received several hundred letters and manuscripts from all over central and eastern Europe. These dealt with aspects of Saul's career in finance and commerce, as a civic leader in Lithuania, with his royal election, and with the laws he is supposed to have rushed through to improve the legal status of the Jews. When Prince Radziwill proposed Saul to the deadlocked electors to be king for a day in order to gain time for a resolution of the impasse, Saul is supposed to have insisted as a condition of accepting the honour that certain laws should be enacted forthwith, that in future the spilling of Jewish blood was to be treated in the same way by the courts as the murder of a Christian, and that no further blood libel allegations (to which there was no basis) were to be considered.

Other legends grew up around Saul's name. The story that Sigismund had an affair with his daughter Hanele has a degree of plausibility. Saul married her off in a hurry to an elderly widowed kinsman, Rabbi Ephraim Zalman Shor. This story is discussed in more detail in a following essay.

CONCLUSION

In this essay I have attempted to sketch in the state of Poland–Lithuania in the later sixteenth century against the general European background. The salient points were the political balance between the king, the magnates, the lesser nobility, and the other estates of the land, the economic importance of the Jewish community, the great wealth of Saul, his influence at court and with the higher nobility, and particularly the patronage of the Radziwills.

Against this historical background and with the documented facts of his life, it is likely that Saul should have played an important role after the death of Stefan Bathory. Many of the principal players would have been beholden to him.

The long interregnum of 1586–7 saw an intense struggle between the parties of the leading candidates. The crown was the prize to be

Chart 7.1 Saul Wahl and some of his children

1	R. Isaac of Katzenellenbogen m. daughter of R. Jechiel Luria of Alsace and Brest
2	Meir Judah Katzenellenbogen (1483–1565), Chief Rabbi of Padua m. Hannah Minz, granddaughter of Judah Minz (1411–1508), Chief Rabbi of Padua
3	Samuel Judah Katzenellenbogen (1521–1597), Chief Rabbi of Padua and Venice m. Abigail Yaffe (d.1594)
4	Saul Katzenellenbogen, known as Saul Wahl (1545–1617) in Poland–Lithuania m. Deborah Drucker. Some of their 13 children are listed in Neil Rosenstein's, *The Unbroken Chain*, v.i.
5.1	Their eldest son, Meir Wahl Katzenellenbogen (d. 1631), Chief Rabbi of Brest m Heinde, daughter of Pinchas Halevi Ish Horowitz (1535–1617), President of the Council of the Four Lands. Among their numerous issue was Rabbi Moses Katzenellenbogen of Chelm, father of Rabbi Saul Katzenellenbogen of Pinczow who married Yente, a daughter of Rabbi Jacob Shor (see below under 5.8)
5.6	Samuel Judah m. daughter of Moses Reb Lazers (i.e. son of Eliezer Isserles, a brother of the great Rabbi Moses Isserles of Krakow) among the children of this couple was Dinah Katzenellenbogen who married [1] Rabbi Naftali Hirsch Katz of Frankfurt etc. and [2] Abraham Joshua Heshel, the Chief Rabbi of Krakow – from the first marriage we have connections going back to Rabbi Judah Loew of Prague and the Chayes family and descent via Katz, Horowitz, Margolies etc. to my immediate family
5.8	Hanele m the elderly kinsman Rabbi Efraim Zalman Shor (d. 1633), whose wife had died in 1589 [note – legends surrounding Hanele and King Sigismund III Vasa] Hanele's son, Rabbi Jacob Shor (*c.*1600–1655) m Hannah, daughter of Isaiah, a son of Moses Reb Lazers of Vilna (who was a descendant of Rabbi Solomon Luria and Israel Isserles) – among the issue of Jacob Shor was Yente who married Rabbi Saul Katzenellenbogen of Pinczow (1617–1692) (v.s.)

won by a Catholic prince who could take the required coronation oath after gaining the support of the magnates and the acclaim of the nobility.

Sigismund Vasa was backed by his aunt, Queen Anna Jagiellonka (the widow of Stefan Bathory), by the Primate, and by the Zamoyski faction. They were ultimately successful against the Habsburg candidate, the Archduke Maximilian, brother of the Emperor Rudolph II, who was supported by the Empire, Spanish silver, the Zborowskis and others. Sweden and the Papacy were in the front rank of players; Muscovy and the Duke of Ferrara were also involved in the struggle. Lithuania pursued its own line within the Union with a delaying policy.

The Swedish prince was chosen in August 1587 and crowned in December of that year. When it came to a crucial vote on 18 August, the delaying tactics in which Saul was involved redounded to Sigismund's advantage. His services were certainly appreciated, not least by Sigismund, who showed him marked favour soon after his accession to the throne.

Saul Wahl combined Talmudic learning, a classical education, outstanding business ability, and leadership of the Jewish community with an important role in the councils of state. He died around the year 1617. One of his sons, Rabbi Meir Katzenellenbogen Wahl, was among the founders of the Council of Lithuania in 1623. Saul's children left numerous progeny and later descendants included many leading personalities in Jewish communities throughout Europe.

BIBLIOGRAPHY

Balaban, Majer, 'Shaul Wahl: Der Yidischer melekh in Poyln: Emes un legende' (The Jewish king in Poland: Truth and legend) in *Yidn in Poyln*. (The Jews in Poland) (Wilno: B. Kietzkin 1930); also cited in Yakov Leib Shapiro, *Mishpachot Atikot BeIsrael*. (Ancient Families of Israel) (Jerusalem: Chulyot 1981).

Bershadski, S. A., in *Voskhod* 1889 *et seq*. (a number of articles in Russian).

Edelmann, Hirsch, Gedullat Shaul, *The Glory of Saul*. (London 1854).

Karpeles, Gustave, *A Jewish King in Poland*. (Jewish Publication Society of America 1895).

Katzenellenbogen, Pinchas, *Yesh Manhilin*. (eighteenth-century MS in Bodleian Library, Oxford, published in Jerusalem 1986).

Marcus, B., & Sons, unpublished manuscript, Vienna 1911, cited by J. Bunford Samuel, *Records of the Samuel Family*. (Philadelphia 1912).

Rosenstein, Neil, *The Unbroken Chain: The Katzenellenbogen Family and its Origins*. (Avotaynu 1990) and *The Lurie Legacy – The House of Davidic Royal Descent*. (Avotaynu 2004).

Rosenstein, Neil and Dov Weber, 'The Edelmann Hoax and the Origins of Anglo-Jewish Aristocracy', *Avotaynu*, Vol. 14, No. 2 (1998).

Roth, Cecil, *Venice*. (Philadelphia: Jewish Publication Society of America 1930).

Walden Ahron, *Shem Hagedolim Hachadash*. (Warsaw 1864).

Wasserzug, D., 'A king for a night. The Polish Jew who reigned', *Jewish World*, 24 July 1903

Zalman Margolies Ephraim, *Ma'aloth Hayochasin*. (Lemberg 1900).

Chapter 8

A Polish affair

Sigismund III Vasa and Hannele Wahl

S
AUL BEN Samuel Judah Katzenellenbogen of Padua, who is known to history as Saul Wahl, was a protégé of Prince Radziwill. He became an influential Jewish community leader in Poland and a prominent entrepreneur with powerful connections. He appears to have played a significant role in the interregnum of 1587 and was subsequently favoured by the new ruler, King Zygmunt III. An examination of a family history written in the early eighteenth century by his descendant Rabbi Pinchas Katzenellenbogen, together with oral tradition in my grandmother's Wahl family suggests that Sigismund Vasa and Hannele, a daughter of Saul Wahl, may have had an affair with interesting genealogical consequences.

FAMILY BACKGROUNDS

King Sigismund III Vasa of Poland, and Hannele Wahl, daughter of Saul ben Samuel Judah Katzenellenbogen of Padua and Brest-Litovsk are the *dramatis personae* of this tale of two countries – Poland and Italy. My descent from Hannele is very probable and my descent from Sigismund Vasa becomes plausible as pieces of circumstantial evidence begin to link related family traditions.

My mother, Regina Griffel, and her brothers, Zygmunt and Edward, were the children of David Mendel Griffel and Chawa Wahl.

My grandmother Chawa was a daughter of Shulem Wahl and Sarah Safier of Tarnobrzeg in Galicia. This Wahl family was widely believed by their Jewish contemporaries to be descended from Saul Wahl, the sixteenth-century Jewish community leader in Poland and Lithuania who, according to legend, carried out royal functions as *rex pro tempore* during the interregnum that led to the election of the Swedish Prince Sigismund Vasa in 1587.

Sigismund Vasa (1566–1632) or Zygmunt III, to give him his Polish name, was King of Poland from 1587 to 1632. He was also Grand Duke of Lithuania and numerous other lands, as well as King of Sweden from 1592 to 1599, and claimant to the title of King of Jerusalem through his grandmother, Bona Sforza of Milan.[1]

Saul Wahl (1545–1617) was the scion of a rabbinical dynasty that began with his grandfather Meir Katzenellenbogen, the eminent Chief Rabbi of Padua, whose family came from the eponymous town in Hesse-Nassau. Saul was the son of Rabbi Samuel Judah Katzenellenbogen of Venice and his wife, Abigail Yaffe. The dynasty was linked with the Treivish, Shapiro, and Luria rabbinic families in their claim of Davidic descent through the great scholar and biblical commentator Rabbi Solomon ben Isaac of Troyes (1040–1105), known as Rashi.

Saul was called 'Wahl' in Poland – in other words, Saul the Italian. There is a very extensive Jewish literature concerning his ancestry and his distinguished progeny, as well as his semi-legendary role in Polish–Lithuanian affairs of state. He was a protégé of Prince Radziwill and favoured by the newly elected king after 1587. Saul Wahl arranged marriages for his many children with the leading Jewish families. His eldest son, Meir Wahl Katzenellenbogen, who

Photo 11 King Sigismund III Vasa

died in 1631, was Rabbi of Brest. He married Hinde, the daughter of Pinchas Halevi Ish Horowitz, who was President of the Council of the Four Lands (the Head of Polish Jewry).

A hundred years ago, J. Bunford Samuel published his *Records of the Samuel Family* in which he quotes an unpublished manuscript dated 1911 by B. Marcus & Sons of Vienna that mentioned a Meir Wohl of the merchant bank A. Holzer of Krakow and Vienna as being of undoubted descent from Saul Wahl. Early in my research I interviewed descendants of the said Salo Meir Wohl, who married the heiress Feigla Holzer and took over the running of the family bank. This couple were the grandparents of Maryla Suesser, the wife of my uncle Zygmunt Griffel. I confirmed that Salo Meir Wohl was named after Rabbi Meir Wahl Katzenellenbogen.[2]

My genealogical studies led me to the belief that the Samuel family, and several other Jewish families who came to England from Polish Silesia in the eighteenth century, shared with my family common ancestors in Rabbi Moses Katzenellenbogen of Chelm, a son of Meir Wahl, and Rabbi Jacob Shor, the son of Hannele Wahl. We also had some common Heilprin (Halpern) ancestry.[3]

I have written elsewhere (also in Chapter 7 of this book) about the esteem in which Saul Wahl seems to have been held by the Polish magnates and king by virtue of his ancient pedigree, his biblical learning, and his Italian Renaissance background, not to speak of his entrepreneurial skills and leadership of the economically important Jewish community.

King Sigismund's Italian background manifested itself in his artistic talent and taste. Sigismund Vasa was a descendant of the Holy Roman Emperor Sigismund (1433–37), as shown on the appended chart (Chart 8.4). The latter was the great-great-grandson of Rudolf of Habsburg, who laid the foundations for the imperial power of his house. The Habsburgs and the family of Saul Wahl are both believed to go back to descendants of Babylonian Exilarchs of Davidic lineage, whose Carolingian connections are addressed in Chapter 1.[4]

WAHL FAMILY LEGENDS

From the family tradition of the Wohls of Krakow we come to the legends of my grandmother's family, the Wahls of Tarnobrzeg. My mother occasionally said in jest 'we are blue-blooded, you know', sometimes adding 'le roi s'amuse'.

The possible significance of these remarks and the fact that she and her elder brother were called Regina and Zygmunt only became clear to me in the course of my recent genealogical studies.

A principal source of many Wahl legends is the work of Rabbi Pinchas Katzenellenbogen of Boskowitz (1691–1767).[5] He finished *Yesh Manhilin* ('There are those who bequeath') around the middle of the eighteenth century. The original manuscript is in the Bodleian Library at Oxford. It was published in book form in Jerusalem in 1986. It combines an excursive autobiography with a somewhat 'hagiographic' account of his family antecedents.

It presents the oft-repeated tale that King Zygmunt III wanted to marry Saul's daughter Hannele not long after the death of his first wife. To prevent this happening, her parents quickly arranged a match for her with an elderly kinsman, Rabbi Efraim Zalman Shor. These stories featured in later books and have been followed by numerous somewhat bowdlerised versions. The historical facts are that Sigismund Vasa was married firstly in 1592 to Anne of Austria, who died in 1598, and secondly in 1605 to her sister Constance, both daughters of Archduke Charles of Austria.

CRITIQUE OF THE ACCOUNT IN *YESH MANHILIN*

The story in *Yesh Manhilin* about Hannele Wahl is set out on pages 148–9 of the book and it contains two passages that are particularly relevant to my present account, namely that 'at that time the Queen had died' and that 'Hannele was married hurriedly to her 70 year old widowed kinsman'.

The first quote supports my thesis that the events in question occurred around the year 1600. The second quote is problematic because an approximate date of 1550 has been suggested elsewhere for Rabbi Efraim Zalman Shor's year of birth and, if my conjecture as to the date for his marriage to Hannele is correct, he would have been in his fifties. However, he could well have been born somewhat earlier than 1550. Anyway, around the turn of the century Hannele Wahl was married to her elderly kinsman, Rabbi Efraim Zalman Shor (d.1633) and promptly produced a son. I have not been able to confirm the year of this marriage or the date of birth of Jacob Shor, who became Rabbi of Brest and died around 1655, but the indications are that these events fell in the period between the death of Queen Anna and the king's second marriage to her sister Constance (1598–1605).

Pinchas Katzenellenbogen was a direct fifth-generation descendant of Saul Wahl and his book is clearly a most important source, but some details of the oral history of these events passed down to him by his father appear to bear a 'family' gloss when set against later information. The leitmotif of *Yesh Manhilin* is to pay homage to the author's ancestors, to extol the distinction of his lineage, to preserve the traditions of his family, and to pass these down to future generations.[6]

In the days of Rabbi Pinchas, his family would have regarded marriage to a non-Jew, king or commoner, as a stain on their family honour. Descendants living in a more ecumenical and 'enlightened' age may have different ideas about family honour (as well as the possible benefit of genetic genealogy). The hasty marriage to an elderly widowed relative followed by the birth of a son may indeed have given rise to my version of a Wahl family legend. However, it does seem more plausible than the story in *Yesh Manhilin*.

A branch of the rabbinic Shor family directly descended from Rabbi Efraim Zalman Shor became followers of Jacob Frank and converted to the Catholic faith in the middle of the eighteenth century, changing their name to Wolowsky. Several members of this family subsequently had brilliant careers in Poland and elsewhere, as I describe in a later essay (Chapter 13).

NOTES

1   Bona Sforza (1494–1557) was a daughter of Duke Gian Galeazzo Sforza of Milan and Isabella of Naples, who was a descendant of the Crusader King of Jerusalem, Baldwin II. Bona Sforza became Queen of Poland as the second wife of King Sigismund I Jagiellon.

2   *Wohl* is a Polish word meaning 'ox' and indeed we had close relatives called *Shor*, which is the Hebrew word for 'ox'. The Wohl family name was also sometimes written as Wahl.

3   Samuel and related families settled in England in the eighteenth century and are descended from Saul Wahl – see N. Rosenstein, *The Unbroken Chain*, Volume 1, pp. 65–74 (1990).

4   David Hughes, *Habsburg Dynasty* (2004), discusses the theories of Habsburg origins, many of which involve an early Jewish Davidic admixture. These several theories explore possible descent from the ancient Colonna, the Pierleone, and the 'desposynic' (direct descendants of Christ) descent line linked to the Merovingians and hence to the Carolingian and other later lines.

5   Pinchas was a brother of Eliezer Katzenellenbogen (1700–71) the Rabbi of Hagenau and Bamberg, who married Jached, the daughter of my ancestor Chief Rabbi Shmuel Helman of Mannheim and Metz (d.1764). Shmuel Helman also had Katzenellenbogen and Halpern forebears. Pinchas and Eliezer Katzenellenbogen were grandsons of Rabbi Saul Katzenellenbogen of Pinczow, who married Yente, a

daughter of Rabbi Jacob Shor of Brest (see Chart 8.2, which indicates relevant lines of descent from Saul Wahl via his son Meir and daughter Hannele).

6   Julia Haarmann, *Hüter der Tradition* (Göttingen: Vandenhoeck & Ruprecht 2013) considers *Yesh Manhilin* as an autobiographical work, including the history of his lineage and comments on selected passages in terms of the light they throw on Jewish customs and traditions. The selected passages include the account of Saul Wahl's 'election to be King for a day' (pp. 162–3) and the account of Hannele Wahl's marriage to the elderly Rabbi Efraim Zalman Shor (pp. 173–4). The latter passage is categorised by Julia Haarmann as among 'Wundergeschichten', accounts of miraculous happenings that are meant to enhance (or preserve) the family honour – such as the blessing of a son born soon after Hannele's marriage to her elderly husband.

Chart 8.1 Wahl of Tarnobrzeg and Wohl of Krakow

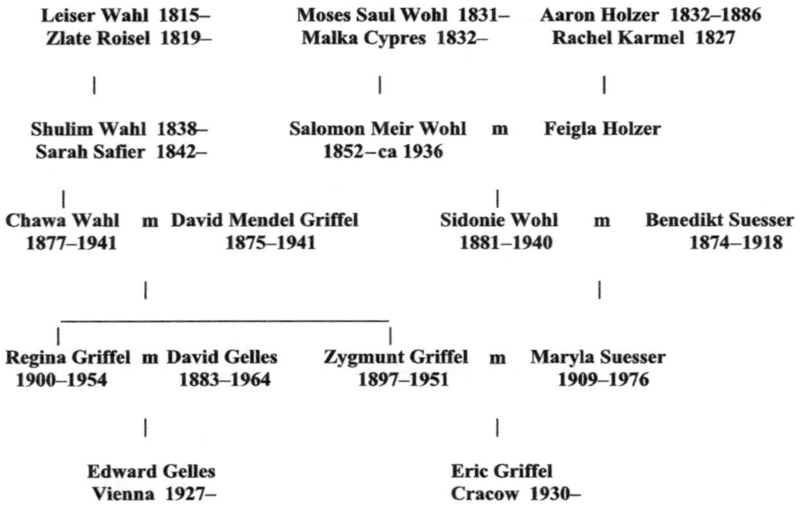

| Leiser Wahl 1815– | Moses Saul Wohl 1831– | Aaron Holzer 1832–1886 |
| Zlate Roisel 1819– | Malka Cypres 1832– | Rachel Karmel 1827 |

| Shulim Wahl 1838– | Salomon Meir Wohl   m   Feigla Holzer |
| Sarah Safier 1842– | 1852–ca 1936 |

| Chawa Wahl   m   David Mendel Griffel | Sidonie Wohl   m   Benedikt Suesser |
| 1877–1941 | 1875–1941 | 1881–1940 | 1874–1918 |

| Regina Griffel m David Gelles | Zygmunt Griffel   m   Maryla Suesser |
| 1900–1954 | 1883–1964 | 1897–1951 | 1909–1976 |

| Edward Gelles | Eric Griffel |
| Vienna 1927– | Cracow 1930– |

Notes

Rachel Wahl (1879–1965) was the younger sister of my grandmother Chawa Wahl. Her first marriage was to Abraham Taube, by whom she had a son and a daughter called Zyga and Rega, being diminutives for Zygmunt and Regina. Zyga Taube was the father of our second cousin, Thaddeus Taube, *see* E. Gelles, *An Ancient Lineage* (London: Vallentine Mitchell 2006).

Bluma Wahl (1861–1903) was the elder sister of Chawa and Rachel Wahl. She married Lazar Loew, and their nine children included Dr Abraham Low, who was the father of our second cousin Marilyn Low. Their descent from Saul Wahl is referred to in the biography of Dr Low, who was a distinguished psychiatrist in Chicago, *see* Neil and Margaret Lau, *My Dear Ones* (Chicago: Recovery Inc. 1971), page 1.

Chart 8.2 Katzenellenbogen and Saul Wahl family connections

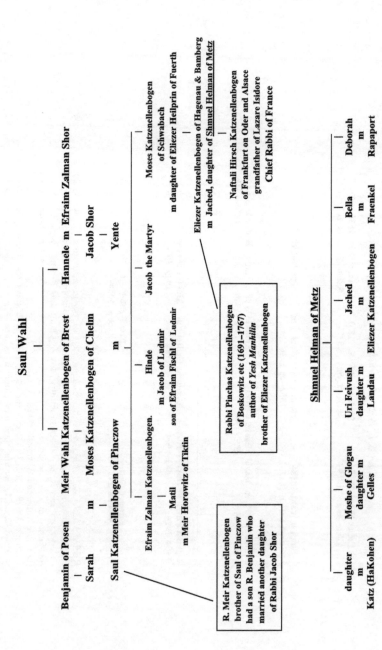

Chart 8.3 Polish kings and the interregnum of 1586–7

Sigismund I Jagiellon m (2nd) **Bona Sforza of Milan**
King of Poland 1508–48   *Duchess of Bari, etc*

Sigismund II August m (2nd) **Barbara Radziwill**   **Anna**   m   **Stefan Bathory**   **Catherine**   m   **John III Vasa**
King of Poland 1548–72   *Queen*   *Prince of Transylvania*   *King of Sweden 1568–92*

                                                            1575–86   *King of Poland 1576–86*

no issue   *no issue*

Henry III Valois   **Maximilian II Habsburg**   **Sigismund III Vasa**
King of Poland 1573–74   *elected King of Poland 1575*   *King of Sweden 1592 – deposed 1599*
King of France 1574–89   *but opposing nobles forced him to leave*   *King of Poland 1587–1632*
                                    Holy Roman Emperor 1564–76   *m 1592 Anne of Austria 1573–1598*
                                                                                                         m 1605 Constance of Austria 1588–1631
                                                                                                         daughters of Arch–Duke Karl

<u>Descent of Queen Bona Sforza from Duke Francesco Sforza of Milan</u>

Duke Francesco I Sforza (1401–1466) married Bianca Maria Visconti.
Duke Galeazzo Maria Sforza (1444–1476) and his mistress Lucretia Landriani
Duke Gian Galeazzo Sforza (1469–1494) married Isabella of Naples
Bona Sforza (1494–1557) Duchess of Bari etc, Queen of Poland
mother of Sigismund II Augustus (1520–1572), the last Polish King of the Jagiellon dynasty

Chart 8.4 Descent of King Sigismund III Vasa

Rudolf I 1218–1291 — Founder of Habsburg Imperial dynasty, King of Germany ('King of the Romans') 1273–1291 married Gertrude of Hohenburg

|

Judith — married Wenceslaus II Przemyslid King of Bohemia 1278–1305 and King of Poland 1300–1305

|

Elizabeth — married John of Luxemburg, King of Bohemia 1310–46, son of Holy Roman Emperor Henry VII

Charles IV 1316–1378 — King of Bohemia 1346–1378, Holy Roman Emperor 1355–1378. married Elizabeth of Pomerania their daughter Anne married King Richard II of England 1377–1399

Sigismund I 1368–1437 — Last Holy Roman Emperor of the House of Luxemburg 1433–37. King of Hungary 1387–, of Germany 1411– of Bohemia 1419–, of Italy 1431–/married (2) Barbara of Celje

Elizabeth of Luxemburg 1409–1442 — Duchess of Austria and later Queen Consort of Hungary, Bohemia, and Germany through marriage with Albert of Habsburg, Duke of Austria, later King of Hungary, Bohemia, and Germany ('King of the Romans')

Elizabeth of Austria 1436–1505 — Queen of Poland through marriage with King Casimir IV, Grand Duke of Lithuania and King of Poland

Sigismund I Jagiellon 1467–1548 — Grand Duke of Lithuania and King of Poland married (2) Bona Sforza of Milan

Catherina 1526–1583 — A sister of King Sigismund II Jagiellon of Poland. Queen of Sweden and Grand Princess of Finland through marriage with John III Vasa, Duke of Finland and King of Sweden

Sigismund III Vasa 1566–1632 — King of Poland and Lithuania 1587–1632 and King of Sweden 1592–1599.

PART 3

Eighteenth century and later

Chapter 9

Capitalists and rabbis

Galician social and economic background

THE ANCIENT LAND of Galicia was part of the Austrian Empire from the time of the first partition of Poland in 1772 to the end of World War I, after which it reverted to the newly reconstituted Polish Republic. During this period of Austrian rule, a Jewish upper class evolved, whose successful entrepreneurs were close to the land and developed its natural resources. They became leaders of their respective communities, and were highly conservative in their religious observances and allegiance to the Habsburg monarchy. Such were the heads of the Griffel, Wahl, Loew, Taube, and other families, who arranged intermarriages of their progeny to maintain the cohesion of their class across the length and breadth of the province.

INTRODUCTION

My maternal ancestors prospered in the Galician province of the Austro-Hungarian Empire from the time of the eighteenth-century partitions of Poland to the outbreak of the World War I. Censuses, tax lists, birth, marriage, death, and other municipal records, and memorial books, as well as biographies and literary works, have provided information to link a number of families sharing a similar cultural and economic background. Generations flourished in towns like Brody, Stanislau, Nadworna, and Kolomea, lying beyond Lemberg in eastern Galicia, and in Tarnobrzeg and Szediszow, to the north-east of the capital city of Krakow at the western end of the province.

Under Austrian rule, a measure of local autonomy and a relatively liberal regime encouraged commercial development. Galician Jews shared in the Enlightenment and emancipation which continued its pan-European progress. At the same time, the religious revival of the Chasidic movement attracted many devoted followers. Traditional orthodoxy was the norm, but as the nineteenth century progressed, Enlightenment ideas made themselves increasingly felt in education and other areas of culture. On the other hand, the Chasidic rabbis retained their hold over devoted flocks throughout the period.

A number of their dynasties established themselves in various centres, and the more famous of these attracted followers from far and wide. The Jews were quite mobile in those days. Branches of prominent families were often found in more than one town. Marriages were frequently arranged on the basis of kinship or business connections which might span the entire province.

FAMILY CONNECTIONS

This chapter is concerned with the Griffel, Wahl, Safier, Loew, and Taube families, their marriages, their commercial enterprise, and their religious allegiances. They had close connections with the land, in the sense that they were involved in the management of estates and dealt in landed property. Jews were not permitted to own freeholds until the second half of the nineteenth century, but there were several categories of exceptions to this rule [1, 2]. For example, a Taube family, based at one time in Belz, not far from Lemberg, owned substantial estates in the early 1800s. In any case, Jewish merchants who had accumulated some capital from trading with farmers or managing the estates of aristocratic landowners became increasingly involved with the exploitation of the land's natural resources, such as timber, oil, and minerals. They would lease land, negotiate concessions, buy the standing wood, and so on. They would plough back the profits from their activities into loans to estate owners. Some remained timber merchants and the like, others went on to acquire estates of their own, and in due course their mortgage lending might grow into more broadly based merchant banking.

The village of Dzikow was absorbed within the town of Tarnobrzeg. A royal charter dates from 1593. It was during the reign of Sigismund III and in the heyday of Saul Wahl, the Jewish community leader who played a leading role in the Polish–Lithuanian state at the time [3]. Wahls are recorded in the Tarnobrzeg archives from the beginning of the nineteenth century [4]. Families descended from Saul Wahl were to be found in numerous Galician towns. Zvi Aryeh Wahl, the Chief Rabbi of Nadworna in the nineteenth century, had a pedigree going back to Wahl and his Katzenellenbogen forebears, who had been Chief Rabbis of Padua and Venice in the sixteenth century [5].

Leiser Wahl was born in Tarnobrzeg in 1815 and married Zlate Roisel of Nisko, who was born in 1819. The bare facts recorded in the town archives, including data from the 1880 census, can be supplemented by a graphic description of Leiser's commercial activities as set down in the memoirs of Jan Slomka, the contemporary mayor of the town [6]. We are told that he obtained the liquor monopoly from Count Tarnowski and later began to deal in timber, buying the standing forest and shipping the wood by raft to Danzig. He was able to set up his sons and give his numerous daughters dowries of tens of thousands of gulden. He remained banker to many tradesmen in trouble, and the probate to his will came in at 300,000 gulden, mostly in mortgages on peasant and gentry properties. His occupation is given in the archives as timber merchant. However, his son Shulim Wahl, born in Tarnobrzeg in 1838, is described as a 'capitalist'. The latter's wife was Sarah Safier, born in 1842, and they had six children.

There are scattered references to the Safiers of Tarnobrzeg from the eighteenth century to the outbreak of World War II. A Safier is listed in the taxation records of 1822 [7]; there are about a dozen families in the Tarnobrzeg census lists of 1880 and 1925, and numerous entries in the birth and death records kept in the nearby town of Sandomierz [5], in the records of high school graduates up to 1939, and in the Dzikow-Tarnobrzeg Memorial Book [8]. The latter refers to two brothers by the names of Chayim and Elimelech Safier, who were apparently among the wealthiest people in the town during the period between the two world wars. They owned forests and were prominent in the timber trade, as indeed had been their forebears a century earlier.

A collection of Chasidic stories includes the tale of Reb Ahron Safier, a timber merchant from Krakow, who benefited from the blessing of Rabbi Yechezkel Halberstam of Siniawa [9]. The Radziechow Memorial Book refers to an Isaac Safier who owned an estate at Shtruvitz and was a follower of the Chasidic Rabbi Yehoshua Rokeach of Belz [10]. There were Safiers also in Opatow, a town not very far from Tarnobrzeg.

Sarah Safier may have been the daughter of Samuel and Chaya Safier of Tarnobrzeg, recorded in the 1880 town census as having been born there in 1823 and 1827. The census lists also confirm the birth dates of her children, including Blume, Rachel, and Chawa Wahl.

THE WAHL MARRIAGES

These three daughters of Shulim Wahl and Sarah Safier married into families who were involved in the same kind of merchant venturing and had a similar social background, with rabbinical antecedents and Chasidic connections.

Blume Wahl became the wife of Lazar Loew, a son of Nathan Nata Loew, who owned estates and was the president of the Jewish community of Sedziszow. He and his brother were successively mayors of that town. Their father Jacob Yoshua Loew was already well established there. As leaders of the community they would have many poor families to dine with them on Saturdays and festival days.

Photo 12 Rachel Wahl (great-aunt)

Their paternalism was also evidenced by marrying off orphan girls of the community at their expense. Although the rabbi of Sedziszow was a Horowitz related to them by marriage and to the Chasidic Horowitz dynasty of Tarnobrzeg, the Loews gave their religious allegiance to the Rabbi of Chortkow, who belonged to the famous Friedman dynasty of Ruzhin, Sadegora, and Chortkow. Old Loew used to take his carriage with four horses, flying the Ruzhin flag, to drive to the rabbi for the festivals. In the days of his sons, the rabbi visited the area of Sedziszow with his entourage, and the Loews bore the entire cost of the visit [11].

The majority of the Chasidic rabbis adopted a simple lifestyle. The Friedmans, by contrast, lived in great splendour, in a quasi-regal style supported by their ecstatic followers. Some rabbis of the Gelles family had collateral connections with the Chortkow 'wonder-rabbis' and with the celebrated sage Phineas Shapiro, known as Pinchas of Koretz, whose life and works are described in Martin Buber's *Tales of the Chasidim* [12, 13].

My grandfather and the Chortkower Rebbe Israel Friedman coincidentally both died in Vienna in 1933/34. Rabbi Nahum Uri Gelles had many responsa addressed to him by leading rabbis of his day. One of these refers him sitting as a judge of a Rabbinical Court at Sedziszow. The Chortkow connection may have had something to do with that particular appointment [14].

Blume Wahl's sister Rachel married Abraham Taube, who was a Talmud scholar of independent means. His father Josef Taube was a rich jute merchant with an international business. Abraham and Rachel knew that they were cousins, and this is a pointer to the ancestral connections of the Wahls of Tarnobrzeg.

A third sister, Chawa Wahl, married David Mendel Griffel, who was named after his grandfather and was one of the numerous children of Eliezer Griffel and Sarah Chayes. Eliezer was the son of David Mendel and Taube Griffel and was born in Nadworna in 1850 [15, 16]. His wife Sarah was the daughter of Isaac Chayim Chayes of Kolomea, who belonged to the family of that name based in Brody [17, 18]. Sarah survived until 1940. The Griffels claimed descent from a seventeenth-century Chief Rabbi of Lvov, David Halevi Segal, known as *Taz* from the title of his principal work.

Photo 13a   Tad Taube (mother's first cousin) and wife at dinner with the author

Photo 13b   Lucia Ohrenstein (mother's first cousin)

The Chayes had been distinguished rabbis for centuries, culminating in Dr Hirsch Perez Chayes, who was Chief Rabbi of Vienna from 1919 to 1927 [19]. They also produced community leaders and men of affairs. A branch flourished in Livorno and Florence from the eighteenth to the twentieth centuries. They became rich in the coral trade, ran a successful merchant bank in Florence called Berenstein, Chayes & Co, and one of their number, Guido Chayes of Livorno, was made a count by the King of Portugal in 1904 [20].

Photo 14   View of Stanislau, 1912

Leiser Griffel (Zeida or Zeidele) was a man of energy and vision. He built up an empire based on the two basic commodities of the area, timber and oil. He owned saw mills and ran a large timber

Photo 15 Dr Jacob Griffel, book cover (mother's first cousin)

export business. He and his sons and partners owned oil wells in the areas of Nadworna, Stanislau, Kolomea, Piasiecna, and further afield in Austria, at Korneuburg near Vienna. He was the largest employer of labour in Nadworna, and his interests extended first to Stanislau and then to Lemberg and Krakow. He had a dominant economic, social, and political influence in his native town.

While the Wahls were rabbis of Nadworna, Eliezer was a follower of the Chasidic rabbis of Otoniya, who were of the Hager family. He and his sons and sons-in-law used to pray regularly in their synagogue. The Griffels and Hagers were also linked by marriage. David Mendel and Isaac Chayim Griffel and their children

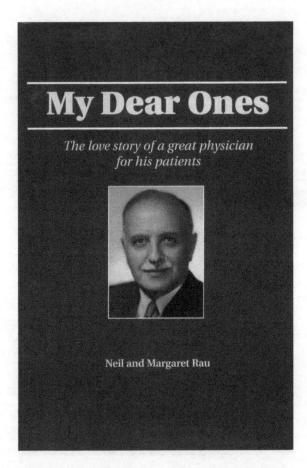

Photo 16 Dr Abraham Low, book cover (mother's first cousin)

succeeded to different parts of the family enterprise, which at a later stage included a bank [21, 22]. The family was ultra-conservative in religion, paternalist in Jewish communal affairs, and monarchist in their sentiment towards Austrian rule. It is said that Eliezer got on famously with Kaiser Franz Joseph during one of the Emperor's visits to his distant province.

These entrepreneurs flourished for a brief period. The pillars of support were a benevolent imperial regime and social cohesion backed by strong Chasidic faith.

The favourable economic climate certainly helped, but I believe that, given a different picture, such as a more rapid industrialisation, these people would have had no difficulty in adapting to changing circumstances, as their surviving descendants have done in other parts of the world. The pillars of the old establishment crumbled at the time of World War I. Economic and political circumstances were very different in the Poland of the inter-war years. The intellectual currents of the nineteenth and early twentieth centuries, the rise of nationalism, along with assimilation and Zionism, weakened the hold of the ancestral faith, although some branches of these families have maintained their unqualified Chasidic adherence.

REFERENCES

[1] C. A. McCartney, *The Hapsburg Empire 1770–1918.* (London: Weidenfeld & Nicholson 1968), p. 502.

[2] Tomasz Gasowski, *From Austeria to Manor. Jewish Landowners in Autonomous Galicia.* Polin, Vol 12. (Oxford: Littman Library of Jewish Civilisation 1999).

[3] Edward Gelles, 'Saul Wahl. A Jewish Legend', *Judaism Today*, 14, Winter 1999–2000. pp. 36–42.

[4] Tarnobrzeg Archives, *Odziel w Sandomierzu*, 27–600 Sandomierz, Ul. Zydowska 4, Poland. (relevant extracts supplied by Mr Tadeusz Zych, the then deputy mayor of Tarnobrzeg).

[5] Edward Gelles, 'The Wahls of Nadworna', *Shemot*, Vol. 8, No. 3, September 2000, pp. 26–2 & Vol. 8, No. 4, December 2000, pp. 31–2.

[6] Jan Slomka, *From Serfdom to Self Government. Memoirs of a Polish Village Mayor, 1842–1927.* (London: Minerva 1941), pp. 98–100.

[7] Michael Honey, 'Propinacya and Koncygnacya Listings for Tarnobrzeg -Dzikow'. *Shemot* Vol. 2, No. 4, October 1994.

[8] Y. Y. Fleisher (ed.), *Kehilat Tarnobrzeg-Dzikow.* (Tel Aviv: Tarnobrzeg-Dzikow Society 1923).

[9] Y. N. Wagschal, *Yud Gimel Oroth* (Thirteen Lights). (New York 1994).

[10] G. Kressel (ed.), *Radziechov Memorial Book.* (Tel Aviv: Society of Radikhov, Lopatyn, and Vicinity 1976), p. 10.

[11] Zeev Wolf Loew, Low family private MS.

[12] Edward Gelles, *Gelles Rabbinical Ancestry*, to be published.

[13] Martin Buber, *Die Erzaehlungen der Chassidim.* (Zurich: Manessa Verlag, Conzett & Huber 1949), p. 218 – Pinchas von Koretz, pp. 520–4 – David Moshe Friedman von Czortkow.

[14] Meir Wunder, *Meorei Galicia* (Institute for the Commemoration of Galician Jewry, Jerusalem 1978), Vol. 1, columns 699–700.

[15] Rabbi Kolesnik of Stanislau has some Nadworna records. His home address is Pushkina Street 75, apartment 1, Ivano-Frankivsk, Ukraine 284000.

[16] Tsentral'n yi Derzhavnyi Archiv u.m. L'vovi, 290004 L'viv 4, Ukraine. pl. Vozz'iednannia 3'a (searches undertaken by Alexander Dunai)

[17] The Kolomea branch of the Chayes family: *An Eternal Light: Brody In Memoriam*. The Organisation of Former Brody Residents in Israel, 1994. p. 324, referring to Chaim Chayes.

[18] Rabbi Chaim Zvi Theomim, *Zikaron Le'Rishonim* (Kolomea 1913), referring to Isaac Chayes.

[19] Edward Gelles, 'Chief Rabbis in the Genes'. *Manna*, No. 69, Autumn 2000, pp. 34–6.

[20] Livorno records from the director of the town archives, Dr Paolo Castignoli, and Portuguese records kindly supplied by the director of the National archives, Dr Bernardo Vasconcelos e Sousa (private correspondence – see Edward Gelles, *An Ancient Lineage*. (London: Vallentine Mitchell 2006), pp. 50–2).

[21] Nadworna (Stanislau District) *Memorial & Records*. Landsmannschaft of Nadworna in Israel and the United States. (Tel Aviv 1975), pp. 25–26.

[22] Y. L. Maimon (ed.), *Arim ve-imahot be-Ysrael* (Mother Communities of Israel). (Jerusalem Rav Kuk Institute 1952), Vol. 5, pp. 63, 212, 213, 219, 233, 311, 314.

Chart 9.1 My mother's family connections

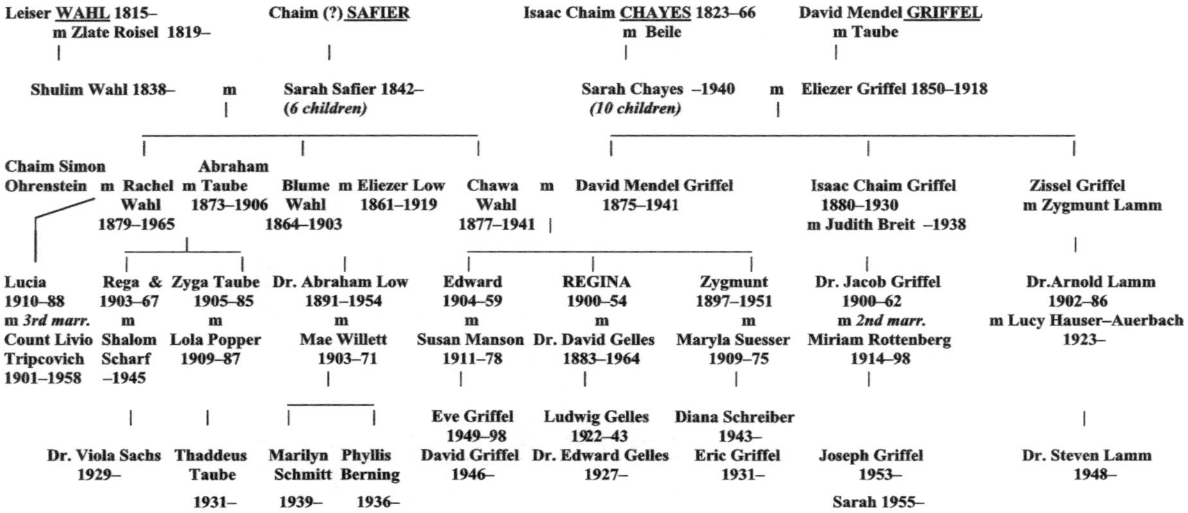

Leiser WAHL 1815– m Zlate Roisel 1819–

Chaim (?) SAFIER

Isaac Chaim CHAYES 1823-66 m Beile

David Mendel GRIFFEL m Taube

Shulim Wahl 1838–   m   Sarah Safier 1842– (6 children)

Sarah Chayes –1940 (10 children)   m   Eliezer Griffel 1850–1918

Abraham

Chaim Simon Ohrenstein m Rachel Wahl 1879–1965   m Taube Wahl 1873–1906

Blume Wahl 1864–1903 m Eliezer Low 1861–1919

Chawa Wahl 1877–1941   m   David Mendel Griffel 1875–1941

Isaac Chaim Griffel 1880–1930 m Judith Breit –1938

Zissel Griffel m Zygmunt Lamm

Lucia 1910–88 m 3rd marr. Count Livio Tripcovich 1901–1958

Rega & Zyga Taube 1903–67

Shalom Scharf –1945 m Lola Popper 1909–87

Dr. Abraham Low 1891–1954 m Mae Willett 1903–71

Edward 1904–59 m Susan Manson 1911–78

REGINA 1900–54 m Dr. David Gelles 1883–1964

Zygmunt 1897–1951 m Maryla Suesser 1909–75

Dr. Jacob Griffel 1900–62 2nd marr. Miriam Rottenberg 1914–98

Dr. Arnold Lamm 1902–86 m Lucy Hauser–Auerbach 1923–

Dr. Viola Sachs 1929–

Thaddeus Taube 1931–

Marilyn Schmitt 1939–

Phyllis Berning 1936–

Eve Griffel 1949–98

David Griffel 1946–

Ludwig Gelles 1922–43

Diana Schreiber 1943–

Dr. Edward Gelles 1927–

Eric Griffel 1931–

Joseph Griffel 1953–

Sarah 1955–

Dr. Steven Lamm 1948–

Chapter 10

Jewish community life in Brody

'The Jerusalem of Austria'

THE CITY OF KRAKOW at the western end of Galicia was once the capital of a greater Poland. The capital of eastern Galicia was the city of Lvov, which was called Lemberg during the period of Austrian rule. To the north-east of Lvov lay the town of Brody, which at the beginning of the eighteenth century enjoyed an economic upswing, becoming for a century or so an important trade entrepôt between the Austrian and Russian Empires.

The Jewish community grew to be the second largest in Europe. Social, cultural, and economic conditions are revealed by the civil and Jewish records, marriage contracts, property transactions, the purchases and sales of synagogue seats, and other activities. The college known as the Brody Klaus was a distinguished feature of a vibrant religious community life.

A fragment of the Brody Beth Din Records from the early nineteenth century has survived and I obtained a copy of this manuscript through the courtesy of the Jewish Theological Seminary in New York [1]. It has proved to be an invaluable source of genealogical and sociological material for a town within the Austro-Hungarian Empire which had a large Jewish community and was also for a considerable time an important centre of Jewish learning. For ten years from 1808 to 1817 the Records detail all manner of transactions that make up the warp and weft of the social fabric, such as the purchase and sale of houses, land, and other property, wills and bequests, marriage contracts, and much else.

The names of people and the details involved in these transactions, when combined with the civil records of births, marriages, and deaths, and the registers of landed property, throw much light on family connections and the life of the community [2].

The procedure followed in the study of the Gelles family is of general applicability, and so are some of the conclusions. For example, Moses Gelles of Brody was a scholar of the study group called the Brody Klaus around the middle of the eighteenth century [3]. He was variously referred to as Gelles and Levush. I have suggested that the epithet *Levush* recalled a descent from the sixteenth-century Rabbi Mordecai

THE MARKET, BRODY

Photo 17a The market, Brody
After 19th century drawing by Joseph Pennell.

THE JEWISH CEMETERY, BRODY

Photo 17b The old cemetery, Brody
After 19th century drawing by Joseph Pennell.

Yaffe of Prague and the title of his magnum opus, *The Levushim*. This Hebrew epithet is noted for four generations and is quite distinct from the vernacular trade soubriquets, such as *Woskoboinik* (wax chandler or candle maker) used by some members of the Gelles family. There is evidence of other Levushes who were known to be descendants of Mordecai Yaffe. A perusal of the Beth Din Records reveals that, at least in this place and period, it was general practice to refer to men of distinguished ancestry by adding the ancestor's epithet or the title of his major work of scholarship [4]. This custom of recalling famous forebears clearly provides useful pointers in rabbinical genealogy. It also indicates the importance attached to lineage [*yichus*] and to standing in the Brody community, in which learning tended to take precedence over wealth in determining social position. Families like the Babad, Chayes, Margolioth, Shapiro, and others combined ancient lineage, intellectual distinction, and wealth. The balance between lineage and learning on one hand and more material attributes on the other was delicately struck in arranged marriages. The leading rabbis featured prominently in the social hierarchy.

The Gelles family owned some land, several houses, and a chandlery [Vaskievonia]. They appear to have had a monopoly on the supply of candles to the community [2]. From the mid 1700s to the early 1800s, a part of which is covered by the Beth Din Records, the family was quite prosperous. Membership of the Klaus certainly carried considerable prestige. This is the period for which there are records of marriage alliances with the families of Brody Rabbis Heschel Hakohen, Meir Fraenkel, Yehuda Leib Zundel, Berach Margoshes, and others. Our connections with Rabbi Pinchas Shapiro of Koretz are documented and discussed elsewhere.

A marriage contract [*Kethuba*] from the year 1817 between the Gelles and Margoshes families contains several points of interest, namely, the relative status of the participating families, the apparent youth of the bridegroom, the use of the Russian rouble, among other currencies, in a town which was an entrepôt between the Austrian and Russian Empires, and an undertaking by the bridegroom's brother to carry out the *chalitza* ceremony [5].

The community was strong in its religious faith, the winds of Enlightenment blowing from post-revolutionary France not yet having made much impact in this distant outpost of the Austrian Empire. The synagogue was central to the life of the community and there were many smaller houses of prayer to cater for special groups. Synagogue seats were bequeathed, sold, and rented. A good example is provided by Finkel, a daughter of R. Dov Ber Fraenkel and the wife of Reb Wolf Bolechower, who purchased 35 seats, later selling some or using the funds from their rental for charitable purposes [6].

Many houses and plots of land stayed in the same family for several generations and the numerous entries for property transactions refer to owners passing property to their heirs, and to later subdivisions. An analysis of names, property numbers, and dates of transactions has confirmed a number of family links.

Moses Gelles had died before the period covered by the Beth Din document. His property was divided between his children and in-laws and then went to their children and grandchildren. Their houses and parcels of land were therefore often adjoining to one another or to the land on part of which stood the family *Vaskievonie* or waxworks.

In the short span of ten years, the Beth Din Record encompasses information on four generations of related families. Several entries show that Moses Gelles of the Klaus was one and the same person as Menachem Levush and that his sons Michel Levush or Gelles, Joseph Gelles *Vaskievonie*, and Mordecai Gelles had numerous issue known by various names. R. Moshe Gershon, a son of Joseph Gelles, sometimes referred to as R. Moshe, can be distinguished from the R. Moshe Gelles whose name is given on the Brody tombstone of his son, Rabbi David Isaac Gellis. This R. Moshe was probably a son of the above-mentioned R. Mordecai Gelles, who was a *mechutan* [in-law] of Rabbi Pinchas of Koretz. More light is thrown on other in-laws. Thus, Rabbi Yehuda Zundel, grandfather of another Moshe Levush or Gelles, appears to be identical with the Rabbi Yehuda Leib Zundel Ramraz, who belonged to the circle of the wise men of Brody and died in 1804. Reb Berach Margoshes' granddaughter married a Gelles and Berach's wife may have been the daughter of R. Shmuel Gelles. The family of Reb Ahron Benish seem to be connected through the wives of Ahron's sons, Reb Simcha and Reb David Hertz. The two couples sold their separate interests in two houses to the brothers-in-law, Meir Fraenkel and Moses Gershon Gelles [7].

The prosperity of the Gelles family declined as candle gave way to gaslight, and as Brody suffered from the siting of the new railways, the decline of its importance as a trading centre, and the loss of its status as a free city. Many Jews left their ancient hometown. Some, like the Brodskys, flourished in Odessa and elsewhere in Russia. In the closing decades of the nineteenth century, the influx of refugees from Russian pogroms led to overcrowding and poverty in Brody, but by that time, many of the old families had been dispersed throughout Galicia, Austria, and beyond.

REFERENCES

[1] Records of the Beth Din of Brody 1808–17. MS 4037, Jewish Theological Seminary, New York.
[2] Edward Gelles, 'Finding Rabbi Moses Gelles', *Avotaynu*, Vol. 18, No. 1, Spring 2002.

[3] Nathan M. Gelber, *Brody: The Jerusalem of Austria* in *An Eternal Light: Brody in Memoriam*, publ. by the Organisation of Former Brody Residents in Israel,1994 (containing a footnote on the Brody Klaus).

[4] Instances of such epithets are entries No. 1116 for R. Zalman Margoshes *Shach* (descendant of the *Shach* – an acronym for Rabbi Shabbatai Katz), and No. 1172 for Chaim Zvi Hersh, son of R. Moshe Efrayim *Chacham Zvi* (descendant of Chacham Zvi Ashkenazi).

More relevant to the interpretation of the *Levush* name, as referring to descent from Rabbi Mordecai Yaffe and to the title of his book, are instances of other epithets derived from famous rabbinical works, namely Nos. 1132, 1138, 1278 for Reb Mendel *Tevuos Shor*, Reb Alexander Chaim *Tevuos Shor*, and Reb Yosef Yisrael *Tevuos Shor* [members of the Shor family descended from the author of *Tevuos Shor*], and No. 1350 for Leah, daughter of R. Avrohom Yitzchak Halevy *Turei Zahav* (after his ancestor David Halevy Segal, the author of the book *Turei Zahav*). The case for the derivation of the epithet *Levush* is certainly strengthened by these examples from the Beth Din Record. The civil birth, marriage, and death records of Brody confirm that Gelles and Levush were alternative or additional names in the family for several generations. There is a previous record of this epithet attached to known progeny of the Levush. The tombstone of a R. Nehemia Levush of Svierz and later of Vilna has an inscription stating that his father Rabbi Zvi Levush was a descendant of Rabbi Mordecai Yaffe [2].

Marriage contracts

[5] Marriage contract No. 1420. Kethuba of Abraham, a (bachelor) son of Rabbi Moshe Gelles, son of Reb Joseph *Vaskievonie* (owner of the waxworks and one of the sons of Moses Gelles–Levush of Brody), married Taube, daughter of Rabbi Josef Kalischer, son of R. Berach Margoshes, on Friday 6th Tammuz 5577 (July 1817). Reb Moshe Gelles promised to pay the sum of 450 Russian roubles, support the couple for the first three years of their marriage, and pay for their clothing, as well as tuition fees (this may indicate the extreme youth of the bridegroom), Reb Josef Kalischer gave the sum of 100 Russian roubles. The bridegroom's brother Reb Yankel Gelles

gave an undertaking to carry out the *chalitza* ceremony (release of a childless bride by the brother of the bridegroom in the event of the bridegroom's death) if necessary.

Other marriage contracts of the period refer to varying sums of money and years of support. Thus, in entry No. 277, the marriage of Yitzchak, a son of Reb Benjamin Zeev Bolechover, which took place in 1808, was endowed with 1980 reinish and a promise of five years' support by the father of the bridegroom and separately by the mother of the bride. Entry Nos. 1391, 1395, 1397, and 1412 refer to 2,700 silver roubles and six years' support, 675 roubles and three years' support from the bride's father, 1425 new roubles with each side supporting the couple for four years, and 1125 Russian roubles with support of two years from the bride's father and five years from the bridegroom's father. While the most common currency of the period was the Russian rouble, Austrian ducats (Kaiserliche dukaten) are mentioned in entry No. 1258 dated 1814, Prussian currency (Preussisch) in No. 447 dated 1808, and Dutch coinage (rendelech Hollander) in Nos. 424 and 429 in 1808.

Synagogue seats etc.

[6] No. 394. Finkel, daughter of R. Dov Ber Fraenkel and wife of Reb Wolf Bolechower, purchased 35 seats in the synagogue. No. 1133. 'A sale by the wealthy Finkel … of a seat in the women's section of the New Synagogue … in memory of the soul of the late Feiga, daughter of Reb Yehoshua Heshel Hakohen, the wife of Rabbi Michel, son of Reb Moshe Gelles … so that this should be an everlasting memorial to her soul, never to be sold. The rental income from the seat is to be used to pay for a Jahrzeit lamp [candle lit on the anniversary of the deceased's death] and the remainder to be distributed to the local poor on the day of her Jahrzeit. She appointed a Trustee … Ellul', 5573 (September 1813). (Finkel was the sister of Rabbi Meir Fraenkel, a son-in-law of R. Josef Gelles *Vaskievonie*, who was a son of R. Moses Gelles.)

The husband of the above-mentioned Feiga is identified in No. 270. Reb Michel, son of Reb Menachem Levush (son-in-law of Reb. S. Gelles (Menachem Levush in No. 270 is thus one and the same person as Moses Gelles in No. 1133)) signed and sealed to his wife Feiga, daughter of Rabbi Yehoshua Heshel, that if she passes away before him, he is obliged to return to her heirs, or to whoever she instructs, half of the value of her *shterentuchel* (the customary jewelled head-dress), and all clothing, bedding etc., immediately after her death ... 27th Tishri 5568 (October 1808). An entry in 1808 gives the value of a *shterentuchel* as at least 200 *rendelech Hollander*, and an entry for the wedding in 1813 of Benjamin Wolf, son of Zvi Hirsch Schonblum of Lvov, to Rikel Landau, daughter of R. Yosef ben R. Shachna, refers to a *shterentuchel*, earrings and pearls being worth at least 900 Russian roubles. No. 401. Gittel Malka, the widow of Reb Todros ben Ramraz (of the Zundel family) sold a seat on the eastern wall in the women's section, next to the seat belonging to Malka Margoshes. Iyyar 5568 (May 1808). No. 1308. Sale by Chaya, widow of R. Shmuel Gelles, of half a seat in the women's section of the synagogue to Ektish, wife of the wealthy R. Yehoshua Margalioth. 28th Menachem 5575 (August 1815).

Property transactions

[7] Parts of houses and parcels of land were conveyed very frequently between the heirs of Moses Gelles and their descendants. These transactions involved Leah and Bonna, and their in-laws of the Benish family (Nos. 713, 813, see also Nos. 1064, 1067), Reb Moshe Gershon Gelles, a son of R. Joseph Gelles *Vaskievonie* and his brother-in-law Rabbi Meir Shlomo Fraenkel (Nos. 713, 786, 813), the latter's wealthy sister Finkel and her husband Reb Benyamin Wolf Bolechover (Nos. 574, 922), and other sons of R. Joseph Gelles, namely Reb Yaakov Hersh Feigang and Rabbi Abraham Yonah Reich with the Reich family (No. 786). These two Gelles were referred to by the names of their fathers-in-law, which was a common custom at the time. Yonah Reich is perhaps identifiable as the father of R. Isaac Reich who married a granddaughter of R. Joseph Landau, ABD of Zolkiew, who became head of the Brody Klaus in 1757 [8]. R. Moshe Gershon Gelles was probably Bonna's brother.

   Reb Mordechai Gelles, a brother of Reb Joseph *Vaskievonie*, is mentioned (Nos. 762, 1035) and Reb Shmuel may be a kinsman of Moshe Gelles of the Klaus (Nos. 481, 530, 953). His daughter married Reb Berach Margoshes. The Margoshes also had marriage links with the Shapiro family (Nos. 860, 863). The identity of Rabbi Yehuda Zundel, whose daughter Sarah Bathya married Mordecai Levush, son of R. Michel Gelles, is indicated by the entries for a property sale to their son Reb Moshe Levush in March 1814 (No. 1194) and the entries relating to land belonging to the heirs of the late R. Zundel Ramraz (No. 1131), and again to the heirs of Reb Zundel son of R.M. Reb Zelig's in December 1814 (No. 1260). Rabbi Yehuda Leib Zundel carried the epithet *Ramraz*, an acronym for Rabbi Moshe Reb Zelig.

[8] Neil Rosenstein, *The Unbroken Chain*. (New York: CIS Publishers 1990), pp. 755–7.

Note on currencies

In this period the use of a variety of coins was widespread and by no means confined to Brody. For a century from 1779, Brody was a 'free city' with a flourishing trade between eastern and central Europe. Money in the above-mentioned documents included the Rhenish, a term for the contemporary German gulden or Netherlandish guilder. The latter was the standard Dutch coin, but many other coins were used in Holland (for references to the ryder, worth 14 guilders, see www.giacomo-casanova.de/catour16.htm. This web page contains interesting information on late eighteenth-century coinage and prices across Europe, drawn from various sources, including Casanova's *Memoirs*, Thomas Nugent's *Grand Tour*, and other writings). The pound sterling was worth about 11½ Dutch guilders and about 5½ Russian roubles, which were of similar value to the rixdollar. The new Russian silver rouble, introduced under Tsar Alexander I in 1810, was clearly popular in Brody. The money settlements in the quoted marriage contracts are in the range of a few hundred to a few thousand Russian roubles or the equivalent in other currencies. Among the few indications of wages paid in that period (Entry No. 1275 – for March 1815) is the fee of one rouble per week paid to the part-time prayer leader of the New Synagogue.

Chart 10.1 Some scholars of the Brody Klaus

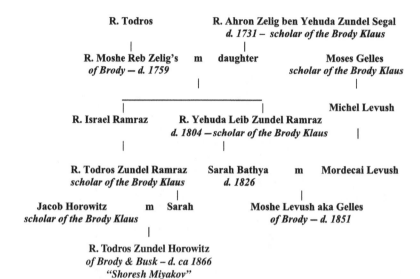

Footnotes

[1] R. Todros was a descendant of the Abulafia scholars and courtiers of medieval Spain.

[2] R. Yehuda Leib Zundel Ramraz was also grandfather of Shalom Rokeach (1779–1855), the first Grand Rabbi of the Belz Chasidic dynasty. Ramraz is an acronym of his father's name – Rabbi Moshe Reb Zelig and became the family name.

[3] Jacob Halevi Horowitz was a son of Yehuda Aryeh Leibush Halevi Horowitz of Apt. They claimed descent from Rabbi Isaiah Halevi Ish Horowitz (c.1568–1627), known as the Holy *Shelah*.

See Arim Veimahot Beyisrael, Vol. 6 (Brody), pp. 54,56, 69–70, Meir Wunder, *Meorei Galicia*, Vol. 2: 217, Vol. 4: 844–907 and 967–9, Vol. 6: 475,

Yitzchak Shlomo Yudlof, *Sefer Yichus Belza*, pp. 25–35, 311–315.

Chart 10.2 Gelles of Brody

Partial family tree showing some rabbinical connections

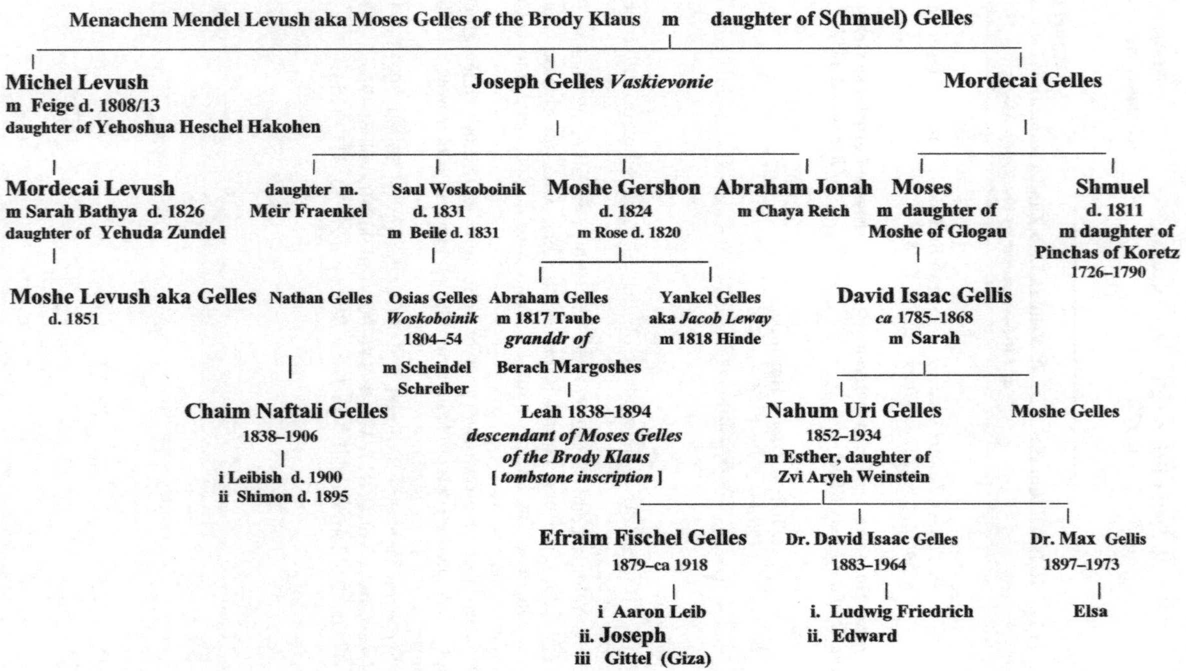

Menachem Mendel Levush aka Moses Gelles of the Brody Klaus   m   daughter of S(hmuel) Gelles

Joseph Gelles *Vaskievonie*

Mordecai Gelles

Shmuel
d. 1811
m daughter of
Pinchas of Koretz
1726–1790

Moses
m daughter of
Moshe of Glogau

Abraham Jonah
m Chaya Reich

Moshe Gershon
d. 1824
m Rose d. 1820

David Isaac Gellis
ca 1785–1868
m Sarah

Moshe Gelles

Nahum Uri Gelles
1852–1934
m Esther, daughter of
Zvi Aryeh Weinstein

Dr. Max Gellis
1897–1973

Elsa

Michel Levush
m Feige d. 1808/13
daughter of Yehoshua Heschel Hakohen

Mordecai Levush
m Sarah Bathya d. 1826
daughter of Yehuda Zundel

daughter m.
Meir Fraenkel

Saul Woskoboinik
d. 1831
m Belle d. 1831

Moshe Levush aka Gelles
d. 1851

Nathan Gelles

Abraham Gelles
m 1817 Taube
grandtr of
Berach Margoshes

Osias Gelles
Woskoboinik
1804–54
m Scheindel
Schreiber

Yankel Gelles
aka *Jacob Leway*
m 1818 Hinde

Leah 1838–1894
descendant of Moses Gelles
of the Brody Klaus
[tombstone inscription]

Chaim Naftali Gelles
1838–1906

i Leibish d. 1900
ii Shimon d. 1895

Efraim Fischel Gelles
1879–ca 1918

i Aaron Leib
ii Joseph
iii Gittel (Giza)

Dr. David Isaac Gelles
1883–1964

i. Ludwig Friedrich
ii. Edward

Footnotes

Moses Menachem Mendel Levush, a scholar of the Brody Klaus, was called *Levush* in recognition of his descent from Mordecai Yaffe of Prague (1530–1612), who was known as the *Levush* after the title of his major work. Menachem Mendel Levush married a daughter of Rabbi S. Gelles of Brody, who was probably connected with the line of Lithuanian rabbis descending from Uri Feivush Ashkenazi of Vilna and Jerusalem. The latter's great-grandson was Shmuel Gelles, the Chief Rabbi of Siemiatycze.

The name of Yehoshua Heschel Hakohen recurred in the family descended from a son-in-law of Abraham Joshua Heschel of Krakow, to whom the Gelles son-in-law of this name may well belong. Moshe Hakohen was the author of a family genealogy *Assfat Hakohen*.

Yehuda Leib Zundel Ramraz of Brody (d.1804) was a scholar of the Brody Klaus, as were his grandfather and Moses Gelles. Yehuda Zundel was the father-in-law of Mordecai Levush (Gelles) and of Eleazar Rokeach, whose son Shalom Rokeach (1779–1855) became the first Rebbe of the Belz Chasidic dynasty. Todros Zundel Ramraz was a nephew of Rabbi Yehuda Leib Zundel of Brody. There is a connection with Rabbi Todros Zundel Horowitz, the author of *Shoresh Miyakov* (Lvov 1858).

Meir Shlomo Fraenkel's sister Finkel, wife of Reb Wolf Bolechower, endowed a trust in memory of Feige Heschel Hakohen, underlining the Fraenkel–Gelles connection. A later Finkel, namesake of the aforementioned, is in the Brody birth records of 1853 as the daughter of Jacob Fraenkel and Chane Gelles.

Margoshes' descent from Efraim Fischl of Lvov (d.1653), President of the Council of the Four Lands, is recorded by Joseph Margoshes in his *Memoirs of my Life*. This Efraim Fischel was the father-in-law of Aryeh Leib Fischls, aka *der Hoiche Rebbe Leib* (d.1671), Chief Rabbi of Krakow and scion of the Kloisner line. One of the latter's sons was Efraim Fischel of Ludmir.

Abraham, son of Joseph Gelles, was a son-in-law of Jonah Reich, who appears to have been a *mechutan* of Jacob Simcha Landau, ABD of Apt and son of Joseph Landau, Head of the Brody Klaus (in 1757).

Shmuel, son of Mordecai and grandson of Moses Gelles, married a daughter of Rabbi Pinchas Shapiro of Koretz. He was a direct descendant of the Shapiro line including Chief Rabbi Nathan Nata Spiro of Krakow (1585–1633) and his grandfather Nathan Nata of Grodno (d.1577). From Pinchas Shapiro there is a line of descent to Rabbi Yehuda Meir Shapira (1887–1934), founder of the Lublin Sages Yeshivah, who taught my cousin Joseph, son of Rabbi Efraim Fischel and grandson of Rabbi Nahum Uri Gelles. The progeny of Shmuel Gelles and Sarah Rachel Scheindel Shapiro were rabbis in Podolia for five generations. They had a connection by marriage with the Chasidic Friedman dynasty of Czortkow. My grandfather and Rabbi Yehuda Meir Shapira were close followers of Rabbi Israel Friedman of Czortkow (1854–1933), who died in Vienna.

My grandfather Nahum Uri was the grandson of Moses Gelles, who was a son-on-law of Moshe of Glogau, eldest son of Shmuel Helman of Metz. There are grounds for believing that this Moses Gelles was the brother rather than first cousin of Shmuel Gelles. Rabbi Nahum Uri's eldest son was Efraim Fischel, possibly named after Efraim Fischel Horowitz (c.1800–1860), ABD of Munkacz. Rabbi Nahum Uri's second son was my father, Dr David Gelles, named after his paternal grandfather.

Data from the Brody Beth Din Records, the civil records in the Lviv archives, and from tombstone inscriptions have been augmented recently (2012) by the new Brody Cemetery Database (Gesher Galicia – Ami Elyasaf).

Photo 18 Rabbi Nahum Uri Gelles (grandfather)

Chapter 11

From the Baltic to the Black Sea

Jewish migrations in eastern Europe

T HE PATTERN of the Gelles name traced across the huge tract of land between the Baltic and Black Seas reflects the economic and political changes in this part of eastern Europe over a period of several hundred years. The fortunes of individual families were affected by periods of armed conflict, changing frontiers and patterns of trade, the beginnings of industrialisation and the coming of the railways, with the consequent declining prosperity of some old towns and the rise of important new ones. The political conditions of Jews in these territories were primarily determined by the three eighteenth-century partitions of Poland and varied from the benign liberal regime of the Habsburgs to the outbreaks of pogroms in the later Russian Empire.

The history of the Jews in Europe has many different facets and I have tried to touch upon some of them in a recent genealogical study. I traced age-old migrations across the continent in a predominantly west–east direction from the Atlantic to the Russian Pale and back again. Within this overarching picture there were numerous diversions, reversals and individual transplantations. The physical character of the continent set natural barriers and also provided openings along the great rivers and stretches of coastline where ancient and not so ancient port cities became centres of commerce and of Jewish culture. The geographic and demographic background had much influence on the socio-political changes over the centuries. Important migrations also took place in a south–north direction, from Italy across the Alps and from Constantinople and its coastal littoral along various routes to a wide area of south-eastern Europe. While some of these migrations were in the distant past, there were significant movements in more recent centuries that fell within the ambit of my family studies.

I have indicated here and elsewhere that the name of Gelles or Gellis was to be found scattered between such landmarks as Memel on the Baltic coast to several Lithuanian towns, including Vilna and Grodno, then on to Silesia and to Volhynia, Podolia, and Galicia, where the city of Brody was for a time of special significance for Jewish culture. From Czernowitz in the neighbouring province of Bukowina the traces turn westwards to Hungary and Austria and south-eastwards to Moldavia with its capital city of Kishinev. Old trade routes led from there to the Black Sea, where the great port of Odessa was founded at the end of the eighteenth century. Some of these families that appear so separate in space and time will have had ancient connections. The origin of others of the same name remains unresolved pending further studies, to which DNA analysis might perhaps make a useful contribution.

The Baltic and Black Seas provide two vital outlets to the world at either end of the vast stretch of land which had been fought over for centuries by people of different cultures and religions and in which generations of Jews had tried to make their home. While the great Polish–Lithuanian commonwealth was in the ascendant many Jewish communities flourished under its protection. The incursions of Bogdan Chmielnicki's Cossacks in the mid seventeenth century marked the beginning of Poland's decline and the rise of the power of Muscovy. Polish Jewry continued to suffer through the following period, which was marked by the war of the Polish succession and the power struggles leading up to the three partitions between the Prussian, Austrian, and Russian Empires in 1772, 1792, and 1795. Large parts of Silesia and western Poland came under Prussian rule, much of Lithuania became Russian, and Galicia was incorporated in the Austro-Hungarian Empire. These frontiers remained by and large until the end of World War I when a new Polish republic was reconstituted.

At the same time, the power of the Ottoman Empire had been in steady decline since the siege of Vienna was lifted in 1683 with the timely help of the Polish cavalry led by their king, Jan Sobieski. In the subsequent period, a series of Turkish wars extended the power of Austria in the Balkans and that of Russia in its southern borderland. These political upheavals and their economic consequences, including changing patterns of trade, improving communications, and rising birth rates, had a major impact on Jewish migrations, to be followed in due course by the effects of the late nineteenth-century Russian pogroms.

The demographic pattern of my extended family connections has inevitably been a consequence of these upheavals. The Holocaust all but put an end to the millennial presence of the Jews in eastern Europe. It remains now as a vital history lesson. We can learn much about great cultural achievement and also much about intolerance and greed and other forms of human folly. At the time of writing, the Jews have largely left the arena, but the great line from the Baltic to the Black Sea, spanning many countries and cultures, is as historically important as it ever was. The Baltic economy is on an upswing and even Brody has risen from the ashes of World War II as a terminal of the Odessa–Brody pipeline.

The old Prussian port of Memel was but a short distance over the border from the Lithuanian trade entrepôts of Kretinga (Krottingen) and Gorzd (Garsden). Gellis and related families who later flourished in England, America, and South Africa came from this area. Isaac Gellis of Memel (d.1906), who developed the Kosher food industry in nineteenth-century New York, may well have been of the same stock as Aaron Gellis, *traiteur* of Baden near Vienna, who was granted permanent residence there in 1805. At one time or another, some of these people moved on from Lithuania to the Silesian towns of Lissa and Krotoschin.

They included the families of Rabbis Siegfried and Benjamin Gelles, who came to England as refugees before World War II.

My immediate family was based in Brody 300 years ago, and some time before that they appear to have been in Prague, which in the sixteenth century lay at the crossroads between Italy and the Rhineland on the one hand and Galicia, Silesia, and points further east on the other. One of the great rabbis of Prague in that distant period was Mordecai Yaffe (1530–1612), known as the *Levush* after the title of his famous work. He became in turn Chief Rabbi of Grodno, Prague, and finally of Posen in Silesia. Descendants of the Levush were to be found in the seventeenth and eighteenth centuries in an arc from Grodno north to the Baltic coast and west to Silesia. The names of Yaffe, Levush, and Gelles (Gellis) were linked by marriage in several instances. One rabbinical Gellis family from Grodno left for the Holy Land in these early times and has now been there for at least ten generations. When Brody in Galicia came to be of some importance early in the eighteenth century as a trading entrepôt between the Russian and Austrian Empires, its Jewish population increased and its rabbis and scholars came from far and wide. Shmuel Gelles, Chief Rabbi of Siemiatycze, was a direct descendant of Uri Feivush Ashkenazi, Chief Rabbi of Vilna and later *Nasi* in Jerusalem. Rabbi Shmuel may be the Rabbi S. Gelles who was the father-in-law of Moses Menachem Mendel Levush, also known as Moses Gelles, who was a scholar of the distinguished study group known the Brody Klaus. The latter is the progenitor of my immediate paternal line. One of his grandsons married the daughter of Rabbi Pinchas Shapiro of Koretz (d.1790), one of the greatest of the eighteenth-century Hasidic rabbis, and another descendant married a granddaughter of Chief Rabbi Shmuel Helman (d.1764) of Metz. Collateral and later lines of the Gellis rabbinical family spread across Galicia, Podolia, Moldovia, and Hungary.

Gelles were widespread in Hungary. Some had been established since the eighteenth century in the so-called seven communities around Eisenstadt in the Burgenland and were probably kinsfolk of ours. Others may have come later from Galicia, such as the printer Moshe Eliyahu Gelles of Ungvar, whose family was decimated in the Holocaust. The Yeshiva at Munkacz also featured in the family annals.

In the nineteenth and early twentieth centuries, Gelles and related Weinstein, Brenner, and Horowitz are found in the Bukowina, including its capital, Czernowitz and in neighbouring Bessarabia (Moldavia). A nexus linking Kishinev and Czernowitz bears evidence to family movements in the twentieth century. A noted American cardiologist links his Gelles line to the Chalfan (Halfin) of Kishinev, harking back to earlier days in Western Europe.

One of the outstanding achievements of the Empress Catherine of Russia was the establishment of the seaport of Odessa in 1794. This city became one of the jewels of the Russian imperial crown and the home of a large and flourishing Jewish community. Galician Jews flocked to this new port with its promise of comparative freedom and liberal economic regime. Among these were many from Brody. Indeed the earliest Jewish synagogue and school in Odessa bore the *Broder* name. A family to whom we are distantly related was that of Meir Shor, who later adopted the name of Brodsky. His descendants were among the richest Jews in Russia. His son, the industrialist Abraham Brodsky (1816–84), was a leader of the Odessa community, which also included families by the name of Gellis.

From this new port city many Jews in due course set sail for America or made their way to Israel. As for Constantinople, the ancient capital of the Byzantine and Ottoman Empires, how many of our forefathers came here a thousand or more years ago? Local records of the Gellis name include Ashkenazi Jews who died in the early years of the twentieth century, so these may have been relatively recent arrivals from Galicia or neighbouring lands during the migration that gathered pace in the late eighteenth century.

BIBLIOGRAPHY

Cesarani, David and Gemma, Romain, *Jews and Port Cities* (London: Vallentine Mitchell 2006).

Gelles, Edward, *An Ancient Lineage: European Roots of a Jewish Family*. (London: Vallentine Mitchell 2006) [Chapters: 30 (Brody), 32 (Prague), 38 (Gelles families); tables: 26 (Gelles of Brody), 27 & 43 (Brodsky), 39 (Chalfan); map: 4 (incidence of Gelles name); bibliography: lists monographs on numerous towns].

Herlihy, Patricia, *Odessa: A History 1794–1914* (Harvard University Press 1985).

Private communications regarding family presence in Grodno, Gorzd, Kretinga, Lissa, Krotoschin, Czernowitz, Kishinev, and Odessa from (among others) Rabbi I. Gellis, H.C. Gellis, J. S. Gelles, J.M. Gelles, and Z. D. Gellis.

Figure 11.1 Incidence of the Gelles family name in central and eastern Europe with some approximate dates

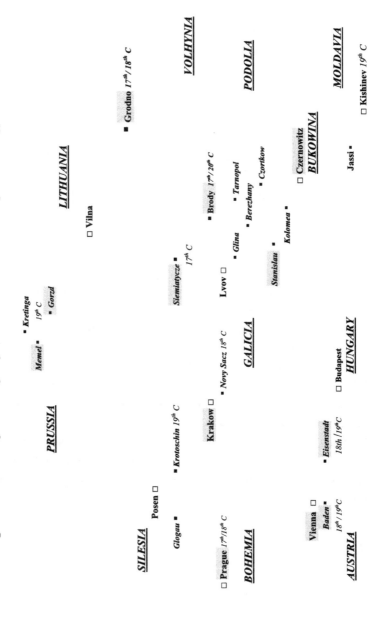

SILESIA

PRUSSIA

LITHUANIA

VOLHYNIA

■ Kreinga
  19ᵗʰ C
Memel ■   ■ Gorzd

□ Vilna

■ Grodno 17ᵗʰ / 18ᵗʰ C

Posen □

■ Krotoschin 19ᵗʰ C

Siemiatycze ■
           17ᵗʰ C

■ Brody 17ᵗʰ / 20ᵗʰ C

PODOLLA

Krakow □

■ Novy Sacz 18ᵗʰ C

GALICIA

Lvov □   ■ Glina

■ Tarnopol

■ Berehany   ■ Czortkow

Stanislau ■
           ■ Kolomea

□ Czernowitz

BUKOWINA

MOLDAVIA

□ Prague 17ᵗʰ / 18ᵗʰ C

BOHEMIA

■ Eisenstadt
  18th / 19ᵗʰ C

□ Budapest

HUNGARY

Jassi ■

□ Kishinev 19ᵗʰ C

Vienna □
■ Baden
  18ᵗʰ / 19ᵗʰ C

Glogau ■

AUSTRIA

Chapter 12

Rabbi Shmuel Helman of Metz

Connections of an influential eighteenth-century rabbi

THE COMPLEX PATTERN of Jewish migrations across the continent reveals major political, social, and economic influences. Among the leading rabbinic families of the eighteenth century none is likely to have been more peripatetic than that of Chief Rabbi Shmuel Helman, who came from Glogau in Silesia, studied in Prague, and was subsequently Chief Rabbi of Kremsier in Moravia, Mannheim in Germany, and Metz in Lorraine. He acquired a pan-European standing through his leadership in religious affairs and his influence is evident in the positions occupied by his progeny and their arranged marriages. His children and grandchildren and their in-laws were spread across Silesia, Galicia, the Burgenland, Austria, Moravia, Bohemia, Germany, and France.

INTRODUCTION

For centuries, rabbis moved about Europe from one appointment to another, but few can have been more peripatetic than Shmuel Helman of Metz and his family. References to him and to his distinguished rabbinical connections are scattered about in Hebrew, German, French, and English texts. It is high time that this corpus of information is brought together, not only to direct the different branches of this widespread family to their source material, but also to throw light on a number of gaps and questionable links.

Shmuel Helman of Metz was called Samuel after the ancient prophet and Helman which is a German Jewish name meaning claivoyant or seer. His descendants adopted this name as their family name in the form of Hillman. Shmuel Helman was born in Krotoschin in the province of Posen around 1670 and lived to be nearly a hundred years old. His extensive family provides a paradigm for the pan-European character of the eighteenth century Ashkenazi rabbinate. Helman is remembered for the great influence he acquired through his many years in important posts at Mannheim and Metz, for his learning, his initiative in matters of education, including the setting-up of a Hebrew printing press at Metz, and for his part in the Eibeschuetz controversy which rocked the mid eighteenth-century rabbinical world.

The emphasis of the present study is on the genealogy of his family, highlighting the continent-wide links between the Jewish communities of his time.

THE IMMEDIATE FAMILY

A primary source for Helman's life is the contemporary manuscript by his friend and kinsman Phineas ben Moses Katzenellenbogen [1]. Helman studied in Prague under Rabbi Abraham ben Saul Broda in the early years of the eighteenth century. His first wife came from Glogau in Silesia, not far from Krotoschin. When she died, her wealthy father supported Helman while he continued his studies at Prague until a younger daughter came of age to take her place. That was not a particularly unusual custom at a time when so many young wives died in childbirth. Helman's wife Sarah, who outlived him by ten years, was his second or possibly third spouse. From Prague, Helman went on to become Rabbi of Kremsier in Moravia in 1720 and Chief Rabbi of Mannheim in 1727. This period is covered in the writings of Frankl-Gruen and Leopold Löwenstein [2, 3]. Gruen avers that the Kremsier town records give Helman as 'son of Feivel of Krotoschin'. However, general opinion held him to be the son of Israel Halpern of Krotoschin, the son-in-law of Nathan Nata Spiro of Krakow. In 1751 Helman moved to Metz in Lorraine where he held the Chief Rabbinate until his death in 1764. The French records are limited in scope [4, 5]. They do not include any transcriptions of the lost tombstones of him or his wife Sarah at Metz, which should have given the names of their respective fathers.

Glogau was the Helman home base. Not only was at least one of his wives from that town but his son Uri Feivush was the son-in-law of the locally prominent Saul Parnes and his wife Henelle, daughter of Rabbi Naftali Cohen, who had been *ABD* of Glogau [6]. Helman's grandson, Naftali Hirsch Katzenellenbogen, married Rachel, daughter of a Feivel of Glogau [7].

Rabbi Moshe of Glogau

Helman's son Moshe, a leading member of the community, was always known as Moshe of Glogau. R. Eleazar Kallir refers to his son-in-law 'the great luminary R. Moshe Halevi, ABD of Libna, son of the famous Gaon R. Michel Halevi, ABD of Eisenstadt, son of the late great Gaon R. Asher Lemel Halevi, ABD and Head of the Yeshiva at Eisenstadt and Head of the Beth Din of Glogau, son-in-law of the late great sharp minded scholar R. Moshe of Glogau, son of the great Gaon, famous in his generation, R. Hillman, ABD and Head of the Yeshiva at Metz' [8]. Moshe of Glogau's daughter married Yechiel Michal Segal, son of Asher Lemel Halevi, who succeeded his father as Chief Rabbi of Eisenstadt in the Burgenland. Bernard Wachstein's work on the tombstone inscriptions from the old Jewish cemetery at Eisenstadt contains much valuable information. (Tombstone Nos 412, 426, 515, 594, 802, 933, 1013, and 1039 give details of Jached, the wife of Asher Lemel Halevi, of her father, of Asher Lemel (described as a descendant of Joel Sirkes), of Chana, the daughter of Moshe Hillman of Glogau, of her husband, and of several kinsfolk by the name of Gelles, including

Jacob Gelles, who died in 1858, of his son Moses Elias Gelles, and of their respective wives.) Chana Hillman appears to have died at a relatively young age in 1805, and her father is referred to as the great luminary Rabbi Moshe, son of the great Gaon Rabbi Shmuel Hillman, ABD of Metz [9]. Moshe of Glogau was a forebear of my grandfather Rabbi Nahum Uri Gelles, as several standard reference works on the Galician Rabbinate testify [10, 11]. This Gelles rabbinical line flourished for a long time in Galicia, but there were other Gelles elsewhere in Poland and Hungary, and specifically in Eisenstadt and its associated villages of the so-called Siebengemeinde (Seven Communities). For example, Ahron Ber Gelles of Loretto signed an Eisenstadt document in 1859 and his name appears in a list of the representatives of the Burgenland [12]. The Jewish Museum in Vienna has a Torah mantle presented by Rabbi Ahron Ber Gelles and his wife Feila on the occasion of their son Mordecai's Bar Mitzvah in 1858.

Rabbi Uri Feivush

Helman's son Uri Feivush became in turn Chief Rabbi of Hanau, Lissa, Bonn, and Cologne. Louis Lewin's *History of the Jews* in Lissa, and the Memorbücher of Hanau, Deutz, and Metz should be consulted for details of his life [13, 14]. He died in his prime during a visit to his father's grave in Metz. Uri's wife was Chaya Jutlé, otherwise Chaya Ittel Parnes. The Memorbuch of Metz gives the date of death of Samuel Helman as 30 December 1764, of his wife Sorle [Sarale] as 27 July 1774, and of his son Uri Schraga Feivush as 20 October 1771. Details of four of Uri Feivish's children and later progeny are to be found in the records of Metz. The children's births are listed as Hendlé 1752, Fratié 1753, Jutiel 1755, and Salomon Léon 1757 [15, 16]. A son of the last of these married Vögele Emerich in 1780. Uri's daughter Hinde became the daughter-in-law of the distinguished Chief Rabbi of Prague, Yechezkiel Landau, who delivered a memorial address on 10 February 1765 following the death of Shmuel Helman [17].

Rabbi Helman's daughters

Four of Rabbi Helman's daughters made alliances with distinguished rabbinic families, as shown in Chart 12.1. They included Jached, wife

Chart 12.1 Chief Rabbi Shmuel Helman of Metz: his children and some of their descendants

(ABD is an acronym for Av Beth Din = Head of the Rabbinical Court - who sometimes also had the title of Chief Rabbi)

1 **Daughter** m **Shimson Katz** of Kremsier, grandson of Naftali Hirsch Katz, Chief Rabbi of Frankfurt and Posen,
   who was a descendant of Judah Loew of Prague and Saul Wahl Katzenellenbogen

2 **Moshe** of Glogau, ABD of Glina m ?

   i)   a daughter, Chana m Yechiel Michal Segal, ABD of Eisenstadt,
         son of Asher Lemel, ABD of Glogau and Eisenstadt

   ii)   another daughter m Moses Gelles of the Brody rabbinical line
         who was the grandfather of Nahum Uri Gelles, ABD of Solotwina

3 **Uri Feivush**, ABD of Hanau, Lissa, Bonn, and Cologne m   Chaya Ittel Parnes

   i)   their daughter Hinde m Shmuel Landau,
         son of Ezekiel Landau, Chief Rabbi of Prague

   ii)   their son Salomon Leib Hillman was the progenitor of a line to
         Shmuel Isaac Hillman, Rabbi of Glasgow, Dayan in London,
         whose daughter Sarah Hillman m Yitzhak Halevi Herzog,
         Chief Rabbi of Israel,
         and their son, Chaim Herzog, became 6th President of Israel

4 **Jached** m **Eliezer Katzenellenbogen**, ABD of Bamberg and Hagenau
   their son Naftali Hirsch Katzenellenbogen, Head of the Consistory of the
   Upper Rhine, was the grandfather of Lazare Isidore, Chief Rabbi of France

5 **Bella** m **Judah Leib Fraenkel**, son of David Mirels Fraenkel, Chief Rabbi of Berlin

6 **Deborah** m **Isaac Rapaport**, son of Israel Ashkenazi, ABD of Offenbach and Hanau

Edward Gelles, a grandson of Nahum Uri Gelles, is a direct 6th generation descendant of Moses Gelles of the Brody Klaus,
and a 6th generation descendant of Shmuel Helman (Hillman), Chief Rabbi of Kremsier, Mannheim and Metz
(see Edward Gelles, *An Ancient Lineage* (2006) and *Meeting my Ancestors: Genealogy, Genes and Heritage* (2011)
for details of the marriage of Shmuel Helman's eldest daughter to Shimshon Ka tz of Kremsier see chart 0.5 in the
Introduction "A Mirror of the Past")

of Eliezer Katzenellenbogen of Alsace, who was Rabbi of Bamberg and Hagenau, Beila, wife of Juda Leib Fraenkel of Dessau, son of David Mirels-Fraenkel, the noted Chief Rabbi of Berlin, and Deborah, wife of Isaac Rapaport of Hanau.

Jached Helman's son, Naphtali Hirsch Katzenellenbogen of Frankfurt-on-Oder and Winzenheim, became Chief Rabbi of the Palatinate. Also known to the French as Naphtalie Lazare Hirsch, Grand Rabbin Président du Consistoire Israélite, he was a member of the Great Sanhedrin called together by the Emperor Napoleon in 1806. His grandson, Isidore Lazare, became Chief Rabbi of France in 1867.

Details of Beila Helman and of other marriages of the Fraenkel family are to be found in the two-volume work on Jewish marriages in Berlin by Jacob Jacobson [18].

The Rapaports of Hanau and their marriage connection with Deborah Helman are treated by Leopold Löwenstein in his essay on the Rabbinate of Hanau, by Chaim Josef David Azulai, and others [19–22].

The provisions made for Helman's daughters are exemplified by an interesting deed drawn up by Shmuel Helman and his wife Sarah in 1749 shortly before they left Mannheim for Metz. It is in favour of their daughter Jached. It indicates the family's wealth and Sarah's independent means [23].

ANCESTRY OF SHMUEL HELMAN

In the absence of the Metz tombstones of Shmuel Helman and his wife Sarah or of any transcriptions, some doubts must remain concerning the identity of their respective parents. The recurrence of the name of Uri Feivush or Feivel in both the Hillman and Gelles lines of descent lends some support to the theory that Shmuel Helman's father-in-law was an Uri Feivush who settled in Glogau. The questions concerning Helman's father might start with the previously mentioned *History of the Jews of Kremsier*, which quotes an entry from the town's *Pinkas* (Jewish records) reading 'son of Feivel of Krotoschin', apparently referring to a Rabbi Samuel Helman. The ancestry of the Rabbi of Metz has for long been taken on the authority of *Da'at Kedoshim* [24] and other reference works, which rely on various sources such as a memorandum written by a relative shortly before Helman's death [25]. This letter by Eliezer Lipman Zak is the primary source for believing that Shmuel Helman was a member of the rabbinical Halpern clan and that he was the son of Israel Halpern, the descendant of Rabbi Moses Halpern of Lvov, author of *Ahavat Zion*, who was the son of Zebulon Ashkenazi Halpern. According to Meir Wunder's *Elef Margoliot*, the latter traced his lineage back to Isaac of Dampierre in the twelfth century [26]. Rabbi Israel Halpern of Krotoschin was married to Lifsha, a daughter of Chief Rabbi Nathan Nata Spiro of Krakow, author of the Kabbalistic work *Megaleh Amukot*. The Spiro line goes back to Rashi of Troyes via the nexus of the Spiro, Luria, and Treivish families.

There are some scholars who have interpreted the entry in the *Pinkas* of Kremsier as meaning that there were two rabbis by the name of Shmuel Helman from Krotoschin, and that the one who became Rabbi of Metz was not the son of Israel Halpern. This is the line taken by David Leib Zinz [27]. This argument is discussed by Rabbi Dov Weber [28]. There is a document from the Council of the Four Lands signed in 1692 by 'Samuel Helman, son of Israel Halpern of Krotoszyn' that would make the Rabbi of Metz a very young man at the time or suggest that his birth might be earlier than the accepted date of 1670. We do know that Shmuel Helman died in 1764/65 and that he reached a very advanced age. The evidence of the aforementioned contemporary Heilprin document, taken together with some biographical details as recorded by Helman's kinsman, friend, and fellow student, Phineas Katzenellenbogen, might be considered more persuasive than a possibly misleading entry in the Kremsier records and any problems with Helman's date of birth. This remains a controversial issue.

In accepting the traditional view that Helman's father was Rabbi Israel Halpern of Krotoschin, one should be mindful of the previous connections between the Halperns and Katzenellenbogens and the marriages that Helman's children contracted with prominent families. These are more compatible with Helman himself being of a distinguished Halpern parentage. Further backing comes from entries in *Ohalei Shem*, which are largely based on information supplied around the publication date of 1912 by the rabbis concerned [30]. The entry for my grandfather has already been mentioned. Another instance is the pedigree given for Eliyahu Chaim Meisels of Lodz, whose mother was descended from Rabbi Eliezer Lipman of Chelm, a brother of Rabbi Shmuel Helman of Metz, stated to be the son of Rabbi Israel Halpern, called 'Charnash', of Krotoschin (acronym for son-in-law of Rabbi Nathan Shapiro).

SHMUEL HELMAN'S ACHIEVEMENTS

Helman was considered a great Talmud scholar in his time, but few of his writings were published. One of his novellae appeared in *Kol Yehuda* by Rabbi Yehuda ben Chanina Selig of Glogau. During his long sojourn in Mannheim, he did much to further Torah education and to encourage literary activity. Other noteworthy achievements included the setting-up of a flourishing Hebrew printing press in Metz in the 1760s [31]. He was involved in a long drawn-out controversy centred on the prominent Rabbi Jonathan Eibeschuetz, whom he succeeded in the Metz Rabbinate in 1751. Suspicions had been aroused that Eibeschuetz was a secret Shabbataian (that is, a follower of the false messiah, Shabbatai Tzvi), and in 1752 Helman joined with the Rabbis of Frankfurt, Amsterdam, and Hanover in pronouncing a ban on Eibeschuetz. Incidentally, the latter was, like Helman himself, a descendant of Nathan Nata Spiro of Krakow. A list of approbations from Helman's time in Mannheim and in Metz is to be found in Leopold Löwenstein's *Index Approbationum* [32].

Helman became the patriarch of an extended family spread over Lorraine and Alsace, Germany, Poland, Austria and Hungary. Many close relatives held senior rabbinical appointments, and a few were rabbis of some consequence. As the respected leader of an important and wealthy community and at the centre of continent-wide Jewish affairs, Helman exerted considerable influence on doctrinal matters and rabbinical appointments, and by arranging marriages with other prominent rabbinical families.

RABBINICAL CONNECTIONS

Shmuel Helman was the father-in-law of Eliezer of Alsace, who was a son of Moses Katzenellenbogen of Anspach (1670–1733). Eliezer's mother was a daughter of Eliezer Halpern (Heilprin) of Fuerth (1649–1700), a cousin of Helman's ancestral line.

Moses of Anspach (near Schwabach) was a direct descendant of Meir Katzenellenbogen, known as the Maharam of Padua, via Meir Wahl Katzenellenbogen of Brest. Rabbi Abraham Joshua Heschel of Krakow (1596–1663) was a grandson of the latter.

Abraham Joshua Heschel was a great-great-grandfather of the Chief Rabbi of Prague, Ezekiel Landau (1713–93). Helman's granddaughter Hinde married Ezekiel's son, Samuel Landau.

Ezekiel Landau was the grandson of Rabbi Zvi Hirsch Witeles Landau of Opatov (1643–1714), who, according to David Tebele Efrati, was the brother-in-law of Rabbi Gershon of Vilna. The latter was a grandfather of Rabbi David Tebele of Lissa, who died in 1792. Rabbi Tebele was a Gelles cousin and also a cousin of Ezekiel Landau [33].

LATER PROGENY

Helman's two sons and four daughters, as shown on Chart 12.2, had numerous progeny which are still largely unexplored. We have French records relating to the Katzenellenbogen descendants of his daughter Jached and to the offspring of his son Uri Feivush. There are some German references to the family of his daughter Beila. The family of his daughter Deborah must be sought in Germany and Moravia.

Details of the life of Helman's son Moshe are very sparse indeed. Little assistance could be gained from works on the Jews of Silesia and of Glogau [35–37] but I have managed to gather a sufficient number of other references to show that Moshe was a leader of the Jewish community in Glogau, and that he was a learned and well-respected figure. His only recorded daughter Chana married the Rabbi of Eisenstadt, whose family came from Glogau. The beginning of this rabbinical line in the Burgenland community is shown in Chart 12.1. The gaps in the available records make it well-nigh impossible to discover Moshe of Glogau's other issue. Another as yet unidentified daughter may be the link with my family. The entry on my grandfather Rabbi Nahum Uri Gelles in *Ohalei Shem* states that Moshe Hillman was ABD at Glina, and *Otzar Harabbanim* has it that he was at Glina in 1780. My great-grandfather Rabbi David Isaac Gelles, from the Brody rabbinical family of that name, studied at Glina under Rabbi Meir Krasnipoler (*c.*1740–1820), who

Chart 12.2 Edward Gelles and Chaim Herzog (6th President of Israel)

Chief Rabbi Shmuel Helman (Hillman) of Mannheim and Metz (d. 1764)

m (1) -wife (d. young)

R. Moshe of Glogau

m (2) - younger sister, Sarah (d. 1774)

R. Uri Feivush (d. 1771)

Chana (d. 1805)
m Yechiel Michal Segal
ABD of Eisenstadt
(1740–1819)

daughter
m Moses Gelles
of Brody

R. David Isaac Gellis
of Glina & Brody (d. 1868)

R. Nahum Uri Gelles
ABD Solotwina (1852–1934)

Dr. David Isaac Gelles
of Vienna (1883–1964)

Dr Edward Gelles
(b. 1927)

Hinde (d. 1835)
m Shmuel Landau (d. 1834)
s. of R. Ezekiel Landau
Chief Rabbi of Prague
(1713–1793)

Salomon Leib Hillman (b. 1757)

Shmuel Isaac Hillman (b. ca 1780)

Shimkhel Hillman (b. 1805)

Avraham Chaim Hillman (1840–1897)

R. Shmuel Isaac Hillman (1868–1953)

Sarah Hillman (1898–1979)
m Yitzhak Halevi Herzog
Chief Rabbi of Israel
(1888–1959)

Chaim Herzog (1918–1997)
6th President of Israel

Isaac Herzog (b. 1960)
Leading Israeli Politician

Chaim Herzog succeeded the 5th President of Israel, Yitzhak Navon, in 1983
President Navon married Ofira Resnikov (1936–1993)
Bertha Gelles, paternal aunt of Edward Gelles was also an aunt by marriage
of Ofira, who became a much loved First Lady of Israel
(see Edward Gelles, *An Ancient Lineage*, pp 189 & 192)

later became ABD in Brody. There is also a reference to David Isaac Gelles in the Memorial Book of Glina [38–40]. From David Isaac's tombstone in Brody we know that he died in 1868 and that his father was Rabbi Moshe. From the birth records of my grandfather at Narayow we know that his mother was called Sarah, but no records have as yet been found identifying the families of David Isaac's wife or mother. However, from the Eisenstadt records we know that Moshe of Glogau's daughter Chana died in 1805 at a relatively young age. Moshe of Glogau might have been born in the period 1700–20. We do not know when he died, although Stuart Steinberg has argued from the dates of his grandson, Moshe Halevi, that it must have been not later than the 1760s. The births of David Isaac Gelles and of his father Moses can be put in the 1790s and 1760s. The conjunction of Moshe of Glogau's supposed sojourn in Glina, my great-grandfather's study there under Meir Krasnipoler, the connection by marriage between the Krasnipoler and Kallir families of Brody and with Moshe of Glogau's Halevi in-laws in Eisenstadt, and what we know about the Gelles family forms the background to the links of my Gelles line with Moshe of Glogau.

A brief word is appropriate here about the ancient connections between Glogau in Silesia, Brody, and neighbouring towns in Galicia, and Eisenstadt in the Burgenland, which was for a long time in Hungary but later became part of Austria. In earlier centuries, German and Austrian Jews sought refuge at various times in Silesia, where Breslau was the principal centre, and in Krakow, whence they would have found their way to eastern Galicia and elsewhere. Some Jews expelled from Vienna in 1670 went to Eisenstadt, where they enjoyed the protection of the Esterhazys. Following the expulsion of the Turks from Hungary in 1686, Jews were forced to leave Ofen (Budapest) and many joined those who had settled earlier in the so-called Siebengemeinde. During the first half of the eighteenth century there was an influx of Moravian and Galician Jews into Hungary. Eisenstadt grew at that time into a notable centre of Jewish learning.

Other descendants of Moshe Helman were to be found in Poland, Lithuania, and Russia as well as in Austria-Hungary before World War I [41].

Among those who joined the flow of emigration to America was Sidney Hillman (1887–1946), who received a rabbinical education in Lithuania, fell foul of the Tsarist government when he became involved in the trade union movement, but rose to prominence in America as a leader of the Congress of Industrial Organizations, a member of Franklin Roosevelt's Labor Advisory Board, and an influential figure in the Democratic Party. At the time of his death, he was vice-president of the World Federation of Trade Unions [42].

After two and a half centuries, descendants of Shmuel Hillman are flourishing in America, Israel, England, and elsewhere. A few years ago, more than a score attended a Hillman reunion in America. Among descendants with an active interest in the history of this family are Harold Rhode in Washington, DC and Stuart Steinberg in California. Dr Harold Hillman, who is resident in England, is the grandson of Samuel Isaac Hillman, who was born in Lithuania in 1868 and held appointments as Chief Rabbi of Glasgow in Scotland and judge of the Rabbinical Court in London before finally settling in Jerusalem, where he died in 1953. The latter's daughter Sarah married Yitzchak Halevi Herzog, who became Chief Rabbi of Israel. Their son Chaim Herzog (1918–97) was a distinguished diplomat and politician who became the sixth president of Israel in 1983 (see Chart 12.2).

Harold Rhode, whose extensive family website can be easily accessed under his name, has also written much about Lithuanian Hillman descendants. He has noted the personal recollections of Sarah Hillman, embracing numerous kinsfolk and including the aforementioned Sidney Hillman, who turned out to be her second cousin [43].

This outline of ancient family connections offers numerous pointers towards further links spanning many centuries of rabbinical history.

REFERENCES

[1] Phineas ben Moses Katzenellenbogen, *Yesh Manhilin* (MS in the Bodleian Library, Oxford. Published in book form Jerusalem 1984), pp. 84–85,109, 192–3, 195, 197, 208, 219, 311–2, 375.
[2] Adolf Frankl-Gruen, *Geschichte der Juden in Kremsier*. (Breslau: S. Schottländer 1896), pp. 84–5.
[3] Leopold Löwenstein, *Geschichte der Juden in der Kurpfalz*. (Frankfurt 1895), pp. 198–202.
[4] Abraham Cahen, 'Le Rabbinat de Metz pendant la periode francaise', *Revue des etudes juives*, xii, pp. 289–94.

[5] Nathan Netter, *Metz et son grand passé: Vingt siècles d'histoire d'une communauté juive*, pp. 113–14.

[6] R. Meir ben Isaac of Horochow, *Kosnoth Or*. (Frankfurt-on-Oder 1753), Introduction.

[7] Neil Rosenstein, *The Unbroken Chain*. (New York: CIS Publishers 1990), Vol. 1, p. 102.

[8] R. Eleazar Kallir, *Chavot Yair Chadash*. (Prague 1792), p. 114a.

[9] Bernhard Wachstein, *Die Grabschriften des alten Jüdenfriedhofs in Eisenstadt* (Vienna: R. Loewit 1922).

[10] Shmuel Nach Gottlieb, *Ohalei Shem*. (Pinsk 1912), pp. 261–2.

[11] R. Meir Wunder, *Meorei Galicia*. (Jerusalem 1978), Vol. 1, p. 699.

[12] Bernhard Wachstein, *Urkunden und Akten zur Geschichte der Juden in Eisenstadt*. (Vienna and Leipzig: Wilhem Braumüller 1926), pp. 214, 706.

[13] Louis Lewin, *Die Geschichte der Juden in Lissa*. (Pinne: N. Gunderman 1904), pp. 189–92 and p. 379.

[14] Adolf Jellinek, *Märtyrer und Memorbuch. Including: Das alte Memorbuch der Deutzer Gemeinde von 1581 bis 1784*. (Vienna: Loewy & Alkalay 1881).

[15] Jean-Claude Bouvart-Martin, Memorbuch of Metz (1720–1849), Nos. 2202, 2340, 2282.

[16] Pierre-André Meyer, *Tables du Register d'Etat Civil de la communauté juive de Metz 1717–1792*. (Paris 1987).

[17] R. Yechezkel Landau, Ahavas Zion. *A Collection of Sermons Delivered by Rabbi Ezekiel Landau, ABD of Prague*. (Jerusalem 1966), Sixth Sermon, pp. 18–21.

[18] Jacob Jacobson, *Jüdische Trauungen in Berlin 1759–1813*. (Berlin: Walter de Gruyter 1968), Vol. 1 [1759–1840], pp. 296–7 and pp. 445–6.

[19] Neil Rosenstein, *The Unbroken Chain*. (New York: CIS Publishers 1990), Vol. 2, p. 723.

[20] Chaim Josef David Azulai, *Diaries [Ma'agal Tov]* Part I, translated by Benjamin Cymerman. (Jerusalem: The Bnei Issakhar Institute 1997), p. 74.

[21] Leopold Löwenstein, *Das Rabbinat in Hanau*. Jahrbuch der Jüdisch-literarischen Gesellschaft. (Frankfurt am Main 1895), Vol. 14.

[22] D. Feuchtwang, 'Epitaphien des Gräberfeldes zu Nikolsburg', *Mittteilungen zur Jüdischen Volkskunde*, (1907), Vol. 21, No. 1.

[23] Deed executed by Rabbi Shmuel Hillman and his wife Sarale in 1749, MS Or.12333 [Gaster Collection at British Library], p. 28.

[24] I.T. Eisenstadt (suppl. S. Wiener), *Da'at Kedoshim*. (St. Petersburg 1897–98), pp. 59–68.

[25] Eliezer Lipman Zak, MS R.761 at Jewish Theological Seminary, New York.

[26] R. Meir Wunder, *Elef Margoliot*. (London & Jerusalem: Institute for the Preservation of the Galician Jewish Heritage and the Margulies family 1993).

[27] David Leib Zinz, *Gedullath Yehonathan*. (Pietrkow 1930), p.249.

[28] R. Dov Weber, *Kol Todah* (New York 1998), pp. 40–2.

[29] Yaakov ben Shmuel's Book of Responsa, Beth Yaakov. (Duerenfürth 1696).

[30] Shmuel Nach Gottlieb, *Ohalei Shem*. (Pinsk 1912), pp. 352–3.

[31] Edouard Privat (ed.), *Histoire des Juifs de France*. Collection Franco-Judaica (Paris, 1972), pp. 115, 319.

[32] Leopold Löwenstein, *Index Approbationum*. (Berlin 1923), p. 71.

[33] David Tebele Efrati, *Toldot Anshei Shem*. (Warsaw 1875), pp. 32–4.

[34] Edward Gelles, 'Finding Rabbi Moses Gelles', *Avotaynu*, Vol. 18, No. 1 (2002).

[35] R. Berndt, *Geschichte der Juden in Gross-Glogau*. (Glogau 1873).

[36] M. Brann, *Geschichte der Juden in Schlesien*. (Berlin 1917).

[37] Franz D. Lucas & Margret Heitmann, *Stadt des Glaubens. Geschichte und Kultur der Juden in Glogau*, (G. Olms 1991), pp. 242–244.

[38] Natan Zvi Friedman, *Otzar Harabbanim*. (Israel: Bnei Brak 1973), No. 14602.

[39] H. Halpern (ed.), *Memorial Book of Glina*. (New York: Emergency Relief Committee for Glina 1950), p. 17.

[40] Edward Gelles, 'My Father's People', *Sharsheret Hadorot* (2003), Vol. 17, No. 1.

[41] Shmuel Nach Gottlieb, *Ohalei Shem*. (Pinsk 1912), pp. 342, 352, 450.

[42] Sidney Hillman, subject of numerous biographies, a long entry in the *Encyclopedia Judaica*, 1971, Vol. 8, pp. 493–4 and many references on the internet.

[43] Harold Rhode, 'Jewish Culture, History, and Religion', *Avotaynu*, Vol. 14, No. 1 (1998) – www.familytreemaker.genealogy.com/users/r/h/o Harold Rhode-MD.

Chapter 13

Frankists

A heretical Jewish sect in eastern Europe

THE STRUGGLE BETWEEN ORTHODOX JUDAISM and heresies of a mystical pseudo-messianic nature led in mid-eighteenth-century Poland to the rabbinical excommunication of the followers of Jacob Frank. Thousands of these Frankists were welcomed by the Catholic Church and in due course many of them married into the Polish nobility. Some influence of the Frankist movement made itself felt in Western Europe. A branch of the rabbinic Shor family were prominent followers of Frank and under their later name of Wolowski had distinguished careers in Poland and in France, while a descendant of Jacob Frank, the Reverend Joseph Wolff, came to England in the nineteenth century and attained prominence as a preacher, author, and Christian missionary.

The Frankists were an eighteenth-century Jewish sect in eastern Europe with a legacy that stretched across the continent. This essay illustrates the pan-European reach of the movement by focusing on French connections of the Wolowski family, who were among the most prominent of the early Frankists, and on the British connections of Jacob Frank's descendant, Joseph Wolff.

JACOB FRANK AND THE FRANKISTS

Jacob ben Judah Leib (1726–91), later known as Jacob Frank, was born in Poland, in the province of Podolia, which is now part of Ukraine. He died in Germany at Offenbach am Main. Some of his formative years were spent in Smyrna and Salonica (then in the Ottoman Empire) where there was a strong Shabbataian following.[1] Inspired by the extreme mystical strands in Judaism and in opposition to Talmudical orthodoxy,[2] Frank returned to Poland where he gathered a large following that later spread to Moravia and then to Germany. The beliefs and usages of the Zoharists,[3] or Frankists as they were called, came under strident condemnation and ultimately led to their excommunication by the Polish Rabbinate in 1756.

Their doctrine had a Trinitarian element that eased Frank's approaches to the Catholic Church and finally led to the baptism of the majority of his followers, with the Polish gentry and nobility acting as their godparents. Jacob Frank himself was baptised in 1759, with King Augustus III as his sponsor. For a while Frank enjoyed the support of several European monarchs, who thought that his movement might lead to a mass conversion of the Jews, but disillusionment ultimately set in.

By the end of the eighteenth century, Frankist descendants were numbered in tens of thousands. The majority gradually merged with Christian families in Poland over several generations and some spread across Europe. The resulting genetic admixture and the historical importance of the movement were played down by generations of orthodox Jews and by some Frankist descendants who may have wished to hide their Jewish roots or were unaware of them.

The acrimonious disputes between the contra-Talmudist Frankists and the Polish Rabbinate, involving outrageous accusations and counter-accusations, are not to be viewed as purely theological arguments between champions of the Talmud and the Zohar. The millennial rabbinical orthodoxy had always encompassed both rationalist and mystical elements. The travails suffered by Polish Jewry from the middle of the seventeenth century onwards provided a fertile ground for the mystical tradition to come to the fore.

In the later eighteenth century, the Chasidic[4] movement of Rabbi Israel ben Eliezer, known as the *Baal Shem Tov* (Master of the Good Name), became a powerful force in bringing a renewed spirituality to the Jewish masses. It divided communities and individual families at the very time when the message of the Enlightenment from France and Germany was beginning to be heard in eastern Europe.

But the Chasidic Jews, led by some great charismatic rabbis, maintained a more or less peaceful co-existence with other Jews within the orthodox tradition. In some eastern Jewish *shtetls* (small towns) there might have been separate prayer houses with an orthodox town rabbi as well as a rabbi (called *Rebbe* or *Admor*, meaning leader) for the Chasidim. Both the community Rabbi and the Chasidic leader might have come from the same group of ancient rabbinic families (see my following essay on 'Chasidism in the Age of Enlightenment').

Jacob Frank, on the other hand, had a message and motives that went far beyond religious heresy. It was an open attack on the leadership of the old rabbinical elite which he attempted to displace. Nor was it just a political struggle between Frank and the rabbinate. The Catholic Church and the rulers of Poland and other countries inevitably became involved. The end result was that the rabbis retained power over their flocks, while most of the Frankists became Christians, and in due course some of the latter made positive contributions to European culture and to its gene pool.

It is to these later contributions that this essay is addressed. For the extraordinary history of the early Frankist movement, the reader is directed to the recent work by Pawel Maciejko (discussed in more detail later in this chapter), which reviews the voluminous literature on the tumultuous events leading up to the mass baptism of the Frankists.

MY FAMILY INTEREST

I am descended from the main stream of the millennial rabbinical elite, some of whom became associated with different branches of the Chasidic movement in the eighteenth century.

My ancestor Saul Wahl was a scion of the Katzenellenbogen rabbis of Padua and Venice. They shared with the Shor family ancestral links going back to the Treves medieval rabbis of France and thence to the eleventh-century scholar known as Rashi and the Kalonymos, who were believed to be of Davidic descent. Saul Wahl and Rabbi Efraim Zalman ben Naftali Hirsch Shor of Lublin and Brest had a common ancestor in Matityahu Treves, the fourteenth-century Chief Rabbi of Paris.

In an earlier chapter I examined the link between the Katzenellenbogen and this Rabbi Shor through the latter's marriage *en secondes noces* to Hannele, a daughter of Saul Wahl. I cited the early-eighteenth-century writings of Rabbi Phineas Katzenellenbogen, a fifth-generation descendant of Saul Wahl, as well as the oral traditions of my grandmother's Wahl family and of our closely related cousins, the Wohls of Krakow, and reached the conclusion that the child produced by Hannele, soon after her hurriedly arranged marriage to the elderly widowed Shor, was quite possibly the natural son of the Polish king, Sigismund III Vasa. The likely date was about 1600–1605.

SHOR–WOLOWSKI

From the Shor line of orthodox and learned rabbis there fell away in the mid eighteenth century a branch that became prominent followers of Jacob Frank.

Elisha Shor was a rabbi in Rohatyn in Galicia. He had long harboured Shabbataian sympathies and in about 1755 he and his sons joined Frank, whom they regarded as the worthy successor of Shabbatai Zvi. His children adhered to the Frankist sect until they became Catholics in 1759, when they changed their name to Wolowski (from the Hebrew *Shor* to the Polish *Wol* for ox).

The most recent major study of Jacob Frank and his followers is by Pawel Maciejko,[5] in which he says:

> *Frank came to Rohatyn, where he established contact with the Shorrs, probably the most important Sabbatian family in Podolia. The family descended from Rabbi Zalman Naftali Shorr, whose book Tevu'at Shorr was held in high esteem by rabbinic scholars, and the Shorrs enjoyed a high status among all Jews. Elisha*

Shorr, the doyen of the family, was known as a principal leader of the Sabbatian
movement in the region; his daughter Haya was considered a prophetess. Through
marriages, the Shorrs were tied to Sabbatians in all the major towns of the province.
If Frank managed to win them over, his success in Podolia would be assured.
Indeed, before long, Elisha's three sons, Salomon, Nathan, and Leyb, accepted
Frank as their leader. (p. 18)[6]

A grandson of Elisha Shor, Franciszek Lukasz Wolowski, became secretary to Stanislas August Poniatowski (1732–98), the last king of the independent Polish Commonwealth. Franciszek Lukasz was ennobled in 1791. His son, Jan Kanti Wolowski (1803–64), was a secretary of state in Congress Poland (created by the Congress of Vienna in 1815 and under Russian suzerainty until World War I). He was one of the draftsmen of the Polish Civil Code. He was raised to the nobility by Tsar Nicholas I in 1839, and in 1861 he became dean of the faculty of law of Warsaw University.

Another great-grandson of Elisha Shor, Franciszek Wolowski (1776–1844), was a member of the Polish parliament. After the abortive Polish uprising of 1830 he emigrated to France. His son Louis Francois Wolowski (1810–76) became a notable political scientist in the country of his adoption. He published the *Revue de legislation et de jurisprudence* and later wrote several books on economics. He was one of the founders of the bank Crédit Foncier, a member of the legislative and constituent assembly of the second French Republic from 1848 to 1851 and of the National Assembly of the third Republic in 1871.

Maria Szymanowska, born Marianna Agata Wolowska, came from another branch of this Wolowski family. She was born in Warsaw in 1789 and died in St Petersburg in 1831. She was a composer and one of the first professional virtuoso pianists of the nineteenth century. She received acclaim on many foreign tours that included several visits to England and was appointed pianist to the Tsarinas in St Petersburg, where she maintained a celebrated salon frequented by the leading musicians and literary figures of the day. She is thought to have influenced Chopin's musical development. Her daughter Celina married the renowned Romantic poet Adam Mickiewicz (1798–1855), whose mother, née Majewski, may also have had a Frankist background. The Wolowski were by all accounts the most able of the latter-day

Photo 19 Louis Wolowski (Frankist and distant relative)

Frankist families, who increasingly married into other Catholic families as the nineteenth century progressed.

A FRANKIST CONNECTION TO BRITAIN

Important Frankist connections also stretched from Poland and Germany to British shores. At the time of the internecine struggle between the Frankists and the orthodox rabbinate in eastern Europe, the United Kingdom had to contend with the aftermath of the Jacobite uprisings of 1715 and 1745 that followed the Protestant Hanoverian succession to the ousted Catholic Stuarts. These two upheavals, so separate in geography and ethnic background, both involved religious strife and had far-reaching political consequences. One link between them was the Polish connection, as illustrated in the story of Joseph Wolff, a German Jew of Frankist ancestry.

JOSEPH WOLFF

Joseph Wolff (1795–1862) was the son of an orthodox Bavarian rabbi. His mother was a descendant of Jacob Frank. The story of his life touches on some personal aspects of the later Stuart line.

Joseph Wolff's mind was set on conversion to the Catholic faith at an early age and his education at several centres of higher learning was eased by Catholic patrons. He studied Greek, Latin, Hebrew, Aramaic, Syriac, Arabic, and Persian. Throughout his life he exhibited great intellectual ability, immense faith, and moral and physical courage of a high order, as well as a considerable measure of eccentricity. He came to England after meeting the equally eccentric Henry Drummond, with whom he formed a lasting friendship. Drummond influenced Wolff to the extent of his becoming an Anglican priest and a leading light in the Irvingite Church that was integral to Drummond's Catholic Apostolic movement. Its objective was to bring Catholic, Anglican, and Orthodox Christians under one roof.

Wolff was a polemicist, prolific writer, and intrepid missionary in the Middle East, to Egypt, Palestine, Persia, Uzbekistan, Afghanistan, and other countries. He signed himself at one time as 'Apostle of our Lord Jesus Christ for Palestine, Persia, Bokhara, and Balkh'. He published accounts of his adventurous missions, and among the books and articles on his life, the article in the Jewish Encyclopedia (1906) is noteworthy for its unusually friendly assessment of a Jewish convert. Wolff's first wife was a daughter of the 2nd Earl of Orford and descendant of Prime Minister Robert Walpole. Their son, named after his friend and patron, was Sir Henry Drummond Wolff, who became a distinguished ambassador, Tory politician, and founder of the Primrose League.

THE STUART LINE

For the later Stuart line the French Catholic connection was of the greatest political importance. Mary of Guise, Francis II of France, and Henrietta Maria, the daughter of Henry IV of France and Marie de Medici, were the spouses of James V of Scotland, Mary Queen of Scots, and Charles I.

James II and VII married firstly the Protestant Anne Hyde (mother of the future queens Mary II and Anne) and secondly the Catholic Mary of Modena of the ducal d'Este family, who was a niece of Cardinal Mazarin, the powerful minister of Louis XIV of France. This second marriage was a crucial factor in bringing about the so-called Glorious Revolution of 1688, the exile of James II, the accession of the protestant Mary II and her husband William III of Orange, followed in due course by Queen Anne and then, in accordance with the Act of Settlement of 1701, by the Protestant Hanoverian line. The Catholic son of James II, styled by his followers James III and VIII, was called the Old Pretender. He married a granddaughter of the great Polish king Jan Sobieski, who lifted the Ottoman Turkish siege of Vienna in 1683.

The sons of the Old Pretender were Charles Edward Stuart, known as Bonnie Prince Charlie or the Young Pretender, and Henry Benedict Stuart, Cardinal York, neither of whom left legitimate issue.

Bonnie Prince Charlie

Before his marriage to Princess Louise of Stolberg-Gedern, Prince Charles Edward had issue by his Scottish mistress, Clementine Marie Sophie Walkinshaw. A recent account of their descendants is Peter Peninski's *The Stuarts' Last Secret.*[7]

Cardinal York

Prince Henry Benedict Stuart remained unmarried, but in crypto-Jewish circles it was thought that as a young man he had a liaison with Reyna Barzillai of Venice. The footnotes to chart 13.1 deal with suggestions made by Athol Bloomer in his blog *Hebrew Christians and Crypto Jewish Connections* that there was issue of this liaison in the persons of James Modin and Elizabeth Rennie. This is wide of the mark as far as Elizabeth Rennie is concerned, as Scottish documents and correspondence show her to have been the daughter and co-heiress of the wealthy India Captain David Rennie (or Rannie). With Modin, Maiden, or Maidman there are interesting Anglo-Italian connections, but there does not appear to be any accessible documentary evidence of a link to Cardinal York.

Chart 13.1 Jacobites and Frankists

STUART DYNASTY

John III Sobieski
King of Poland
(1629–1696)

James Louis Sobieski
(1667–1737)

Maria Klementina Sobieska
(1702–1735)

James II & VII m (1) **Anne Hyde**
(1633–1701)   (2) **Mary of Modena**

James Francis Edward (the Old Pretender) m **Maria Klementina Sobieska**
(1688–1766)

(1) **Charles Edward Stuart, Bonnie Prince Charlie**
(the Young Pretender) (1720–1788)
no legitimate issue

(2) **Henry Benedict Stuart**
Cardinal York (1725–1807)
no legitimate issue[1]

Elizabeth Bailey m Captain David Rennie or Rannie (1716–1764)[1]

Elizabeth Rennie (1750–1843) m 1st Viscount Melville (1742–1811)

Lady Anne Dundas m (1) Henry Drummond (1762–1794)
s. of Hon Henry Drummond (1730–1795)
and Elizabeth Compton[2]

Henry Drummond (1786–1860) m Lady Henrietta Hay-Drummond, daughter of 10th Earl of Kinnoul[3]

Daniel Leibowitz
his daughter became
a Catholic on marriage

his great nephew
Jacob ben Judah Leib
aka **JACOB FRANK**
(1726–1791)

Frank and his large Jewish following
were received into the Catholic Church

JOSEPH WOLFF[4]
(1795–1862)

son of Rabbi David Halevi and Esther Mayer
who was a grand-daughter of Jacob Frank
Wolff was an important preacher & Anglican missionary
a protege of Henry Drummond (1786–1860)
of the Catholic Apostolic movement

Wolff married firstly Lady Georgiana Mary Walpole
(daughter of Horatio Walpole, 2nd Earl of Orford)
their son Sir Henry Drummond Wolff (1830–1908)
diplomat, politician, and founder of the Primrose League

Notes

For Jacob Frank and his movement, see, among others:

YIWO Encyclopedia of Jews in eastern Europe (Yale University Press 2005).

Articles in the Jewish Virtual Library etc.

Joseph Wolff – article in the Jewish Encyclopedia (1906)

A fascinating vignette of the Reverend Doctor Wolff is to be found in Karl E. Meyer and Shareen Blair Brysac, *Tournament of Shadows: The Great Game and the Race for Empire in Central Asia* (Counterpoint 1999), pp. 126 and 129–32.

On Henry Drummond – see, for example, R. Thorne (ed.), *The History of Parliament: the House of Commons* (Boydell & Brewer 1986)

See also articles in the *Oxford Dictionary of National Biography* (Oxford University Press 2004) on Joseph Wolff and his son Sir Henry Charles Drummond Wolff, on Joseph Wolff's patron Henry Drummond (1786–1860) and his eponymous grandfather (1730–95) and on Henry Dundas, 1st Viscount Melville.

[1] The suggestion that Henry Stuart, Cardinal York had a liaison with Reyna Barzillai of Venice and that James Modin (Maiden) and Elizabeth Rennie came of this union has been put forward by Athol Bloomer in his blog (miriamhakedosha.blogspot/ 'Hebrew Christians and Crypto Jewish connections' (December 2007) and 'James Bartram of Emerald Hills' (December 2009).

There were certainly Barzillay, Modin, and related Jewish families in Venice, Amsterdam, and elsewhere. Their connections with Benveniste and Mendes may point to ancient and distinguished Iberian origins. Sir James Wright (1716–85), the last Royal Governor of Georgia and first baronet of his line, married Sarah Maiden or Maidman (d.1763), as listed in the burial records of Westminster Abbey and the Oxford Dictionary of National Biography, 2004. Their grandson Sir Robert Bartram (1761–1844) married his cousin Anne Maidman (Modin). She is given as the daughter of James Modin and Sarah de Medina (Modena?). The Wright and Bartram families had roots in Norfolk and branches that stretched respectively to the Americas and to Italy. According to the digitised 'Calendar of the Stuart Papers belonging to His Majesty the King', preserved at Windsor Castle, Richard Bartram (c.1749–1826) of Civitavecchia, who was a relative of Sir Robert Bartram, was involved in securing this archive prior to its transmission to England. Bloomer's suggested connections of Barzillay and Modin, Maiden, or Maidman to Henry Stuart, Cardinal York do not appear to be based on readily accessible documentation. The name of Modin could well be derived from Modena where there was an old Jewish community.

As for the alleged Stuart connection of Elizabeth Rennie, who became the first wife of Henry Dundas, the 1st Viscount Melville, there is adequate documentation that she was in fact one of the two daughters of Captain David Rennie or Rannie (1716–64) and his wife Elizabeth Bailey. David Rennie was the son of John Rannie (d.1728) and Janet Stark. His daughter Elizabeth Rennie (born 1750) had a sister Janet (born 1754) who married Archibald Cockburn. The two daughters were co-heiresses of their father, a captain and ship owner who had made a fortune in India and bought Melville Castle. See the Complete Peerage, Burke's Peerage and other reference works and the following web pages:

www.merchantnetworks.com.au/genealogy/web/darvall/pafg04.htm

www.merchantnetworks.com.au/genealogy/web/dundas/pafg04.htm

www.merchantnetworks.com.au/genealogy/web/dundas/pafg05.htm

[2] Prime Minister Spencer Perceval (1760–1812) was a son of John Perceval, 2nd Earl of Egmont (1711–70) by his second wife Catherine Compton, Baroness Arden, a sister of Elizabeth Compton.

[3] The Hay and Drummond families were already joined by the marriage of Thomas Hay (1660–1719), the 7th Earl of Kinnoul and the Hon Elizabeth Drummond (1668–96).

[4] Athol Bloomer (see above) asserts that Jacob Frank's Catholic great-aunt had a Sobieski connection by marriage, but gives no references.

There was some Jewish admixture in the earlier Stuart line as in most European ruling houses. Some goes back to descendants of Davidic Exilarchs. Mary of Guise and the ducal house of Lorraine have such a Davidic–Carolingian connection and so did the d'Este of Ferrara and Modena. The mother-in-law of Charles II was from the ducal house of Medina-Sidonia of allegedly crypto Jewish background.

HENRY DRUMMOND AND HIS ANCESTRY

Chart 13.1 shows some of the ancestry of Joseph Wolff's patron, Henry Drummond. He belonged to a Scottish family with ancient royal and aristocratic links. His immediate forebears from the time of the Hanoverian succession were successful bankers and members of parliament. He married his cousin, Lady Henrietta Hay-Drummond. His father, also called Henry Drummond, had married Lady Anne Dundas, a daughter of Henry Dundas, the 1st Viscount Melville and his wife Elizabeth Rennie. Dundas became an important minister in William Pitt's administration. Some of the earlier Drummond relatives had Jacobite sympathies. The eldest of the three Henry Drummonds in the appended chart was a son of William Drummond, 4th Viscount Strathallan (1690–1746) who, like his father, espoused the Jacobite cause. He was killed at Culloden.

Out of the vagaries of sectarian religious strife, with their grievous political repercussions, there emerged in the early part of the nineteenth century seeds of ecumenical progress. The mind boggles at the thought of how the Reverend Joseph Wolff would fare today if he were to attempt to preach to the Taleban. But what was played out in Europe and the Middle East in his lifetime may perhaps be translated one day on to the global stage in the idiom of the twenty-first century.

NOTES TO CHAPTER 13

1   Followers of the false Messiah, Shabbatai Zvi (1626–76) in the Ottoman Empire, known as the *Dönmeh*.
2   The *Talmud* (instruction or learning) is the central text of Rabbinical Judaism after the Torah (the five books of Moses).

3   The *Zohar* (book of Splendour), a commentary on the mystical aspects
    of the Torah attributed to the thirteenth-century Moses de Leon.
4   From the Hebrew *Hasidut* = piety/ *Chasidim* = pious men.
5   Pawel Maciejko, *The Mixed Multitude: Jacob Frank and the Frankist Movement
    1755–1816*. (University of Pennsylvania 2011).
6   I have retained Maciejko's spelling of names in the above quotation.
7   Peter Peninski, *The Stuarts' Last Secret. The Missing Heirs of Bonnie Prince
    Charlie* (East Linton: Tuckwell Press 2001).

Chapter 14

Chasidism in the Age of Enlightenment

Rational and mystical strands in eighteenth-century Jewry

I N THE EIGHTEENTH CENTURY, the ideas of the Enlightenment gradually spread from France and Germany to eastern Europe. The movement's most prominent Jewish philosopher was Moses Mendelssohn, who came from the same group of leading rabbinic families as some of the leaders of the Chasidic movement that grew in importance in Poland at that time. The mystical strand of this popular movement competed with the rationalism of the Enlightenment. The writings of the great sixteenth- and seventeenth-century rabbis of Krakow, Moses Isserles and Nathan Nata Shapiro, exemplified these two strands in Jewish thought, and their descendants included Moses Mendelssohn and Chasidic leaders such as Rabbi Pinchas Shapiro of Koretz.

INTRODUCTION

The preceding essay on the heretical movement led by Jacob Frank indicated how it drew on the mystical beliefs of the false messiah Shabbatai Zvi (1626–76) and of his followers. The Frankists directly challenged rabbinical Talmudism and were ultimately excommunicated. But the same social and economic conditions in Poland that alienated the Jewish masses at that time also influenced the growth of the Chasidic movement.

During the second half of the eighteenth century, the ideas of the Enlightenment gradually spread from France to Germany and eastern Europe. They were challenged by the movement whose Polish origins date from the teachings of Israel ben Eliezer (1700–60), known as the *Baal Shem Tov* (Master of the Good Name). His immediate follower was Dov Ber, the *Maggid* (preacher) of Meseritz, while a near contemporary was Pinchas Shapiro of Koretz. The ancestral background of these men is indicated in a chart that includes Menachem Nachum Twersky and the descendant Friedmans of Ruzhin, Sadagora, and Czortkow. These Chasidic sages came from a tightly knit group of rabbinical families [1–6]. Interestingly, the philosopher of the Enlightenment, Moses Mendelssohn, sprang from a similar background [7].

HISTORY OF IDEAS

The rationalist and mystical strands in Jewish thought since the Middle Ages can be traced from Moses Maimonides on the one hand and from Kabbalistic writings, particularly the influential *Zohar*, on the other. In the sixteenth century, exponents of these two strands were Moses Isserles (the *Rema*, d.1572) and Isaac Luria (the holy *Ari*, d.1574). Both strands were based on the Talmud and traditional Jewish learning, but the rationalists drew on Aristotle while the mystics had affinity with Neo-Platonic and Pythagorean ideas. These two strands were not mutually exclusive and many rabbis had greater or lesser sympathy with a study of the Kabbalah. Luria's teaching of the contraction of the Infinite before the creation of the world and of the creative power of numbers and letters was carried further by Nathan Nata Spiro of Krakow. Rabbi Loew of Prague showed sympathy with

Kabbalistic thought, and Rabbi Isaiah Halevi Horovitz (1568–1627) wrote an ethical-mystical work that earned him the title of the *Holy Sheloh* and aroused much interest in eastern Europe. The pedigree of eighteenth-century Chasidism is thus a long one. It goes back to the mysticism of the Bible and Talmud and arrived in Poland via the medieval Kabbalists of Spain, Provence, and Germany, and to the school of Safed, where Isaac Luria's teachings took root. This continuing tradition of Jewish mysticism is mirrored in the lineage of some of the aforementioned families.

SOCIO-ECONOMIC BACKGROUND

In the sixteenth century, the Jewish communities in Poland enjoyed a high point of local autonomy and economic well-being. Many centres of learning attracted the leading rabbis of the day. Then the Polish–Lithuanian state went into gradual political decline and finally fell to Prussia, Austria, and Russia in the three late eighteenth-century partitions. The Jews had already suffered the catastrophe of the Chmielnicki massacres in the mid seventeenth century, and the following period brought further depredations. Rabbinical learning and leadership declined and the wretched state of the poor Jewish masses provided fertile ground for the new message of hope and joy brought by the Baal Shem Tov and his followers.

CHASIDIC TEACHING

The message was revealed to the masses in simple stories and parables and spoke of the sparks of God's holiness in all things. It encouraged the Chasidim to express their joy in his all-pervading presence through worship in which singing, dancing, and story-telling played an important part. Ecstatic enthusiasm and constant devotion were emphasised in their prayers. The influence of the Kabbalah was apparent in their liturgy, which drew particularly on the practice of Isaac Luria's school. Their beliefs included that of the transmigration of souls, and the basis of their ethics was humility and love. The people flocked to the charismatic leader or *Tzaddik*, who was held to have attained a degree of religious perfection. The founder's disciples and successors were men of great personal charisma whose emphasis on different aspects of religious piety gave their communities an individual character. Dov Ber of Meseritz took the lead in organising the movement after the founder's death. Pinchas Shapiro of Koretz was a towering figure of sublime ethical teaching who enjoined his following to love the evil-doer more in order to compensate for the diminution in the power of love the sinner had caused in the world. Some masters like Menachem Nahum Twersky believed that there is no place empty of the divine, everything that exists comes from God, and the power of the creator resides within each created thing. In such teaching Chasidism comes close to a pantheistic world view. Other leaders, not shown in the chart, included Jacob Joseph of Polonnoye, Schneur Zalman of Liadi, who founded the *Chabad* school in Lithuania, and Nahman of Bratslav.

In the nineteenth century, scores of Chasidic communities grew around their *Tzaddikim*, who generally founded enduring dynasties These rabbi-saints had a spiritual cohesion notwithstanding their differences and doctrinal squabbles. Among the most famous was the Rokeach dynasty of Belz. The Rokeach were uncompromising in their rejection of any reformist and Enlightenment ideas. Of equally ancient family were the Friedmans of Ruzhin, Sadagora, and Czortkow. Their semi-regal style contrasted strangely with the saintly simplicity of the Court of Belz, but their extraordinarily charismatic leadership drew followers from all over Galicia and beyond. Israel of Ruzhin was venerated in his time, and even in 1934, his grandson Israel Friedman of Czortkow was mourned by thousands as they followed him to his grave in Vienna.

The ancestral roots of the eighteenth-century rationalist Moses Mendelssohn were very similar to those of the Chasidic leaders. Mendelssohn was a descendant of Moses Isserles and the Katzenellenbogens. Saul Wahl Katzenellenbogen was the progenitor of so many important lines. Some of these came together with other clans such as the Horowitz and Shapiro to bring forth important leaders of the Chasidic movement. For example, the Wahl descendant Meir Horowitz of Tiktin was the forebear of Schmuel Schmelke Horowitz of Nikolsburg and of his younger brother Pinchas Horowitz of Frankfurt, who were both prominent disciples of Dov Ber of Meseritz. However, within these old rabbinical families, there were often sharp divisions between adherents of Chasidism and opponents of the movement, particularly in the first two generations after its foundation.

CHASIDIC CONNECTIONS OF THE GELLES FAMILY

My ancestors were very much embedded in this great genealogical tapestry. Moses Gelles was a scholar of the prestigious Brody Klaus in the early part of the eighteenth century. He was also known as *Levush*, possibly after the epithet of Rabbi Mordecai Yaffe of Prague [8]. Moses Gelles was the great-grandfather of R. Moshe Gelles aka Levush, who was a grandson of Rabbi Yehuda Leib Zundel *Ramraz*, whose other grandsons included R. Shalom Rokeach (1779–1855), the first *Tzaddik* of the great Belz dynasty [9]. The elder Moses Gelles was also the grandfather of Rabbi Shmuel Gelles, who married Sarah Rachel Scheindel, daughter of Rabbi Pinchas Shapiro of Koretz and whose progeny were later known by the name of Polonsky. Various sources give Shmuel as the son of Rabbi Mordecai, son of Moses Gelles of Brody, whose tombstone inscription refers to him as a 'servant of God' [10–11]. Shmuel's letter of appointment in 1793 to the rabbinate of Kolibolet and the surrounding area describes him as the son of Rabbi Mordecai, and as the son-in-law of Pinchas, 'the holy flame, the royal wonder of our generation ... Rabbi of Shepetivka'. Shmuel's rabbinical post passed from father to son for five generations, as shown in the charts [12–13]. His grandson, Rabbi Eliyahu Pinchas, married Sima Wertheim, thus linking the Polonsky – essentially a Gelles–Shapiro line – with Menachem Nahum Twersky's Shapiro–Katzenellenbogen ancestry [14–15].

My great-grandfather Rabbi David Isaac Gellis and his line were cousins of the Polonsky rabbis. His father, Rabbi Moshe Gelles, was a brother or first cousin of Rabbi Shmuel ben Mordecai Gelles (see Chart 14.1). David Isaac Gellis studied at Glina and was buried in Brody. His son, my grandfather Rabbi Nahum Uri Gelles (1852–1934), was descended from Rabbi Shmuel Hillman of Metz. The latter is generally taken as a grandson of Nathan Nata Spiro, the Chief Rabbi of Krakow and author of the important Kabbalistic work *Megaleh Amukot* (Revealed Depths) [16–18]. The direct Shapiro line leads to Pinchas of Koretz, and then to Yehuda Meir Shapiro

Photo 20 Rabbi Israel Friedman of Czortkow

(1887–1934), who was one of the most important Polish rabbis of the twentieth century. Meir Shapiro founded the Lublin Yeshiva where he taught my cousin Joseph Gelles, grandson of Nahum Uri and the last of our rabbinical line [19]. Joseph's brother Leo (Aryeh Leib) Gelles was a descendant of another Chasidic sage, Rabbi Meir of Przemyslany (the younger) [20–22]. The latter was a close friend of Israel Friedman of Ruzhin, whose grandson and namesake Rabbi Israel Friedman of Czortkow had a large following that included my grandfather and Rabbi Meir Shapiro.

The Czortkow connection has survived the Holocaust, as indeed have many other Chasidic families in their worldwide dispersion. The links between several of the great Chasidic leaders encompass distinct lines of Gelles cousins. These sages made a unique contribution to the history of Jewish mysticism which connected with other ancient philosophies and had a significant impact on Christian thought through the ages.

REFERENCES

[1] Yehuda Klausner, 'The Hasidic Rabbinate', *Sharsheret Hadorot*, Vol. 16, Nos. 1 & 3, October 2001 & June 2002. Regarding Rabbi Nathan Nata Shapiro of Krakow (1585–1633) and his Kabbalistic work *Megaleh Amukot* – a quotation from his entry in the YIVO Encyclopedia of Jews in eastern Europe is also very relevant to my preceding essay on the Frankists: 'Although Spira died before the rise of the Sabbatian movement and its subsequent Jewish and Christian incarnations, the fact that Jewish, Jewish-Sabbatian, and Jewish-Christian sources all link him to messianism and to Christianity arouses interest, and points to the complexity of the connection between the Jewish and Christian worlds in the seventeenth and eighteenth centuries.'

[2] Martin Buber, *Tales of the Chasidim. Thames & Hudson 1956 Die Erzählungen der Chassidim*. (Zurich: Manesse Verlag, Conzett & Huber 1949). Martin Buber wrote on Pinchas of Koretz: 'In the period between the Baal Shem Tov and his great-grandson Nahman of Bratslav he has no equal in fresh and direct thinking, in daring and vivid expression. What he says often springs from a profound knowledge of the human soul and it is always spontaneous and great-hearted' (pp. 19–20 of the English and pp. 218–42 of the German edition).

[3] Jiri Langer, *Nine Gates*. (London: James Clarke & Co. 1961) (Czech edition first published in 1937).

[4] Gabrielle Kohlbauer-Fritz, *Zwischen Ost und West: Galizische Juden in Wien*. (Vienna: Jüdisches Museum 2001).

[5] Neil Rosenstein, *The Unbroken Chain*. (London: CIS Publishers 1990), pp. 291, 1184–5.

[6] Isidore Epstein, *Judaism*. (London: Penguin Books 1959).

[7] Alexander Altmann, Moses Mendelssohn, *A Biographical Study* (Philadelphia: Jewish Publication Society 1973).

[8] Edward Gelles, 'Finding Rabbi Moses Gelles', *Avotaynu*, Vol. 18, No. 1, Spring 2002.

[9] *Idem*, Jewish community life in Brody.

[10] Levi Grossman, *Shem U She'erith*. (Tel Aviv 1943), p. 92.

[11] Shimson Ahron Polonsky, *Chidushei Horav MiTeplik*. (Jerusalem 1984).

[12] Metityahu Yechezkel Guttman, *Rabbi Pinchas mi Koretz*. (Tel Aviv 1950).

[13] Yaakov Y Wahrman, 'Sefer Yuchasin' (www.pikholz.org/Families/Wahrman).

[14] A. J. Heshel, *Yivo Bletter*, Vol. 36, pp. 124–5.

[15] Yechezkel Shraga Frankel (ed.), *Imrei Pinchas* (Israel: Benei Brak 2003), Vol. 2, pp. 486–8. The letters of appointment of Rabbi Shmuel (Gelles)

in 1793 and of his grandson Rabbi Eliyahu Pinchas in 1831 to the
position of Av Beis Din [head of the Rabbinical Court] of Kolibolet
and the surrounding area (including the towns of Zvenigorodka,
Tolna, Shpole, and Kalerka) add much to the information provided
in references 10–14. The first document defines the new rabbi's duties
and his emoluments, specifying payments for sermons, contributions
from inn-keepers, traders, and tailors, the exclusive right to the sale
of candles, and other duties and privileges. The appointment of the
grandson had similar provisions including that relating to the sale
of candles (cf. reference 8 to the chandlery owned by their ancestor,
Moses Gelles of Brody. The family appear to have enjoyed a monopoly for the sale of candles in Brody.)

[16] Shmuel Nach Gottlieb, *Ohalei Shem*. (Pinsk 1912), pp. 261–2.

[17] Edward Gelles, *Rabbi Shmuel Helman of Metz and his Family Connections*,
Sharsheret Hadorot, Vol. 18, May 2004.

[18] Stuart Steinberg, 'Shmuel Helman of Metz is the Son of Israel
Heilprin', *Avotaynu*, Vol. 19, No. 4, Winter 2003.

[19] Yehuda Meir Shapira, *Imrei Da'as*. (Israel: Bnei Brak 1990). Josef
Gelles, son of Rabbi Ephraim Fischl Gelles, is listed as a student at the
Lublin Yeshiva.

[20] Ahron Leib (Leo) Gelles, died New York 1973, son of Rabbi Ephraim
Fischel Gelles, the eldest son of Rabbi Nahum Uri Gelles of Solotwina
near Stanislau. Leo's mother was descended from R. Meir of
Przemyslany through the Leifers of Nadworna – see chapter 18)

[21] Neil Rosenstein, *loc. cit.*, p. 490

[21] Meir Wunder, *Meiorei Galicia*, Vol. 3, p. 521.

[22] Dan Ben-Amos and Jerome R Mintz, *In Praise of the Baal Shem Tov*
(New York: Schocken Books 1984), p. 219. In the English translation
of the collection of stories about the saintly founder of the Chasidic
movement, the Baal Shem Tov, there is a tale that he was travelling
from Polonnoye to the 'new town' and that on passing a Jewish cemetery he perceived a pillar of fire marking the grave of a *Tzaddik* (a
wholly righteous man) whose epitaph read 'Moses the servant of God'.
The translators suggested that this 'new town' was Novograd Volynsky
(known to the Jews as Zvihl), which was some distance to the north of
Polonnoye. However, my Hebrew translator drew my attention to a
passage in Imrei Pinchas (see Ref 15), the book of sayings and teaching
of Rabbi Pinchas Shapiro of Koretz and Shepetivka, describing how
Rabbi Pinchas went from the 'new town' to the 'old town' to visit the
Rabbi of Polonnoye. This suggests that the 'new town' was an exten-
sion of Polonnoye and that 'Moses the servant of God' died while in

Polonnoye and was buried there. He is tentatively identified as Moses
Gelles of the Brody Klaus. Levi Grossman, who describes himself as
a descendant, quotes his epitaph (see Ref 10). This would tie in with
the family of Rabbi Shmuel ben Mordecai Gelles having a connection with Polonnoye and therefore becoming known by the name of
Polonsky.

[23] Yechezkel Shraga Frankel (ed.), *Imrei Pinchas* (see Ref 15), p. 221.

Chart 14.1 Descent from Moses Gelles of Brody

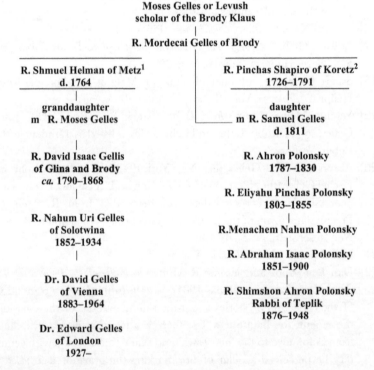

Footnotes

1 Rabbi Shmuel Helman of Metz is widely believed to have been the grandson of
Nathan Nata Shapiro (1585–1633) the Chief Rabbi of Krakow.
2 Rabbi Pinchas Shapiro of Koretz was a direct male line descendant of **Nathan
Nata Shapiro**, the author of the Kabbalistic work *Megaleh Amukot* (Revealed
Depths).

Chart 14.2 An Enlightenment philosopher and some Chasidic sages

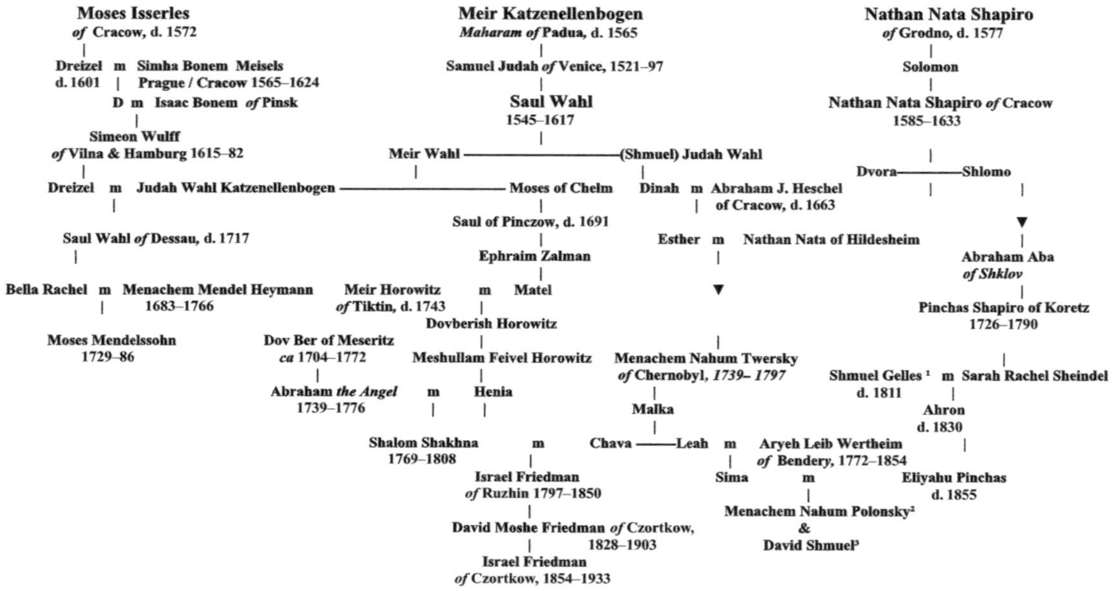

Moses Isserles *of* Cracow, d. 1572

Dreizel m **Simha Bonem Meisels**
d. 1601 | Prague / Cracow 1565–1624
D m **Isaac Bonem** *of* Pinsk

Simeon Wulff
of Vilna & Hamburg 1615–82

Dreizel m **Judah Wahl Katzenellenbogen**

Saul Wahl *of Dessau*, d. 1717

Bella Rachel m **Menachem Mendel Heymann**
1683–1766

Moses Mendelsohn
1729–86

Meir Katzenellenbogen
Maharam of Padua, d. 1565

Samuel Judah *of Venice*, 1521–97

Saul Wahl
1545–1617

Meir Wahl ———— (Shmuel) **Judah Wahl**
Moses of Chelm

Saul of Pinczow, d. 1691

Ephraim Zalman

Matel m **Meir Horowitz**
of Tiktin, d. 1743

Dov Ber of Meseritz
ca 1704–1772

Abraham *the Angel*
1739–1776

Dovberish Horowitz

Meshullam Feivel Horowitz m **Henia**

Shalom Shakhna
1769–1808

Nathan Nata Shapiro
of Grodno, d. 1577

Solomon

Nathan Nata Shapiro *of Cracow*
1585–1633

Dvora ——— **Shlomo**

Dinah m **Abraham J. Heschel**
of Cracow, d. 1663

Esther m **Nathan Nata of Hildesheim**

Abraham Aba
of Shklov

Pinchas Shapiro of Koretz
1726–1790

Menachem Nahum Twersky
of Chernobyl, 1739–1797

Malka

Chava ——— **Leah** m **Aryeh Leib Wertheim**
of Bendery, 1772–1854

Shmuel Gelles ¹ m **Sarah Rachel Sheindel**
d. 1811

Sima
m

Ahron
d. 1830

Eliyahu Pinchas
d. 1855

Menachem Nahum Polonsky²
&
David Shmuel³

Israel Friedman
of Ruzhin 1797–1850

David Moshe Friedman *of Czortkow,*
1828–1903

Israel Friedman
of Czortkow, 1854–1933

Footnotes

1 Son of R. Mordecai Gelles and grandson of Moses Gelles of Brody.
2 Father of Abraham Isaac Polonsky (1851–1900). Fifth-generation Rabbi of Kolibolet and surrounding area.
3 Father of Levi Isaac of Nigrest, whose branch was also linked by marriage to the lines from **Levi Isaac** of **Berdichev** (1740–1810) and **Meir** of **Przemyslany** (1780–1850). A line from Moses Gelles of Brody led to my grandfather R. Nahum Uri Gelles (1852–1934), whose grandson, Ahron Leib Gelles, was descended through his mother from **Meir** of **Przemyslany**. The rabbis of the Gelles–Shapiro or **Polonsky** line were cousins of the **Gelles** line to my grandfather R. Nahum Uri Gelles as well as cousins of the **Friedman** line descended from Israel Friedman of Ruzhin.

PART 4

Various roads to modern times

Chapter 15

Mendelssohn, Marx, Buber

And other descendants of Saul Wahl

SAUL BEN SAMUEL JUDAH KATZENELLENBOGEN is known to history as Saul Wahl. He was a scion of the Katzenellenbogen Chief Rabbis of Padua and Venice. Saul Wahl played an important role in the sixteenth century Polish–Lithuanian Commonwealth (as discussed in Chapter 7).

His numerous progeny were allied by marriage to the leading Jewish families of their time. Their descendants, who continued to intermarry over the ensuing centuries, included historic personalities such as the Enlightenment philosopher Moses Mendelssohn and his grandson, the composer Felix Mendelssohn-Bartholdy, Karl Marx, Martin Buber, and many others. Their genealogical backgrounds are examined and reveal interesting connections, not only to the Wahl–Katzenellenbogen line but also to Horowitz, Jaffe, Guggenheim, Oppenheimer, Wertheimer, and their related families.

INTRODUCTION

Saul Wahl's ancestral background and the distinction of his progeny may be without equal in Jewish history. The glamour of enduring legend surrounds his life in the Polish–Lithuanian Commonwealth. These legends, as well as the core of recorded history, have been written about for centuries. My book *An Ancient Lineage* summarises the literature on the subject, while Chapters 7 and 8 of the present volume offer a critique of some details in 'hagiographies' such as *Yesh Manhilin* and *Gedullat Shaul*, written respectively by Saul Wahl's descendant Rabbi Pinchas Katzenellenbogen in the first part of the eighteenth century and by Hirsch Edelman in the mid nineteenth century [1].

Saul ben Samuel Judah Katzenellenbogen, later known in Poland as Saul Wahl, was born in Padua around 1545 and died in 1617. His parents were Samuel Judah ben Meir Katzenellenbogen, the Chief Rabbi of Venice, and his wife Abigail Yaffe. The Yaffe (Yofe, Jaffe etc.) are an ancient family who were known in Spain and became prominent in Bologna and other north Italian cities long before they shone on the wider European stage. Saul's grandfather, Meir Katzenellenbogen, married the granddaughter of Rabbi Judah Mintz and became the Chief Rabbi of Padua. He was considered to be a scholar of pan-European importance. Meir's father was Isaac of Katzenellenbogen, whose wife was a daughter of Jechiel Luria of Alsace, the Rabbi of Brest-Litovsk. Through this marriage, the Katzenellenbogen go back via Luria, Spira, and Treivish rabbis to the eleventh century scholar and bible commentator Rabbi Solomon ben Isaac of Troyes, known as Rashi, who is believed to be a descendant of King David.[1]

DESCENDANTS OF SAUL WAHL

Saul Wahl and Deborah Drucker had 13 recorded children whose issue has multiplied over four centuries. Hundreds of notable descendants and their lateral family connections fill two large volumes in the well-known reference book *The Unbroken Chain* [2].

Many descendants perpetuated the Wahl name, some using Saul's family name of Katzenellenbogen, and there were many branches

Chart 15.1 Some lines of descent from Saul Wahl

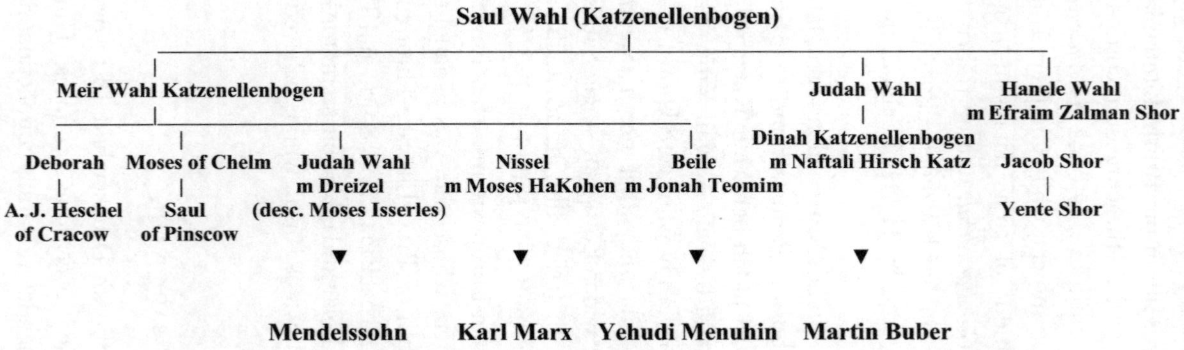

Saul Wahl (Katzenellenbogen)

Meir Wahl Katzenellenbogen

Moses of Chelm

Judah Wahl
m Dreizel
(desc. Moses Isserles)

Deborah

A. J. Heschel
of Cracow

Saul
of Pinscow

Nissel
m Moses HaKohen

Beile
m Jonah Teomim

Judah Wahl

Dinah Katzenellenbogen
m Naftali Hirsch Katz

Hanele Wahl
m Efraim Zalman Shor

Jacob Shor

Yente Shor

▶

▶

▶

▶

Mendelssohn

Karl Marx

Yehudi Menuhin

Martin Buber

Chart 15.2 From Saul Wahl to Moses Mendelssohn

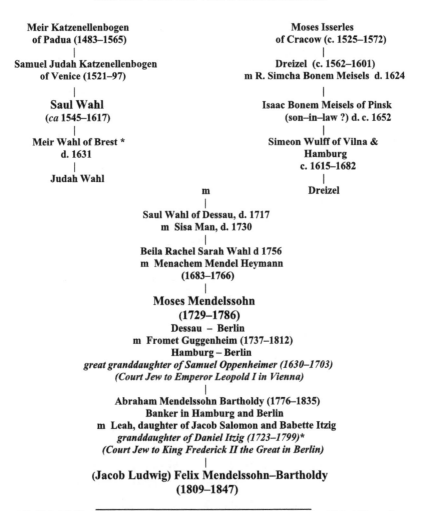

Meir Katzenellenbogen
of Padua (1483–1565)
|
Samuel Judah Katzenellenbogen
of Venice (1521–97)
|
Saul Wahl
(*ca* 1545–1617)
|
Meir Wahl of Brest *
d. 1631
|
Judah Wahl

Moses Isserles
of Cracow (c. 1525–1572)
|
Dreizel (c. 1562–1601)
m R. Simcha Bonem Meisels d. 1624
|
Isaac Bonem Meisels of Pinsk
(son–in–law ?) d. c. 1652
|
Simeon Wulff of Vilna &
Hamburg
c. 1615–1682
|
Dreizel

m
|
Saul Wahl of Dessau, d. 1717
m Sisa Man, d. 1730
|
Beila Rachel Sarah Wahl d 1756
m Menachem Mendel Heymann
(1683–1766)
|
**Moses Mendelssohn
(1729–1786)**
Dessau – Berlin
m Fromet Guggenheim (1737–1812)
Hamburg – Berlin
great granddaughter of Samuel Oppenheimer (1630–1703)
(Court Jew to Emperor Leopold I in Vienna)
|
Abraham Mendelssohn Bartholdy (1776–1835)
Banker in Hamburg and Berlin
m Leah, daughter of Jacob Salomon and Babette Itzig
*granddaughter of Daniel Itzig (1723–1799)**
(Court Jew to King Frederick II the Great in Berlin)
|
(Jacob Ludwig) Felix Mendelssohn–Bartholdy
(1809–1847)

---

* R. Meir Wahl of Brest married Hinde Horowitz, daughter of Pinchas Halevi Horowitz
(1535 Prague–1618 Cracow), and his wife Miriam Beila, who was the sister of Chief
Rabbi Moses Isserles of Cracow known as the REMA
Daniel Itzig aka Jaffe was of a line descended from Rabbi Mordecai Jaffe of Prague
(1530–1612) known as the LEVUSH

who were known by other names. Scores of rabbis were followed
in later centuries by philosophers, scientists, writers, musicians,
men in the liberal professions, and men distinguished in public life.
Marriages between the leading Ashkenazi families were reinforced
in the case of Saul Wahl's descendancy by intermarriages between

many distinct family lines. The result of this inbreeding is that latter-day descendants may have their specific inheritance reinforced to varying degrees. For example, I am a descendant of Saul Wahl through different routes on both sides of my family.

The variety of Wahl descendancies is illustrated in the genealogical charts for the philosopher Moses Mendelssohn and his grandson, the composer Felix Mendelssohn-Bartholdy, Karl Marx, arguably the most important political thinker of his age, the musician Yehudi Menuhin, and the sociologist and historian Martin Buber.

Of Saul Wahl's 13 recorded children and their innumerable lines of descent, some of the above are particularly relevant to my own Wahl connections on my paternal side and to my maternal Wahl grandmother. Numerous intermarriages are exemplified by the union *en secondes noces* between Abraham Joshua Heschel of Krakow and Dinah Katzenellenbogen and by the marriage of Hanele Wahl's granddaughter Yente Shor to Rabbi Saul Katzenellenbogen of Pinscow, the son of Rabbi Moses of Chelm. The descent of the Mendelssohns, Karl Marx, Yehudi Menuhin, and Martin Buber is now discussed in more detail.

The Mendelssohns

Moses Mendelssohn was a notable German philosopher of the Enlightenment. He was also the leading polemicist in the struggle for Jewish emancipation and as such he was called 'the third Moses' by some of his many admirers (following Moses the Lawgiver and the medieval philosopher Moses Maimonides). However, his efforts were opposed by religious traditionalists, who correctly foresaw that his attempts to reconcile biblical teaching with Greek philosophy would accelerate the trend towards assimilation.

In my earlier books (and in the previous chapter in this volume) I presented a very brief outline of the history of the eighteenth-century Chasidic movement in eastern Europe that in its mysticism was diametrically opposed to Mendelssohn's rationalistic philosophy. Mendelssohn and some Chasidic leaders had a very similar ancestral background, as shown in *An Ancient Lineage*, Chapter 35, *Enlightenment and Chasidism*, pp. 253–63, quoting Martin Buber's books and Alexander Altman's *Biographical Study of Moses Mendelssohn*.

Photo 21 Moses Mendelssohn

Chart 15.2 shows Mendelssohn family descent from great rabbis, the Katzenellenbogen of Padua and Venice and Moses Isserles of Krakow. Saul Wahl was the scion of the Katzenellenbogen who later rose to eminence in Poland. Later generations of the line were strengthened through further inflow from notable families.

Moses Mendelssohn won an essay competition on a metaphysical subject set by the Berlin Academy against competitors that included Immanuel Kant (1763). Then followed the publication of *Phaedon: On the Immortality of the Soul* (1767). A translation of parts of the Bible (1783) and *Jerusalem* both had an enormous impact: the first on his German co-religionists and the latter on the wider world, when he argued that the state had no right to interfere with the religion of its citizens. Three men who were of most importance in his life were King Frederick II 'the Great', his friend the playwright Gotthold Ephraim Lessing, who in *Nathan the Wise* modelled his principal character on Mendelssohn, and the theologian John Kaspar Lavater.

Photo 22 Felix Mendelssohn

Felix Mendelssohn-Bartholdy, the composer of the Romantic movement, possessed a quintessential European culture. Leading musicians, writers, and scientists of the time frequented the salon of his parents in Berlin. His music drew its major inspiration from Bach, Beethoven, and Mozart, but traces of Jewish influence can be detected in some of his work, such as the Violin Concerto in E Minor. He met Goethe and set a number of his poems to music. Goethe also inspired his romantic cantata *Die erste Walpurgisnacht*. Mendelssohn wrote music for productions of Sophocles' *Antigone* and *Oedipus at Colonus*, Shakespeare's *Midsummer Night's Dream*, and Racine's *Antigone*. He visited Britain ten times and became Queen Victoria's and Prince Albert's favourite composer. His strong connections with Scotland gave rise to the overture *The Hebrides* (*Fingal's Cave*) and the *Scottish Symphony*.

As Chart 15.2 shows, Felix Mendelssohn's paternal line went back to Saul Wahl and Moses Isserles of Krakow. It also included

Pinchas Horowitz, the distinguished forebear of my own branch of that family. From his paternal grandmother and mother, Felix Mendelssohn had influential forebears in Samuel Oppenheimer and Daniel Itzig (Jaffe).

Edward Gelles and Felix Mendelssohn have a common descent from Saul Wahl and his Katzenellenbogen ancestors of Padua and Venice. The Mendelssohn in-laws Itzig and my Levush lineages descend from Rabbi Mordecai Jaffe of Prague (1530–1612), known as the 'Levush' after the title of his magnum opus. Pinchas Halevi Horowitz (Prague 1535–Krakow 1618) married Miriam Beila Isserles, the sister of one of the most important rabbis of his age, Chief Rabbi Moses Isserles of Krakow (1520–72).

Their father was the Talmudist Israel Isserl, whose family came to Poland from Prague, as did the Horowitz and other important families. Israel Isserl was a common ancestor of Edward Gelles and of the composers Felix Mendelssohn and Giacomo Meyerbeer (1791–1864). A detailed 'Ascendancy' of Felix Mendelssohn was published by Lars Menk in the French genealogical journal *Gen Ami* (see Chart 15.3).

Chart 15.3 Descent from Samuel Oppenheimer to Felix Mendelssohn

42 **Oppenheimer,** Samuel   b.: 21/06/1630 Heidelberg d.: 03/05/1703 Vienna
                              Kaiserl. Hof-faktor in Vienna sc. 1679
43 **Carcassone,** Sandela   b.: 1640 ? Mannheim d.: 16/02/1705 Vienna
         |
21 **Oppenheimer,** Frummet b.: 1675 ? Vienna d.: 14/04/1713 Frankfurt
20 **Guggenheim,** Josef   b.: 1670 Frankfurt am Main d.: 03/02/1735
                              Frankfurt / money changer in Frankfurt

         |
10 **Guggenheim,** Abraham b.:1700 ? Frankfurt d.:1766 Hamburg
11 **Cleve,** Miriam Glueckel b.~ 1705   d.: 28/10/1738 Hamburg
         |
5 **Guggenheim,** Fromet   b.: 06/10/1737 Hamburg d.: 16/03/1812 Berlin
4 **Mendelssohn, Moses**   b.: 06/09/1729 Dessau   d.:   04/01/1786 Berlin
         |
2 **Mendelssohn** Bartholdy, Abraham   b.: 10/12/1776 Berlin
                  d.: 19/11/1835 Berlin, Banker in Hamburg & Berlin
3 **Salomon,** Lea 'Lilly'   b.: 26/03/1777 ? Berlin m : 26/12/1804 Berlin
             d.: 12/12/1842 Berlin [*granddaughter of Daniel Itzig or Jaffe*]

1 **Mendelssohn Bartholdy, Felix**   b.: 03/02/1809 Hamburg
                              d.: 04/11/1847 Leipzig

175

Samuel Oppenheimer (1630–1703) and his nephew Samson Wertheimer (1658–1724) were the great Court Jews of Habsburg Vienna. Oppenheimer's son Wolf married a daughter of Leffman Behrends (1630–1714), Court Jew of Hanover. The Hanover family nexus included Salman Gans (d. 1654) and his descendants, Glueckel of Hameln (1646–1724), who wrote famous memoirs, her sister Hendele, who married the Court Jew of Brandenburg, Mordecai Gumpel of Cleves (father of Elias Cleve Gomperz, the banker), and her cousin Schoene, whose husband Elias Cohn was the son of Hamburg's first Chief Rabbi, David ben Menachem HaKohen. From this couple and from Salman Gans follow later family connections, including Warburg, Loeb, Herz, Hirsch, and Breuer [3]. Oppenheimer, Gans, and Mendelssohn have connections to the family of the great poet Heinrich Heine.

Pointers to my connections with this bedrock of German Ashkenaz come from a study of autosomal DNA segments shared with some people from the aforementioned family nexus. A group of probands who have many of these names in their ancestry show matches between themselves and me and thus give a convincing impression of distant family links in the Rhineland. Many of these families had connections with the old Jewish community of Frankfurt.[2]

Some ancestral names recorded for a number of probands are listed in Chart 15.4. The intermarriages of their families become apparent from the striking recurrence of some names. Chart 15.4 also shows the total autosomal DNA matches and longest shared DNA segments (in cM)[3] of Edward Gelles with the several probands, providing strong support for the affinity of my paternal line with this great Ashkenazi family nexus. Most of the autosomal DNA tests were carried out by Family Tree DNA of Houston, Texas, and are discussed further in Chapter 21 of the present volume.

The names of many probands in this chart derive from medieval towns of origin or names of houses. The German Spiegel may be connected with the later eponymous Galician family who intermarried with Gelles and Weinstein. Branches of some of these families, including Oppenheimer, Stern, Rothschild, Guggenheim, Wertheimer, and Salomon, produced noteworthy pan-European financial dynasties.[4]

Chart 15.4 Common ancestral names and DNA matches with Edward Gelles

Ralph N. Baer   138.46 cM,   8.10 cM
Oppenheim, Carcassone. Guggenheim, Baer, Hess, Kohn
Alan Guggenheim
Guggenheim, Brilin, Bluhm, Cohen, Goldschmid of Hameln, Gompertz
Julia P Guggenheim   98.46 cM,   9.40 cM
Guggenheim, Phillips Wertheimer, Oppenheim, Bernheimer, Einstein,
Dreifuss, Hess, Kohn, Baer, Spiegel, Loewenstein, Levi, Heyman, Neuberger
William M Oppenheim   99.14 cM, 14.95 cM
Oppenheim, Goldschmidt, Kahn, Herz, Hess, Daub Dewald
Debra Calzareth   116.30 cM, 10.05 cM
Baer, Krieger, Blum, Loewenstein, Rothschild, Wertheimer
Lorie Krieger   106.99 cM, 15.52 cM
Krieger, Baer, Blum, Herz, Hirsch, Loeb, Marx, Reis, Rothschild,
Oppenheimer, Salomon, Wertheimer, Kallman
William R Wertheimer   86.52 cM, 11.29 cM
Wertheimer, Guggenheim, Stern,Loewenstein, Baer, Spiegel, Rothschild
Michael Aaron Wertheimer   92.98 cM,   7.73 cM
Wertheimer, Brilin, Bruelle, Goldschmidt, Gomperz, Oppenheimer, Salomon,
Roy H Stern   111.31 cM, 10.61 cM
Stern, Strauss,Hirsch, Susskind, Bamberger,
Gerald Stern   110.22 cM, 10.23 cM
Stern, Strauss, Loewenstein, Loeb, Hecht, Kahn, Marx, Wertheimer
J.Lowenstein   122.23 cM, 11.29 cM
Loewenstein, Baer, Rothschild, Oppenheim, Hirsch, Klein, Sternfels
Ronald Stephen Loewenstein   (110.80 cM,   9.20 cM)
Loewenstein, Oppenheim, Baer, Krieger, Meyerson, Spiegel, Wertheimer,
Guggenheim, Rothschild, Kohn, Salomon
Ralph F Rothschild
Rothschild, Bernheimer, Oppenheim, Katz, Marx, Wachs,
Joy B. Rothschild   116.45 cM, 10.61 cM
Rothschild, Kahn, Cohen, Schloss, Baer, Werthemer, Guggenheim, Krieger,
Loewenstein, Stern, Spiegel
Walter Spiegel   70.88 cM, 11.12 cM
Spiegel, Calzareth, Krieger, Guggenheim, Gumperz, Loewenstein,
Schlesinger, Wallach, Schloss, Salomon
R.Salomon
Salomon, Baer, Stern, Loewenstein, Guggenheim
R. A. Jaffe   77.02 cM, 13.84 cM
Jaffe, Jofe, Feldman, Kushner, Weisss, Zundel
R. Adelson   62.12 cM, 16.56 cM
Adelson, Almoslino, Halfon, Shapiro

As for the immediate Mendelssohn line, it is thoroughly documented, but there is a lack of relevant genetic data. In an approach to fill this gap in our knowledge I persuaded Sheila Hayman to take a *Family Finder* autosomal DNA test. Sheila is a direct descendant of Fanny Mendelssohn-Bartholdy. Fanny was a highly

Chart 15.5 Ancestry of Sheila Hayman

8 Beila Rachel Sarah <u>Wahl</u> d. 1756 (descendant of Saul Wahl)
   m Menachem Mendel Heyman d. 1766
7 Moses <u>Mendelssohn</u> d 1786
   (philosopher & leading spirit of the Jewish Enlightenment)
    m Fromet <u>*Guggenheim*</u> d. 1812
   (desc *Samuel Oppenheimer* related to *Samson Wertheimer*)
6 Abraham Mendelssohn Bartholdy (banker) d 1835
   m Leah <u>*Salomon*</u>
   (desc David *Itzig* aka *Jaffe*)
5 Fanny Mendelssohn – Bartholdy (composer) d 1847
    m Wilhelm Hensel (painter) d 1861
   (Fanny was a sister of Felix Mendelssohn-Bartholdy)
4 Sebastian Ludwig Friedrich Hensel d 1898
   m Julie von <u>*Adelson*</u> d 1901   (dr of Fanny *Adelson*)
3 Kurt Hensel (mathematician) d 1941
   m Gertrude Hahn (dr of Kurt Hahn of Gordonstoun School)
2 Ruth Hensel   d 1979
   m Franz K. A. S, Haymann (Professor of Law) d 1947
1 Walter Kurt Hayman (mathematician)
    m Margaret Crann
   (Parents of Sheila Hayman)

talented musician and composer whose work was overshadowed by that of her famous brother Felix.

As may be seen from Chart 15.5, Sheila Hayman is the daughter of a Jewish Professor of German extraction and an English Quaker mother. Her genetic roots are very much mixed European and Eastern, as confirmed by the testing company's picture of her genetic origins. The story of her distinguished Hensel and Hayman families has been related by Sheila. My personal interest presently focuses on the earlier generations of her family tree, involving old Jewish connections that should have given rise to some shared DNA segments in their present-day descendants. I refer to the mother of Moses Mendelssohn, who was a descendant of Saul Wahl, and to the succeeding generations of in-laws and their connections, namely Guggenheim, Oppenheimer, Wertheimer, Salomon, Itzig (Jaffe), and others.

In Table 15.6 the autosomal DNA matches of relevant probands with Sheila Hayman are compared with the matches I and my paternal first cousin, Elsa Gellis Schmaus, have with the same probands. Bearing in mind that Sheila Hayman is less than

Table 15.6 – *Family Finder* autosomal DNA matches of Edward Gelles with Oppenheim and others

(total DNA matches and longest shared segment in cM)

	Sheila Hayman	Edward Gelles	Elsa Schmaus
			Gelles 1st cousin
Sheila Hayman			
Ralph N. Baer	68.51/9.12	138.46/8.10	125.82/8.42
Alan Guggenheim	46.92/9.29		
J.P. Guggenheim		98.46/9.40	90.72 /10.89
W.M. Oppenheim		99.24/14.95	113.03/12.69
Charles Oppenheim	52.06/10.52		71.29/9.77
W.R. Wertheimer	77.71/13.06	86.50 /11.29	100.28/8.11
M.A. Wertheimer		92.98/7.73	108.39/25.95
L. Krieger	72.52/15.86	116.09/15.52	115.73/11.50
D. Calzareth	61.43/14.98	116.30/10.05	145.74/10.14
R. Salomon	54.85/12.48	81.87/9.61	123.10/11.36
Eugenie Salomon	38.71/13.33		
Hillel Jaffe	39.44/9.20		85.90/12.64
R.A. Jaffe		77.92/13.24	72.71/11.85
Roy H. Stern	91.22/10.72	111.31/10.51	
Ralph F. Rothschild	79.88/8.69		
Olga Rothschild		85.98/8.45	72.11/9.49
Joy B. Rothschild		116.45/13.61	110.16/8.85
J. Löwenstein	53.57/10.05	122.23/11.29	109.12/7.82
R. Adelson	43.06/11.19	62.12/16.56	

As Sheila Hayman has a non-Jewish mother and numerous forebears of mixed descent, her total DNA match with Jewish probands is generally at a reduced level. The manner in which DNA is jumbled in passing down the generations can sometimes result in test matches with a proband but none for a close cousin.

While my father and mother are distantly related, DNA tests show that the parents of my paternal first cousin Elsa Gellis Schmaus do not have any noticeable commonality. It follows that where Elsa and I show a similar genetic affinity with other probands, this can be ascribed to connections with our Gelles line.

half-Jewish and that our common genetic background may be many generations in the past and really beyond the effective range of the available DNA tests, these data support the assertion that we have an area of genetic interest in this nexus of old German Jewish families. The size of some of the shared autosomal DNA fragments suggests some common ancestors a few hundred years ago but this does not establish their individual identities.

179

Table 15.7 – GEDmatch matrix of Oppenheim and other families:

Matches of DNA segments above 7 cM (total shared DNA, longest shared segments, genetic distance to MRCA)

	Sheila Hayman			Edward Gelles		
Edward Gelles	42.4	8.9	5.3			
Ralph N. Baer	33.7	12.8	4.4	164.7	11.0	3.2
Alan Guggenheim	36.0	11.4	4.3	78.3	8.8	4.7
Steven Guggenheim				37.1	12.6	4.3
Wm.M. Oppenheim				100.2	15.0	3.6
W.R. Wertheimer	70.9	17.4	3.8	87.2	13.0	3.7
L. Krieger	62.6	17.6	3.9	115.3	16.0	3.5
D. Calzareth	38.6	16.8	4.3	116.3	9.0	4.5
R. Salomon	34.2	13.7	4.4	24.4	8.7	5.9
Joy Rothschild	40.6	7.6	6.2	114.0	9.8	3.7

Table 15.7 shows the results of uploading the autosomal and X-DNA data from the Family Finder and from other providers such as 23andme and Ancestry.com on to the website of GEDmatch to produce estimates of genetic distance (in number of generations) to the most recent common ancestor. These are generally underestimates due to inadequate allowance for extensive inbreeding in these families.

Sheila and I are only distantly related. Interestingly, she has similar matches with my paternal first cousin, Elsa Gellis Schmaus, and with Susan Lee Weinstein, who is my paternal second cousin once removed, being descended from my great-grandfather Hirsch Leib Weinstein, Chief Rabbi of Solotwina. The Weinsteins (also sometimes found as Reinstein) and our mutual in-laws of the Spiegel family may well have come originally from the Rhineland nexus (see Table 15.4 above and Chapter 18). My paternal ancestry is further discussed in Chapter 21 and set out in Chart 21.8.

The descent of Karl Marx from Meir Katzenellenbogen and Gershon HaKohen is set out in Chart 15.8. Josef Katz, the son of Gershon HaKohen, was an important scholar and brother-in-law of Rabbi Moses Isserles of Krakow. Josef's wife was Shprinze Altschuler, descendant of the Chayes-Altschulers of Provence and Prague and of the Treivish rabbis of medieval France.

From Nissel Wahl and Moses HaKohen runs through the female line to Galician rabbis called Lwow (Lemberger), after the capital of eastern Galicia, whence they retraced their millennial journey to become Chief Rabbis of Treves (Trier). Karl's grandfather, Meir

Chart 15.8 From Saul Wahl to Karl Marx

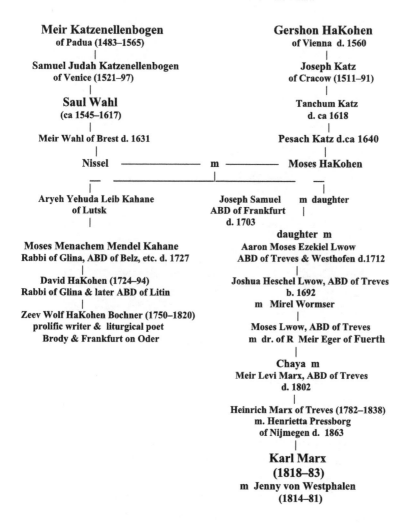

Meir Katzenellenbogen
of Padua (1483–1565)
|
Samuel Judah Katzenellenbogen
of Venice (1521–97)
|
Saul Wahl
(ca 1545–1617)
|
Meir Wahl of Brest d. 1631
|
Nissel ————————— m ————————— Moses HaKohen

Gershon HaKohen
of Vienna d. 1560
|
Joseph Katz
of Cracow (1511–91)
|
Tanchum Katz
d. ca 1618
|
Pesach Katz d.ca 1640
|

Aryeh Yehuda Leib Kahane
of Lutsk
|
Moses Menachem Mendel Kahane
Rabbi of Glina, ABD of Belz, etc. d. 1727
|
David HaKohen (1724–94)
Rabbi of Glina & later ABD of Litin
|
Zeev Wolf HaKohen Bochner (1750–1820)
prolific writer & liturgical poet
Brody & Frankfurt on Oder

Joseph Samuel   m daughter
ABD of Frankfurt |
d. 1703
daughter m
Aaron Moses Ezekiel Lwow
ABD of Treves & Westhofen d.1712
|
Joshua Heschel Lwow, ABD of Treves
b. 1692
m Mirel Wormser
|
Moses Lwow, ABD of Treves
m dr. of R Meir Eger of Fuerth
|
Chaya m
Meir Levi Marx, ABD of Treves
d. 1802
|
Heinrich Marx of Treves (1782–1838)
m. Henrietta Pressborg
of Nijmegen d. 1863
|
Karl Marx
(1818–83)
m Jenny von Westphalen
(1814–81)

Levi, who succeeded his father-in-law as Rabbi of Treves, added the surname Marx.

Another line from Nissel Wahl and Moses HaKohen goes via Aryeh Yehuda Leib Kahane to Moses Menachem Mendel Kahane, who was Rabbi at Glina, Chief Rabbi of Belz etc. His son David HaKohen was Rabbi of Glina in the late eighteenth century. Incidentally, the major encyclopedia on Galician scholars and sages by Rabbi Meir Wunder of Jerusalem states that my grandfather Rabbi Nahum Uri Gelles was a descendant of Rabbi Moses Kahane.

Photo 23 Karl Marx

My great-grandfather Rabbi David Isaac Gellis of Brody studied in Glina. He is mentioned together with other rabbis in the Glina Memorial Book and rabbinical reference works, which appear to form the basis of this intriguing assertion [4].

Rabbi Samuel Levi Marx (an uncle of Karl Marx) and Rabbi Naftali Hirsch Katzenellenbogen (a cousin of Rabbi David Isaac Gelles) were Nos. 45 and 19 respectively among the 71 delegates (plus alternates) who attended the Emperor Napoleon's Grand Sanhedrin held in Paris in 1807. The chart shows how the marriage of Nissel Wahl and Moses HaKohen of Brest united the line of Katzenellenbogen and Saul Wahl with the ancient priestly line.

The ancestry of Henrietta Pressborg of Nijmegen, the mother of Karl Marx, is also of more than passing interest. The great poet Heinrich Heine (1797–1856) was her third cousin. Her father was Rabbi Isaak Heyman Pressburg (whose family came from Bratislava). Her mother Nanette (1754–1833) was born in Amsterdam and belonged to the rabbinical Barent-Cohen family, who were linked to the Rothschilds through the marriage of Nathan Meyer Rothschild (1777–1836) to Hanna Barent-Cohen (1783–1850).

The descent of Yehudi Menuhin is shown in Chart 15.9. The father of Rabbi Moses Ahron Teomim was Simeon Teomim Lemel of Prague. Rachel and Hinde Horowitz were the sister and daughter of Pinchas Halevi Ish Horowitz (1535–1618), President of the Council of the Four Lands.

For connections between the descendants of Levi Isaac of Berdichev and Shmuel Gelles (called Polonsky) grandson of Moses Gelles of Brody and son-in-law of Pinchas Shapiro of Koretz see table 34 in my book *An Ancient Lineage*.

Shneur Zalman of Liadi (1745–1812), *der Alte Rebbe*, was the founder and first Rebbe of Chabad, a branch of Chasidic Judaism.

His grandson, Menachem Mendel Schneersohn (1789–1866), shown in the chart, was the ancestor of the seventh Lubavitcher Rebbe, Menachem Mendel Schneerson (1902–94), spiritual leader of the worldwide Chabad-Lubavitch movement.

Photo 24 Yehudi Menuhin

Chart 15.9 From Saul Wahl to Yehudi Menuhin

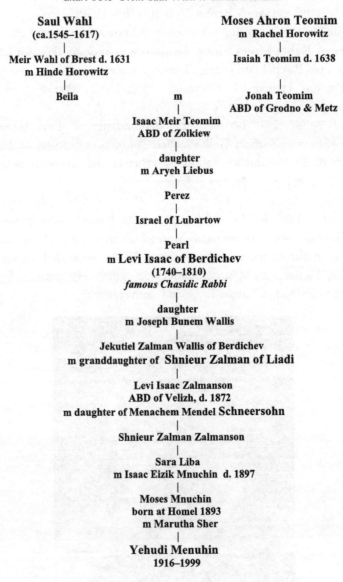

Saul Wahl
(ca.1545–1617)

Moses Ahron Teomim
m Rachel Horowitz

Meir Wahl of Brest d. 1631
m Hinde Horowitz

Isaiah Teomim d. 1638

Beila   m

Jonah Teomim
ABD of Grodno & Metz

Isaac Meir Teomim
ABD of Zolkiew

daughter
m Aryeh Liebus

Perez

Israel of Lubartow

Pearl
m **Levi Isaac of Berdichev**
(1740–1810)
famous Chasidic Rabbi

daughter
m Joseph Bunem Wallis

Jekutiel Zalman Wallis of Berdichev
m granddaughter of **Shnieur Zalman of Liadi**

Levi Isaac Zalmanson
ABD of Velizh, d. 1872
m daughter of Menachem Mendel **Schneersohn**

Shnieur Zalman Zalmanson

Sara Liba
m Isaac Eizik Mnuchin d. 1897

Moses Mnuchin
born at Homel 1893
m Marutha Sher

Yehudi Menuhin
1916–1999

Chart 15.10 From Saul Wahl to Martin Buber

SAUL WAHL

Judah Wahl　　　　　　　　　　　**Meir Wahl**

　　　　　　　　　　　　　　　　　　Deborah

Dinah Katzenellenbogen　　m　　**Abraham Joshua Heschel**
widow of Naftali Hirsch Katz　　　　　*of Cracow 1596–1663*

daughter
m **Samson HaKohen**

daughter
m **Joel Heilprin**
of Zamosc

Uri Heilprin

Joel Heilprin

Zvi Hirsch Heilprin

Isaiah Heilprin

Zeev Dov Schiff
of Cracow 1768–1842

Gittel
m **Solomon Rubinstein**
of Zolkiew

Sarah Leah
m **Isaiah Abrahan Buber**
of Lvov d. 1870

Solomon Buber
of Lvov 1827–1906

Kalman Buber

Martin Buber
Vienna – Jerusalem
1878–1965

Yehudi Menuhin and Sir Isaiah Berlin (1909–97), the Oxford philosopher and historian of ideas, who are descended from Saul Wahl, share with the Lubavitcher Rebbe a descent from Shneur Zalman of Liadi.

The descent of Martin Buber from Saul Wahl is shown in Chart 15.10

Martin Buber absorbed traditional Jewish learning from his grandfather Solomon Buber, who was a distinguished scholar and prolific author in Austrian Galicia. He later studied philosophy and other subjects at Vienna University, but he spent the years up to the

Photo 25 Martin Buber (stamp)

outbreak of World War I in a deep engagement with Chasidism, publishing numerous works such as the *Legends of the Baal Shem Tov* and *Tales of the Chasidim*.

While he was active as a translator, publicist, and academic teacher, as well as a cultural Zionist, it was not until the 1920s that he began to publish his philosophical ideas including *Ich und Du* (I and Thou). His philosophy of the role of the individual and society has deep roots in his Chasidic background and has made a lasting impact in sociological and theological circles. Martin Buber left Germany in 1938 and became a professor at the Hebrew University in Jerusalem where he lectured on anthropology and sociology and played an active role in political dialogue as a supporter of a bi-national Jewish–Arab state.

Buber's genetic and cultural background is similar to mine, from Galician Chasidism to Viennese Enlightenment, descent from Saul Wahl, connections with different branches of the Heilprin family, and with the descendants of Samson Hakohen (see my book *An Ancient Lineage*, particularly table 45). Buber's ancestors also included Yomtov Lipman Heller (1578–1654), the Chief Rabbi of Vienna, Prague, and Krakow.

186

NOTES

1 Wahl = possibly from medieval German for 'the Italian'; Katzenellenbogen = from the eponymous town in Hesse-Nassau; Mintz = from city of Mainz; Spira or Shapiro = from city of Speyer; Treivish = from city of Treves/Trier.

2 See The History of the Jewish Community of Frankfurt-am-Main, http://goldschmidt.tripod.com/history.htm and www.jewsofFrankfurt.com/dna-2/.

3 See the Jewish Virtual Library article on 'Banking and Bankers' at www.jewishvirtuallibrary.org/jsource/judaica/ejud_0002_0003_0_01978.html.

REFERENCES

[1] Pinchas Katzenellenbogen, *Yesh Manhilin* (1730s), MS in the Bodleian Library Oxford (published in Jerusalem 1986); Hirsch Edelman, *Gedullat Shaul* (London 1844).

[2] Neil Rosenstein, *The Unbroken Chain*. (London: CIS Publishers 1990).

[3] See N. Rosenstein in 'The Breuer Family Background – Tzemach David' on the internet, originally published in *The Jewish Press*, 2 May 1980), p. 28D.

[4] Meir Wunder, *Meorei Galicia*, Vol. 6. (Jerusalem 2005), p. 345; H. Halpern (ed.), *Memorial Book of Glina*. (New York 1950), p. 17; Shmuel Noach Gottlieb, *Ohalei Shem*. (Pinsk 1912), pp. 261–2; Nathan Zvi Friedman, *Otzar Harabbanim*, *# 5168, # 15904, # 14602*. (Israel: Bnei Brak 1973).

Chart 15.11 Some of the ancestral background of Edward Gelles from the sixteenth-century Ashkenazi Rabbinate

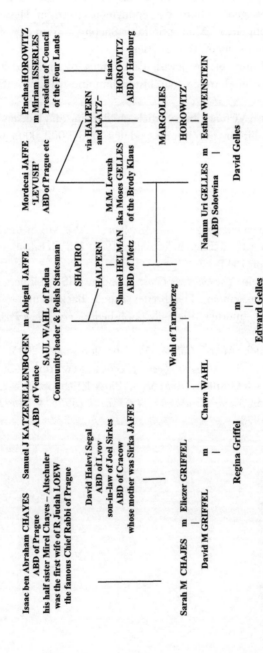

Isaac ben Abraham CHAYES
ABD of Prague
his half sister Mirel Chayes – Altschuler
was the first wife of R Judah LOEW
the famous Chief Rabbi of Prague

Samuel J KATZENELLENBOGEN   m   **Abigail JAFFE** –
ABD of Venice

SAUL WAHL of Padua
Community leader & Polish Statesman

Mordecai JAFFE
'LEVUSH'
ABD of Prague etc

Pinchas HOROWITZ
m Miriam ISSERLES
President of Council
of the Four Lands

SHAPIRO

HALPERN

via HALPERN
and KATZ –

Isaac
HOROWITZ
ABD of Hamburg

David Halevi Segal
ABD of Lvov
son-in-law of Joel Sirkes
ABD of Cracow
whose mother was Sirka JAFFE

M.M. Levush
aka Moses GELLES
of the Brody Klaus

Shmuel HELMAN
ABD of Metz

MARGOLIES

HOROWITZ

Nahum Uri GELLES   m   **Esther WEINSTEIN**
ABD Solotwina

Wahl of Tarnobrzeg

David Gelles

Sarah M CHAJES   m   **Eliezer GRIFFEL**

Chawa WAHL

David M GRIFFEL   m

Regina Griffel

m

Edward Gelles

note : ABD stands for Av Beth Din
head of the Rabbinical Court/Chief Rabbi.

Footnotes

Following the above chart, Edward Gelles is a sixth-generation descendant of the scholar Moses Gelles of Brody and of Chief Rabbi Shmuel Helman of Metz, a seventh-generation descendant of Chief Rabbi Isaac Horowitz of Hamburg, and a thirteenth-generation descendant of Pinchas Halevi Ish Horowitz of Prague and Krakow, who married Miriam, the sister of the great Krakow Rabbi Moses Isserles and became President of the Council of the Four Lands (the semi-autonomous governing body of Polish Jewry). Edward Gelles is a fifteenth-generation descendant of Chief Rabbis Judah Loew, Isaac Chayes, and Mordecai Jaffe of Prague and of Chief Rabbi Samuel Judah Katzenellenbogen of Padua and Venice, who was the father of Saul Wahl.

Rabbinic lines of Chayes, Katzenellenbogen, Loew, Halpern, Shapiro, and others go back to the scholar Rashi (eleventh century) and Kalonymos of Narbonne (eighth century). They are considered to have claims to Davidic descent.

Horowitz are Levites descended from Shem Tov Halevi of Gerona (tenth century), whose ancestry is deemed to go back to the Prophet Samuel.

The Kohanic line of Judah Loew's son-in-law, Isaac ben Samson Katz, has been claimed to go back to Eli the Priest. Edward Gelles appears to be 31 generations from Shem Tov Halevi of Gerona and 14 generations from Isaac ben Samson Katz of Prague.

The Narbonne Kalonymos line from Makhir, a descendant of Babylonian Exilarchs of Davidic lineage, is believed to have links with the Carolingian line via a daughter of Charles Martel, the grandfather of Charlemagne, and there are consequently connections to some royal and noble European houses.

Chapter 16

Chayes: Prague, Brody, Livorno and Vienna

Pan-European connections from the fifteenth to the twentieth century

AN OUTLINE HISTORY of the ancient Chayes family follows them for over five hundred years from Portugal to Italy and Provence, thence to Prague, to Poland, and Lithuania, to Brody in Galicia, to Livorno and Trieste in Italy, to Vienna, and in more recent times back to Western Europe, America, and Israel. A long line of notable rabbis, including Chief Rabbis of Prague and Vienna, ennobled merchant bankers in Tuscany, and many doctors, scientists, professors of law and humanities, a modern composer, and a world-class chess player bear their name. Their achievements and marriage connections show the Chayes to be one of the less well-known but exceptionally talented and distinguished of the major rabbinic families.

INTRODUCTION

The Chayes were originally called by the Hebrew name Chayut. The history of this ancient family takes in their journey from Portugal to Italy and the south of France. From Provence some came to Prague and thence to Poland and Lithuania, and in due course settled in the Galician city of Brody. There they flourished for many generations as scholars and community leaders. Some also did well in business that took them to Livorno and Florence in the early nineteenth century. A Tuscan branch was ennobled by the King of Portugal. While the family was best known for its great rabbis, the Age of Enlightenment opened their manifold talents to science, arts, and the liberal professions and brought them to Vienna and other Western cities. In the twentieth century, Chajes have distinguished themselves as lawyers and scholars in various disciplines. They have produced a world-class chess player and a notable musician. After World War II and the Holocaust, most of the present generation are to be found in the United States and Israel [1].

When a family shows such undiminished intellectual energy over so many generations their genealogical connections and genetic heritage must inevitably become the subject of reassessment and this is the purpose of the present essay.

Chief Rabbi Zwi (Hirsch) Perez Chajes was Chief Rabbi of Vienna between the two world wars. This essay was written for the commemoration of the 80th anniversary of his death in 1927. Rabbi Chajes was the thirteenth-generation descendant of Isaac Chayes, a son of Rabbi Abraham, known as Eberel Altschuler. Isaac's sister married the *Maharal*, Judah Löw, otherwise known as *der hohe Rabbi Löw*. Isaac Chayes and his famous brother-in-law were in turn Chief Rabbis of Prague in the late sixteenth century.

The Chayut, who described themselves as 'of the pious men of Provence', were transplanted to Bohemia when ancient Jewish communities in the south of France were being expelled. Legend has it that members of this family came to Prague with stones from their destroyed house of prayer that were incorporated into the synagogue which they helped to build and from which they took their Altschuler name.

Photo 26 Rabbi Zwi Perez Chajes of Vienna

This was the period when Prague was at the crossroads of Jewish migration from west to east. In this city, where for a while Habsburg emperors held their Court, the Chayut mingled with Judah Löw's family from Worms and met such contemporaries as Mordecai Yaffe, whose family hailed from Bologna and who was in turn Chief Rabbi of Grodno, Prague, and Posen, Rabbi David Gans from Westphalia, and the descendants of an ancient Spanish Levitic clan who had added the town name of *Horovice* near Prague to become the Halevi Horovitz.

Meisels were outstanding among families of community leaders. The sacerdotal family of Katz (an acronym of Kohen Zedek or *righteous priest*) and some of the aforementioned were connected by marriage. Their names and others, including Gelles, are found on Prague tombstone inscriptions [2].

While the sixteenth century overall was a glorious period for the Jews of Prague, there were frequent temporary expulsions from the city. The rise of Poland–Lithuania to power and affluence impelled many Jews to seek new homes in a country that appeared to offer a measure of religious toleration, communal self-government, and economic opportunities. The high point of Jewish community life had thus shifted from Prague to Poland and Lithuania by the seventeenth century. The political and economic fortunes of the region largely determined migrations to Silesia and to Galicia, where the town of Brody gained in economic importance. The Chayes established themselves as one of its leading families. Others in Brody included the Horowitz and the Babad, whose head, Isaac Krakower, the ABD of Brody, was a descendant of Chief Rabbi Abraham Joshua Heschel of Krakow and of the Katzenellenbogens of Padua and Venice. At that time my immediate Gelles line and members of the Katz family were also to be found there. The first of the three partitions that dismembered the Polish state in the later eighteenth century incorporated the ancient land of Galicia into the Austro-Hungarian Empire (1772–1918).

The ancestry of Hirsch Perez Chajes in the direct male line is well known through the writings of Dr N. M. Gelber and Moritz Rosenfeld [3, 4]. The first appended chart (16.1) shows this Chajes line side by side with a line descending from Judah Löw and a sister of Isaac ben Abraham Chayes.

It is my contention that the outstanding intellectual gifts of Hirsch Perez Chajes and of his grandfather Zwi Hirsch of Zolkiew might be ascribed in part to immediately preceding Chajes marriages that reinforced the genetic inheritance. Two of these marriages and their wider connections are shown in the Chart 16.2. The unions of Isaac Chajes with a daughter of Natan Nata ben Aryeh Leib and of their son Menachem Meinish Chajes with a daughter of Isaac Wolf Berenstein brought about infusions from the Klausner line, which goes back to the family of Judah Löw, and from the Katzenellenbogen.

While the story of the Chajes family in Brody is fairly well known, little systematic work has been done on the numerous branches that developed over the course of time in other Galician towns. The Chart 16.3 shows some connections of branches at Drohobycz and Kolomea.

The Altschuler–Löw descendancy takes in some of the important connections to the priestly Katz family from which confluent

Horowitz and Zausmer lines emerge and whose ramifications are examined in some detail.

The Chajes family is clearly one of the major rabbinical families and through its connections with so many other historic families it is revealed as a microcosm of the millennial Jewish presence in Europe.

FROM ISAAC BEN ABRAHAM TO HIRSCH PEREZ CHAYES

The direct line of descent shown in the first chart follows the literature [3, 4]. Eberel Altschuler died around 1587. His son Isaac Chayes (c.1538–1617) was Rabbi of Prague from 1584. He also spent some years at Prossnitz in Moravia where he was head of an important Yeshiva [5]. His son Menachem Manish was called to be Chief Rabbi of Vilna in 1617 and died there in 1636. His son Jacob was the father of the second Isaac Chayes of the line, who became Rabbi of Skole. The latter's issue included Eliezer (d.1766) and Jacob Koppel (d.1782), who were noted Kabbalists in Brody. Their tombstone inscriptions were preserved by Dr N. M. Gelber [6]. Eliezer's son, the third Isaac Chayes, was also an ardent Kabbalist and leading member of the Council of the Four Lands. Isaac's son, Meir Chayes, the Rabbi of Tysmienica, was a saintly mystic about whose wondrous deeds many tales were told by the Chassidim. Meir Chayes was the father of the fourth Isaac Chayes (d.1807), leader of the Jewish community in Brody, whose wife was a daughter of its Chief Rabbi, Nathan Nata ben Aryeh Leib. From this couple came the second Menachem Manish of the line (d.1832), who married a daughter of Isaac Wolf Berenstein of Brody, a son of Aryeh Leib Berenstein (1708–88), who was appointed to the post of Chief Rabbi of Galicia by the Austrian authorities. Menachem Manish Chayes became a merchant in Livorno and the family business developed in Florence where the house of Berenstein, Chayes and Co. was established. Meir ben Menachem Manish (d.1854) also married a Berenstein. He later returned to Brody but maintained his connections with Tuscany, where a family branch flourished for several generations. Meir's son, Zvi Hirsch Chayes of Brody (d.1855), was the noted Rabbi of Zolkiew. His wives are given as Riva Pshivogarsky [7] and Golda Berenstein [8]. Zvi Hirsch had five sons, Leon (1828–91), Chaim (1830–86), Solomon (1835–96), Isaac (1842–1901), and Wolf

Photo 27 Villa Chajes in Livorno

(1845–1901). Isaac Chajes, the fifth Isaac of the direct line, became ABD of Brody. His brother, the scholar and merchant Solomon Chajes, and his wife Rebecca Shapiro had three sons, Abraham (1853–1911), Max (1855–98), and Hirsch Perez Chajes (1876–1927). Max married his cousin Anna, the daughter of Chaim Chajes, who after her husband's early death ran the household for her cousin, the Chief Rabbi, in Trieste (1912–18) and later in Vienna (1918–27).

ISAAC BEN MEIR OF BRODY AND HIS SON MENACHEM MANISH OF BRODY & FLORENCE

As the second chart shows, Isaac ben Meir Chajes of Brody married a daughter of Nathan Nata, son of Aryeh Leib, the ABD of Slutsk and Grodno, who was a son of Nathan Nata, ABD of Tarnigrad [9–11]. The wife of the said Aryeh Leib *Sheitels*, was a granddaughter of Aryeh Leib *Fischls*, also known as the *der Hoiche Rebbe Leib* of Krakow, where he was Chief Rabbi in succession to Abraham Joshua Heschel. The connection of Aryeh Leib Fischls to the family of Judah Löw of Prague is through the Klausner line to Zacharia Mendel Klausner Hazaken, who was a brother-in-law of the *Maharal*. Isaac Chajes' mother-in-law was a daughter of Gershon Vilner of Shklov, an uncle of Shmuel Gelles, the ABD of Siemiatycze. The marriage of Menachem Manish Chajes to a Berenstein descended from Chief Rabbi Abraham Joshua Heschel of Krakow combined a line of mystics and scholars with another of outstanding intellectual credentials but of a more worldly disposition. Aryeh Leib Berenstein' appointment to be Chief Rabbi of Galicia was very much a political one.

Berenstein was married to Chaya, descended from Efraim Fischl of Ludmir, whose wife's antecedents included the Katz line from Prague and the Katzenellenbogen. I believe that the fortunes of the ensuing Chayes branch in Tuscany support my assessment of the Berenstein marriage and its influence on later generations.

In the course of the long Chajes saga there have been many marriages with families mentioned in this essay. One granddaughter of Isaac ben Abraham Chayes married Jacob Halevi Horowitz (*c.*1604–43), a son of Isaiah ben Abraham Halevi Ish Horowitz (1568–1627), the Chief Rabbi of Frankfurt and Prague and later *Nasi* in the Holy Land, who was known as the *Holy Shelah*. Another Chayes granddaughter married Josef Halevi Horowitz (d. *c.*1680), a descendant of the earlier Isaiah ben Moshe Halevi Horowitz (*c.*1440–1515), who originally bought the *Arenda* of Horovice and moved to nearby Prague around 1480 [12]. Later Chajes marriages to Katzenellenbogen and Rapaport are quoted by Rosenstein [13].

DAVID TEBELE CHAJES OF DROHOBYCZ AND ISAAC CHAIM CHAJES OF KOLOMEA

Lines of descent from David Tebele Chajes of Drohobycz and Isaac Chaim Chajes of Kolomea are shown on the third chart. The earliest known Chayes connection with Drohobycz was provided by Rabbi Isaac Chayes of Skole (the second Isaac of the main line), who moved to Drohobycz, where he died around 1726. Much information on the later Chayes of Drohobycz is provided by the admirable Lauterbach Family Chronicle [14]. David Tebele Chajes was known to have come from the Brody family, but his precise connection to the main line was obscure. Neil Rosenstein has suggested that he might have been a brother of Rabbi Zvi Hirsch of Brody and Zolkiew [15]. My study of name patterns, set out in Chart 16.4, starts with a brother of Aryeh Leib Fischls of Krakow, who was a Rabbi David Tebele. As the chart shows, his name recurs over many generations, its introduction into the Chayes family being through the marriage of the fourth Isaac Chajes to a sister of the Rabbi of Lissa, David Tebele ben Nathan Nata. There is therefore clear support for the supposition that David Tebele Chajes of Drohobycz was a descendant of the fourth Isaac Chajes of Brody or of his issue.

From Drohobycz some Chajes went to Kolomea, whose Memorial (Yizkor) Book records a number of Chajes families [16]. My great-great-grandfather Isaac Chaim Chajes was a well-connected businessman there [17]. His children married into the Hermann, Lichtenstein, and Sternhel families of Kolomea as well as into my maternal Griffel family [18]. Sarah Matel Chajes became the wife of my great-grandfather Eliezer Griffel, the community leader and patriarch of the Griffel clan in Nadworna. Their grandchildren included my mother Regina and my uncle Zygmunt, whose wife Maryla Suesser belonged to a prominent Krakow family. The Suessers were also in-laws of the Chajes of Drohobycz. The first names of Isaac Chaim were passed down from my Chajes ancestor to my great-uncle Isaac Chaim Griffel (1880–1930) and then to my uncle Edward (Isaac Chaim ben David Mendel Griffel).

Chana Chajes, who died in Vienna, was the first wife of Wolf Leib Lichtenstein, a son of Baruch Bendet and a grandson of Hillel Lichtensten, who came from Hungary and was Rabbi of Klausenburg before becoming Chief Rabbi of Kolomea in 1867. In his day he was a leading spokesman of the ultra-orthodox school [19]. The family claimed descent from Isaiah Horovitz and Mordecai Yaffe among others [20].

The literature on the Sternhels includes an account of Reb Shaltiel Isaac Sternhel of Kolomea, who was related to prominent Chasidic rabbis. He retired to the Holy Land and died there in the 1840s [21]. His great-grandson Reb Yakov Sternhel married a descendant of Rabbi Meir Chayes of Tysmienica.

The vital records of Kolomea show that Isaac Chaim Chajes died just before the birth of his son in 1866. The latter could therefore be named Isaac according to ancient custom, suggesting an ancestral link to the fourth Isaac Chayes of Brody, as is also indicated for his kinsman David Tebele Chajes. Other material on the Chajes family in *An Ancient Lineage* [1] includes references to subscription lists in support of Jewish publications in which the name of Reb Isaac Chaim Chajes of Kolomea is to be found [22].

THE ALTSCHULER CONNECTION TO JUDAH LÖW OF PRAGUE

The literature on the marriages of Rabbi Judah Löw of Prague would benefit from further clarification. Meir Perels' work *Megillath Yuchasin Mehral mi Prag* dwells on the marriage to Perel, daughter of Schmelke Reich [23]. It appears that Judah Löw was 32 years of age when he took Perel as his second wife [24–25]. His first wife, whose name is given as Mirel [26] was a sister of Isaac ben Abraham Chayes. The children of this first marriage included Vögele Löw (d.1629), who was the second wife of Isaac ben Samson Katz (d.1624). Isaac Katz of Prague came from a priestly family (also called Kohen Zedek or HaKohen), whose lineage goes back to biblical times [27].

DESCENT FROM JUDAH LÖW VIA KATZ, HOROWITZ, AND ZAUSMER

Vögele Löw and Isaac Katz were the parents of Naftali Katz, ABD of Lublin (d.1649). He married Dinah Katzenellenbogen, a granddaughter of Saul Wahl (*c.*1545–1617). After her first husband's death, Dinah became the second wife of Chief Rabbi Abraham Joshua Heschel of Krakow. Naftali Katz and Dinah were the parents of Isaac Katz, ABD of Stepan in Volhynia, whose sons included Naftali Hirsch Katz (ABD of Stepan, Ostrog, Frankfurt am Main, and Posen, died 1719) and Isaiah Katz, who was a judge in Brody. The son of Isaiah Katz was Menachem Meinish, whose daughter married Meir Horowitz (d.1743), the ABD of Tykocin, known as the *Maharam of Tiktin*. Their descendants included a line via Jacob Jokel Horowitz (d.1755), ABD of Brody and Glogau, to Isaac *Hamburger* Horowitz (1715–67), ABD of Brody and Hamburg. The latter's daughter Beile was the wife of Menachem Mendel Rubin (d.1803), the ABD of Lesniow and Lesko, and one of their sons was Jacob Jokel Horowitz (1772–1832), the ABD of Bolechow.

Naftali Hirsch Katz of Frankfurt had a daughter, Shprintze, who was the wife of Jacob Ashkenazi-Katzenellenbogen of Posen. Their daughter married Efraim Fischl of Ludmir (see first and second charts). Shprintze's brother Bezalel Katz (d.1717) was ABD of Ostrog and his son Isaac Katz (d.1734) followed him to become ABD of the Ostrog Klaus. One of the latter's daughters married Nahum Zausmer, ABD of Sandomierz. Their son was Menachem Nahum Zausmer, and his children included Rabbi Enzel Zausmer of Stryj (d.1858) and a daughter who was the first wife of the aforementioned Jacob Jokel Horowitz, ABD of Bolechow. From this marriage came Efraim Fischel Horowitz, ABD of Munkacz (c.1790–1860), who was thus doubly descended from Judah Löw and Mirel Altschuler. He had a half-brother Yehuda Aaron, who was the son of Jacob Jokel Horowitz by his third marriage to Hinde, a daughter of Yehuda Aaron Fraenkel of Brody [28, 29].

Evidence for Gelles descent shown in the first chart is considered in my first book and articles [1, 30]. Yehuda Aaron Horowitz was Rabbi in Solotwina near Stanislau before moving to the neighbouring province of Bukowina in 1859. His successors at Solotwina were Hirsch Leib Weinstein (d.1884), his son-in-law Nahum Uri Gelles (1852–1934), and finally Yoel Babad (d. c.1941). Stanislau was the stronghold of an unbroken Horowitz rabbinical line from 1784 to the eve of World War II and most of the little *shtetls* in the area had rabbis who were either Horowitz or related to them. Rabbinical succession by a qualified son or son-in-law was the rule rather than the exception. The pattern of personal names, particularly Efraim Fischel and Nahum, of place names, dates, and individual biographical details adds up to a very plausible hypothesis of Gelles ascent via the Katz family to Löw and Altschuler of Prague, but the search for direct documentary proof of the Horowitz connection has so far proved elusive.

VIENNA AND BEYOND

Our genealogical journey from sixteenth century Prague, shared by the Chajes with a number of other families, led us to Brody and some other Galician towns. In the later nineteenth century, our families spread to a wider arena and participated more fully in the social and cultural life of their time through the sciences, arts, and liberal professions. Among members of the Chajes family who attained distinction in various walks of life are the grandchildren of Rabbi Zwi Hirsch Chajes of Zolkiew and descendants of his siblings or cousins. Many of these lived and worked in Vienna at some time or another.

For an orthodox rabbi of his time and place Zwi Hirsch Chajes had an extraordinarily wide cultural background and pan-European perspective. From his five sons, one recalls the issue of *Chaim Chajes* including Dr Hermann Chajes, a physician who died in Vienna in 1928, and his sister Sophie, who married Professor Solomon Frankfurter (1856–1941), the philologist, director of Vienna University Library, and uncle of US Supreme Court Judge Felix Frankfurter. Another sister, Chana, was the wife of Max (Meir), a son of *Solomon Chajes* and brother of Vienna's Chief Rabbi Hirsch Perez Chajes (v.s). From *Isaac Chajes*, the Chief Rabbi of Brody, came Saul Chajes (1884–1935), the distinguished bibliographer and archivist of the Jewish community in Vienna. Benno Chajes (1880–1938), a son of *Wolf Chajes*, was Professor of Social Medicine at the Technical University of Berlin-Charlottenburg. *Leon Chajes* died in Vienna in 1891 where he had issue.

Descendants from siblings or cousins of the Rabbi of Zolkiew included Markus Chajes, whose son Dr Josef Chajes (1875–1944) was born in Lemberg, studied in Vienna and worked there as a gynaecologist before moving to Palestine in 1934. He and Valerie Roth (1893–1970) had two sons, Dr Richard Chajes, a physician who died in Detroit in 1966, and the music teacher and composer Julius Chajes (1910–85), whose distinguished career began in Vienna. My book includes more biographical details and a photograph with his son Yossi Hillel Chajes (b.1965), who is now Professor of History at Haifa University [1].

CONCLUSION

This chapter has attempted to furnish a genealogical backcloth to the rich tapestry of the Chajes family history, which has involved close ties with Löw, Katz, Horowitz, Katzenellenbogen, and others from early times.

From Prague to Brody and Vienna the genius of the Chajes inheritance found expression in 14 generations of mystics, scholars, and community leaders. The outstanding figures were undoubtedly the three Rabbis – Isaac ben Abraham of Prague, who was receptive to both rationalist and mystical strands in Jewish learning, Zwi Hirsch of Zolkiew, who combined orthodoxy with secular culture and modern ideas on social and educational reform, and his grandson, Zwi Hirsch Perez of Vienna, the scholar, educationist, Zionist, and political leader of a great community, whose name is forever enshrined in the history of European Jewry [3, 31, 32]. The remarkably enduring intellectual energy of this ancient family has been ascribed, in part, to the genetic enrichment of the line brought about by several marriages, particularly those of Isaac ben Meir Chajes of Brody and of his son Menachem Manish Chajes of Brody and Florence. The ancient virtues of several lineages seem to have come together in the person of Zwi Hirsch Perez Chajes. It is fitting that attention should also be drawn to the influence of the Rabbi's mother, Rebecca, daughter of Perez Shapiro, whose name recalls another long and famous rabbinical line.

The funeral service for Chief Rabbi Zwi Perez Chajes was attended by the then Austrian State President Dr Michael Hainisch and other dignitaries. After 80 years and the Holocaust that ravaged the Jewish community and transformed the Austrian state, the legacy of the greatest rabbi of the Chajes line is secure, not least in the high school he originally founded and the other institutions that bear his name.

REFERENCES

[1] Edward Gelles, *An Ancient Lineage: European Roots of a Jewish Family.* (London: Vallentine Mitchell 2006).

[2] Simon Hock, *Die Familien Prags nach Epitaphien des alten Jüdischen Friedhofes,* Adolf Alkalay, Pressburg (1892). From about 1600 to 1750 numerous tombstone inscriptions for Gelles and variants on the name are listed, e.g. the honourable Rabbi Mendel, son of Zalman Gelles, 'emissary of the Beth Din' (1651), and some are of priestly connection, e.g. Freidel, wife of Rabbi Benjamin Gallis Katz (1727).

[3] N. M. Gelber, 'Aus Oberrabbiner Prof. Chajes' Ahnensaal', *Die Stimme,* No 2. (Vienna 1927).

[4] Moritz Rosenfeld, *Oberrabbiner Hirsch Perez Chajes. Sein Leben und Werk.* (Vienna 1933).

[5] B. Wachstein, *Notizen zur Geschichte der Juden in Prossnitz*, Jahrbuch der Jüdisch-literarischen Gesellschaft, Frankfurt am Main, Vol. 16 (1924).

[6] N. M. Gelber, Tombstone inscriptions in the Gelber file at the Central Archive of the History of the Jewish People, Jerusalem.

[7] Meir Wunder, *Meorei Galicia*, Vols 1–6. (Jerusalem 1978–2005).

[8] Neil Rosenstein, *The Unbroken Chain*, Vol. 2. (London: CIS Publishers 1990), p. 983.

[9] *Idem*, Vol. 1, p. 219. Also *Arim Veimahot (Brody)*, pp. 56–57 and David Tebele Efrati, *Toldot Anshei Shem.* (Warsaw 1875), pp. 34–5.

[10] Ahron Walden, *Shem Hagedolim Hachadash.* (Jerusalem 1965), pp. 43, 52.

[11] Louis Lewin, *Die Geschichte der Juden in Lissa.* (Pinne 1904), pp. 192–204.

[12] Michael Honey, *Jewish Historical Clock. The Horowitz Family.* (London 1993).

[13] Rosenstein, *loc. cit.*, Vol. 1, pp. 583–4; Vol. 2, pp. 716–27.

[14] Leo Lauterbach, *Chronicle of the Lauterbach Family 1800–1991*, new edition by Bernard S. Lauterbach. (El Paso, Texas 1992).

[15] Rosenstein, *loc. cit.*, Vol. 2, p. 806.

[16] D. Ney and M. Schutzman (eds), *Sefer Zikaron (Kolomea Memorial Book).* (Tel Aviv, Israel 1972).

[17] JewishGen, JRI-Poland Data Base for Kolomea.

[18] JewishGen, JRI-Poland Data Base for Nadworna (ed.), Israel Carmi, *Nadworna Memorial Book and Records* Landsmanschaft of Nadworna in Israel and America (1975).

[19] Jewish Encyclopedia, 'Article on Hillel Lichtenstein' (New York & London 1904).

[20] L. Rakow, Tzefunot, Vol. 12. (Israel: Benei Brak 1992); Y.Y. Cohen, *Chachmei Transylvania.* (Jerusalem: Machon 1989); Reuben Gross, private communication on Lichtenstein descent.

[21] M.Y. Schwerdscharf, *Hadras Zvi.* (Sziget 1909); Y. Sternhel, *Kochvei Yitzchok.* (New York 1977).

[22] Shmuel Schmelke Horowitz of Nicolsburg and his son Zvi Yehishua of Trebitch *Nezir Hashem* and *Semichas Moshe* (*the subscription lists printed in the book include Reb Isaac Chaim Chajes of Kolomea*).

[23] Meir Perels, *Megillath Yuchasin Mehral miPrag.* (Warsaw 1864 & 1889), German translation in the Jahrbuch der Jüdisch-literarischen Gesellschaft, Frankfurt am Main (1929).

[24] David Nachman Rutner, Beth Ahron Beyisrael, Vol. 18, No. 2, pp. 170–5 (Dec/Jan 2002–3) (published in Jerusalem by the Chasidim

of the Karlin-Stolin dynasty); Yair Chaim Bacharach, MS in Bikurim, publ. by Naftali Keller in Vienna (1864–5), quoted by Rutner.

[25] L. Rakow, *Keren Yisrael*. (London & Jerusalem 2000), pp. 57–66.

[26] Yehudah Klausner, private communication.

[27] Ahron Samuel ben Naftali Hirsch Katz, *VeTzivah HaKohen*. (White Field 1823). The family claimed descent from Eli the Priest. Akiba Katz fled from Spain around 1391. The family went to Constantinople and were in Hungary before settling in Prague by *c*.1500. Yocheved (d.1552), a daughter of Akiba Katz, grandson of the above, married Shabbatai Sheftel Horowitz of Prague(1480–1555), a son of Isaiah ben Moshe Halevi Ish Horowitz from Provence, who first settled at Horovice near Prague v.s. The latter's eighth-generation descendant, Meir Horowitz of Tykocin (d.1743) married a daughter of Menachem Manish Katz, son of Isaiah Katz of Brody (see first chart).

[28] Wunder, *loc. cit.*

[29] Rosenstein, *loc. cit.*

[30] Edward Gelles, 'Rabbis of Solotwina near Stanislau Gelles of Brody and some Fraenkel-Horowitz Connections', *Sharsheret Hadorot*, 19, 4 (Nov 2005) and 20, 1 (Feb 2006) 'Marriages between some Rabbinical families in Galicia', *The Galitzianer*, 14, 1 (Nov 2006).

[31] V. Aptowitzer and A.Z. Schwarz (eds), *Abhandlungen zur Erinnerung an Hirsch Perez Chajes*. (Vienna: Alexander Kohut Foundation 1933).

[32] Hugo Gold, *Zwi Perez Chajes. Dokumente aus Seinem Leben und Wirken*. (Olamenu, Tel Aviv: Zwi Perez Chajes Institute 1971).

Chart 16.1 *Rabbi Abraham Chayes of Prague, known as Eberel Altschuler*

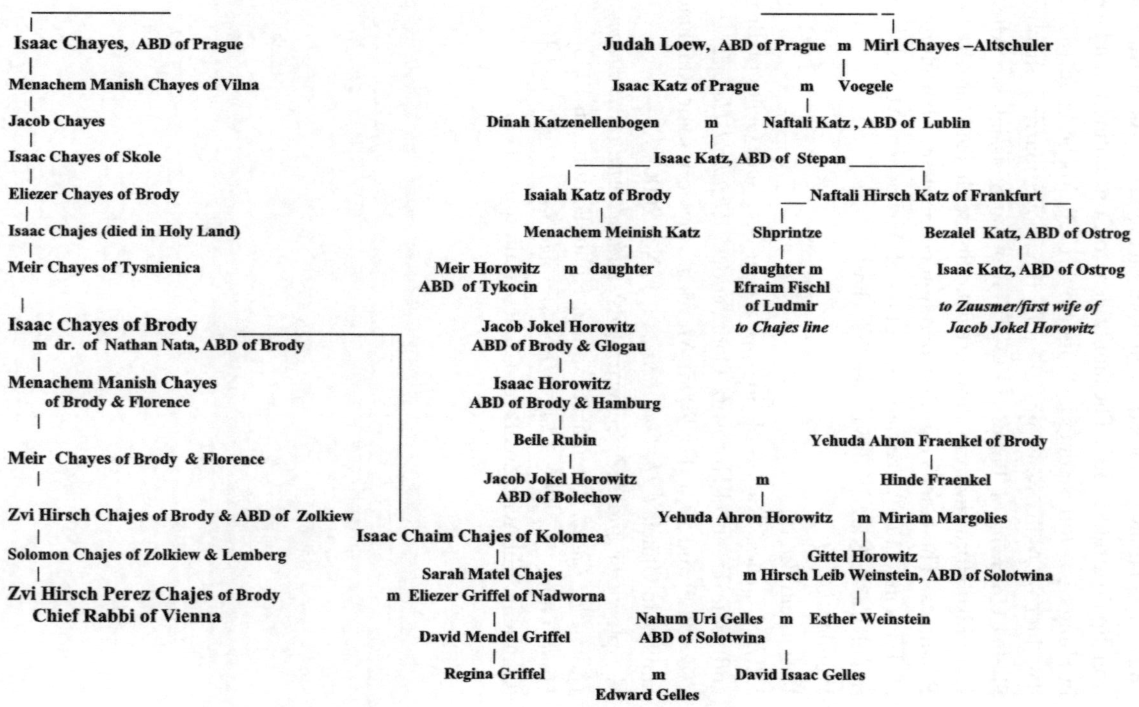

Isaac Chayes, ABD of Prague

Menachem Manish Chayes of Vilna

Jacob Chayes

Isaac Chayes of Skole

Eliezer Chayes of Brody

Isaac Chajes (died in Holy Land)

Meir Chayes of Tysmienica

Isaac Chayes of Brody
m dr. of Nathan Nata, ABD of Brody

Menachem Manish Chayes
of Brody & Florence

Meir Chayes of Brody & Florence

Zvi Hirsch Chajes of Brody & ABD of Zolkiew

Solomon Chajes of Zolkiew & Lemberg

Zvi Hirsch Perez Chajes of Brody
Chief Rabbi of Vienna

Judah Loew, ABD of Prague m Mirl Chayes –Altschuler

Isaac Katz of Prague

Dinah Katzenellenbogen m

Isaiah Katz of Brody

Menachem Meinish Katz

Meir Horowitz m daughter
ABD of Tykocin

Jacob Jokel Horowitz
ABD of Brody & Glogau

Isaac Horowitz
ABD of Brody & Hamburg

Beile Rubin

Jacob Jokel Horowitz
ABD of Bolechow

Isaac Chaim Chajes of Kolomea

Sarah Matel Chajes
m Eliezer Griffel of Nadworna

David Mendel Griffel

Regina Griffel

Voegele

m

Naftali Katz , ABD of Lublin

Isaac Katz, ABD of Stepan

Naftali Hirsch Katz of Frankfurt

Shprintze

daughter m
Efraim Fischl
of Ludmir
to Chajes line

Yehuda Ahron Fraenkel of Brody

Hinde Fraenkel

Yehuda Ahron Horowitz m Miriam Margolies

Gittel Horowitz
m Hirsch Leib Weinstein, ABD of Solotwina

m

Nahum Uri Gelles m Esther Weinstein
ABD of Solotwina

m

Edward Gelles

David Isaac Gelles

Bezalel Katz, ABD of Ostrog

Isaac Katz, ABD of Ostrog

to Zausmer/first wife of
Jacob Jokel Horowitz

Chart 16.2 Chayes Family Connections I

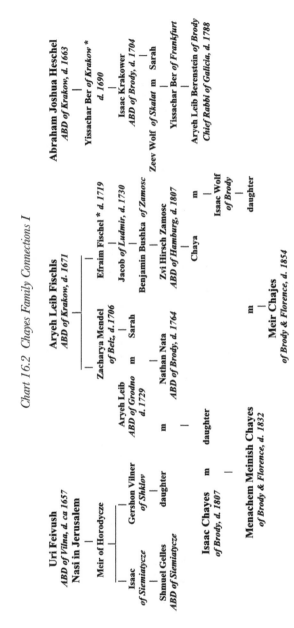

Notes

Uri Feivush was a son of David, Chief Rabbi of Vilna. Aryeh Leib (ben Zacharya Mendel Hanavi) Klausner was descended from the family of Judah Löw of Prague. After his marriage to Jutta, daughter of Efraim Fischel of Lvov (d. 1653), he was known as Aryeh Leib Fischls. The Fischel line goes back to fifteenth-century Frankfurt. Efraim ben Aryeh Leib Fischel of Ludmir married a granddaughter of Naftali Hirsch Katz of Frankfurt, a descendant of Judah Löw and Mirel Altschular. Abraham Joshua Heschel, scion of the Katzenellenbogen line from Padua and Venice, and Aryeh Leib Fischls were Chief Rabbis of Krakow.

* Their sons, Yissachar Ber of Krakow and Efraim Fischel of Ludmir, were Presidents of the Council of the Four Lands.

Chart 16.3 Chayes Family Connections II

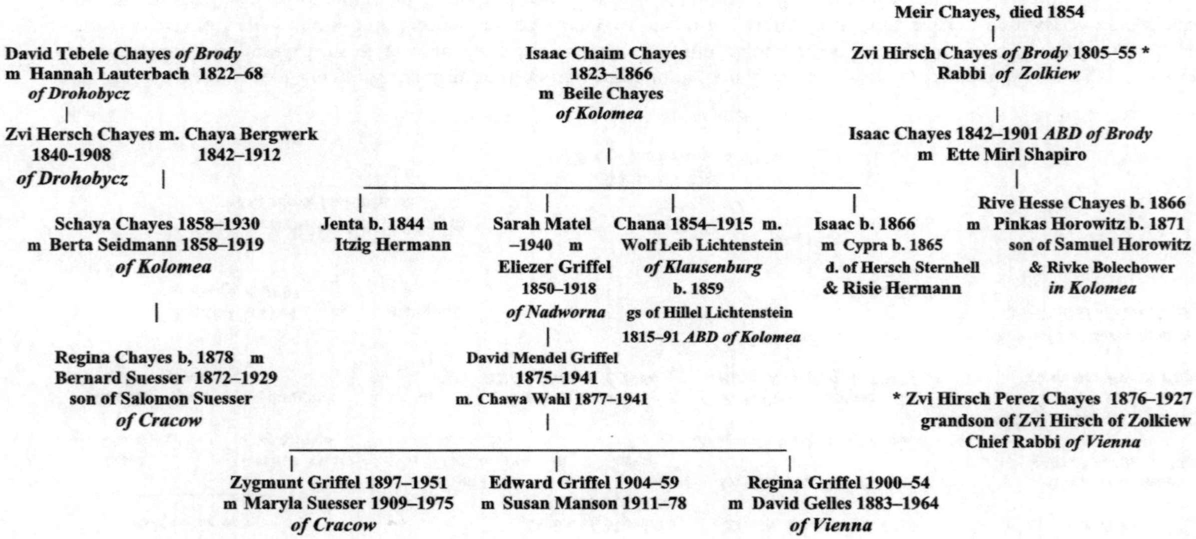

Meir Chayes, died 1854

Zvi Hirsch Chayes *of Brody* 1805–55 *
Rabbi *of Zolkiew*

Isaac Chaim Chayes 1823–1866
m Beille Chayes *of Kolomea*

Isaac Chayes 1842–1901 *ABD of Brody*
m Ette Mirl Shapiro

David Tebele Chayes *of Brody*
m Hannah Lauterbach 1822–68
of Drohobycz

Zvi Hersch Chayes m. Chaya Bergwerk
1840–1908   1842–1912
of Drohobycz

Rive Hesse Chayes b. 1866
m Pinkas Horowitz b. 1871
son of Samuel Horowitz
& Rivke Bolechower
in Kolomea

Isaac b. 1866
m Cypra b. 1865
d. of Hersch Sternhell
& Risie Hermann

Chana 1854–1915 m.
Wolf Leib Lichtenstein
of Klausenburg
b. 1859
gs of Hillel Lichtenstein
1815–91 *ABD of Kolomea*

Sarah Matel
–1940   m
Eliezer Griffel
1850–1918
of Nadworna

Jenta b. 1844 m
Itzig Hermann

Schaya Chayes 1858–1930
m Berta Seidmann 1858–1919
of Kolomea

David Mendel Griffel
1875–1941
m. Chawa Wahl 1877–1941

* Zvi Hirsch Perez Chayes 1876–1927
grandson of Zvi Hirsch of Zolkiew
Chief Rabbi *of Vienna*

Regina Griffel 1900–54
m David Gelles 1883–1964
of Vienna

Regina Chayes b, 1878   m
Bernard Suesser 1872–1929
son of Salomon Suesser
of Cracow

Zygmunt Griffel 1897–1951
m Maryla Suesser 1909–1975
of Cracow

Edward Griffel 1904–59
m Susan Manson 1911–78

Notes

The Chayes family spread from their base in Brody to other Galician towns and they also flourished in Tuscany. Meir Chayes was a merchant banker in Brody and Florence, and one of his sons was the famous Rabbi Zvi Hirsch of Zolkiew. Numerous family members in Kolomea included my great-great-grandfather Isaac Chaim Chayes.

The Drohobycz and Kolomea branches had connections including marriages with the Suesser family of Krakow.

Chart 16.4 Chayes Family Connections III: David Tebele name patterns

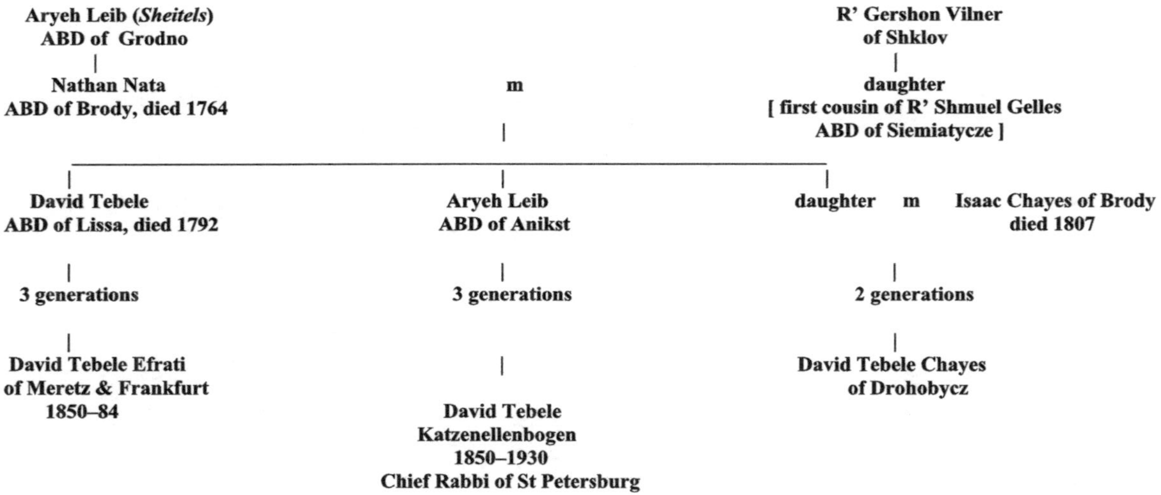

Aryeh Leib (*Sheitels*)
ABD of Grodno

R' Gershon Vilner
of Shklov

Nathan Nata
ABD of Brody, died 1764   m   daughter
[first cousin of R' Shmuel Gelles
ABD of Siemiatycze]

David Tebele
ABD of Lissa, died 1792

Aryeh Leib
ABD of Anikst

daughter   m   Isaac Chayes of Brody
died 1807

3 generations

3 generations

2 generations

David Tebele Efrati
of Meretz & Frankfurt
1850–84

David Tebele
Katzenellenbogen
1850–1930
Chief Rabbi of St Petersburg

David Tebele Chayes
of Drohobycz

Rabbi **David Tebele** of Brisk was a brother of the Chief Rabbi of Krakow, known as the Hoicher Rebbe Leib or Leib Fischls.

Two great-grandsons of Aryeh Leib Fischls were Nathan Nata, a Chief Rabbi of Brody; and Zvi Hirsch Berlin, who was known as Rabbi Hart Lyon while he was Chief Rabbi in London. The latter's grandson was **David Tebele** Berliner. The Chayes line clearly derives the name of **David Tebele** from the marriage of Isaac Chayes of Brody to the daughter of Nathan Nata ben Aryeh Leib.

Chapter 17

They met in Trieste

Christians and Jews in an ethnic melting-pot

WHEN THE AUSTRIAN EMPIRE was dismembered at the end of World War I, the city of Trieste, its ancient outlet to the Adriatic and Mediterranean seas, became part of the Kingdom of Italy. For centuries it had been a fascinating crucible where Austrians, Italians, Slovenes, Croats, Greeks, and Jews came together in a spirit of tolerance and in furtherance of mutual commercial interests.

This is the setting for the story of a Dalmation seafaring family, who established a shipping empire in Trieste. Diodato Tripcovich and Ermenegilda Pozza di Zagorje had a daughter who married Baron Geoffrey de Banfield, an Irish-Bohemian World War I hero in the Austrian service. Their son, Raffaello de Banfield Tripcovich, who was born in Newcastle upon Tyne, became a well-known composer. Diodato and Ermenegilda's two sons, Counts Mario and Livio Tripcovish, married Jewish girls, Sylvia Mordo of a wealthy Corfiote family, and Lucia Ohrenstein from Warsaw, a daughter of my great-aunt Rachel Wahl.

LUCIA WAHL OHRENSTEIN

There was an unusual range of personalities among my mother's first cousins – from Dr Jacob Griffel, the ultra-orthodox hero of World War II Jewish rescue to Lucia Ohrenstein, a leading light of the post-war Italian *dolce vita*.

Lucia was a Jewish girl from Poland who became an Italian countess and a prominent member of Rome café society. She died over 30 years ago, and it was by no means easy to gather the barest facts on her life.

My quest started in Vienna. The state archives, including the Austrian army records, led me to the family of our cousin Dr Abraham Low, who had become a well-known psychiatrist in Chicago and a pioneer of modern community mental health care. His mother's records in the Strasbourg municipal archives pointed to an origin in the little town of Tarnobrzeg north-west of Krakow in what was then part of Austrian Galicia. From the archives in Lviv and Sandomierz, I finally arrived at a full picture of my great-grandparents, Shulim Wahl and Sarah Safier of Tarnobrzeg. The Wahl family has an ancient history, claiming descent from a scion of the sixteenth-century Katzenellenbogen rabbis of Padua and Venice. Shulim and Sarah had six children, including my grandmother Chava (Eva) and my great-aunts Bluma and Rachel.

Rachel Wahl married Abraham Taube of Lemberg (Lviv). They were the grandparents of my second cousin, Tad Taube.

Rachel married again after being widowed and had a child called Luska. Little information was forthcoming on her second husband. His name was Ohrenstein and he was taken prisoner by the Russians in Lemberg during World War I and sent to Siberia. He returned to Poland after the war but died in the 1920s. Lucia, as she was called later, was reportedly born in Krakow around 1910 and became the wife of an Italian businessman in Warsaw. I heard that Lucia had fled to Italy at the outbreak of war in 1939, and that she had met and later married a Count Livio Tripcovich. Further research led me to the distinguished Triestine family to which Lucia's husband belonged.

THE TRIPCOVICH OF TRIESTE

The recent death of the composer Raffaello de Banfield Tripcovich marks the end of an epoch for that family. Raffaello de Banfield was born in Newcastle upon Tyne in 1922. He was the only son of Geoffrey de Banfield, scion of an Irish-Bohemian family in the Austrian service, who became a famous World War I air ace [1].

As the appended chart (17.1) shows, Raffaello's mother Maria was the daughter of Diodato Tripcovich, who came of an old Catholic family of seafaring folk from Dobrota on the Gulf of Cattaro. Diodato moved to Trieste in 1884 where he built up a highly successful shipping company that became a major force under the Italian flag after World War I. Following his death in 1925, the firm's helm was taken by his sons Mario and Livio and by their brother-in-law, Goffredo de Banfield. The latter developed the Tripcovich interests, such as salvage operations that included the clearing of the Suez Canal after the war of 1956.

Italian titles of nobility were conferred on the Tripcovich family in 1936, Diodato's eldest son Mario becoming a hereditary count while his younger siblings held personal titles. Raffaello de Banfield Tripcovich died without a direct heir, but his sister Maria Louisa de Banfield is married and has issue [2].

The fortunes of this family were intimately connected with those of Trieste. For more than 500 years this city gave the Austro-Hungarian Empire an outlet to the Adriatic and Mediterranean seas. For long it enjoyed the status of a 'free port' and enlightened Habsburg rule [3]. When the Empire disintegrated at the end of World War I, the city became part of the Kingdom of Italy. For centuries it had been a fascinating crucible where Austrians, Italians, Slovenes, Croats, Greeks and Jews came together in a spirit of tolerance and in furtherance of mutual commercial interests. The city's unique culture drew its flavours from north of the Alps as well as from an Italian, Dalmatian, and Byzantine mixture. This variety gave many Triestine families their cosmopolitan outlook and in due course led to marriages across ethnic and religious lines.

MARIO TRIPCOVICH AND SILVIA MORDO

Mario Tripcovich married a Mordo of the Corfiote family that had connections by marriage with the Pavia, Morpurgo, Segrè, and other distinguished Jewish families.

In the fifteenth century, one of Europe's foremost rabbis was Israel ben Pethahiah Ashkenazi Isserlein (*c.*1390–1460). He was known as Israel of Neustadt or Israel of Marburg after the towns near Vienna and in the Austrian province of Steiermark where he spent most of his adult life [4]. The border changes resulting from the two world wars found Marburg just inside the new Republic of Slovenia. Under its Slovene name of Maribor it cherishes its ancient Jewish relics. Israel of Marburg's progeny has flourished. In due course their family name became Morpurgo. By the early seventeenth century, they had advanced to the status of *Hof-juden* or Court Jews. They moved to Gradisca whence they proliferated and were later prominent in Trieste. The economist and poet Giuseppe Lazzaro Morpurgo (1762–1835) took a lead in the founding of the insurance company *Assicurazioni Generali* [5]. From this base, the company has grown to its present-day world status. Other Jewish families that were involved in the development of Triestine commerce included the Frigessi, father and son, who left their imprint on *Riunione Adriatica di Securta*.

THE JEWS OF CORFU

The Jews of Corfu were of separate Greek, Spanish, and Italian origins but in time overcame linguistic and liturgical differences. When all Jews were expelled from the Kingdom of Naples in 1541 many migrated to northern Italy, some taking the circuitous route via Corfu and the Dalmatian littoral. They led a privileged life on Corfu under the protection of the *Serenissima*. When Jews were expelled from Venice after the historic victory over the Ottoman Turks at Lepanto in 1571, those who came from Corfu received special exemption [6]. Their status was further enhanced during the brief period of French rule (1805–15), but the British protectorate (1815–63) was retrograde in that respect, and when the island became part of Greece in 1863 anti-Semitic disturbances occurred that resurfaced in 1891. This later period saw an exodus of many Jews, predominantly to Trieste, with which city they had enjoyed commercial links for centuries.

The Mordo were a Corfiote family of merchants and scholars. Lazare Mordo (1744–1823) studied at Padua and Venice and was a prominent physician and honorary rabbi of the island [7]. Marriage contracts (*ketuboth*) between the de Mordo and de Osmo families (dated 1812 and 1835) are among the Judaic treasures of the US Library of Congress [8]. Nineteenth-century records refer to Rietti Mordo of Corfu exporting olive oil to Trieste, and to Salamon Mordo, who traded in both wine and olive oil and also invested in commercial property [9].

The traffic between Corfu and Trieste might have brought Jewish merchants into early contact with shipowners from Ragusa and Cattaro like the Tripcovich, who also had age-old contacts with Venice [10].

In the years leading up to World War I, the Jews of Trieste tended to harbour irredentist sentiments. Ideas of self-determination that were widespread throughout the Austro-Hungarian Empire inspired the younger generation to see the city as part of a liberal Italian nation state. This naturally led to political, ethnic, and family tensions [11].

Mario Tripcovich was a young man at this time. He met and fell in love with Silvia Mordo, a daughter of Isaac Adolfo Mordo, a wealthy Jewish property owner of Trieste. He was the son of Raffaele Mordo (1822–94) and Carolina Morpurgo (1836–1906) [12]. Silvia's father forbad his daughter to marry a Gentile and threatened to kill himself if she persisted in her plans. James Joyce, who had been a house tutor to the Tripcovich family, acted as go-between for the lovers, and in 1917 Silvia married Mario in Zurich. Shortly thereafter, news came that Silvia's father had committed suicide after disinheriting her. The background to this tragedy may have involved problems in Trieste following the outbreak of war, such as the sequestration by the Austrian authorities of property belonging to those suspected of irredentist sentiments. Silvia Mordo's sister Anna later married Giacomo Treves de'Bonfili of Venice and returned to Silvia the rightful portion of her inheritance, which largely stemmed from her mother's Pavia family fortune.

Mario Tripcovich had a distinguished career in the management of the family shipping interests and served for a time as President of *Generali.*

LIVIO TRIPCOVICH AND LUCIA OHRENSTEIN

A generation passed and Europe was on the eve of World War II. Lucia Ohrenstein, who had married the director of the Warsaw branch of *Riunione Adriatica,* fled to Italy before the German invasion of Poland. She was in a position to help her mother, Rachel Wahl, and her half-sister Rega in their escape from Krakow to Rio de Janeiro via Trieste. Lucia had converted to the Catholic faith and sheltered for a time in a convent. She met Livio Tripcovich through her husband. After the latter's death her romance with Livio eventually led to marriage in 1947. Lucia's character had been shaped by the experiences of her childhood, when she had been left without a father at a tender age, and the privations and anxieties of the war years in Italy. When the clouds of war finally lifted, Lucia and Livio enjoyed a decade of *la dolce vita* in Rome, Venice, and Trieste. They entertained

Photo 28 Lucia Tripcovich (neé Ohrenstein) and husband, Count Livio Tripcovich

lavishly and Lucia mixed her aristocratic friends with stage and screen idols. Her cousins from the New World were warmly received. She and Livio often visited Monte Carlo, where they knew Princess Grace and befriended various celebrities.

Her journey from Poland to the melting-pot of Trieste is a tale that James Joyce might have appreciated [13].

REFERENCES

[1] www.atrieste.org/viewtopic – Goffredo de Banfield, known as *Der Adler von Triest*, was raised to the rank of *Freiherr* (Baron) by the Austrian Emperor and made a Knight of the Order of Maria Theresa in 1917 (see various internet sources on Trieste in World War I, on Banfield's World War I record and subsequent career, Irish soldiers in the Habsburg service, the Mumb von Muelheim family connection, etc.).

[2] Private correspondence with Maria Louisa de Banfield (www.trip-covich.com/Storia) (Tripcovich family titles go back to the Byzantine Empire and were reaffirmed in modern times by the King of Italy in 1936). Raffaello de Banfield (Baron Raphael Douglas von Banfield Tripcovich) 2 June 1922–7 January 2008. www.lipizer.it/conco/de banfield.

[3] Lois C. Dubin, *The Port Jews of Habsburg Trieste: Absolutist Politics and Enlightenment Culture*. (Stanford University Press 1999).

[4] Jewish Encyclopedia, 1904 edition – article on Israel Isserlein: www.jewishcommunity.si/jss/ENG-isser.asp.

[5] Cecil Roth, *The History of the Jews in Italy*. (Philadelphia: Jewish Publication Society of America 1946), p. 486.

[6] Idem, *The Jews of Venice*. (Philadelphia: Jewish Publication Society of America 1930), p. 313 [section on Corfu, pp. 310–31].

[7] Jewish Encyclopedia, 1904 edition, article on *Lazare Mordo*.

[8] Judaic Treasures of the Library of Congress. *The Jews of Corfu:* www.jewishvirtuallibrary.org/jsource/loc/Corfu.

[9] David Cesarani and Gemma Romain, *Jews and Port Cities 1590–1990*. (London: Vallentine Mitchell 2006), p. 183.

[10] Anna Krekic, *Alberi Genealogici*. (Trieste: Associazione Goffredo de Banfield 2007), pp. 82–3.

[11] Commune di Trieste: www.retecivica.trieste.it/joyce; articles on the website of Museo Joyce in Trieste and private correspondence with Erik Schneider.

[12] Vital records supplied by the municipal office (Commune di Trieste). Silvia Mordo's family data obtained by Livio Vizieri by courtesy of the Jewish Community of Trieste. Silvia was a daughter of Isaac Adolfo Mordo and Adela, daughter of Benedetto and Irene Pavia. Isaac Adolfo Mordo was the son of Raffaele Mordo and Carolina Morpurgo (who was a daughter of Isaac Morpurgo and Annetta Segrè).

[13] Edward Gelles, *An Ancient Lineage: European Roots of a Jewish Family*. (London: Vallentine Mitchell 2006) includes chapters on Wahl–Katzenellenbogen in Poland and Italy and on Lucia Ohrenstein. Rachel Wahl was a daughter of Shulim Wahl and Sarah Safier of Tarnobrzeg in Galicia. Rachel's second husband was Chaim Simon Ohrenstein. Attached: a family chart for Diodato Tripcovich and Ermenegilda Pozza di Zagorje. a photo of Count and Countess Livio Tripcovich.

My best thanks are due to a number of correspondents in Trieste and elsewhere, including members of the Tripcovich and Banfield families and my cousins who are descendants of Rachel Wahl from her first marriage to Abraham Taube.

Chart 17.1 Trieste at the crossroads: Tripcovich and Wahl Ohrenstein

Diodato Tripcovich
1862–1925
m
Ermenegilda Pozza di Zagorje
1870–1943

Rachel Wahl 1878 – 1965   m   Chaim Simon Ohrenstein 1881 – *ca* 1923

Lucia Ohrenstein 1910–1988
m 1947
Oliviero Tripcovich 1901–1958

Maria Tripcovich 1897–1976
m 1921
Geoffrey de Banfield 1890–1986

Raffaello de Banfield Tripcovich 1922–2008
brother of
Maria Louisa de Banfield 1927–

Mario Tripcovich 1893–1964
m 1917
Silvia Raffaella Virginia Mordo 1894–1978

Isaac Adolfo Mordo 1863–1917 m Adela Bersabea Benedetta Pavia 1869–1905

Footnotes

Diodato Tripcovich, shipping magnate of Trieste, descended from a Catholic seafaring family of Cataro who claimed ancient Byzantine title.

His wife Ermenegilda came from a Croatian family who held titles of Austrian nobility.

Geoffrey de Banfield (Gottfried von Banfield), of Irish–Bohemian extraction, was a World War I air ace (Der Adler von Trieste). He was raised to the rank of Freiherr and made a Knight of the Order of Maria Theresa (1917).

Raffaello de Banfield (Baron Raphael Douglas von Banfield Tripcovich), the distinguished composer, was born in Newcastle upon Tyne, England. He married Maria delle Grazie dei Conti Brandolini d'Adda in 1986 (who had issue from her first marriage to Count Leonardo Arrivabene Valenti Gonzaga).

Mario Tripcovich married Silvia Mordo, of an old Jewish family from Corfu.

The second wife of Oliviero Tripcovich was Lucia Ohrenstein of Krakow, whose mother's family claimed descent from Saul Wahl and the Katzenellenbogen rabbis of Padua and Venice.

Chapter 18

Rabbis and lawyers

A shared ethos

ABOUT A HUNDRED YEARS ago my paternal Gelles line in Vienna lost touch with relatives who had gone to America and only kept the most tenuous contact with the ultra-orthodox in eastern Europe. The new genealogical methodology, including internet searches for a variety of sources and DNA tests, has enabled me to identify and confirm old and forgotten family connections.

INTRODUCTION

In the nineteenth century, Rabbis Yehuda Ahron Horowitz, Hirsch Leib Weinstein, and Nahum Uri Gelles were connected by marriages in the little Galician town of Solotwina. Some grandchildren of my great-grandfather Rabbi Weinstein emigrated to America a hundred years ago. Two of their descendants were Philip and Howard Weinstein, who served in their country's armed forces during World War II and subsequently became successful attorneys in New York. Philip's son David Weinstein is a corporate lawyer and businessman who became a distinguished educationist in Boston.

My grandfather Rabbi Nahum Uri Gelles and Esther Weinstein had six children. Their eldest son, Efraim Fischel Gelles (given in some records as Fischel Kalman Gelles), trained for the rabbinate but died at a young age just after the end of World War I. A similar fate took his son Josef, who studied at the prestigious Lublin Sages Yeshivah. Efraim Fischel's brothers were my father David and uncle Max, who both became advocates. My father established himself in Vienna, graduating from its university in 1916. He brought his younger brother Max and sister Lotte to Vienna and supported them through their studies. All three gained the degree of Dr Juris. Max wrote a definitive commentary on Austrian Company Law which is now in its seventh edition. Thus the ancient rabbinic tradition was transmuted through emancipation, wars, and worldwide dispersion to these secular 'men of law'. Such family traits might indeed become another case study of the role of nature vs. nurture in the inheritance of special intellectual aptitudes [1].

FAMILY GENEALOGY

Contact between the American Weinsteins and my Viennese Gelles line was lost at the time of World War I, but I was able to arrive at an outline of our family connections in the nineteenth century from my study of Galician vital records, tombstone inscriptions, memorial books, newspaper extracts, family postcards, and other ephemera. This work is recorded in my books, as itemised in the appended notes.

The dates and places of birth and death of some children of Rabbi Hirsch Leib and Gittel Weinstein are shown in the first attached chart (18.1). These provide strong support for the identification of their mother Gittel as the daughter of Rabbi Yehuda Ahron Horowitz and his wife Miriam Rottenberg Margolies. Details of the latter couple's background, their movement from Solotwina to the neighbouring province of Bukowina and to Rabbi Horowitz's post as ABD of Saniawitz (Mihailenai) are given in several sources, such as Meir Wunder's encyclopedia *Meorei Galicia*. Miriam was a daughter of Gittel HaKohen Adlersberg and Zalman Berish Rottenberg Margolies of Brodshin [1–3].

For the later Weinsteins I have had the benefit of correspondence with Elaine Beth Weinstein and, more recently, with Susan Lee Weinstein. They are the daughters of Philip and Howard Weinstein, respectively.

DNA TESTS

Our family links are supported by autosomal DNA tests. I suggested to Susan Weinstein that the *Family Finder* test provided by FamilyTree DNA could confirm our consanguinity. Susan's DNA data and those previously obtained for myself and my 'Gelles' first cousin Elsa Schmaus matched, as set out in a later essay (Chapter 21). Total shared DNA, the largest shared segment (in centimorgans) and the genetic distance to the most recent common ancestor (MRCA) are consistent with the degree of kinship established by traditional genealogy. The three cousins share significant DNA on chromosomes 4, 12, and 22. Elsa Schmaus and I are three generations from our nearest common ancestors, Rabbi Hirsch Leib and Gittel Weinstein.

CONNECTIONS WITH CHASIDIC DYNASTIES IN GALICIA

The recent indexing of many Galician records now published on the JRI-Poland website of *Jewish Gen* has confirmed that the children of my uncle Efraim Fischel Kalman Gelles were descended on their mother's side from the Laufer rabbis of Nadworna. Some of these relationships emerge from the vital records of the Lustman family of

Boryslaw, where Rabbi Zvi Hersch Lustman became Chief Rabbi in 1870 [4].

Efraim Fischel Kalman Gelles was a son-in-law of the Boryslaw Rabbi. So was Rabbi Isaak Efrussi, scion of an Efrussi rabbinic line, as shown on the second chart (18.2) based on the vital records for Boryslaw, a brief extract from which is appended in Chart 18.3 [5]. Details of some of the Efrussi rabbis are given by Meir Wunder [6].

Esther Lea Lustman was the second wife of Efraim Fischel Kalman Gelles. The marriage records of Lvov show details of Efraim Fischel's first marriage to Chaja Sara Kretz in 1906 [7].

CONCLUSION

The immensely strong Chasidic background of Galician rabbinic families linked by centuries of intermarriage was of no avail to those who remained in eastern Europe and perished in the Holocaust, but their assimilated descendants in the West will continue to be sustained by their traditions, which are among the bulwarks of Judeo-Christian civilisation.

REFERENCES

[1] Edward Gelles, *An Ancient Lineage*. (London: Vallentine Mitchell 2006).
[2] *Idem, Ephemeral and Eternal: Josef Gelles, a brief life*. (Maastricht: Shaker Publishing 2010).
[3] *Idem, Meeting My Ancestors*. (Maastricht: Shaker Publishing 2011).
[4] Meir Wunder, *Meorei Galicia*, Vol. 3. (Jerusalem 1986), pp. 426–9.
[5] Searching for surname LUSTMAN in Lwow Wojewodztwo Boryslaw Births, Deaths, Marriages (Ukraine in Fond 300 in AGAD Archives).
[6] Meir Wunder, *Meorei Galicia*. (Jerusalem 1986), Vol. 1, pp. 260–7; Vol. 6, 118–19.
[7] DCJR, Digitised Collection of Jewish Records: Lvov 1906, Gelles, Fischel Kalman + Kretz, Chaja Sara.

Chart 18.1 Rabbis and lawyers: Gelles and Weinstein

Rabbi Israel Jacob Weinstein
of Solotwina

Rabbi Yehuda Ahron Horowitz m Miriam Margolies
moved from Solotwina to the Bukowina in 1858–59

Rabbi Hirsch Leib Weinstein
ABD of *Solotwina near Stanislau* (died 1884)

m

Gittel

Abraham
born *Solotwina* 1856 – died *Kolomea* 1904

Esther
born *Bukowina* 1860 – died 1907
m **Rabbi Nahum Uri Gelles** 1852–1934
ABD of *Solotwina* 1884–1934

Chaim
died *Solotwina* 1927
m Rivka Schechter

Sam Weinstein 1892–1977
emigrated to US in 1906
m 1917
Gussie Spiegel [1]
1893–1978
emigrated to US in 1908

Efraim Fischel Gelles [4]
1879 – ca 1920
m (1) Chaya Sarah Kretz
m (2) Esther Lea Lustman

Dr David Gelles [6]
1883–1964
Advocate in Vienna
m Regina Griffel

Dr Max Gellis [8]
1897–1973
Advocate in Vienna
m Nelly Leinkram

Howard Weinstein
1925–1974
Attorney in New York
m Ruth Framer [2]
1926–1978

Josef Gelles [5]
1912–1941/42
Boryslaw & Stanislawow
m – Spiegel in 1935

Dr Edward Gelles [7]
London

Elsa Schmaus
New York

Philip Weinstein
1922–2001
Attorney in New York
m Molly Rencoff died 1990
Prof. of Philosophy, Queens College NY

David C Weinstein [3]
Lawyer in Boston

Susan Lee Lipsitt
Boston

Footnotes

See Edward Gelles, *An Ancient Lineage* [1], chapter 28, *Meeting My Ancestors* [3], chapter 7, and private correspondence with **Susan Lee**, daughter of **Howard Weinstein** and **Elaine Beth**, daughter of **Philip Weinstein** (Elaine Beth Weinstein also has a law degree).

1 **Gussie and Clara Spiegel** were daughters of Shraga Feivush Spiegel of Solotwina. They married the brothers Sam and Jake Weinstein.

2 **Ruth Framer** was a daughter of Dr Abraham Framer and Molly Menaker, who was a daughter of Abraham Menaker and Lena Horowitz.

3 **David C Weinstein**, business executive, corporate lawyer, and educationist Doctor of Law, Boston University. Senior Fellow – Advanced Leadership Initiative at Harvard, Chairman, Board of Overseers at Boston College Law School and senior roles in other cultural and educational institutions.

4 **Efraim Fischel Gelles** and Bendet Spiegel were comrades in an Austrian army unit (*Juedische Zeitung*, Vienna, 12 May 1916). The name Efraim Fischel recurred in the family (cf. R. Efraim Fischel Horowitz, half-brother of R. Yehudah Ahron Horowitz). See Edward Gelles, *Family Connections: Gelles–Shapiro–Friedman* (Maastricht: Shaker Publishing 2009). Efraim Fischel, referred to in some documents as Fischel Kalman Gelles, married firstly Chaya Sara Kretz in Lwow 1906. His second wife was Esther Lea Lustman of Boryslaw by whom he had three recorded children, Aaron Leib, Josef, and Sara Gittel Gelles (see the following chart).

5 **Josef Gelles** married a Spiegel in Stanislawow. His bride was undoubtedly related to Bendet Spiegel and also to Gussie and Clara Spiegel. Josef was the brother of Giza (Gittel) Gelles (d. *c*.1941) and Leo Gelles, see Edward Gelles, *Ephemeral and Eternal: Josef Gelles, a Brief Life* [2].

6 **David Gelles**, Doctor of Law, University of Vienna, see Edward Gelles, *Family Connections: Gelles–Shapiro–Friedman*, Chapter 6 – Dr David Gelles, A Zionist in Vienna.

7 **Edward Gelles**, brother of Ludwig Gelles (1922–43), 1st cousin of Elsa Schmaus and 2nd cousin once removed of David Weinstein and Susan Lee Lipsitt, née Weinstein.

8 **Max Gellis**, Doctor of Law, University of Vienna, author of *Kommentar zum GMBH Gesetz* (Vienna: Linde Verlag), a definitive commentary on Austrian Company Law. Dr Max Gellis was also a distinguished amateur chess player – see Edward Gelles, *Meeting my Ancestors* [3], 'Family Chess Notes', pp. 73–4.

[ABD = Av Beit Din i.e. Head of Rabbinical Court/Chief Rabbi; R. = Rabbi]

R. David Isaac Gellis
Sarah
Narayov

R. Hirsch Leib Weinstein
Gittel
ABD of Solotwina

Josef Lustman
Lea
Skole

R. Aaron Leib Laufer
Chaje Beile
Nadworna

R. Nahum Uri Gelles
ABD of Solotwina   m   Esther Weinstein

R. Hersh Lustman
ABD of Boryslaw   m (2)   Mariem Jente Laufer
Nadworna

Chaja Sara Kretz   m (1)
in *Lvov* 1906

Efraim Fischel Kalman Gelles
1879– ca. 1920
Boryslaw   m (2)   Esther Lea Lustman
1879–

in *Boryslaw*
Aaron Leib Gelles
Josef Gelles
Sara Gittel Gelles

R. Yeshaya Wilf
Drohobycz

Blume Wilf
Drohobycz

Ruben Efrussi
ABD of Choloyow

R Hersh Lustman
ABD of Boryslaw   m (1)   Rifka Lustman

R. Isaak Efrussi   m   Moses Efrussi

Footnotes

Chief Rabbi Hersh Lustman of Boryslaw was the father-in-law of Rabbi Isaak Efrussi and of Efraim Fischel Kalman Gelles. Hersch Lustman married, firstly, Blume, a daughter of Rabbi Yeshaya Wilf of Drohobycz, who, according to Meir Wunder, was a highly regarded saintly rabbi, and secondly, Mariem Jente Laufer, a daughter of Rabbi Aaron Leib Laufer of the Nadworna Chasidic dynasty (the family name was rendered as Laufer or Leifer).

A daughter of the second marriage, Esther Lea, married Efraim Fischel Gelles. As can be seen from the above chart, their children, Aaron Leib, Josef, and Sarah Gittel were named after their great-grandparents. Sarah Gittel is most probably the Gittel or Giza given in my book *Ephemeral and Eternal* [2].

My immediate paternal Gelles line goes back to early eighteenth-century Brody to a scholar of the Brody Klaus known as Moses Gelles. The Efrussi rabbis of Cholyow are listed by Meir Wunder in *Meorei Galicia*, Vol. 1, pp. 260–7 and Vol. 6, 118–19. The Efrussi were also rabbis in Brody where they established the 'Efrussi Synagogue'. Wunder particularly mentions Rabbi Yehoshua Heshel Efrussi (*c*.1780–1852), who became ABD of Cholyow and had many followers. He was succeeded by Rabbi Ruben Efrussi, whose son Isaak married Rifke Lustman.

Other Efrussi rabbis include Rabbi Mordecai Efrussi (*c*.1860–1930) and Rabbi Yekusiel Efrussi (1880–1935), both Chasidic rabbis in Lvov.

As the eighteenth century drew to a close, changing social conditions and economic opportunities led many Galician Jews to Austria and Hungary, the Ukraine, to Odessa, and later to Baku. Edmund de Waal's best-selling book, *The Hare with Amber Eyes*, traces his Efrussi (Ephrussi) line back to Berdichev and Odessa.

Extracts from the recently published vital data on 'Lustman of Boryslaw' are attached in Chart 18.3. For those who are not familiar with Galician customs of those days, it should be pointed out that orthodox Jews often did not go to the trouble and expense of civil registration for many years after their religious marriage, by which time some of their children might have been registered under their mother's maiden name. Years of birth in civil registers of the period may also be inaccurate for several reasons.

Chart 18.3 Searching for surname Lustmann in Lwow Wojewodztwo

Boryslaw PSA AGAD Births 1878-86,88,89,94-98,1900-12
Deaths 1878-1912, Marriages 1886-1906,08-12
Lwow Wojewodztwo / Ukraine (records in Fond 300 in AGAD Archive) Located at 49°17' 23°25'
Last updated April 2014

Please note that some of the links to the AGAD Images are only APPROXIMATE and should be within a few pages of the correct image.
Use the scrolling arrow buttons at the bottom of each page to move forwards and backwards based on the year and akt number you want to view.

click to view	Surname	Given Name	Year	Type	Akta	Page	Event Date	Sygnatura	Sex	Age	Father	Father Surname	Father Town	Mother	Mother Surname	Mother Town	Spouse	Spouse Surname	Town	House	Comments
View		Chaim Ber	1881	B	183			35	M		Hersch	LUSTMANN		Marjem Jente	LAUFER				Nadwórna		
View		Moses	1883	B	56			37	M		Isak	EFRUSI		Rifke	LUSTMANN						

Given Name	Year	Type	Akta	Page	Event Date	Sygnatura	Sex	Age	Father	Father Surname	Mother	Mother Surname	Mother Town	Town
Ester Lea	1879	B	57	M	33		F	Hersch		LUSTMAN	Marjem Jente		LÄUFER	Nadwórna
Schaje Josef	1879	B	148	M	33		M	Isak		EFRUSY	Rifke		LUSTMAN	

Surname	Given Name	Year	Type	Akta	Page	Sygnatura	Sex	Age	Father	Father Surname	Mother	Mother Surname	Spouse	Spouse Surname
EFRUSI	Isak	1900	M	3		2100	M	40 y., 8 m.	Rubin	EFRUSI			Rachel	EFRUSI
LUSTMANN	Rifke	1900	M	3		2100	F	40 y.	Hersch			LUSTMAN	Blime	WILF
	Rifke	1905	B	229		2384	F			Hersch		LEWIN	Ester Lea	LUSTMANN
	Hendel	1911	B	94	32	2820	F			Natan		RINGEL/ROTH	Chaje Beile	LUSTMANN/LÄUFER
	Josef	1911	B	184	62	2820	M			Fischel Kalman v. Fischel		GELLES	Leicze	LUSTMANN
	Sara	1912	B	379	127	3007	F			Fischel		GELLES	Lea	LUSTMANN

PART 5

A brief look back to our legendary past

Chapter 19

Davidic descent

Historical impact of ancient myth

THE STORY OF King David and the myth of a divinely appointed and consecrated kingship hereditary in the seed of David was not only a part of European culture for many centuries, but with the concept of 'the divine right of kings' it was for long a potent reality of politics. The supposedly Davidic Jewish strain introduced into some ruling families in early medieval times is an aspect of an enduring genealogical interest in the subject that extends well beyond circles of biblical scholars and political scientists.

There is a grey area between legend and documented fact which should be of concern not only to antiquarians but also to serious genealogists and historians, at least in so far as ancient legends have sometimes cast a long shadow over subsequent periods of history.

For a long time most Jews believed that God had assigned rule over their people to King David and that the Messiah would be his descendant. Early Christians were at pains to advance a convincing Davidic pedigree for Jesus. The Jewish idea of a divinely appointed and consecrated kingship, hereditary to the seed of David, provided an inspiring model for the Christian rulers of Europe and had far-reaching political consequences, involving questions such as the divine right of kings and the limitation of their royal power. The legacy of the first great king of Judah and Israel was of significance in the medieval power game. It led to arguments between rival religious factions. It has also had a deep and lasting impact on Western literature and art.

Britain has given hospitality to a complex of legends and romances about the lost ten tribes of Israel, Joseph of Arimathea and the Holy Grail, the origin of the stone of destiny, and so on. They are all part of the religious culture of this country. Claims of Davidic descent for Britain's Royal House go back to ancient Irish chronicles and were elaborated by genealogists in the nineteenth century.

When Jerusalem was overwhelmed by the Babylonian king Nebuchadnezzar, most of the Jews were carried off into captivity. The story goes that two daughters of Zedekiah, the last Jewish king, managed to escape to Egypt with the prophet Jeremiah. After many wanderings they reached Spain. Thence the Princess Tamar or Tea Tephi, with the prophet and a small entourage, finally came to Ireland. They were said to have brought with them Hebrew heirlooms including the breastplate of the high priest and the stone known as Jacob's pillow, the stone of destiny that was later called the stone of Scone after the coronation site of Scottish kings. Tea Tephi married Eochaide the Heremon, who became High King of Ireland. From this royal pair the line of kings of Ireland and then of Scotland continued to Kenneth MacAlpine, followed by a long line of succession to the House of Windsor.

More than half a millennium before the great dispersion of the Jews that followed the destruction of the second temple, the Babylonian conquest gave rise to an outflow of refugees. Their settlements in Europe at such an early date are unsubstantiated, but these are not isolated legends. For example, a Jewish presence in Worms is mentioned by Benjamin of Tudela. The tale has been recounted that these Jews brought with them earth from the Holy Land and claimed that Worms and their synagogue had become their new Jerusalem and temple.

Echoes of the distant past are heard at our sovereign's coronation, when Handel's Messiah recalls Zadok, the priest of David, who anointed his son, Solomon. Zadok and the following high priests of ancient Israel were descendants of Aaron, the brother of Moses. The anointment of kings at their enthronement was only a part of the complex ritual, which evolved in ancient times, and which has been discussed at length by scholars such as Raphael Patai. Conferment of divine authority by the hands of the consecrating priest became a millennial practice at coronations in Europe.

The power thus supposedly conferred was demonstrated by English and French monarchs in the practice of 'touching for the king's evil' in order to heal scrofula, a tubercular condition of the neck. In England this royal ceremony persisted from the beginning of the second millennium into the eighteenth century. The Fitzwilliam Museum in Cambridge has a pierced gold 'angel' from the time of Charles I, a coin which was presented to sufferers by the king, to be hung round their neck as an amulet. Dr Samuel Johnson refers to one of the last of these occasions in the reign of Queen Anne.

It is no coincidence that the case for the divine right of kings came to the forefront of political discourse during the seventeenth century, which brought challenges to the absolutist pretensions of numerous rulers. King James I was an ardent supporter of the theory of divine right and wrote a book about it, while Charles I lost his head in its defence. In the hands of Bossuet and Louis XIV, theory and practice did better in France, at least for a while. The traditions of Davidic descent were an important part of such monarchical pretensions.

In earlier times, the Merovingian kings of France laid claim not just to Davidic descent, but harboured the idea of descent from Jesus himself, or at least from one of his brothers, who was supposed to have reached France and married into a local ruling family. Noble houses subsequently attempted to trace their lineage from this progeny. These assertions and rumours stirred up much religious antagonism and political rivalry during the early medieval period and are supposed to have contributed to the eventual downfall of the Merovingians and the rise of Charlemagne's house.

The Carolingians enjoyed the backing of the Roman Church, which was implacably opposed to the heretical views of those who propagated the Merovingian claims. These continued to strike a chord in later times within societies such as the Rosicrucians and Templars. The beliefs of these groups were heavily influenced by mystical ideas of Gnostic origins and were expressed with the frequent employment of Kabbalistic symbolism. A sceptical view of these fanciful tales does not conflict with recognition of their historical influence.

Assertions made for a number of European royal houses include, for example, that of the descendants of William, Count of Toulouse, whose mother was a sister of Charlemagne's father, Pepin. She is supposed to have married an eighth-century descendant of Babylonian Exilarchs, who were indubitably of the House of David.

Amongst many Jewish families the subject of lineage continues to fascinate. During the millennia of their dispersion and its countless persecutions, vital documentary material has been lost. While there are many claimants to a Davidic connection, there are almost always gaps in the chain of descent. From the time of the Babylonian captivity Jews survived there, and the descendants of the Exilarchs who led them can be traced for the best part of two thousand years until the trail is lost in medieval Spain. Undoubtedly, some Sephardic families had respectable claims. But ancient tradition and partial pedigrees do not amount to proof.

Among the good cases that have been made, a noteworthy recent publication by Moshe Shaltiel-Gracian sets out to trace his family from Princes of the Babylonian Exile to Spain and later to the Ottoman Empire, North Africa, Italy, and England. His studies combine ancient and medieval documentation, artefacts such as tombstones, seals, and escutcheons, and some DNA testing.

The claims of Ashkenazi families face equal difficulties. This is a subject that has naturally interested family historians and has even attracted some of the leading genealogists of the day.

One linchpin in links to the ancient past is the fifteenth-century Rabbi Jechiel Luria of Alsace. From him many old rabbinical families are descended, including the Katzenellenbogen of Padua. A long lost pedigree scroll of the Luria family is supposed to have confirmed their descent from Salomon ben Isaac of Troyes, the great scholar and bible commentator, who lived in the eleventh century and was known as Rashi. This pedigree includes members of other ancient rabbinical clans. From Rashi the ascent is deemed to go back to Johanan Ha-Sandelar, who lived in the second century of our era and came from the circle of Rabbi Akiba.

Johanan Ha-Sandelar was a fourth-generation descendant of the Babylonian Talmudic sage Hillel. The belief that Hillel was of Davidic lineage was expressed by Moses Maimonides in the twelfth century, relying primarily on passages in the Babylonian Talmud. There are other sources supporting the pedigree of Hillel and the connection of the latter to Rashi.

Second only to Rashi as a key figure in genealogical links with the ancient past is Judah Loew the Elder, the great-great-grandfather of the sixteenth-century Rabbi Judah Loew of Prague. Rashi and Judah Loew have been venerated for their wisdom and scholarship, and both have become figures surrounded with potent legends, as indeed were Hillel, Rabbi Akiba, and the sages of their day.

Numerous miracles are associated with the story of Rashi's life. Among the legends about his prophetic gifts, the best known is that of his meeting with Godfrey of Bouillon before the latter set out on the First Crusade.

Rabbi Judah Loew was known as the *Hohe Rabbi Loew* of Prague or the *Maharal*. He was a renowned scholar and a master of the Kabbalah, alchemy, and all other branches of arcane knowledge. He impressed both leaders and common people, who were prepared to credit him with supernatural powers such as the creation of the 'Golem', his servant, reportedly fashioned out of clay and brought to life through magical invocation. This was a time when both Jewish secret lore and alchemy were at the height of their influence and captivated the highest in the land, including the Emperor Rudolf II. Three generations later, the great Sir Isaac Newton was still interested in alchemy. The beginnings of modern chemical science were nearly two centuries in the future.

From ancient times, the potency of many kings, princes, prophets, and sages has been connected with the royal line of David. Legends that have had such an impact from the days of the Bible and the Talmud through millennia of European history surely belong to more than the outer periphery of our cultural inheritance.

My family, in common with many old rabbinical families, can claim descent from Rashi. Such claims might be based on links with Katzenellenbogen, Halpern, Shapiro, Chayes, and others going back to Luria and Treivish rabbis.

Nathan Nata Shapiro, the seventeenth-century Chief Rabbi of Krakow and author of the Kabbalistic work *Megaleh Amukot* (Revealed Depths) was of this company. The name of this scholar and mystic is connected with other legends. His tombstone in Krakow bears an inscription stating that he conversed regularly face to face with the Prophet Elijah. At the time this might have been meant as more than a figure of speech. It was believed that Elijah would put in an appearance to herald the coming of the Messiah.

Nathan Nata's ancestors include Shapiro, Luria, and the medieval Treivish rabbis of France. It is this family nexus which also leads to the line of the Katzenellenbogen of Padua and Venice, whose scion Saul Wahl was, at least according to family tradition, an ancestor of my Wahl grandmother. Certain rabbinical lines intermarried for centuries thus creating multiple connections. Our links with the forebears of Judah Loew are discussed in earlier chapters. Ascent from these figures to biblical times and to King David is discussed in articles that have appeared over the past decade or so, particularly in genealogical journals like *Avotaynu* in America and *Sharsheret Hadorot* in Israel.

BIBLIOGRAPHY: DAVIDIC DESCENT IN JEWISH GENEALOGY

Avotaynu

Einsiedler, David, 'Can We Prove Descent From King David?', Vol. 8, No. 3, Fall 1992.
Idem, 'A Seventeenth Century Luria Manuscript', Vol.7, No. 2, Summer 1991.
Idem, 'Descent From King David – Part II', Vol. 9, No. 2, Summer 1993.
Idem, 'Rashi's Descent From King David', Vol.8, No. 3, Fall 1992.
Idem, 'The (Maternal) Descent of Rashi', Vol. 9, No. 2., Summer 1993.

Rosenstein, Neil, 'A Response to Jacobi's Rashi Article', Vol. 6, No. 2, Summer 1990.
Tauber, Laurence S. , 'From the Seed of Rashi', Vol. 8, No. 3, Fall 1992.

Sharsheret Hadorot

Klausner, Yehuda, 'Torah and Jewish Genealogy', Vol. 15, No. 1, November 2000.
Shaltiel-Gracian, Moshe, 'Tracing a Davidic Line from Babylon to the Modern World', Vol. 16, No. 2, February 2002.

Moment magazine

Epstein, Nadine, 'King David's Genes', March/April 2012 (recent addition).

Other publications

Patai, Raphael, *The Messiah Tree. Jewish Legends of Three Thousand Years*. Wayne University Press. Reprint 1989

Miscellaneous subjects on the internet

Merovingian claims: Who Was Dagobert II? www.dagobertsrevenge.com/articles/dag.html
The Holy Grail: www.thedyinggod.com/holygrail.htm
The King's Evil: www.bbc.co.uk/education/medicine/nonint/renaiss/am/reamgs.shtml
http://www.fitzmuseum.cam.ac.uk/coins/CoinOfTheMoment/angel/angel.html
Queen Elizabeth II's descent from King David & the legend of Tamar, daughter of Zedekiah, King of Judah: www.bibleprobe.com/lineage.htm

Appendix
Onomastics and genetic genealogy

Some staging posts on the millennial journey of European Jews have been described in the preceding pages. The historical account of these episodes and of some of the individuals involved in them went hand in hand with genealogy, which often required recourse to a study of Jewish naming customs and name origins.

The study of genetic genealogy is still at an early stage of development but with refinements in available tests and the rapid growth of databases it will become an increasingly important adjunct to traditional methodology. I have looked at DNA data pertaining to a number of selected probands, both Jews and non-Jews, and found that these can have a significant bearing on previously raised historical and genealogical questions. I have therefore decided to publish a brief account of my pilot studies, notwithstanding the probability that advances in this new field may soon overtake the methodology if not some of my conclusions.

Some of the questions to which presently available commercial DNA tests can be addressed are illustrated in the following chapters:

- Y-DNA matches demonstrating the existence of a common ancestor in direct male line and giving an estimate of his genetic distance;
- finding genetic relationships between probands by studying autosomal and X-DNA matches – for example, testing the degree of relationship of probands with the same family name or indeed with different surnames but a tradition of kinship;
- using autosomal DNA data to obtain a rough idea of a proband's genetic admixture.

Chapter 20

Family names

The study of Jewish family names and their origins is an essential part of genealogical research. Many of these names changed during our millennial journey. They did not become universally settled until the end of the eighteenth and beginning of the nineteenth century. In earlier times, naming patterns varied in different parts of Europe. Members of the same family and even single individuals were sometimes known by more than one second name. Topographical and occupational origins, personal nicknames based on physical characteristics, changes from patronymic to matronymic within a given family line, siblings with different second names to distinguish their respective lineages, and many other onomastic curiosities all had a direct bearing on and contributed to an understanding of our history.

The study of family names and their evolution through the ages is an essential prerequisite for Jewish genealogical research. This chapter is about some of the names in my wider family circle.

Well over a thousand years ago, Greek, Hebrew, and Catalan versions of the 'good name', **Kalonymos**, **Shem Tov**, and **Bonnet** were passed down the generations in southern France and the Spanish March. The names implied distinguished and ancient descent.

Many of the rabbinic dynasties that formed the bedrock of Ashkenazi Jewry took permanent family names from the towns they came from in the Middle Ages. For example, the **Treivish**, **Shapiro**, **Halpern**, **Katzenellenbogen**, and **Landau** originally hailed from Trier, Speyer, Heilbronn, and eponymous towns in Germany. But most Ashkenazi Jews were known by patronymics. This practice was part of their ancient naming tradition.[1]

In later times, first names were adopted as family names, for example the German Hirsch, Wolff, Baer, and Loew (from Zvi, Zeev, Dov, and Aryeh, being the Hebrew names of stag, wolf, bear, and lion).

In some medieval towns, residents were called after the names of their houses. Examples are the *red shield* of the house of **Rothschild** in Frankfurt, the *goose* on the house sign of the **Gans,** and the *ox* that in German and Hebrew gave its name to the **Ochs** and **Schor** families.

Nicknames referring to personal characteristics were common from earliest times. Adaptation to the languages of different countries are shown by the medieval Hebrew Chalfan or **Halfan** (money changer) that became Wechsler or **Wexler** in German. The Jewish Wachsman or **Waxman** (candle maker or wax chandler) became Voskoboinik in Russian. There are many examples of such occupational name origins.

Different spelling customs and name suffixes characteristic of German, Czech, Polish, Lithuanian, and Russian Jews provide obvious clues for genealogical research.

Matronymics within old lineages may pose peculiar problems to genealogists, which DNA studies may sometimes clarify. For example, **Gelles** has been taken as a matronymic of the German medieval girl's name Geyle or Gele (yellow or fair-haired).

It was not until the end of the eighteenth and the early decades of the nineteenth century that the governments of central and eastern Europe were led by the exigencies of taxation and military conscription to impose compulsory registration of permanent family names on their Jewish subjects. In earlier times, Ashkenazi Jews, living in relatively small inward-looking communities, found traditional seemingly haphazard naming practice quite compatible with interest in their own and their neighbours' family connections.

Lineage (*yichus*) has been of importance to Jews since biblical times. Its religious significance is indicated by the age-old phrase 'may the merit of our ancestors protect us' with its implied obligation to be a credit to one's forebears. Rabbinic families in particular valued their lineage and tried to improve it by marriage. There were, of course, some distinguished rabbis or scholars of modest background, but very often they would strive to ally their children to one of these families. The recognition of inbred moral and intellectual qualities was part of the ethos of the Ashkenazi rabbinical elite. It led at times to the establishment of family dynasties in which rabbinical posts and other appointments passed unchallenged to sons or sons-in-law. It was a common occurrence for a promising pupil to marry his teacher's daughter and in due course to inherit his father-in-law's post. This preferment was not so much an exercise of nepotism as an accepted form of recognising talent and honouring the memory of predecessors. The name of a son-in-law might be changed to that of the father-in-law, but occasionally the two names would run side by side for several generations, as, for example, with **Munk/Horowitz**.

Incidentally, Chief Rabbi Meshullam Issachar Horowitz of Stanislau (1808–88), avowed that only members of his family should ever occupy his seat, and his dynasty did survive until World War II. Furthermore, about a dozen little *shtetls* around Stanislau, including Bohorodzany and Solotwina, often had rabbis who were Horowitz or were related to them by marriage.

Arranged marriages between rabbinic families of similar standing are exemplified by the union of Rabbi Samuel ben Mordecai Gelles, a grandson of Moses Gelles of Brody, with the only daughter of Rabbi Pinchas Shapiro of Koretz. The progeny of this marriage adopted the name of **Polonsky** after the town of Polonnoye in Ukraine.

Rabbis of pan-European standing whose influence reached across the continent included my eighteenth-century ancestor Samuel Helman, the Chief Rabbi of Mannheim and later of Metz. He gave one of his daughters in marriage to the son of Chief Rabbi David **Mirels-Fraenkel** of Berlin, another to Rabbi Eliezer Katzenellenbogen of Hagenau and Bamberg, a third to Rabbi Isaac **Rapaport** of Hanau, and a fourth to a grandson of Chief Rabbi Naftali Hirsch **Katz** of Frankfurt and Posen, who was of the ancient Kohanic (sacerdotal) line connected to the Horowitz and to the famous Rabbi Judah **Loew** of Prague. One daughter of Samuel Helman's eldest son, Rabbi Moshe of Glogau, married Jehiel Michael, a son of Asher Lemel **Halevi Segal**, the Chief Rabbi of Glogau and Eisenstadt, and another daughter was the wife of Moses Gelles, a grandson of the Brody scholar of that name. A daughter of Samuel Helman's younger son, Uri Feivush, who was in turn Chief Rabbi of Hanau, Lissa, Bonn, and Cologne, married Samuel, the son of Ezekiel Landau, the Chief Rabbi of Prague.

The progeny of Samuel Helman adopted the first name of Helman as a family name in the form of **Hillman**. Samuel Helman of Metz was traditionally taken to be the son of Israel Halpern of Krotoschin and grandson of Nathan Nata Shapiro of Krakow. He was in any case undoubtedly of the Halpern–Katzenellenbogen family nexus.

His contemporary Moses Menachem Mendel **Levush** of Brody married a daughter of Rabbi S(hmuel) Gelles, and was thereafter known as Moses Gelles. The use of an epithet such as Levush to indicate descent from the author of an important rabbinical work was quite common in certain parts before the era of obligatory family names. In this case, the ancestor was most probably Mordecai **Jaffe**, the sixteenth-century Chief Rabbi of Grodno, Prague, and Posen and author of *Levushim* (Rabbinical robes of learning). The immediate progeny of Moses Gelles were known by either or both names of Levush and Gelles.

The adoption of a mother's family name by her children was not unusual, particularly when her family was perceived to be of higher status by lineage, scholarship, or wealth. When Beile, a daughter of Isaac Horowitz (1715–67), the Chief Rabbi of Brody, Glogau, and Hamburg, married Rabbi Menachem Mendel **Rubin** of Lesniow and Lesko some of their issue opted to be known as Horowitz.

The first name of a female relative had been used as a second name in earlier times by Chief Rabbi Joel **Sirkes** of Krakow, who belonged to the Jaffe family, and Rabbi Samuel **Eidels** of Chelm,

241

Lublin, and Ostrog, who adopted the first name of his mother-in-law in appreciation of her support. A mother's first name was used as an epithet for Rabbi Aryeh Leib *Sarah*, an eighteenth-century Chasidic mystic. Occasionally a father-in-law's first name was added as an epithet, as in the case of Rabbi Moshe Reb Zelig of Brody, who married a daughter of Rabbi Ahron Zelig ben Yehuda Zundel Segal. An acronym of Rabbi Moshe Reb Zelig's (**Ramraz**) became the family name of his descendants. His son, Rabbi Yehuda Leib Zundel Ramraz, was a grandfather of Shalom **Rokeah** (1779–1855), the first of the Rokeah Grand Rabbis of Belz, and of Moshe Levush, aka Gelles, a great-grandson of Moses Gelles.

In old families, the descendants of siblings sometimes adopted different second names for their respective lines (e.g. **Fraenkel**, **Ornstein**, and **Ashkenazi**). Changes of name could distinguish progeny of a particularly important member of the main line or of the branch of a family that established itself in a new location.

Thus, the descendants through the male line of the *Maharam* of Padua, Meir Katzenellenbogen, were known by the eponymous name of the German town of their origin. The *Maharam*'s grandson, was known as Saul **Wahl**, and his Wahl–Katzenellenbogen descendants retained the epithet as a family name (Wahl meaning 'the Italian' in medieval German).

The noted Chief Rabbi of Krakow, Abraham Joshua **Heschel**, son of a Rabbi Heschel had progeny that used the Heschel name. This notable rabbi was descended through his father and mother from Saul Wahl and Saul Wahl's grandfather Meir Katzenellenbogen. Abraham Joshua Heschel's son was referred to simply as Yissachar Ber of Krakow. The latter's son was known as Isaac **Krakower**, after the city of his birth, though he became Chief Rabbi of Brody and the progenitor of a separate family called **Babad**. This name was an acronym of the Hebrew for 'sons of the Av Beth Din' (head of the Rabbinical Court) and rendered in the vernacular as **Rabinowitz**. So his family are sometimes referred to as Rabinowitz-Babad.

The Horowitz family are believed to be a sprig of the Shem Tov Halevi of Gerona (Levites of the Good Name), who were allied with a number of other ancient families such as the **Benveniste**. From the Spanish March and Provence a family of these Levites found their way to Bohemia in the late fifteenth century and settled at the little town of Horovice near Prague from which they took their new name.

The Halevi Ish Horowitz (the Levites, men from Horovice) flourished in Prague and subsequently in Krakow and elsewhere. They married with other leading Prague families.

Of particular interest in the present study are their marriages with the Chayoth (**Chayes**) family, whose Isaac ben Abraham Chayes had been a Chief Rabbi of Prague and whose sister was the first wife of the famous Rabbi Judah Loew.

The Chayes family, like the Horowitz, had ancient roots in Iberia and Provence. A branch of this family were called **Altschuler** after the Prague synagogue they helped to build with stones of their old prayer house which they had brought from Provence (*Schul* = the German word for school, which is Yiddish for synagogue).

A daughter of Judah Loew and Mirel Chayes-Altschuler married Isaac ben Samson Katz, of the millennial sacerdotal family. From the offspring of that marriage there descended Katzenellenbogen, **Margolies**, **Fischel**, **Zausmer**, and Horowitz lines. In the glory period of Prague Jewry that extended into the first part of the seventeenth century, Gelles are also recorded in that city and on its tombstones. One tombstone refers to the honourable Rabbi Mendel, son of Zalman Gelles, emissary of the *Beth Din* (the Rabbinical Court). Other tombstone inscriptions refer to Gelles Katz. The Katz (**HaKohen**) connect a number of families that mingled in sixteenth-century Prague and came together again in eighteenth- and nineteenth-century Galicia.

My mother's family name of **Griffel**, being the German word for the writing implement called stylus in Latin, suggests that they had an ancestral maker or user of the same. The names of my maternal grandmother and great-grandmothers were Wahl, Chayes, and **Safier**. Close cousins on this side of the family included Low and **Taube**.

In view of the variety of ways surnames developed over the centuries, it is not surprising that there are numerous instances of families sharing the same or a very similar surname who are not closely related. For example, if Gelles is a matronymic indicating descent from Gele or Geyle, a not-uncommon German/Jewish name, various families could be descended from different ladies called Geyle.

Referring again to another example from my family, our cousinly Gelles–Shapiro line adopted the family name of Polonsky after the town of Polonnoye in Ukraine, but there are other Polonsky families of quite different origin.

The derivation of some of the above-mentioned 'family' names can be categorised as follows.

Ancient descent

Kalonymos, Shem Tov, HaKohen, Halevi, *from kings, prophets, ancient priests and their attendants*

Babad, Levush, etc., *from specific distinguished rabbis*

Country of origin

Fraenkel, *from Germany (Frank = Ashkenaz)*, pan-European branches including Teomim-Fraenkel, Mirels-Fraenkel, and Fraenkel-Heller-Wallerstein

Wahl, *from Italy – descent from Katzenellenbogen of Padua and Venice*

Towns of origin

Katzenellenbogen, Treivish, Shapiro, Halpern, Landau, Horowitz, Krakower, Polonsky – see text

Luria, *of Italian origin and linked with Katzenellenbogen, Shapiro, and Treivish back to Kalonymos*

Epstein, *after the town of Eppstein and perhaps descended like the Horowitz from Shem Tov Halevi and Benveniste*

Oppenheim(er) and Wertheim(er), *after Oppenheim and Wertheim in the Rhineland*

Rapaport, *from the Renaissance union of German Rapa [raven] and Italian family from Porto*

Zausmer, *from the Jewish name for Polish town of Sandomierz*

House signs

Rothschild, Gans, Schor, *red shield, goose and ox*, see text

Stern, Spiegel, Schloss and many others derived from house names in Frankfurt – see Chapter 21

Occupational connections

Griffel, *stylus*, see text

Safier, *from sapphire (a sapphire was one of the 12 precious stones set in the ancient high priest's breastplate symbolic of one of the 12 tribes of Israel)*

From a male first name

Hillman, Ramraz, see text

Benveniste, *Sephardic first name and also family name, e.g. Benveniste ibn Benveniste of Saragossa, fl. c. 1200, held the Jewish title of Nasi and was an envoy to the King of Morocco*

From a female first name

Eidels, see text

Margolies (Margulies, Margolioth), *from Margole (Pearl), daughter of Naftali Hirsch Shor*

Matronymic

Sirkes, see text

Taube, *child of Taube (German–Yiddish girl's name meaning dove)*, ditto the name Taubes and Taubman, but the latter can have other derivations

Gelles (Gelles, Gellis, Gelis, etc.), *from child of Geyle (medieval German Jewish girl's name meaning the fair-haired)*, but see below for other derivations of the name

Chayes, *from child of Chaye*, but according to the legend of this ancient rabbinic family, who trace their name back to their Portuguese and Provencal roots before they came to Prague and thence to Galicia and became known as Chayes (Chajes), their original Hebrew name of Chayyut was a nickname with the meaning 'wild animal' that was given to four brothers whose commonly used first names were those of the four animals, namely the lion (Aryeh), the stag (Zvi), the wolf (Zeev), and the bear (Dov)

Topographic

Popper, *after the river Poprad (Popper)*

Tauber, *after the river Tauber*, cf. matronymic Taube or Taubes of different derivation

Miscellaneous

Altschuler, see text

Loew, *from the lion, symbol of the tribe of Judah*

Jaffe, *Hebrew meaning 'beautiful' with various spellings ancient family in medieval Spain and Northern Italy, in the fifteenth century to Bohemia and thence to Poland*

Mordecai Jaffe of Prague, *whose descendants had a variety of names, viz Jaffe, Levush (as in Gelles–Levush) and Itzig (as in the family of the eighteenth-century Court Jew Daniel Itzig – see Chapter 15)*

MORE ON GELLES NAME ORIGINS

Transliteration from the Hebrew into the vernacular produced variant spellings of my family name in seventeenth- to twentieth-century Jewish and civil records. These included Gelles, Gellis, Geles, Gelis, Guelis, or Gillies. These variants within one and the same family may confuse latter-day readers but was fully understood within Jewish communities. The principal reference works on Jewish onomastics (such as those by Beider and Guggenheimer) take the Gelles name to be a matronymic of the medieval German or Yiddish Geyle or Gele. I have no doubt that some Gelles families are indeed descended from an ancestral Geyle. Such a family may be the Gellis from Grodno who emigrated to the Holy Land and have now been there for over ten generations (see my first book, *An Ancient Lineage*, London 2006, pp. 317–19).

My historical reading indicates that some Gelles ancestors flourished in sixteenth- to eighteenth-century Prague. Some of these Gelles later moved to Lithuania. So did Jaffe descendants of Mordecai Jaffe of Prague. The Levush, as he was known after the title of his magnum opus, became in turn Chief Rabbi of Grodno in Lithuania, Prague in Bohemia, and Posen in Silesia. Gelles and Jaffe were both in Grodno, moved north to Kretinga, Gorzd, and other towns near the Baltic coast, to Memel in East Prussia, then westwards to Silesia and Germany. Around 1700, some Lithuanian Jews went south to Galicia. Among these were Gelles who flourished in Brody for a couple of centuries, and spread further afield to Ukraine, the Bukowina, Austria, Hungary and the Burgenland, Moldavia, and to Odessa on the Black Sea. The incidence and approximate dates of the Gelles name in central and eastern Europe is shown on a chart in Chapter 11.

Tracing my Gelles ancestors back from Bohemia becomes more speculative and so does the derivation of the Gelles name. The migration patterns of related families suggests that the European part of our millennial migrations in earliest times began in Italy and the Rhineland, the Iberian peninsula, and southern France, and that the migrations of the Norsemen, the history of the Crusades, and the expulsions of Jews from Spain and Portugal were major factors in taking us to Holland and Britain in the west and to eastern Europe including the Ottoman Empire in the east.

Possible linchpins in our journey from the historical and onomastic perspective may include St Gilles (between Nimes and Arles) in the south of France, where there was a Jewish rabbinical Yeshivah, and the nearby Abbey of Gellone (St Guilhem-le-désert) associated with the name of Charlemagne's cousin William of Gellone, aka Guillaume d'Orange (755–812), Count of Toulouse, who was a grandson of Charles Martel. His lineage, according to ancient writings, was believed to have been linked to that of descendants of Jewish Exilarchs from Baghdad who were of royal Davidic descent (see Chapter 1 on the Kalonymos of Narbonne).

My paternal Gelles forebears in later times were related to a nexus of families descendant from Samuel Oppenheimer, whose geographical origins included the land between the old Duchy of Guelders–Gelderland – and North Rhine–Westphalia (see Chapter 15 and notes on Cleves and on Heinrich Heine's connections through his maternal van Geldern).

The name of Gelles with variant spellings was found in the British Isles from the time of the Norman conquest and seems to have had several different origins. Possible links to the Low Countries appear to be of particular interest in so far as my ancestral background shows traces of early genetic connections that have so far not been fully explored by traditional genealogical methodology. Chart 20.1 (in the colour plates between this chapter and the next) shows my ancestral origins across Europe as derived from autosomal DNA tests by FamilyTree DNA. I go into more detail of my genetic admixture in a later chapter, but the chart indicates that my DNA matches in the United Kingdom and the coastline of Northern France and the Low Countries are genetically significant, but, amounting as they do to no more than a few per cent of my total admixture, go back many hundreds of years.

GELLES IN YORKSHIRE AND THE LOW COUNTRIES

The sources at the end of the chapter refer to some of the records relating to a Gelles family who had connections with York, Bradford, Wakefield, Pontefract, and other places in the West Riding of Yorkshire, extending over a period from the fourteenth to the sixteenth centuries, a period that coincided with the most important time for

English commerce with the Low Countries in which the wool trade was paramount.

This family was quite possibly from Hainault or Brabant. According to articles on the history of Vorst, the first houses built in this forested area south of Brussels along the Geleysbeek, a tributary of the Zenne, date from the seventh century. The village's first church was dedicated to Dionysius (Denis) the Areopagite. In the thirteenth century, the Romanesque church of Saint Denis was rebuilt in the newer Gothic style. These details strike a chord with the references to Sir Dionysius or Denis Gelles of Bradford.

Towns in Yorkshire such as Bradford, and Ghent, Bruges, and Ypres in Flanders and in Hainault played significant roles in this period, and not only in economic life but also in the family fortunes of our Plantagenet kings. King Edward III and his Queen Philippa, descendant of Counts of Hainault and Holland and of St Louis IX of France, took personal interest in furthering economic ties with the continent. Their son, John of Gaunt, Duke of Lancaster, was born in Ghent. He and some distinguished descendants from his marriages to Blanche of Lancaster, the Infanta Constance of Castile, and Katherine Swynford have some bearing on this family story. John of Gaunt and his first wife Blanche were both descended from Henry II Plantagenet and Eleanor of Aquitaine. Blanche of Lancaster's ancestry included Earls of Leicester and Earls (and a Duke) of Lancaster. She brought vast estates to her marriage. These included the manor of Bradford, which later passed for a time to the Beaufort descendants of John of Gaunt and Katherine Swynford, a daughter of Paon de Roet, also referred to as Sir Gilles de Roet of Hainault, knight and herald, who became attached to the court of King Edward III. The Beauforts became earls and dukes of Somerset.

Gelles came to the fore in Yorkshire in the fifteenth century. Dionysius Gelles, chaplain, is mentioned in local records. He was appointed Vicar of Bradford in 1432 and was followed there by his nephew Henry Gelles in 1464. Both were recommended by the College of Leicester. Some of their old family connections are indicated in the appended references. Henry Gelles studied at Oxford University and was one of two scholars of that name who became principals of schools linked to major Oxford colleges.

Their church preferments indicate, at the very least, their adherence to the House of Lancaster in the dynastic struggles of that period.

The Yorkshire connections extended beyond Bradford and Wakefield. Thomas Swynford, a son of Katherine Swynford by her first marriage, was Constable of Pontefract Castle. William Gelles was a bailiff and later Robert Gelles served as mayor of Pontefract.

The latter helped to put down a local rebellion a few years after the battle of Bosworth. In 1492, Thomas Howard, Earl of Surrey, fought a pitched battle and defeated the insurgents at Ackworth. Elizabeth, the widow of Robert Gelles, is recorded as having received a grant of £13.18s.8d in recognition of her husband's assistance.

The Gelles connections in West Yorkshire appear to go back to the late fourteenth century. In 1402 Gelles was associated with del Chaumbre (later Chambers or Chamberlain) as plaintiffs in a court action. The latter name evolved from the 'valet de chambre' of the royal households. The herald Sir Gilles de Roet was called a 'knight of the chamber'. His daughter Katherine, the third wife of John of Gaunt, had a sister Philippa, whose husband Geoffrey Chaucer was referred to as 'of the king's chamber'.

It is possible that there is a Gelles connection with the later Gelles line descended from an Agnes Chambers in Angus, but the Gelles name, at least in this line, could also be related to the Baltic trade that flourished in 17th century Scotland.

REFERENCES

GELLES in medieval Oxford

A.B. Emden, A Biographical Register of the University of Oxford to AD 1500 (Oxford, 1957).

Entries for Gelles on page 754:

Gelys, John M. A. (a recent immigrant according to the University Register), Rector of school rented from Exeter College, 1390.

Gellys, Henry (**Gelles, Gellis, Gyllys**) M.A., adm 1450, B.A.,Ordained 1452, Keeper of the Four Keys Chest 1457
Principal of Staple Hall (attached to Lincoln College) 1458
Vicar of Bradford 1464 to his death in 1476
Nephew of Sir Dionysius Gelles (v.i.)

Gellys, Thomas plaintiff with Henry Gellys and Richard Lancastre before the Chancellor's Court 1463 when they were granted a cession of debt 'ad exhibiciones suas in Universitate Oxonie'

Entry for Lancaster on page 1089:

Lancastre, Richard (Lancaster, etc.) M.A., Queens College, BA 1456, Ordained 1462, chaplain 1464–67, fellow 1467–68, Vicar of Tadcaster, Yorkshire 1468–69, subsequently Rector and Vicar in Dorset and Hants. Died 1507

GELLES in medieval Yorkshire

Index of Wills in the York Registry – internet archive www.archive.org/stream/ indexwillsinyor01collgoog/indexwillsinyor01collgoog_djvu.txt
   Gelles, Sir Dionysius, chaplain, Adm, 4 252., Henry, M.A. Vicar of Bradford, Mar. 20, 1475. 4 106 Aug.25, 1476., Thomas, Pontefract, Adm. 4 237.

Henry VI, Vol. 5, p. 726 [index] – SDRC sdrc.lib.uiowa.edu/patentrolls/ h6v5/index/Henry6vol5page0726.pdf
   Gelles, Gellis, Denys or William, Vicar of Bradford ... **William**, of Bradford or Pontefract, draper, 317. commissioner,. 443.

Full text of 'The History and Topography of Bradford' – internet archive archive. org/stream/historyandtopog00jamegoog/historyandtopog00jamegoog_djvu.txt
   Henry Gelles, M.A., Vicar of Bradford, (Will proved 2nd April, 1476) gave his soul as above, and bis body to be buried in the chancel of *Bradford* church.
   Sir Dionysius Gelles became Vicar of Bradford in 1432 and was succeeded by his nephew **Henry Gelles** in 1464. The latter's Will identifies **William Gelles** as his brother and **Thomas Gelles** as the latter's son.
   In the Continuations and Additions to the History of Bradford it is recorded that the manor of Bradford was held by John of Gaunt, Duke of Lancaster and his first wife Blanche and in the fifteenth century it was held briefly by Beaufort descendants of John of Gaunt and his third wife Katherine Swynford.

From 'Yorkshire Fines – 1546–50', pp.120–53, Francis Collins (editor) (1887)
   Thomas Gelles, gent. Messuage or burgage in Wakefeld. (British History Online – www.british-history.ac.uk.)

Figure 20.1 Ancestral origins of Edward Gelles according to Family Tree DNA tests confirming traditional genealogy of Ashkenazi Jewish roots in central and eastern Europe and earlier roots in a large swathe of southern Europe but also revealing traces of ancestral matches in the Low Countries and the British Isles

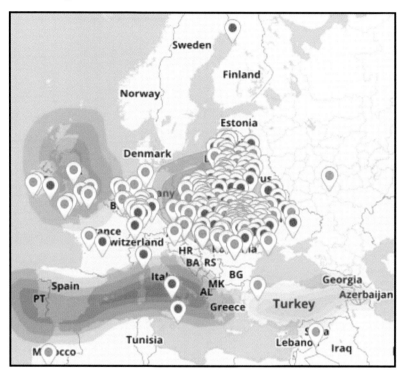

Shaded areas indicate regions of ancestral origins. Orange and green dots show locations of the most distant known paternal and maternal ancestors of those having significant autosomal DNA matches with Edward Gelles on the Family Finder database.

Chart 21.8 Ancestry of Edward Gelles through paternal grandparents

Halpern–Shapiro	Jaffe– Gelles–Weinstein	Horowitz	Margoliouth	Halpern–HaKohen

Halpern line

R. Moshe Heilprin
of Berdichev & Solotwina
d. 1752
m Mindel Katz, desc. of
R. Shabbatai Katz

four generations
of Katz rabbinic line

R. Isaac Dov Ber Margolioth
of Jaslowitz
m granddaughter of
Jacob of Posen & Shprintze Katz
desc of Saul Wahl & Judah Loew

R. Jacob of Tlust

R. Isaac Horowitz
ABD of Brody, Glogau
and Hamburg, d. 1767
m Reitze Babad of Brody

R. Eliezer Lipman Halpern
of Lvov

R. Israel Halpern
m Lifsha Shapiro
?

R. Shmuel Helman
ABD of Metz, d. 1764

R. Moses Gelles
of the Brody Klaus
aka Levush (Jaffe)
grandfather of Moses Gelles

Beile Horowitz
m R. Rubin, d.1803
ABD of Lezniow & Lesko

R. Abraham Mordecai Margolies
of Ustechko

Gittel Hakohen Adlersberg
d. 1862

Zalman Berish Rottenberg   m
Margolies of Brodshin

Mordecai Gelles
and siblings

R. Jacob Jokel Horowitz
ABD of Bolechow, d. 1832

Miriam Margolies

R. Moshe of Glogau

daughter
m R. Moses Gelles

R. Israel Jacob Weinstein
of Solotwina

R. Yehuda Ahron Horowitz
of Solotwina, ABD of Mihaileni

m ?

Gittel Horowitz

m

R. David Isaac Gellis

R. Zvi Aryeh Weinstein
ABD of Solotwina, d. 1884

m

Esther Weinstein
1861–1907

R. Nahum Uri Gelles
of Glina & Brody
ca 1790–1868

ABD of Solotwina
1852–1934

Dr. Max Gellis
1897–1973

Dr. David Isaac Gelles
1883–1964   *Advocates in Vienna*

Elsa Gellis Schmaus
1929–

Dr. Edward Gelles
1927–

ABD = Head of Rabbinical Court / Chief Rabbi
Katz = Acronym for Kohen Zedek (Righteous Priest)

Gelles male line –subject of Y–DNA tests
Female line –from whom some X–DNA can reach
cousin Elsa but not Edward Gelles

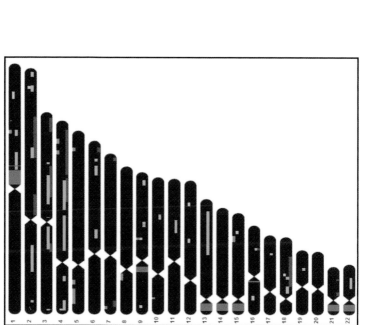

Chart 22.3 Autosomal DNA matches (above 5 cM) of Thaddeus N. Taube with Nosson Wahl (orange), Shawn Weil (blue), Edward Gelles (green), and Marilyn Low Schmitt (pink)

Chart 22.4 Autosomal DNA matches (above 5 cM) of Elsa Schmaus with Nosson Wahl (orange), Susan Lee Lipsitt (blue), and Edward Gelles (green)

Note matches between Nosson Wahl and Edward Gelles

Chart 22.5 *Autosomal DNA matches (above 5 cM) of Nosson Wahl with Jeffrey D. Wexler (orange), Bruce Fetter (blue), Elsa Schmaus (green), Peter A. Pitzele (pink), and Sandra Aaronson (yellow)*

Feet of Fines: CP 25/1/279/149. Number 30 www.medievalgenealogy.org.uk/ fines/abstracts/CP_25_1_279_149.shtml

3 Henry IV 27 January 1402. Plea of Covenant: A moiety of the manor of Kelfield.

Parties to the action: Nicholas Gascoigne, Richard Gascoigne, Robert de **Gelles** ('thorp'), chaplain, William Scotte, Henry del Chaumbre and John del Chaumbre querents, and William de Ryther, knight, and Sibel his wife, deforciants

Index of Wills in the York Registry www.archive.org/stream/indexwillsinyor 01collgoog/indexwillsinyor01collgoog_djvu.txt

482., Peter, **Colthorp**, gentleman, Adm. 455. 5.Ardern ... **Gellesthorp, Robert, Rect. of Burwales Gelsthorp, Henry, Merston (bur. Hoton)**

Pontefract and Ackworth www.ackworth.w-yorks.sch.uk/ack/lhistfd.html

William Gelles, recorded as bailiff of Pontefract in 1439.

Robert Gelles, was mayor of Pontefract. He helped to put down an insurrection at Ackworth in 1492.

Chapter 21

A study in genetic genealogy

COMMERCIALLY AVAILABLE DNA tests are becoming a routine part of genealogical research. The support such tests can give to traditional methodology is illustrated in Chapters 21 and 22, mainly by studies of Y-DNA and autosomal DNA matches.

Chapter 21 focuses on comparisons between cousins of my paternal Gelles line with more distant connections, while Chapter 22 is concerned with my maternal grandmother's Wahl family and eponymous probands.

INTRODUCTION

The support that commercially available DNA tests can now provide for traditional Jewish genealogy is illustrated in this essay, which deals with aspects of my family background.

Jewish genealogy in Europe has its peculiar difficulties. A primary obstacle is the loss of many written records and the destruction of tombstones during the Holocaust. Another problem area is the fluidity of second names in earlier times. Only a small minority had family names that passed down the generations. During certain periods, the adoption of a father-in-law's name was quite common. There was also a genealogical problem with second or third marriages at a time when many young mothers died in childbirth. Surviving records for wives and children have often been dispersed and uncertainty sometimes persists as to the attribution of a husband's recorded progeny to separate known wives.

Some of these issues can be addressed by various DNA tests. It should be emphasised that these tests are not likely to be very revealing in isolation. However, when applied to a group of related probands and accompanied by 'paper-trails' of family background, they can make a valuable contribution to genealogical research.

GENEALOGICAL BACKGROUND

The founder of the eighteenth-century Chasidic movement (the *Baal Shem Tov* or 'Master of the Good Name') considered the Shapiro, Horowitz, and Margolioth to be of specially distinguished lineage. Other families such as the Luria, Treivish, Halpern, Jaffe, Loew and Katzenellenbogen are worthy of that company. The priestly *Kohanim* and the *Levites* have special places in Jewish history and genealogy. The ancient priestly caste and their assistants were called HaKohen (Kahane or by the acronym Katz standing for Kohen Zedek or 'righteous priest') and Halevi (also Halevi Segal or simply Segal, meaning the Levite 'assistant to the priest'). Prominent rabbinic families of priestly descent include the Hakohen Rapaport, while Levitic families include the Halevi Horowitz and Segal Landau.

The paternal and maternal lines of my ancestry are linked in many ways. My maternal grandmother and a great-grandmother were from the Wahl and Chayes (Chajes) families. The Katzenellenbogen, who originally hailed from the eponymous town in Hesse-Nassau, were Chief Rabbis in Renaissance Padua and Venice. Their scion, Saul ben Samuel Judah Katzenellenbogen, known to history as Saul Wahl, played a significant role in the sixteenth-century Polish–Lithuanian Commonwealth. His later descendants included Moses Mendelssohn, Karl Marx, Martin Buber, Isaiah Berlin, Felix Mendelssohn-Bartholdi, Yehudi Menuhin, and many others [1].

The Chayes journeyed from Portugal to Provence, Bohemia, Poland, Italy, and Austria. The sixteenth-century Chief Rabbi of Prague, Isaac ben Abraham Chayes, was followed by a dozen rabbis of his family, ending with Hirsch Perez Chajes, the Chief Rabbi of Vienna between the two world wars. There have been notable Chajes scientists, doctors, lawyers, musicians, and a world-class chess player [2].

Chapter 22 has more to say about aspects of my maternal forebears while the present chapter concentrates on descent from my paternal grandparents.

These families and some of their in-laws trace their lineage back to the eleventh-century scholar and bible commentator Rabbi Solomon ben Isaac, known as *Rashi*, and to the Kalonymos of Narbonne, who are believed to have a Carolingian connection through descendants of Babylonian Exilarchs of the House of King David [3].

My paternal background includes connections to Levush (Jaffe), Halpern, Weinstein, Horowitz, Margolies (Margolioth), and HaKohen (Katz). These are shown on the colour Chart 21.8. The two following charts (21.9 and 21.10) set out some Shapiro connections and descent from the Katzenellenbogen of Padua and Judah Loew of Prague.

I am a direct sixth-generation descendant of Moses Menachem Mendel Levush, who became known as Moses Gelles after his marriage to a daughter of Rabbi S(hmuel) Gelles, He was a scholar of the Brody Klaus, a Talmudic study group of pan-European reputation that flourished in the mid eighteenth century at a time when Brody had the second-largest Jewish community after Amsterdam [4]. The name of Levush is believed to relate to descent from Rabbi Mordecai Jaffe of Prague (1530–1612), generally known as the *Levush* after the title of his magnum opus *The Levushim* [5].

The eponymous grandson of this Moses Gelles married a daughter of Rabbi Moshe of Glogau, the eldest son of the Chief Rabbi Shmuel Helman of Mannheim and Metz (d.1764). The latter's descendants include Lazare Isidore, the nineteenth-century Chief Rabbi of France, and Chaim Herzog, the sixth president of the State of Israel [6].

There is conflicting documentary evidence as to whether Rabbi Shmuel Helman (Hillman) was a son of the Israel Halpern of Krotoschin, the son-in-law of Chief Rabbi Nathan Nata Shapiro of Krakow (1585–1633). However, Helman certainly had a Halpern and Katzenellenbogen family background [7].

The Gelles line descending from Moses Gelles of the Brody Klaus had other connections with ancient Shapiro lines, as indicated in Chart 21.9. Grandsons of the elder Moses Gelles included Rabbi Shmuel ben Mordecai Gelles. He married Sarah Rachel Scheindel, the only daughter of Rabbi Pinchas Shapiro of Koretz (1726–91), who was one of the leading figures in the eighteenth-century Chasidic movement. This Gelles–Shapiro line was known by the name of Polonsky (after the town of Polonnoye). Their line continued for five generations as rabbis of Kolnibolet and Zvenigorodka, with some oversight at Shpole, Tolna, and Kalerka in Ukraine. Y-DNA matches with a descendant of this line support the genealogical picture shown in the chart. They confirm that my great-great-grandfather Moses Gelles must have descended through a son rather than a daughter of his eponymous grandfather, the elder Moses Gelles of Brody. He was very probably a brother rather than a first cousin of the aforementioned Shmuel ben Mordecai Gelles [8].

My paternal grandmother Esther Weinstein was a daughter of Hirsch Leib Weinstein, the Chief Rabbi of Solotwina in Galicia, and his wife Gittel. The Weinsteins had links with the neighbouring province of Bukowina. My grandfather Nahum Uri Gelles succeeded his father-in-law Rabbi Weinstein as Chief Rabbi of Solotwina on the latter's death in 1884 [9].

I have presented circumstantial evidence that Esther Weinstein's mother Gittel was a Horowitz and it is indeed possible that my paternal grandparents were second cousins through their Horowitz connection. Recent DNA tests are supportive of these connections [10].

Gittel Weinstein's putative father, Rabbi Yehuda Ahron Horowitz, came from the ancient family that went back a thousand years from Galicia to Prague, Provence, and Spain. He and his half-brother Rabbi Efraim Fischel Horowitz of Munkacz were sons of Rabbi Jacob Jokel Horowitz of Bolechow. Their ancestor Isaac Horowitz (1715–67), the Chief Rabbi of Hamburg, was a descendant of Pinchas Halevi Ish Horowitz of Prague and Krakow (1535–1618), who married the sister of Chief Rabbi Moses Isserles of Krakow and became President of the Council of the Four Lands, the semi-autonomous governing body of Polish Jewry. Over the course of several centuries, the Horowitz intermarried with many of the other leading families, including the Chayes and Katzenellenbogen. Thus, one wife of Isaac (Hamburger) Horowitz was Reitze Babad, granddaughter of Isaac Krakower, the Chief Rabbi of Brody, who was a grandson of Chief Rabbi Abraham Joshua Heschel of Krakow, and thence a descendant of Saul Wahl and the Rabbis of Padua. Through such marriages my family tree acquired additional connections to Saul Wahl and his lineage [11].

Rabbi Yehuda Ahron Horowitz lived in Solotwina before moving from Galicia to Bukowina to become ABD of Mihaileni (on the borders of present-day Moldova). He married Miriam, the daughter of Zalman Berish Rottenberg Margolies of Bohorodzany (Brodshin), an old town lying between Solotwina and the larger city of Stanislawow (called Stanislau while in the Austrian Empire and now in Ukraine and renamed Ivano-Frankivsk). A part of this Margolioth line is shown in Chart 21.8 (in the colour plates)[12].

The mother of Miriam Margolies Horowitz was Gittel HaKohen Adlersberg. She was of a priestly (Kohanic) line from Mindel Katz, a descendant of the notable Rabbi Shabbatai Katz (1621–63), otherwise Shabbatai ben Meir HaKohen, known as the *Schach*. Mindel Katz was the wife of the saintly Rabbi Moshe Heilprin of Berdichev and Solotwina (d.1752). Moshe Heilprin's forebears of the Halpern line go back to Bella Epstein, daughter of the aforementioned Rabbi Mordecai Jaffe, who was in turn Chief Rabbi of Grodno, Prague, and Posen, and one of the founders of the Council of the Four Lands [13].

These connections with my ancestral Gelles line, as shown in the charts, were established through searches that included the study of birth, marriage, death, and property records in various European archives, as well as tombstone inscriptions, documentation of various kinds including the rabbinic literature, contemporary newspapers, private correspondence, and other ephemera.

BACKGROUND TO DNA TESTS

We have 23 pairs of chromosomes. There are 22 pairs of autosomal DNA which are mixed in the process of passing down the generations, and there is one pair that carries the male and female chromosomes. Males have one Y-chromosome from their father and one X-chromosome from their mother, while females have two X-chromosomes, one from each parent. A mother passes X-DNA to her sons and daughters, a father can pass his X-DNA only to a daughter.

There are Y-DNA tests which indicate descent through an all-male father-to-son line going back for centuries, subject to occasional mutations, and also mitochondrial DNA tests which can reveal matches along all-female mother-to-daughter lines.

X-DNA passes down the generations in a complicated way (an X-chromosome from a mother comes from recombined X-DNA inherited from her mother and father, while an X-chromosome from a father is the same as the X-chromosome he inherited from his mother). Where a line of descent comes to a father–son link the transmission of paternal X-DNA ceases. The identification and dating of common ancestry is necessarily difficult, but X-DNA matches can sometimes throw light on relatively close or quite ancient admixtures.

Autosomal DNA tests can reveal common ancestry irrespective of sex on either side of a family. This test is useful but at the same time problematic for Ashkenazi Jews because their inbreeding complicates estimates of nearest common ancestry. It is best used in testing as large a number as possible in a related group and its reliability decreases as one goes back over the centuries.

Only precise or partly overlapping segments of adequate length on specific chromosome positions can give some assurance of shared ancestry and then only if confirmed with a number of probands. This is the problem of *half-identical regions* (HIR) when two people share a DNA segment that half matches and confirmation is required that it is identical by descent (IBD) and indicative of a common ancestor.

Autosomal DNA tests can reveal a wide picture of a family's ancestral background. They can search for a common ancestry for probands where the specific father-to-son male descent studied by Y-DNA tests is not applicable.

In the past couple of years I have brought together results of DNA tests for myself and some of those related to me in one way or another. Tests of my Y-DNA, mitochondrial DNA, and autosomal DNA and those of close cousins were carried out by Family Tree DNA of Houston, Texas. Other commercial test providers are 23andme and Ancestry.com. Uploading the results of autosomal DNA tests from these providers onto the (free) website of GEDmatch enables one to compare the matches of probands across the several substantial databases. Results from other test providers are being added to GEDmatch, which boasts many other useful facilities, such as comparison of X-DNA data and genetic admixture analysis.

Y-DNA TESTS

The appended Chart 21.9 incorporates genealogy of the cousinly Gelles and Polonsky in the light of Y-DNA tests on Drs Edward Gelles and Jeffrey Mark Paull, who are latter-day descendants of these two lines. From the thousands of records on Family Tree DNA's database these two probands were, at least until recently, the only pair with Y-DNA matches on 36 of 37 and 65 of 67 markers. The genealogy shows Dr Gelles to be the sixth-generation descendant of the eighteenth-century scholar Moses Gelles of the Brody Klaus and Dr Paull as a tenth-generation descendant, in separate direct male lines. The Y-DNA tests strongly support this Moses Gelles or his son Mordecai Gelles of Brody as the nearest common ancestor. For the Y-DNA match my great-great-grandfather Moses Gelles had to be a grandson of the eponymous scholar of Brody through a son rather than a daughter. The known brothers of Mordecai Gelles (the father of Rabbi Shmuel Gelles Polonsky) are Michel Levush, whose recorded son was known by the name of Levush, and Joseph Gelles, one of whose sons is recorded as Moses Gershon Gelles (see Chapter 10 on Jewish Community Life in Brody and the Gelles family chart). So the younger Moses Gelles was most probably a son of Mordecai Gelles and hence a brother of Shmuel Gelles Polonsky.

Genealogical evidence suggests that the Levush of my paternal Gelles–Levush line goes back to the distinguished sixteenth-century Rabbi Mordecai Jaffe of Prague, who was known as the *Levush*. Gelles and Levush connections in eighteenth-century Brody were echoed by Gelles–Jaffe marriages in earlier centuries in Lithuania, in Grodno where Mordecai Jaffe was Chief Rabbi for a time, and in other Lithuanian towns, such as Gorzd, where the *Pinkas HaKehilot Lita* mention Rabbi Moshe Jaffe, who occupied the rabbinical seat from 1840 to1885.

His son Joseph Jaffe was a rabbi in Manchester, where he died in 1897. The tradition of this family was that they descended from the *Levush*.

A third-generation descendant of Rabbi Joseph Jaffe is one of the members of the Jaffe Y-DNA project at Family Tree DNA, who was found to be of haplogroup R2a (M124). Dr Jeffrey Mark Paull and I are of this haplogroup, which is relatively rare among Ashkenazi Jews and suggests that many thousands of years ago our distant ancestors might have come from regions of the Persian Empire to Mesopotamia and further afield before moving to Europe in larger numbers in the days of the Roman Empire.

The Jaffe were in medieval Spain, as noted in Pere Bonin's book *Sangre Judia* – names of Jafa, Jafe, Jaffa, Jaffe Jofa, Jofe, Jaffia, Jafia are recorded from 1175 to 1404 (the first letter of the name was traditionally written as Y as there is no J in the Hebrew alphabet). Jaffe flourished in northern Italy in the later Middle Ages, in Bologna and other towns. Some moved from Italy to Bohemia in the fifteenth century and later prospered in Poland and beyond. From these sprang Mordecai Jaffe who, before becoming Chief Rabbi of Grodno, Prague, and Posen, spent ten years of his life in Venice. He was a close relative of Abigail Jaffe, wife of the Rabbi of Venice. Abigail Jaffe was the mother of my ancestor Saul Wahl. There are about a dozen probands on the *Family Finder* database who are called Jaffe or lay claim to Jaffe descent. Some of these share autosomal DNA segments of significant size with me and my Gelles–Levush cousins, indicating a probable genealogical connection, but my Jaffe story presently rests primarily on a synthesis of family history, genealogy, and results of the Y-DNA test.

AUTOSOMAL DNA TESTS

The Ashkenazi families of my wider ancestral background intermarried for centuries. Some of these connections are set out in Charts 21.8 to 21.10. My close cousins and I share DNA segments with many relevant probands. When these common segments are of sufficient size they may indicate significant genealogical links. Pairs of related probands, each having a DNA admixture drawn from different sources, may share a number of DNA segments on the same or different chromosomes. It then becomes very difficult to ascribe matches to a particular family source. However, it is often possible to obtain an indication of the family origins of these several matching segments by comparing as many proband pairs of known family background as can be found. This procedure is illustrated below for some of my genealogical links, particularly with the Halpern and Horowitz of my paternal ancestry.

Halpern

The ancient Halpern family from Heilbronn in Germany had many branches with variants of the old name, including Heilbron, Halpern, Halperin, Heilprin, Alperin, Alpert, and Alperowitz. These proliferated in central and eastern Europe over many centuries.

A study group of probands who are descendants of the Halpern line or who have claims to such connections is coordinated by Steven D. Bloom and Andi Alpert Ziegelman on Family Tree DNA. Table 21.1 shows that I have matches with numerous probands of this group, and in particular with Leibish Halpern and Carmel Halperin, whose genealogical descent from ancestors of their family name is fairly well established. DNA matches such as those on chromosomes 10 and 11 are shown in Table 21.1.

These DNA matches are sufficiently supportive of the Gelles–Halpern connections that are set out on subsequent family charts. The two eponymous Halpern probands and I also have Horowitz connections and these show up by comparing matching DNA segments of related Gelles and Halpern with a common Horowitz proband.

Table 21.1 Gelles–Halpern autosomal DNA matches (GEDmatch)

Edward Gelles and Elsa Schmaus are Gelles first cousins and cousins of Naftali Horowitz

Edward Gelles with	Segment	
	on chromosome 11	length (cM)
Leibish Halpern	36,426,334–42,704,558	5.2
Carmel Halperin	36,426,334–44,662,337	7.8
	on chromosome 10	
Leibish Halpern	104,199,067–112,421,310	6.3
Carol Joan Baird (Heilborn)	106,613,*** –114,102,***	6.7
Priscilla Newman Bloom	101,355,*** –110,330,***	6.7
Kurt Alexander	106,156,*** –112,198,***	5.3
Moshe Geller	101,153,*** –114,080,***	12.2
Philip Roscher	108,037,*** –115,303,***	8.6
Debra Calzareth	106,770,*** –112,307,***	5.6
William M Oppenheim	99,350,*** –115,364,***	15.0
DNA matches of Gelles and Halpern with Horowitz		
	on chromosome 8	
E. Gelles & L. Halpern	116,739,602–121,456,106	4.3
Elsa Schmaus & L. Halpern	116,739,602–121,656,346	4.4
N. Horowitz & C. Halperin	119,745,926–123,154,424	3.7
	on chromosome 9	
E. Gelles & L. Halpern	128,657,074–131,094,103	3.6
Elsa Schamus & L. Halpern	129,274,874–131,276,520	3.2
N. Horowitz & L. Halpern	128,952,327–131,151,451	3.4
	on chromosome 13	
E. Gelles & L. Halpern	91,889,819–94,137,941	3.9
Elsa Schmaus & L. Halpern	90,551,384–93,841,289	4.5
N. Horowitz & L. Halpern	91,927,400–94,137,941	3.9
	95,610,858–97,766,534	3.1
Elsa Schmaus & C. Halperin	93,197,257–98,572,725	8.6

Shapiro

Table 21.9 shows me as a sixth-generation descendant of Rabbi Shmuel Helman of Metz, who is of a Halpern–Katzenellenbogen line. Widely accepted tradition based on a contemporary document would have Shmuel Helman's mother as a daughter of Chief Rabbi Nathan Nata Shapiro of Krakow. If this is the case, I would be the latter's eighth-generation descendant (Dr Jeffrey Mark Paull, of a cousinly Gelles–Shapiro line through Rabbi Pinchas Shapiro of Koretz is 15 generations from Rabbi Nathan Nata Shapiro).

Table 21.2 Gelles–Shapiro DNA matches (GEDmatch)

Edward Gelles with	Segment	length (cM)
	on chromosome 19	
Jeffrey Mark Paull	4,231,186–9,861,306	16.1
Judith Shapiro	7,177,144–9,111,370	5.8
Shaine Shapiro	7,177,144–9,222,196	6.1
Lawrence Horowitz	7,190,555–9,111.170	5.8
	on chromosome 17	
Judith Shapiro	13,669,474–14,856,672	6.5
Shaine Shapiro	13,642,035–14,855,745	6.7
N. Leppo	13,669,917–14,887,326	6.8
Judith Shapiro with J. Leppo	13,564,943–14,660,868	6.0
X-DNA matches with Judith Shapiro		
Judith Shapiro & Shaine Shapiro &	2,321–154,886293	196.1
Rebecca Shapiro *ditto*		
total segments = 196.1 cM, largest segment = 196.1 cM		
Judith Shapiro & Edward Gelles	40,626,824–67,945,799	20.4
total segments = 20.4 cM, largest segment = 20.4 cM		
Judith Shapiro & Elsa Schmaus	48,542,832–53,448,908	3.3
	55,099,743–68,238,423	3.7
total segments = 37.4 cM, largest segment = 10.2 cM		
Judith Shapiro & N. Leppo	50,762,221–67,541,734	4.4
total segments = 31.8 cM; largest segment = 4.9 cM		
Judith Shapiro & Jeffrey M Paull	138,287,834–141,487,164	12.0
total segments = 12.0 cM, largest segment = 12.0 cM		

Of the few Shapiro probands with available autosomal DNA test results, Judith Shapiro and her daughters Shaine and Rebecca are of interest. Judith and her family are somewhat confusingly listed under her married name of Krupp on the *Family Finder* but under Judith's maiden name of Shapiro on GEDmatch. Judith's family tree shows the names of her paternal grandparents to be Asher Shapiro of Teofipol and Malke Golder, while the names of her maternal grandparents were Gurevich (Horowitz) and Bick. So both Horowitz and Shapiro will have contributed to their descendants' autosomal DNA matches. The X-DNA matches of Shaine and Rebecca could have arisen from their Horowitz–Bick side but not from the Shapiro grandfather.

Table 21.2 lists interesting X-DNA matches in the second section of the table that is preceded by matching autosomal DNA segments on chromosomes 17 and 19 with two Leppo brothers of known Shapiro descent and with Edward Gelles and Jeffrey Mark Paull.

Weinstein

My paternal grandmother Esther was a daughter of Rabbi Hirsch Leib Weinstein of Solotwina, some of whose descendants emigrated to the United States in the early days of the twentieth century. In Chapter 18 entitled 'Rabbis and lawyers' I describe my Gelles connection with these American Weinsteins and show Susan Lee Lipsitt née Weinstein as the second cousin once removed of myself and my first cousin Elsa Gellis Schmaus. Our nearest common ancestors are my great-grandparents Rabbi Hirsch Leib (Zvi Aryeh) Weinstein and his wife Gittel Horowitz.

HOROWITZ CONNECTIONS WITH MY PATERNAL GELLES LINE

A line from Isaac Halevi Horowitz, the eighteenth-century Chief Rabbi of Brody, Glogau, and Hamburg, descending through his daughter Beile, to Rabbi Jacob Jokel Horowitz of Bolechow, and then to Rabbi Yehuda Ahron Horowitz of Solotwina led to the latter's daughter Gittel. Circumstantial evidence suggests that she is the same Gittel who married Rabbi Hirsch Leib Weinstein. Their daughter Esther was the wife of my grandfather Rabbi Nahum Uri Gelles, who succeeded his father-in-law as Chief Rabbi of Solotwina.

A study of autosomal DNA matches using the *Family Finder* of Family Tree DNA in association with the facilities provided by GEDmatch is now lending support to the inferences drawn from traditional methodology. We have test results from several probands bearing the Horowitz name and of others who are believed to have connections with branches of this family. The inbreeding of these Ashkenazi families often results in pairs of probands who are cousins of different degree on both paternal and maternal sides. We need probands who have sufficiently close Horowitz connections and whose pedigrees are known to the extent that the contribution of DNA from other family sources to their genetic make-up can be assessed.

Naftali Horowitz of Brooklyn is believed to be a descendant of Rabbi Isaac Horowitz of Hamburg through his son Abraham Aryeh Leib Horowitz. Naftali and I would thus have a common ancestor in Isaac 'Hamburger' Horowitz, or indeed possibly closer.

The ongoing work on Levite Y-DNA initiated by Jeffrey Wexler is clarifying the connections between members of different Horowitz branches who are descended in direct male line.

Y-DNA 111 marker tests for Naftali and Harvey Horowitz show that they belong to the Levite R1a1a haplogroup, and that Harvey has a 106/111 match with Naftali Horowitz.

Lawrence Horowitz, whose parents were named Shlomo and Sima Czerwic in a 1921 ship's manifest, is of Y-DNA haplogroup G, while having significant autosomal matches with Naftali and Harvey Horowitz. It seems that a male ancestor of Lawrence called Czerwic or Czerwiec (a Polish name meaning June), may be responsible for the Y-DNA haplogroup, and he could have married into a family with Horowitz connections which show up in the autosomal DNA matches. In the absence of adequate documentation of his Horowitz ancestry, the inclusion of Lawrence in the tables of Horowitz probands is to be regarded as an enquiry into his genetic background rather than as an assertion of Horowitz family status, but his autosomal DNA matches are quite persuasive. The matches of the three above-mentioned probands bearing the Horowitz family name are shown in Table 21.3.

The following Table 21.4 lists the total shared DNA and the longest shared segment in cM (above 3 cM and 500 SNP[1]) for a series of probands with Naftali, Harvey, and Lawrence Horowitz. It also has values for MRCA – generations to most recent common ancestor – a measure that is not to be taken too seriously for these highly inbred Ashkenazi families.

I and my two nearest paternal cousins have strong DNA matches with Naftali Horowitz. Interestingly, Jeffrey Mark Paull, who belongs to a cousinly Gelles–Shapiro line, called Polonsky after the town of Polonnoye in Ukraine, is closer to the line of Lawrence Horowitz from the nearby town of Teofipol. Shawn A. Weil (formerly Wahl) and Nosson Wahl are distant cousins on my mother's side. While they may have some connection to my Wahl grandmother's ancestors, they have a common Kohanic ancestor, as shown by Y-DNA tests

Table 21.3 Some autosomal DNA matches of three Horowitz probands (GEDmatch) showing their total shared DNA and longest shared segment (above 3 cM) and MRCA (the estimated generational distance of their nearest common ancestor)

	Naftali Horowitz	Harvey Horowitz	Lawrence Czerwic aka Horowitz
Naftali Horowitz		54.0 6.7 6.0	106.8 17.3 3.5
Harvey Horowitz	54.0 6.7 6.0		83.2 10.7 3.7
Lawrence Czerwic aka Horowitz	106.8 17.3 3.5	83.2 10.7 3.7	

and they also derive DNA from other family sources. Thus Shawn Weil seems to have quite a lot of 'Horowitz' DNA.

Tables 21.5 and 6 present the DNA matches between Gelles cousins and some Horowitz probands. The primary Horowitz proband is Naftali Horowitz, whose Y-DNA test results and family tradition give him a firm place as a direct descendant of Rabbi Isaac Horowitz of Hamburg. The numerous DNA matches between him and Edward Gelles, as well as with the latter's closest paternal cousins lends very strong support to the Gelles–Horowitz connection.

There appears to be a common ancestor at about the genetic distance of Chief Rabbi Isaac Horowitz of Hamburg. The latter was a first cousin of two of the great eighteenth-century Chasidic rabbis, Pinchas Horowitz of Frankfurt and Shmuel Schmelke Horowitz of Nikolsburg. These three cousins were grandsons of Meir Horowitz, the Chief Rabbi of Tykocin (also known to Jews as the *Maharam of Tiktin*).

Chart 21.7a shows the two marriages of Rabbi Meir Horowitz and how the Friedman Grand Rabbis of Ruzhin, Sadagora, and Czortkow are descended from him. The Friedman pedigree not only goes back to Horowitz and Katzenellenbogen but to Twersky and to the ancient Shapiro rabbinic line, including Rabbi Nathan Nata Shapiro of Krakow, as set out on Chart 14.2 (Chapter 14). Any assessment of the importance of the Friedman dynasty in the history of Chasidism must take account of their ancient lineage that contributed not a little to the 'royal' aura that held their devoted followers spellbound for generations.

Table 21.4 Autosomal DNA matches of Gelles cousins with several Horowitz probands (GEDmatch)

Name and relationship to Edward Gelles	Naftali Horowitz			Harvey Horowitz			Lawrence Czerwic aka Horowitz		
	Total cM	Longest segment cM	MRCA	Total cM	Longest segment cM	MRCA	Total cM	Longest segment cM	MRCA
Edward Gelles	**112.0**	**9.9**	**3.6**	**85.0**	**8.6**	**5.1**	107.3	8.8	4.7
Elsa Gellis Schmaus paternal 1st cousin	**141.2**	**14.4**	**3.3**	**94.5**	**10.3**	**3.6**	95.9	6.8	5.6
Susan Lee Weinstein Lipsitt paternal 2nd cousin ×1 removed	**122.0**	**10.7**	**3.4**	**89.3**	**11.6**	**3.7**	45.0	7.3	6.2
Jeffrey Mark Paull paternal distant cousin	65.5	7.6	5.9	**81.3**	**12.1**	**3.7**	**111.2**	**12.2**	**3.5**
Tad Taube maternal 2nd cousin	81.0	7.0	5.7	57.3	8.4	5.6	**90.3**	**14.9**	**3.7**
Shawn A Weil distant cousin	**112.4**	**12.1**	**3.5**	**64.5**	**11.8**	**3.9**	**114.0**	**11.3**	**3.5**
Nosson Wahl distant cousin	141.9	8.2	5.2	70.2	6.8	5.8	65.0	7.5	5.9
Jeffrey D Wexler distant cousin	**110.4**	**11.3**	**3.5**	**76.7**	**11.6**	**3.8**	108.9	8.5	5.0
Sandy Aaronson Horowitz connection	**87.1**	**10.6**	**3.7**	**65.2**	**12.8**	**3.9**	88.5	8.6	5.1
Ilya Gurevich Varnavati Horowitz connection	77.8	7.1	5.8	**112.2**	**10.7**	**3.5**	82.6	7.6	5.7

Table 21.5 Gelles–Weinstein–Horowitz autosomal DNA matches (GEDmatch)

Edward Gelles, Elsa Schmaus née Gellis (1st cousin), **Susan Lee Lipsitt née Weinstein** (2nd cousin once removed), **Jeffrey Mark Paull** (distant Gelles cousin), **Naftali Horowitz**

	E. Gelles / E. Schmaus	E. Gelles / S.L. Lipsitt	E. Schmaus / S.L. Lipsitt	N. Horowitz / E. Gelles	N. Horowitz / J.M. Paull	N. Horowitz / E. Schmaus	N. Horowitz / S.L. Lipsitt
Total DNA shared	949	241	222	112	65	141	122
Longest segment (cM)	105	33	52	10	8	14	11
MRCA (generations)	2.0	2.9	3.0	3.6	5.9	3.3	3.4 –
chromosome 4	61,566 92,907,163 105.5 cM	7,663,415 22,307,903 20.4 cM	7,546,875 22,320,567 20.9 cM	180,585,542 183,826,817 7.9 c M	181,729,177 183,619,587 5.0 cM 32,543,295 39,104,690 6.8 cM	181,547,564 183,815,592 6.1 cM	36,602,837 40,466,447 6.7 cM
chromosome 12	52,605,994 63,005,235 9.0 cM	52,605,994 75,938,492 21.2 cM	12,126,485 63,005,235 51.9 cM	94,454,399 97,372,827 3.4 cM	93,681,585 97,794,464 5.7 cM	56,406,622 61,422,310 3.5 cM 703,186 3,490,007 7.8 cM	1,915,901 3,552,050 4.8 cM
chromosome 22	15,973,685 23,595,972 19.8 cM	18,587,825 23,730,511 11.1 cM	18,565,457 23,730,511 11.0 cM	20,776,002 23,727,740 7.2 cM		20,776,002 23,966,680 7.6 cM	20,887,954 23,796,553 7.0 cM

GEDmatch kit numbers F181141, F207755, F271521, F158177, and F249519.

Part of the ancestry of Rabbi Meir Horowitz is common to the Gelles and the Friedman paternal lines and is shown on Chart 21.10. My grandfather, Rabbi Nahum Uri Gelles (1852–1934), was a close adherent of the Czortkower Rebbe Israel Friedman (1854–1933), as recorded by Jewish newspapers in Vienna from about 1915 to 1925 and detailed in my book *Gelles–Shapiro–Friedman* published in 2009. Rabbi Nahum Uri Gelles is buried next to Rabbi Israel Friedman and his wife Bathsheva Ruchama Friedman in Vienna. I remember a story from my childhood in the 1930s that the Gelles rabbis were presumed to be somehow related to the Friedmans of Czortkow. These stories may have been based on common descent from Meir Horowitz, the *Maharam* of Tiktin, or indeed on other distant shared ancestry from either side of our families.

My paternal Gelles ancestry includes more immediately Weinstein, Horowitz, Halpern and Shapiro, and more distantly the priestly Katz (HaKohen), and Katzenellenbogen (including their scion, Saul Wahl). On my mother's side I have a close Katzenellenbogen connection through my grandmother Chawa Wahl and a Chayes connection via my great-grandmother, Sarah Matel Chayes (see Chapter 9).

The Czortkower Rabbe Israel Friedman was the grandson of the dynasty's founder, Israel Friedman of Ruzhin, and the great-grandfather of the eponymous Rabbi Israel Friedman of Manchester, whose autosomal DNA match results have now become available. The latter's distinguished paternal line is shown in my charts. On his mother's side, he has connections to old German rabbinic families such as Berlinger and Bamberger.

Preliminary autosomal DNA tests on the young Rabbi Israel Friedman show matches between him and Edward Gelles located on chromosomes 4 and 22. These are fairly close matches to the ones between Edward Gelles and Naftali Horowitz. As can be seen from Chart 21.7b, Israel Friedman's Horowitz connection is more distant than that of the other two probands, but the three of them share a common ancestor in Rabbi Meir Horowitz.

It must be stressed that each of the above probands will have received DNA from other families on both sides of their families. For example, Israel Friedman has many distant 'DNA cousins' indicative of connections with Ashkenazi families known to have been in the

Table 21.6 Gelles–Horowitz autosomal DNA matches on several further chromosomes (GEDmatch)

CHROMOSOME	2	3	9	17
Edward Gelles **Naftali Horowitz**	46,929,201–51,894,346 4.2 cM	147,645,114–150,161,049 3.5 cM	128,501,733–131,088,774 3.8 cM 132,040.603–134,474,323 4.4 cM	15,450,736–22,994,974 5.2cM 27,915,441–29,496359 4.1 cM
Elsa Schmaus **Naftali Horowitz**	46,902,957–51,884,417 4.2 cM	147,577,316–150, 547,490 4.3 cM	128,980,237–131,103,396 3.2 cM	15,450,736–21,338,557 4.4 cM 27,925,442–29,567,882 4.3 cM
Edward Gelles with **Harvey Horowitz**			128,372,377–131,111,063 4.1 cM	
Elsa Schmaus with **Harvey Horowitz**			129,470,425–132,221,148 5.7 cM	
Elsa Schmaus with **Lawrence Horowitz**			128,997,969–131.294.486 3.6 cM	
Naftali Horowitz and **Harvey Horowitz**			132,907,098–135, 566,915 5.0 cM	
Naftali Horowitz and **Lawrence Horowitz**			133,199,528–136,321, 920 7.2 cM 89,991,559–106,730,356 17.3 cM	
Harvey Horowitz and **Lawrence Horowitz**			133,993,815–136,946, 376 10.7 cM	

Rhineland in medieval times. Some are on the list of my own early German connections with the likes of Oppenheim, Wertheimer, Guggenheim, Rothschild, Löwenstein, and so on (see Charts 15.9 and 15.11). Israel Friedman and I have quite significant matches with, for example, Ralph N. Baer, William M Oppenheim, several Guggenheims, and Walther F. Spiegel.

INTERPRETATION OF DNA MATCHES

Edward Gelles, Elsa Schmaus (his Gelles first cousin), and Susan Lee Lipsitt (his Weinstein 2nd cousin once removed) have common ancestors in Rabbi Hirsch Leib Weinstein and Gittel Horowitz. Edward and Elsa descend from this couple's daughter Esther Weinstein and Susan Lee from Esther's brother Chaim Weinstein. Edward and Elsa have DNA from Gelles, Weinstein, and Horowitz but **Susan Lee has no 'Gelles' DNA input**. The kinship of these three close cousins is reflected in large shared segments. Jeffrey Mark Paull is a distant Gelles cousin from the Gelles–Shapiro line, known by the name of Polonsky, originating with Rabbi Shmuel Gelles, aka Polonsky, who was a grandson of our common Gelles ancestor, the scholar Moses Gelles of Brody. **Jeffrey has no Weinstein connection** and his Horowitz links are more distant and different from those of Edward Gelles and his close cousins. These genealogical differences are reflected in the DNA matches or their absence on chromosomes 4, 12, and 22 of the above charts. Neither Susan Lee Weinstein nor Jeffrey Paull match with Naftali Horowitz on chromosomes 2, 3, 9, and 17 where Edward Gelles and Elsa Schmaus show evidence of Gelles–Horowitz linkage, in addition to their matches with Naftali Horowitz on chromosomes 4 and 22.

The three Horowitz probands share DNA segments on chromosome 9 – with each other, with Edward Gelles and his first cousin Elsa, and with several other probands, for example Naftali Horowitz and Adele Vodovoz Wexler have a shared segment of 3.8 cM (128,521,053–131,090,282).

CONCLUSION

DNA matches between myself and my closest cousins with several Horowitz probands are giving support to the Gelles–Horowitz links put forward by me previously on the basis of a mixture of documented and circumstantial evidence. The results of autosomal DNA *Family Finder* tests, analysed with the help of GEDmatch and with additional information from Y-DNA and X-DNA tests, underwrite Rabbi Isaac Horowitz of Hamburg as my common ancestor with Naftali Horowitz and point to Rabbi Isaac's grandfather, Rabbi Meir Horowitz of Tykocin, as a common ancestor of myself, Naftali Horowitz, and Rabbi Israel Friedman of Manchester. It must be emphasised again that the several shared DNA segments of these three probands cannot, in the present state of our knowledge, be ascribed to a definite family source, though the magnitude of the autosomal matches is consistent with the genetic distances of the three probands from their Horowitz forebears as shown in Table 21.7b. The X-DNA matches reveal the three probands to be distantly related, through their respective maternal lines of descent.

This pilot study also showed the application of Y-DNA tests in confirming nearest common male ancestors, as with my Gelles and Polonsky rabbinic lines. The uses and limitations of currently available commercial DNA tests are further illustrated in the following chapters.

ACKNOWLEDGEMENTS

I am indebted to several correspondents for family information and particularly to Jeffrey Wexler, Dr Ben Weinstock, Susan Lee Lipsitt, Kathleen Desmond, and Rabbi Israel Friedman.

REFERENCES

Referring to my books:
AL   *An Ancient Lineage* (London: Vallentine Mitchell 2006)
GHC   *Family Connections: Gelles–Horowitz–Chajes* (Maastricht: Shaker 2008)
GSF   *Family Connections: Gelles–Shapiro–Friedman* (Maastricht: Shaker 2009)
EE   *Ephemeral & Eternal: A Brief Life of Joseph Gelles* (Shaker 2010)

MMA   *Meeting My Ancestors* (Shaker 2011)

TJJ   *The Jewish Journey: A Passage through European History* (to be
             published)

[1] The story of Saul Wahl and some of his descendants is presented in
TJJ, chapters 7, 8, 15, and 22; see also **AL**, chapters 4, 5, 13, 14 and
numerous references in **MMA**.

[2] The history of the Chayes family is outlined in **AL**, chapters 6, 7, 8, and
genealogical connections are detailed in **GHC**, chapter 3.

[3] Davidic descent – see **AL**, chapter 37 and **TJJ**, chapters 1 and 19.

[4] The scholar of the Brody Klaus, Moses Gelles (*c.*1710–60) married
a daughter of Rabbi S. Gelles (who may have been Shmuel Gelles,
the Chief Rabbi of Siemiatycze). The Gelles–Levush family connections emerge from a study of the fragmentary *Records of the Beth Din of
Brody 1808–1817* (MS 4037) in the Library of the Jewish Theological
Seminary of New York, the Brody vital records in the Lviv archives, and
many other sources – see **AL**, chapters 27–29.

[5] Our ancestral name of Levush and indications of descent from Rabbi
Mordecai Jaffe of Prague (1530–1612) are discussed in **AL**, in a recent
article published in *The Galitzianer* (Vol. 19, No. 3, September 2012) and
in **TJJ**, chapter 10 (Jewish Community Life in Brody).

[6] The principal source for our descent from Chief Rabbi Shmuel
Helman of Metz (d.1764) is the entry for my grandfather Chief Rabbi
Nahum Uri Gelles of Solotwina (1852–1934) in *Ohalai Shem* (pp. 261–2)
by Shmuel Noach Gottlieb (published in Pinsk 1912). A translation of
this entry is given in **AL**, chapter 33, note 9, pp. 236–7. It states that my
grandfather's descent from Rabbi Shmuel Helman (Hillman) was via the
latter's son, Rabbi Moshe of Glogau, and that Rabbi Shmuel Helman
was a son of Rabbi Israel Halpern of Krotoschin, who was a son-in-law
of Chief Rabbi Nathan Nata Shapiro of Krakow (1585–1633). See also
entries in Meir Wunder, *Meorei Galicia*, the authoritative work on the
Galician Rabbinate.

[7] This time-honoured descent of Shmuel Helman going back to the
source book *Da'at Kedoshim* and to a contemporary family letter has
recently been challenged on the basis of apparently conflicting evidence. Rabbi Shmuel Helman was Chief Rabbi of Kremsier in Moravia
before going on to Mannheim and finally to Metz. In the records of
Kremsier he is described as a son of Rabbi Uri Feivush. The latter
may well have been his rich father-in-law from Glogau who supported
him and who gave him (successively) two daughters in marriage. We
do not know the exact date of Shmuel Helman's birth. His tombstone

has not survived at Metz nor has a transcription been found. We know from other writings that he lived to a very old age, so the date of 1692 on a document bearing the signature of Shmuel Helman among other 'Jewish Elders' has to be reconciled with a birth date around 1670 or earlier. This issue is fully discussed in **AL**, chapter 33, pp. 229–42. There is separate documentation that Rabbi Shmuel Helman came from a Halpern–Katzenellenbogen family nexus.

[8] The Gelles–Shapiro connection continued from earlier centuries into the days of my grandfather. Rabbi Yehuda Meir Shapira (1887–1934) was a direct fifth-generation descendant of Rabbi Pinchas Shapiro of Koretz, who was a sixth-generation descendant of Rabbi Nathan Nata Shapiro of Krakow. Rabbi Yehuda Meir Shapira was Chief Rabbi of Lublin, founder of the Lublin Sages Yeshiva, and a member of the Polish Parliament. He and my grandfather were both close adherents of Rabbi Israel Friedman of the Czortkow Chasidic dynasty. My first cousin Joseph Gelles studied at the Lublin Sages Yeshivah where Rabbi Yehuda Meir took him under his wing – see **GSF** and **EE**. Rabbi Shmuel ben Mordecai Gelles (d.1811) and his wife Sarah Rachel Scheindel Shapiro, the only daughter of Rabbi Pinchas Shapiro of Koretz, were the progenitors of a rabbinic Gelles–Shapiro line that went by the name of Polonsky. A book by their descendant Rabbi Shimshon Ahron Polonsky *Chidushei Horav mi Teplik* sets out his descent from Moses Gelles, the scholar of the Brody Klaus. *Rabbi Pinchas mi Koretz* by Rabbi Matityahu Yechezkiel Guttman and *Shem U' She'erith* by Levi Grossman are two further monographs confirming this origin of the Polonsky line – see **MMA** chapters 4 and 5 for the Polonsky rabbinic line and for the Gelles–Shapiro descent of Dr Jeffrey Mark Paull.

[9] For a brief account of Rabbi Zvi Aryeh (Hirsch Leib) Weinstein and his family see **AL**, chapter 28, **MMA,** chapter 7 entitled 'Rabbis of Solotwina near Stanislau', **EE** p. 32, and chapter 18 of **TJJ**.

[10] Rabbi Hirsch Leib Weinstein's family had been in Solotwina for some time. His father Rabbi Israel Jacob Weinstein lived and died there. Rabbi Yehuda Ahron Horowitz resided in Solotwina and his wife Miriam had come from nearby Brodshin. Around 1858–9 the family moved to the province of Bukowina and the Rabbi became ABD of Saniawitz–Mihaileni (see Meir Wunder, *Meorei Galicia*, Vol. 2, p. 220). Records on the JewishGen JRI-Poland database have my grandmother Esther Weinstein as born in the province of Bukowina in 1861. She died in Solotwina in 1907. Her brother Abraham was born in Solotwina in 1856 and died in the nearby town of Kolomea

in 1904. His parents are given as Hirsch Leib and Gittel Weinstein of Solotwina. It was a well-established custom in those days for an expectant mother to go to her parents for the birth of a child. In 1856, Gittel Weinstein had her parents close at hand in Solotwina when Abraham was expected, while in 1861 Gittel had to go to the neighbouring province for Esther's birth.

[11] For Horowitz lineage see **GHC** chapter 2 and **MMA** chart on p. 108. The half-brother of Rabbi Yehuda Ahron was Rabbi Efraim Fischel Horowitz (*c.*1790–1860), ABD of Munkacz in Hungary. Following traditional Ashkenazi naming patterns, the third chart suggests a possible connection with Sarah, the wife of my great-grandfather Rabbi David Isaac Gelles (*c.*1790–1868). My grandfather was born at Narayow in 1852. His eldest son was called Efraim Fischel and his second son was called David Isaac after his paternal grandfather. My father David Isaac studied at the Munkacz Yeshiva at the turn of the century (for Efraim Fischel Horowitz see Meir Wunder, *loc. cit.*, Vol. 2, pp. 176–7, and for the father of the two half-brothers, Jacob Jokel Horowitz (1773–1832), the ABD of Bolechow, see Vol. 2, pp. 235–6).

[12] For Margolies Connection see **MMA** chart on p. 68.

[13] For descent from Rabbi Mordecai Jaffe (Levush) via a Heilprin (Halpern) line to Moshe Heilprin of Berdichev and Solotwina and then via a priestly Kohanic line to Gittel HaKohen Adlersberg and the Rabbis of Solotwina see **MMA** chart on p. 59.

[14] DNA tests and common ancestors *The Galitzianer*, Vol. 18, No. 2, February 2011.

[15] Autosomal DNA matches between close cousins: 'The Genetic Heritage of Some Galician Families: A Précis' is in *The Galitzianer*, Vol. 19, No. 1, March 2012. www.jewishgen.org/galicia/assets/images/AutosomalDNAmatches.pdf.

[16] Autosomal DNA and genetic origins of some Ashkenazi cousins: www.jewishgen.org/galicia/assets/images/AutosomalAshkenazi.pdf.

[17] **MMA**, chapter 5 'Genes and Genealogy'.

[18] For the Gelles family genealogy and the Weinstein connection – see **AL** and **MMA**.

[19] Horowitz connection – see **GHC** and **GSF** for Naftali Horowitz – private communication from Dr Ben Weinstock, and Neil Rosenstein, *The Unbroken Chain*, Vol. 2, p. 1062.

[20] For the Friedman Chasidic dynasty, see my above-mentioned books and for the contemporary geo-political background, see David Rechter, *Becoming Habsburg –The Jews of Austrian Bukowina 1774–1918*. (The Littman Library 2013).

[21] Jeffrey D. Wexler's website *Levite DNA*.org is devoted to the study of the Y-DNA of R1a1a Ashkenazi Levites and has references to many recent and very relevant sources.

Chart 21.7a Horowitz connections including the Friedman Chasidic dynasty

Shmuel Shmelke Horowitz (d. 1694)
ABD of Tarnow

Meir Horowitz (d. 1743)   m (1)   **Matil, daughter of**
Maharam of Tiktin   **Efraim Zalman Katzenellenbogen**

daughter of **Menachem Manish Katz**   m (2)
son of Isaiah Katz of Brody

Zvi Hirsch Horowitz (d. 1754)   **Dov Berish Horowitz**
ABD of Czortkow

Jacob Jokel Horowitz (d. 1755)   **Meshullam Feivel Horowitz**
ABD of Glogau & Brody

Shmuel Shmelke Horowitz ——— **Pinchas Horowitz**
ABD of Nikolsburg (d. 1778)   *ABD of Frankfurt* (d. 1805)

Isaac Horowitz (1715–1767)   **Henia**
ABD of Brody, Glogau, & Hamburg   m **Abraham "the Angel"**
                                                                          son of **Dov Ber of Meseritz**
Abraham Aryeh Leib Horowitz   (1739 –1776)
Brody (d. 1803)

Beile Horowitz   via   **Shalom Shakhna** (d. 1803)
m **Menachem Mendel Rubin**   m **Chawa Twersky**

                                    Naftali Horowitz

Jacob Jokel Horowitz   **Israel Friedman of Ruzhin** (d. 1850)
ABD of Bolechow   **Jacob Horowitz**

                                    Meir Horowitz   **David Moshe Friedman of Czortkow** (d. 1903)

Yehuda Ahron Horowitz   **Israel Friedman of Czortkow** (d. 1933)
ABD of Mihaileni   **Naftali Horowitz**   m **Bathsheva Ruchama Friedman** (1st cousin)
                                    of **Brooklyn**
Gittel   m   **Hirsch Leib Weinstein**
                         ABD of Solotwina   **Dov Ber Friedman of Vienna** (d. 1936)

Esther Weinstein
m **Nahum Uri Gelles** (d. 1934)   **David Moses Friedman of London** (d. 1988)
ABD of Solotwina

David Gelles of Vienna (d. 1964)   **Israel Friedman**
                                                                          of **Manchester**
Edward Gelles
of **London**

Chart 21.7b DNA matches between Edward Gelles, Naftali Horowitz. and Rabbi Israel Friedman

autosomal DNA matches above 500 SNP and 3 cM (GEDmatch Kit numbers F 181141, F249519, and F346463)

CHROMOSOME	2	4	22	X–DNA
Edward Gelles	102,542,843–107,437,956	180,585,442–183,826,817	20,776,002–23,794,319	
Naftali Horowitz	3.8 cM	7.9 cM	7.2 cM	3.3 cM
Total shared DNA 112 cM	114,726,876–119,5–4,086			100,099,888 – 106,825,515
Longest segment 9.8 cM	3.4 cM			
MRCA 3.7				
Edward Gelles	112,138,037–116,518,149	173,713,250–179,601,410	18,292,015–22,038,833	
Israel Friedman	4.0 cM	7.4 cM	8.1 cM	9.0 cM
Total shared DNA 106 cM		179,703,677–182,151,597		95,539,510–106,825,515
Longest segment 8.9 cM		4.7 cM		
MRCA 4.7				

A significant X–DNA match between Edward Gelles and Israel Friedman is also shown between each of these probands and the daughters of Judith Shapiro, who is of Shapiro and Horowitz descent (see Table 21.2). There are clearly ancestral links which, in view of the complex way X–DNA passes down the generations, remains a challenge for further genealogical study.

Judith Shapiro's daughters Shaine and Rebecca show X–DNA matches with the above probands –
both Rebecca Shapiro (M204553) have X–DNA matches with
and Shaine Shapiro (M132809)

Elsa Gellis Schmaus	9.6 cM	(95,116,870 – 108,588,600)
	10.6 cM	(93,021,612 – 104,655,457)
Israel Friedman	9.3 cM	(95,539,519 = 108,595,208)
Naftali Horowitz	3.6 cM	(100,099,888 – 108,595,208)
cf. Naftali Horowitz with Israel Friedman	4.0 cM	(100,099,888 – 109,089,685)

Chart 21.9 Gelles and Shapiro connections

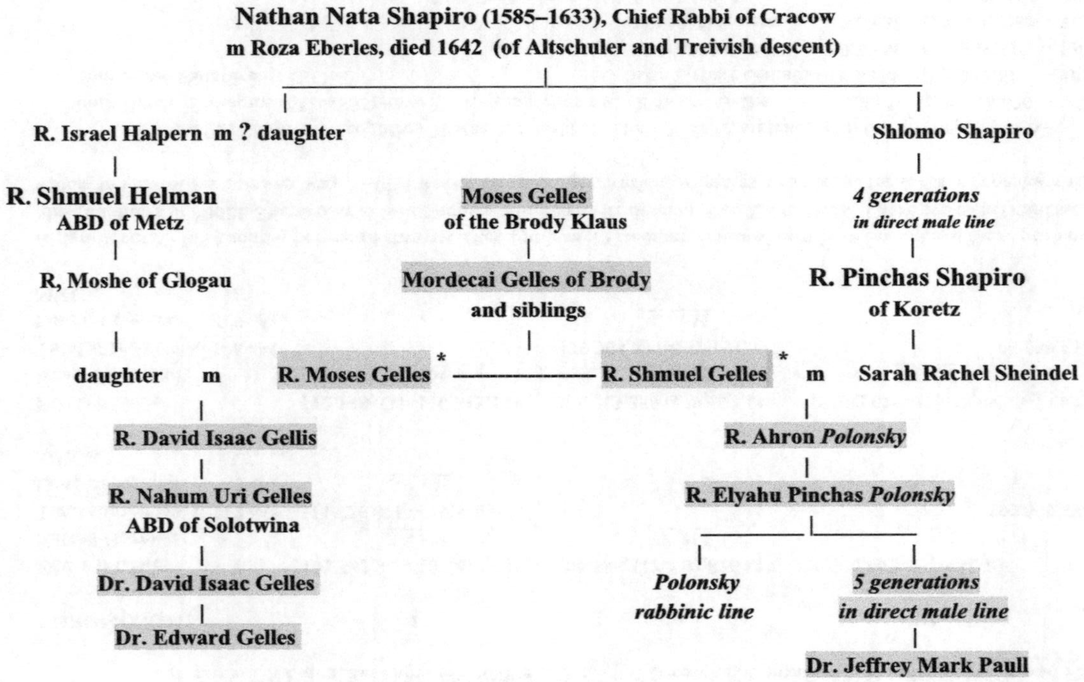

Nathan Nata Shapiro (1585–1633), Chief Rabbi of Cracow
m Roza Eberles, died 1642 (of Altschuler and Treivish descent)

Shlomo Shapiro

4 generations
in direct male line

R. Pinchas Shapiro
of Koretz

Sarah Rachel Sheindel   m

R. Ahron *Polonsky*

R. Elyahu Pinchas *Polonsky*

Polonsky
rabbinic line

5 generations
in direct male line

Dr. Jeffrey Mark Paull

Moses Gelles
of the Brody Klaus

Mordecai Gelles of Brody
and siblings

*   **R. Shmuel Gelles**

R. Israel Halpern m ? daughter

R. Shmuel Helman
ABD of Metz

R, Moshe of Glogau

daughter   m   *   **R. Moses Gelles**

R. David Isaac Gellis

R. Nahum Uri Gelles
ABD of Solotwina

Dr. David Isaac Gelles

Dr. Edward Gelles

* Moses and Shmuel Gelles were brothers or at least first cousins (see text)

Chart 21.10 Descent from Katzenellenbogen of Padua and Venice and Judah Loew of Prague

Saul ben Samuel Judah Katzenellenbogen aka **Saul Wahl** 1545–1617   **Judah Loew** of Prague ca 1525–1609 m Mirel Chayes –Altschuler

Isaac ben Samson Katz of Prague, d. 1624 m Voegele Loew d. 1629

Judah Katzenellenbogen

Naftali Katz of Lublin. d. 1649

Abraham Joshua **Heschel** of Cracow d. 1663   m (2)   Dinah Katzenellenbogen
m (1) Miriam Lazers – *see BABAD chart*

Isaac Katz of Stepan   m.   Margolioth

Isaiah Katz of Brody

Menachem Meinish Katz

Naftali Hirsch Katz of Frankfurt & Posen . d. 1719

Meir Horowitz of Tiktin d 1743   m   daughter

Shprintze   m   Jacob Ashkenazi-Katzenellenpogen of Posen

Bezalel Katz of Ostrog d 1717
m Halpern

Jacob Jokel Horowitz of Brody & Glogau 1755

Abraham of Posen and a daughter m Efraim Fischel of Ludmir d. 1719

Isaac Katz of Ostrog d. 1734

Isaac Horowitz 1715–1767
of Brody, Glogau, & Hamburg
m Reitze **Babad** d 1755 – *BABAD chart*

daughter
m Isaac Dov Ber Margolioth
of Jaslowitz

Jacob of Ludmir d. 1730
m Katzenellenbogen

daughter
m Nahum Zausmer
of Sandomierz

Beile Horowitz m Menachem Mendel Rubin

Jacob of Tlust

Benjamin Bushka of Zamosc

Menachem Nahum Zausmer

Jacob Jokel Horowitz   m (3)   Hinde Fraenkel
of Bolechow 1772 – 1832   daughter of
                                Yehuda Ahron Fraenkel
                                       of Brody

Abraham Mordecai Margolies
of Ustechko

Zwi Hirsch Zamosc 1740–1807
of Brody, Glogau, & Hamburg

Chaya   m   Aryeh Leib Berenstein
of Brody d 1788

daughter   m (1)

Yehuda Ahron Horowitz of **Solotwina**
moved to the Bukowina in 1858–59
ABD of Saniawitz – Mihaileni
m Miriam Rottenberg Margolies

Zalman Berish Rottenberg
of Brodshin
m Gittel Hakohen Adlersberg

Isaac Wolf Berenstein

Efraim Fischel Horowitz
ca 1790 –1861
ABD of Munkacz
possible in-law of
Rabbi David Isaac Gelles

Miriam Rottenberg Margolies
m Yehuda Ahron Horowitz

daughter
m Menachem Manish Chayes
of Brody & Florence d. 1832

——— Continues on Chart 21.8 in the colour plates ———

Chapter 22

The Wahls of Tarnobrzeg

Genealogical links and DNA tests

M Y MATERNAL GRANDMOTHER'S Wahl family had lived in the little Galician town of Tarnobrzeg for many generations. There were about half a dozen families of that name there, as revealed by the town census of 1880, in which names and dates of birth were listed under separate house numbers. A study of contemporary descendants of three of these Wahl families, using Y-DNA and autosomal DNA tests, suggests that a common Wahl ancestor might perhaps be over two centuries in the past. The tests also cast an interesting light on the genetic admixture these probands derive from other family sources in their ancestry.

INTRODUCTION

My maternal grandmother Chawa Wahl was born in Galicia, which was at that time a province of the Austrian Empire. Her family had lived in Tarnobrzeg for many generations. This little town, on the river Vistula north-east of Krakow, incorporated the village of Dzikow where a Jewish community had flourished for three hundred years. Chawa's family claimed descent from Saul Wahl, scion of the Katzenellenbogen rabbis of Padua and Venice, who rose to eminence in the Polish–Lithuanian Commonwealth in the later sixteenth century.

In my grandmother's time, there were about half a dozen families by the name of Wahl in Tarnobrzeg. They were surmised to be related to one another. The town censuses of 1880 and 1925 are important sources for individual families whose lineages can be partly identified from the listed house numbers and dates of birth. Table 22.1 shows entries for three Wahl families from the 1880 census.

Chawa Wahl married David Mendel Griffel, the eldest son of Eliezer Griffel, who was head of Jewish community of Nadworna. Chawa's sisters Rachel and Bluma married Abraham Taube and Lazar Loew, whose forebears had been respective heads of the Belz and Sedziszow communities. The grandchildren of these three Wahl sisters include Edward Gelles, Thaddeus Taube, and Marilyn Low. Autosomal DNA tests carried out by Family Tree DNA of Houston, Texas, confirmed the consanguinity of these three cousins, as indicated in Table 22.2. The purpose of the present study is to examine possible connections with other families in Tarnobrzeg bearing the Wahl name.

Shawn A. Weil and Nosson Wahl are descendants of listed Wahl families from Tarnobrzeg and they have kindly provided results from their recent DNA tests which are discussed below.

Shawn Weil and Nosson Wahl are closely related, but do not at first sight appear to have close Wahl connections with Edward Gelles and his second cousins, Marilyn Low Schmitt and Thaddeus N. Taube. Shawn and Nosson share a total DNA of 118.64 cM with a longest common segment of 24.29 cM. The *Family Finder* estimates that they could be third cousins, but taking the endogamy of our wider family

281

Table 22.1 Tarnobrzeg 1880 town census entries for three Wahl families

Family of Leiser Wahl and Zlate Roisel (to Edward Gelles and his second cousins)

Surname	First name	Page	Entry	House	Birth year	Town of birth
WAHL	Leiser	200	1	108	1815	Tarnobrzeg
WAHL	ZlateReisel	200	2	108	1819	Nisko
WAHL	Shulim	288	8	154	1838	Tarnobrzeg
WAHL	Sarah	288	2	154	1842	Tarnobrzeg
WAHL	Chaim	288	3	154	1869	Tarnobrzeg
WAHL	Moises	288	4	154	1873	Tarnobrzeg
WAHL	Cypra	288	5	154	1875	Tarnobrzeg
WAHL	Chawa	288	6	154	1877	Tarnobrzeg
WAHL	Rachel	288	7	154	1879	Tarnobrzeg

NB: Bluma Wahl, daughter of Shulim Wahl and Sarah Safier, born in 1864, had left home by the time of the 1880 census.

Family of Majer Wahl and Gitla (to Shawn A. Weil)

Surname	First name	Page	Entry	House	Birth year	Town of birth
WAHL	Sarah	212	7	114	1810	Tarnobrzeg
WAHL	Majer	212	1	114	1825	Tarnobrzeg
WAHL	Gitla	212	2	114	1824	Nisko
WAHL	Moises	212	5	114	1855	Tarnobrzeg
WAHL	EsterBluma	212	6	114	1858	Tarnobrzeg
WAHL	Sane	212	3	114	1861	Tarnobrzeg
WAHL	Bruche	212	4	114	1866	Tarnobrzeg

Family of Jacob Majer Wahl and Perel (to Nosson Wahl)

Surname	First name	Page	Entry	House	Birth year	Town of birth
WAHL	Jacob Majer	596	1	343	1835	Tarnobrzeg
WAHL	Perel	596	2	343	1835	Tarnobrzeg
WAHL	Chana Riwa	596	3	343	1855	Tarnobrzeg
WAHL	Aron Josel	596	4	343	1857	Tarnobrzeg
WAHL	Ita	596	5	343	1865	Tarnobrzeg
WAHL	Wolf	596	6	343	1867	Tarnobrzeg

Table 22.2 Descendants of three Wahl families and shared autosomal DNA (*Family Finder*)

	Thaddeus N Taube	Edward Gelles	Marilyn Low Schmitt	Shawn Aaron Weil	Nosson Wahl
Total shared DNA		375	311	78	106
Longest segment (in cM) →		48	57	9	20
		Second cousin	Second cousin	Distant cousin	Distant cousin
	Leiser Wahl b 1815 Zlate Roisel of Nisko b 1819	**Leiser Wahl** b 1815 Zlate Roisel of Nisko b 1819	**Leiser Wahl** b 1815 Zlate Roisel of Nisko b 1819	**Sarah Wahl** b1810	**Jacob Majer Wahl** b 1835 Perel b 1835
	Shulim Wahl b 1838 Sarah Safier b 1842	**Shulim Wahl** b 1838 Sarah Safier b 1842	**Shulim Wahl** b 1838 Sarah Safier b 1842	**Majer Wahl** b1825 Gitla of Nisko b1824	**Israel Eliyahu Wahl** Chana Weisenfeld b 1862
	Rachel Wahl b 1879 Abraham Taube b 1873	**Chawa Wahl** b 1877 David M Griffel b 1875	**Bluma Wahl** b 1864 Lazar Loew b 1861	**Nasanel Wahl** b1863 Yette Abramowitz b 1865	**Shraga Meier Wahl** b 1889 Yehudis Weisenfeld
	Ziga Taube 1905 Lola Popper b 1907	**Regina Griffel** b 1900 Dr David Gelles b 1883	**Abraham Loew** b 1891 Mae Willett b 1903	**Jacob Weil** b 1903 Marian (Mirla) Goldner b 1905	**Shalom Wahl** b 1923 Dina Landman b 1925
	Thaddeus N Taube b 1931	**Dr Edward Gelles** b 1927	**Marilyn Low Schmitt** b 1939	**Stephen P Weil** b 1943 Rochelle (Shelly) Telles b 1945	**R' Feivel Wahl** b 1953 Malka Tauber b 1957
				Dr Shawn A Weil b 1975	**Nosson Wahl** b 1983

circle into account, their matches suggest that their kinship might be slightly more distant.[1]

The ancient Katzenellenbogen and their Wahl descendants were not of a priestly line, but both Shawn Weil and Nosson Wahl, as well as Thaddeus Taube belong to a Y-DNA haplogroup indicative of Cohanic male descent. It would appear that with these probands one of their female forebears might have married a Cohen but that their issue kept the mother's name. Such matronymic patterns were not uncommon in Galician Jewry of the relevant period. The results of Y-DNA 67 marker tests confirm that Shawn Weil and Nosson Wahl are of Y-DNA haplogroup J1 (M267), and their match of 65 out of 67 markers indicates a reasonably close common Cohen ancestor in their direct male line. However, my cousin Tad Taube, while of the same haplogroup J1 (M267), has a different Cohanic forebear. His numerous Y-DNA matches do not include Nosson or Shawn. Interestingly, one of Tad Taube's distant Cohanic Y-DNA matches of 61 out of 67 markers is with Abraham Richter. My own Y-DNA haplogroup is R2a (R-M124). In other words, while I have a number of Cohanic ancestors, they are not in my direct male line, but Tad and I both have autosomal DNA matches with Abraham Richter.

Chart 22.3 (in the colour plates) shows matches on the chromosomes numbered 1 to 22 for Thaddeus Taube with Nosson Wahl (orange), Shawn Weil (blue), Edward Gelles (green), and Marilyn Low Schmitt (pink). There is only slight evidence for a common Wahl ancestor between the three Wahl second cousins and our more distant cousins. Nosson Wahl and Shawn Weil match Tad Taube exactly on chromosome 9. Edward Gelles has small matches with Nosson on chromosome 1 and with Shawn on chromosomes 2 and 4.

Chart 22.4 (in the colour plates) similarly shows matches of Elsa Schmaus with Nosson Wahl (orange), Susan Lee Lipsitt (blue), and Edward Gelles (green). Elsa Gellis Schmaus, a daughter of my uncle Dr Max Gellis and Nellie Leinkram, is my first cousin. Susan Lee née Weinstein is my second cousin once removed. Rabbi Zvi Aryeh Weinstein and Gittel Horowitz of Solotwina were our nearest common ancestors, as set out in the preceding chapter. Small matches between Nosson Wahl and Edward Gelles are apparent on chromosomes 2, 4, 5, and 7.

Chart 22.5 brings out matches of Nosson Wahl with Bruce Fetter (blue), Peter A. Pitzele (pink), and Sandra Aaronson (yellow) on chromosome 14 and with Jeffrey D. Wexler (orange), Elsa Schmaus (green), and Peter A. Pitzele (pink) on chromosome 15.

Simply on the basis of the above comparisons one might conclude that if Nosson Wahl and Shawn Weil have a common ancestor with the family descended from Leiser Wahl of Tarnobrzeg and Zlate Roisel of Nisko, their most recent common Wahl forebear must be some generations further back than those shown in Table 22.2. There is documentary evidence for the presence of Wahls in Tarnobrzeg in the eighteenth century. Shawn and Nosson might be of the order of ten or more generations down from a Wahl ancestor common to all the Wahls in the table, at which distance the *Family Finder* becomes increasingly unreliable in estimating genetic distance for inbred Ashkenazi Jews.

In Table 22.6 I have taken some probands of Gelles, Polonsky (a cousinly Gelles–Shapiro line), Halpern, and Horowitz connection and compared their DNA matches with Tad Taube, myself, my paternal first cousin Elsa Gellis Schmaus and with Nosson Wahl and Shawn Weil. From these somewhat complex interrelationships, it emerges that the cousins Nosson Wahl and Shawn Weil are distantly related through sharing some DNA with me on my paternal Gelles and maternal Wahl sides as well as with my close cousins, and that some of these DNA matches suggest Halpern and Horowitz connections.

The results of the Y-DNA and *Family Finder* autosomal DNA tests discussed above have shed considerable light on family relationships. They have also revealed some limitations, particularly of the *Family Finder* test, that are due to the high degree of inbreeding in our old Ashkenazi families. It becomes apparent that the various probands under study have shared DNA from several family sources which are very difficult to differentiate without considerable background knowledge acquired through the traditional genealogical methodology and cross-checked with other probands of known pedigree. Thus, probands who are close cousins on the paternal side may also be distant cousins on the maternal side, and vice versa.

Some further progress can often be made with the help of the GEDmatch website, which processes the raw autosomal DNA data from the Family Tree DNA *Family Finder* tests as well as those from

Table 22.6 Autosomal DNA matches for Thaddeus Taube, Edward Gelles, Elsa Schmaus, Nosson Wahl, and Shawn A. Weil with probands having Wahl, Gelles, Polonsky, Halpern, Horowitz connections

Total shared DNA followed by longest shared segment above 5 cM

	Thaddeus Taube		Edward Gelles		Elsa Schmaus		Nosson Wahl		Shawn A Weil	
Wahl										
Tad Taube			375	48			105	20	78	9
Edward Gelles	375	48			875	99				
Nosson Wahl	105	20			88	11			119	24
Shawn A. Weil	78	9					119	24		
Gelles–Weinstein										
Elsa Schmaus			875	99			88	11		
Susan L. Lipsitt	69	8	211	31	182	49	72	9	62	16
Polonsky										
Jeffrey M. Paull	59	8	68	10	56	11	82	11		
Danny Dag			115	9	105	9	110	15	56	11
Halpern										
Leibish Halpern	69	12	*93*	*8*	99	18	102	29	93	10
Carmel Halperin	112	10	*94*	*8*	100	15	99	14		
Steven D. Bloom							109	14	83	8
Melvin H. Bloom	72	9	75	8						
Horowitz										
Harvey Horowitz			*85*	*9*	80	9			71	14
Annette M. Sussman	106	10	100	13					70	10
Thomas F. Weiss	80	9	113	9	88	9	99	10	148	10
Other										
Sandy Aaronson	65	12					67	11	103	12
Peter A. Pitzele	121	12	67	9	85	9	118	10		
Jeffrey D. Wexler	92	9	105	14	75	13	154	17		

The comparable figures are from *Family Finder* with shared segments above 5 cM, while the figures in italics are for shared segments of autosomal DNA uploaded on to GEDmatch (of probands that do not show up on the *Family Finder* list of matches for Edward Gelles) For Leibish and Carmel Halpern (see Chapter 21):
Edward Gelles
with Leibish Halpern: Total matches 93 cM, longest segment **[above 3 cM]** 8.2 cM, MRCA 5.4
with Carmel Halperin: Total matches 94 cM, longest segment 8.4 cM, MRCA 5.2
Elsa Schmaus (Gelles 1st cousin)
with Leibish Halpern: Total matches 112 cM, longest segment do 21.2 cM, MRCA 3.5
with Carmel Halperin: Total matches 113 cM, longest segment do 14.8 cM, MRCA 3.5

other test providers such as 23andme and Ancestry.com. GEDmatch has developed a number of ingenious facilities for interpreting these data.

One useful facility can give an indication whether a proband's parents are related to one another (ROH or run of homozygosity). This confirms that my parents, Dr David Gelles and Regina Griffel, were distant cousins, whereas the parents of my first Gelles cousin Elsa seem to have scarcely any common ancestors within the same time frame. Elsa showed no matches with my Wahl cousin Tad Taube.

In order to distinguish the DNA segments shared by Nosson Wahl and Shawn Weil with my paternal Gelles and my maternal Wahl side I employed another GEDmatch facility that throws up all matches on their extensive website that are above a certain size and are shared with a pair of probands and also with either one or the other of this pair.

Taking firstly Edward Gelles and Elsa Gellis Schmaus, I looked for substantial matches over 10 cM with this 'Gelles' pair. A proband's strong matches with both Gelles cousins would point to consanguinity with Gelles and their relations.

The results shown in Table 22.7 confirm the conclusion drawn from the preceding Table 22.6 based on *Family Finder* data that the larger part of Nosson and Shawn's shared DNA with me and my close cousins is of other than Wahl origin. Further interesting pointers continue to emerge from the several GEDmatch facilities.

Nosson Wahl clearly shares DNA with Edward Gelles, Elsa Schmaus, and Tad Taube that includes sources other than the Wahl line.

Shawn Weil has matches with some other Horowitz probands, including Lawrence Horowitz, and Ilya Gurevich Varnavati, and these also share DNA segments with Edward Gelles.

The matches shown by Nosson Wahl and Shawn Weil with my close cousins and me, be they on my paternal Gelles side (Elsa Schmaus, Susan Lee Lipsitt) or my maternal Wahl side (Thaddeus Taube, Marilyn Low Schmitt) appear to come more from such as Halpern, Horowitz, and Cohen ancestry than from Wahl–Katzenellenbogen connections. It should be noted that Edward Gelles, Elsa Schmaus (née Gelles), Susan Lee Lipsitt (née Weinstein), Robert Mansbach, Sandy Aaronson, and also my Wahl cousin Tad Taube have some

Table 22.7 Autosomal DNA matches above 10 cM with one or both probands of a pair: Edward Gelles & Elsa Gellis Schmaus and Shawn Weil & Nosson Wahl (GEDmatch) (total shared DNA/longest shared segment/ and number of generations to a most recent common ancestor (MRCA))

Matching with Edward Gelles and Elsa Gellis Schmaus

Susan Lee Lipsitt	241.3/33.4/2.9	and	221.0/51.9/3.0
Ralph N. Baer	164.7/11.0/3.2	and	142.1/10.6/3.3
Ira R. Alperin	127.2/14.9/3.4	and	85.4/11.4/3.7
Jeffrey D. Wexler	108.1/12.8/3.5	and	100.5/11.1/3.6
Sandy Aaronson	no segment over 10 cM		103.7/11.6/3.6
Robert Mansbach	86.8/11.0/3.7	and	113.1/13.7/3.5
W.M. Oppenheim	100.2/15.0/3.6	and	120.6/13.3/3.4
Julia P. Guggenheim	98.7/9.1/4.5	and	96.8/9.4/3.7
Lorie Krieger	116.3/16.4/3.6	and	114.8/15.9/3.6
Nosson Wahl	84.8/10.4/3.7	and	107.8/13.5/3.5

Matching with Nosson Wahl and Shawn Weil

Susan Lee Lipsitt	70.6/11.8/3.8	and	77.7/16.4/3.8
Ira R. Alperin	92.5/13.0/3.6	and	69.3/11.0/3.8
Julia P. Guggenheim	106.7/14.2/3.5	and	94.9 /11.0/3.6
Sandy Aaronson	11.7/11.7/	and	13.8/13.8/
Thaddeus N. Taube	104.8/22.0/3.5		no segments over 10 cM
Jeffrey D. Wexler	154.4/17.5/3.3		no segments over 10 cM
Robert Mansbach	77.2/10.6/3.8		no segments over 10 cM
Lawrence Horowitz	no segments above 10 cM		11.3/11.3/
Ilya Gurevich Varnavati	no segments above 10 cM		13.6/13.6/

Horowitz ancestry. Ralph Baer, Guggenheim, Oppenheim, Lorie Krieger, Debra Calzareth, and others derive from a medieval family nexus, emanating from the Rhineland, to whose genetic make-up many ancient families contributed. Reference should be made to the tables in the preceding Chapter 21 and to Chapter 15 with tables touching upon our early German connections.

SUMMARY AND CONCLUSION

Several families called Wahl have records going back for more than two hundred years in a little Galician town. One of them is my maternal grandmother's family. Descendants of two neighbouring families bearing the Wahl name have now taken relevant DNA tests. A study of their genealogical data and of the new genetic evidence indicates that these two probands share some DNA with me and my Wahl second cousins, Thaddeus N. Taube and Marilyn Low Schmitt, but also with my paternal Gelles kinsfolk, whose connection with the Wahl–Katzenellenbogen is considerably more distant. A large part of this shared DNA appears to be common with some Halpern, Horowitz, and Cohen probands. Any common Wahl roots must lie some distance in the past. It is interesting that Tad Taube, Shawn A. Weil, and Nosson Wahl turn out to be of Cohanic descent along their direct male lines. Shawn and Nosson have a close Y-DNA match and presumably a common Cohen ancestor whose marriage to a Wahl led to issue that retained their mother's family name. There is no sign of a link between this forebear and the nearest Cohanic ancestor of my close cousin Thaddeus Taube.

NOTE ON THE WAHL NAME

My first book, *An Ancient Lineage*, discusses the origins of our illustrious forebear Saul Wahl and his extensive progeny. It also has several chapters on my grandmother Chawa Wahl, her sisters Rachel and Blume Wahl and their marriage links with the Griffel, Taube, and Low families. Chapters 7, 8, 9, and 15 of the present volume are relevant to this discussion.

I am very dubious about the story originating with Rabbi Pinchas Katzenellenbogen's account in *Yesh Manhilin*, written in the early eighteenth century, that Saul Katzenellenbogen was called Wahl (the German noun meaning 'choice' or 'election') after being made *Rex pro tempore* during the interregnum of 1587. I believe that the Wahl name was acquired by Saul when he travelled from his native Padua to Poland, where his new friends called him Saul Wahl, i.e. Saul the Italian, 'Walen' being the medieval German word for 'Italians'.

My grandmother Chawa Wahl's family and the Hausers were the leading Jewish families in Tarnobrzeg-Dzikow. This Wahl family and their relations, including the Wohls of Krakow, maintained their wealth and social position until World War II, as documented in contemporary town records, memorial books, and monographs. They were very conscious of their lineage, shown, for example, by the first names they gave their children.

Nosson Wahl's family also had multiple ancient connections and a family tradition of descent from Saul Wahl, the legendary 'king for a day'.

Shawn Weil has a close Y-DNA match with Nosson Wahl, indicating a common Cohanic ancestor. He also shares some DNA with Halpern and Horowitz probands, but has only weak DNA matches with my family. He has sent me the appended note on the name change from Wahl to Weil that occurred in his line, and he has asked me to append it to my essay. I can only conclude from this note, and I think that Shawn will agree with me, that his forebears, who came to America as poor immigrants, were most probably unaware of the history of the Wahl name and its origin and were anxious to put behind them all reminders of the old country and the Dzikow community. This seems to be the real motive for the name change and I think that credit is due to Shawn for facing this problem and wishing to lift the shadow of doubt over his lineage that thus arose a century ago.

Shawn A Weil's account of the name change in his lineage

Nasanel 'Sana' Wahl was born around 1864 in Dzikow, Poland. He married Yetta Abramowitz of either Witkowice or Majdan, Poland – the daughter of Aron Abramowitz and Jente Wilkenfeld – c.1884. They had two children in Radomysl-nad-Sanem, Poland: Chaim Mejer (later Matty, 1886–1970) and Reisel (later Rose, 1888–1983). As was common at that time, it is likely that Sana and Yetta did not have a civil marriage; both children are listed as 'Abramowitz' in Polish birth records. Sana immigrated alone to New York on April 18, 1890 aboard the steamships Weimar (Hamburg to Edinburgh) and State of Georgia (Glasgow to New York). Yetta and the two children followed on July 30, 1891 on the SS Veendam (Rotterdam to New York). They settled on Willet St. in the Lower East Side of New York and had seven additional children: Henry/Harry (1893–1979), Abraham/Al

(1895–1984), Sadie/Sarah (1897–1986), Bella (1899–1971), Max (1901–1982), Jacob/Jack (1903–1987), and Moses (1905–1907). Nasanel Americanised his name to Sam.

While possibly apocryphal, family tradition suggests that the surname was changed from Wahl to Weil around 1905 when Matty – who performed in vaudeville in the 1900s and 1910s – decided that Wahl 'sounded too Yiddish.' In contrast, 'Weil' had the air of sophistication of a higher class German surname.

Such a change would have distinguished him from other Jewish actors and thus helped his career. Sadly, the change did not have the desired effect; Matty's success in show business was short lived and he went on to have a long career as a postal employee. Nevertheless, the rest of the family liked the name change and followed suit soon after. The surname was listed as 'Wahl' in the family listings in the US Federal Censuses of 1900 and 1910 and New York State Census of 1905. It is listed as 'Weill' in the death certificate of Moses Wahl (aka Maurice Weill. D. Nov 12 1907; NYC Death Cert #35890), and listed as 'Weil' in the 1912 marriage certificate of Matty Weil and Esther Pearlman (NYC Certificate# 25538), the 1920 US Federal Census, and all subsequent vital records. Yetta died in 1944; Nasanel died in 1954.

Chapter 23

X-DNA matches and European roots

C HAPTERS 23 AND 24 ATTEMPT to assess the facilities provided by the website GEDmatch.com for evaluating X-DNA and autosomal DNA matches between a small group of European Jews and non-Jews.

In the first of these two pilot studies, some Ashkenazi Jewish cousins and a few non-Jews from western and eastern Europe show little shared autosomal DNA in recent generations, but these apparently unrelated probands have X-DNA matches that suggest some common genetic origins, possibly going back to the time of Norse migrations.

INTRODUCTION

There are several widely used commercial tests for autosomal DNA whose results may be uploaded onto the website GEDmatch, where the data obtained from these different tests can be directly compared. GEDmatch provides numerous other innovative facilities, including a convenient way of studying X-DNA matches.

Unlike mitochondrial DNA (mtDNA), which is passed down in a direct female line from mother to daughter, the DNA that is passed down on the X-chromosome follows a more complicated path. Females inherit one X-DNA chromosome from their father and another from their mother. Males have one X-chromosome from their mother and a Y-chromosome from their father. A father–son generation within a lineage will therefore obscure previous X-DNA inheritance and result in zero X-DNA match. With females having two X-chromosomes and males only one X-chromosome the possibilities of X-DNA matches between two females are enhanced, and indeed the majority of my X-DNA probands are female. Because of the particular way X-DNA passes down the generations the trail may be difficult to follow. X-DNA matches may nevertheless be revealing about genetic origins that are too far back in time for help from autosomal DNA tests or traditional genealogical methodology.

My recent studies of autosomal DNA matches between cousins brought me into contact with people of various nationalities and backgrounds who had little or no apparent connection with my family. I then made the serendipitous discovery that some of these probands had X-DNA matches between themselves and with two close cousins of mine. These matches exemplify the complex genetic admixtures of peoples concomitant with the history of Europe from ancient times to the present day.

AUTOSOMAL DNA MATCHES AND GENETIC ORIGINS

The data in Table 23.1 are calculated from the model of Dienekes Pontikos, whose bio-geographical categories indicate genetic admixture proportions that are informative for comparative purposes in selected groups of probands. The numerous models of Eurogenes

Table 23.1 Genetic admixture proportions of some Jewish and non-Jewish probands on GEDmatch

(Dodecad v3 after Dienekes Pontikos)

	W Eur	E Eur	Med	W Asia	SW Asia	NW Africa
Ashkenazi						
Edward Gelles	20.2	5.7	31.1	22.5	13.1	4.3
Elsa Schmaus	18.8	5.1	32.9	23.2	13.8	3.4
Tad Taube	21.3	2.8	33.3	23.4	12.5	3.2
½ Ashkenazi + ½ Norwegian/French						
Marilyn Low Schmitt	33.6	8.7	29.1	17.2	6.3	2.7
¼ Ashkenazi + ¼ German + ½ Norwegian						
Kitty Munson Cooper	44.8	9.2	27.3	10.0	5.6	-
Norwegian						
Lawrence S Munson (father of above)	56.0	14.4	20.5	5.6	-	0.5
English						
Elizabeth Noyes	52.9	12.3	24.7	6.3	1.3	1.0
Irish						
Mary Ellen Desmond	54.8	11.3	24.4	5.7	1.4	0.6
½ Russian + ¼ Ukrainian + ¼ Ashkenazi						
Maryana Panyarskaya	35.9	27.8	17.5	7.7	3.3	1.8
Russian (some Karelian)						
Anna Rumianteeva (mother of above)	37.5	36.0	12.6	3.2	0.9	0.7

Davidski, which are also accessible through the GEDmatch website, have evolved methods for relating data to various bio-geographical reference groups which are also highly suggestive in attempting to gain insights into genetic admixtures. The data from these analyses reflect ancient migrations and intermarriages as well as more recent family history.

I and my paternal first cousin Elsa Gellis Schmaus have ancient Jewish ancestry. We do not know of any non-Jewish ancestors within the past two or three hundred years. My second cousin Marilyn Low Schmitt is of a similar and related Jewish lineage on her father's side, but her mother was Norwegian with French Canadian admixture, as indicated in the table.

Among the outstanding features of Table 23.1 are the West European, Mediterranean, and ancient Middle Eastern admixtures of Ashkenazi Jews. Their East European admixture is generally low because during their long sojourn in that part of Europe, they lived in strictly endogamous communities. The small North-West African admixture may relate to the period in Moorish Spain.

The genetic admixtures of three Ashkenazi Jews, three (non-Jewish) West Europeans, and an East European (Russian) proband are clearly distinguished in the table and are typical of many other probands in their particular categories.

Autosomal DNA matches in Table 23.2 indicate that a few generations back I and my close cousins had some common ancestry with Maryana Panyarskaya, whose father Victor Panyarsky is half-Jewish and emerges from his DNA tests as a not so distant cousin of ours. There is also a trace of common autosomal DNA with Kitty Munson Cooper. Any common ancestry with the other probands appears too remote to be presently identifiable.

X-DNA MATCHES

Table 23.3 shows the X-DNA matches between close cousins Edward Gelles and Marilyn Low Schmitt.

These matches are consistent with the known genealogical relationship of these two second cousins.

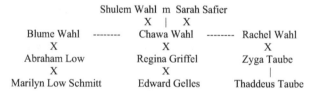

```
                   Shulem Wahl  m  Sarah Safier
                          X   |   X
   Blume Wahl   --------  Chawa Wahl  --------  Rachel Wahl
        X                     X                      X
  Abraham Low            Regina Griffel          Zyga Taube
        X                     X                      |
Marilyn Low Schmitt      Edward Gelles        Thaddeus Taube
```

They do not show X-DNA matches with their second cousin Thaddeus Taube because X-DNA could not pass to him from his father Zyga. For a similar reason, I do not show any shared X-DNA with my paternal first cousin Elsa:

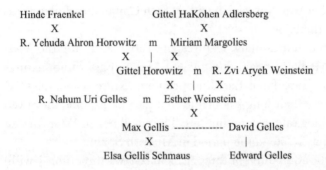

X-DNA lines of descent for men are screened out when they come to a father–son link. However, four of my X-DNA matches have come through and are shown with matches (overlapping or not) of other proband pairs.

It may be noted that all 17 female proband pairs in Table 23.4 have shared X-DNA located at 146–153 and fifteen pairs have shared X-DNA within either or both 45–48 and 50–68. There are also numerous pairs with matches at 118–120. Comparison with the autosomal matches listed in Table 23.2 shows that there is no correlation between the amount of autosomal and X-DNA matching. Indeed, in some cases, significant X-DNA matches have been found for pairs that do not register any autosomal matches above 5 cM in length. The autosomal DNA matches may reveal common ancestors (on either side of families, irrespective of sex) and can support established genealogical connections over a few hundred years. X-DNA matches may or may not originate considerably further back in time. Because of the complex manner in which X-DNA and autosomal DNA are passed down the generations it is presently impossible to do more than speculate as to the origins of common X-DNA or the dates of common ancestors that give rise to these matches. However, if we compare the size of the X-DNA matches between cousins sharing great-grandparents in Table 23.3 with the very small X-DNA fragments for other pairs of probands in Table 23.4, the latter appear to indicate common ancestral origins that go back for quite a long time.

Table 23.2 Autosomal DNA matches between the probands in Table 23.1 DNA segments are measured in centimorgans (cM) and the generational distance is indicated by MRCA (most recent common ancestor)

	Longest block	Total match	MRCA
Lizzie Noyes & Mary Ellen Desmond	4.3 cM (chr1)	18.1 cM	6.8
Lizzie Noyes & Edward Gelles	5.3 cM (chr 22)	13.2 cM	7.0
Lizzie Noyes & Elsa Schmaus	4.6 cM (chr 9)	14.4 cM	7.0
Lizzie Noyes & Marilyn Schmitt	8.2 cM (chr 22)	29.2 cM	6.3
Mary E Desmond & Edward Gelles	4.1 cM (chr 13)	4.1 cM	–
Mary E Desmond & Elsa Schmaus	3.1 cM (chr 16)	3.1 cM	–
Mary E Desmond & Marilyn Schmitt	4.0 cM (chr 3)	7.7 cM	7.4
Mary E. Desmond &Maryana Panyarskaya	4.3 cM (chr 12)	20.6 cM	6.7
Maryana Panyarskaya & Lizzie Noyes	–	–	–
Maryana Panyarskaya & Elsa Schmaus	15.5 cM (chr11)	52.1 cM	4.1
Maryana Panyarskaya & Edward Gelles	9.3 cM (chr14)	20.6 cM	5.4
Kitty Munson Cooper + Edward Gelles	8.8 cM (chr 20)	24.3 cM	5.5
Kitty Munson Cooper + Elsa Schmaus	7.1 cM (chr 16)	13.0 cM	7.1
Kitty Munson Cooper + Marilyn Schmitt	10.1 cM (chr 16)	28.0 cM	4.5

Table 23.3 X-DNA matches between close cousins Edward Gelles and Marilyn Low Schmitt

Chr	Start location	End location	Centimorgans (cM)	SNPs*
X	13,431,098	32,387,789	28.2	2,856
X	86,088,392	100,699,852	16.3	1,468

* Single nucleotide polymorphism, a change in DNA code at a specific point or locus.

Table 23.4 X-DNA matches between probands of different ethnic groups

X-DNA matches between Elizabeth Noyes and Edward Gelles

Chr	Start location	End location	Centimorgans (cM)	SNPs
X	**146,818,012**	**148,413,312**	3.3	208

X-DNA matches between Kitty Munson Cooper and Edward Gelles

Chr	Start location	End location	Centimorgans (cM)	SNPs
X	49,348,271	53,818,269	3.1	308

X-DNA matches between Kitty Munson Cooper and Elsa Schmaus

Chr	Start location	End location	Centimorgans (cM)	SNPs
X	18,287,242	21,921,357	3.9	384
X	111,317,946	114,598,734	5.7	350
X	117,891,777	119,283,125	3.4	200
X	129,378,794	133,541,438	3.6	380
X	134,326,312	137,958,084	3.1	442
X	139,785,574	141,024,884	6.2	241
X	143,464,441	145,397,362	4.2	374
X	**147,227,093**	**149,433,373**	5.2	275

X-DNA matches between Kitty Munson Cooper and Marilyn Low Schmitt

Chr	Start location	End location	Centimorgans (cM)	SNPs
X	3,467,060	5,269,115	3.2	243
X	6,446,087	8,798,982	3.4	299
X	32,228,468	33,119,101	5.4	231
X	49,348,271	53,915,022	3.1	315
X	96,999,352	99,756,864	3.4	247
X	106,153,076	111,267,826	3.7	410
X	118,435,685	119,727,491	3.5	214
X	123,474,023	125,579,389	3.6	201
X	**145,036,073**	**147,012,373**	3.7	329
X	**147,197,392**	**149,433,373**	5.2	276
X	151,841,809	154,056,000	3.8	367

X-DNA matches between Kitty Munson Cooper and Elizabeth Noyes

Chr	Start location	End location	Centimorgans (cM)	SNPs
X	18,709,806	22,065,345	3.6	534
X	32,148,765	32,684,449	3.7	236
X	38,996,765	40,302,137	3.4	263
X	44,940,333	47,266,812	4.4	377
X	48,806,648	53,390,283	3.0	460
X	96,222,232	99,328,471	3.7	418
X	140,797,756	141,959,128	3.7	360
X	**146,458,116**	**149,433,373**	6.0	550
X	**151,574,761**	**154,776,431**	5.0	1,125

Table 23.4 (*cont.*)

X-DNA matches between Kitty Munson Cooper and Mary Ellen Desmond

Chr	Start location	End location	Centimorgans (cM)	SNPs
X	18,548,003	21,711,190	3.1	330
X	22,279,098	22,929,238	3.1	206
X	34,930,981	37,956,140	3.4	280
X	41,030,869	43,801,623	3.3	405
X	95,825,238	99,768,232	4.9	388
X	112,104,112	114,764,437	4.5	262
X	**147,660,329**	**149,433,373**	4.1	210

X-DNA matches between Kitty Munson Cooper and Maryana Panyarskaya

Chr	Start location	End location	Centimorgans (cM)	SNPs
X	16,474,673	20,446,593	5.1	649
X	112,841,080	114,764,437	3.1	304
X	130,238,646	135,251,995	4.9	755
X	138,390,034	139,807,973	4.2	332
X	**150,191,653**	**154,886,292**	9.5	1,480

X-DNA matches between Kitty Munson Cooper and Anna Rumianteeva

Chr	Start location	End location	Centimorgans (cM)	SNPs
X	16,475,931	20,281,379	4.9	619
X	32,508,439	33,119,101	3.5	215
X	44,101,254	45,550,550	3.1	245
X	53,968,194	68,138,735	3.8	924
X	96,999,352	99,665,183	3.2	331
X	123,441,813	125,392,308	3.5	266
X	138,390,034	139,532,272	3.2	247
X	**150,962,510**	**154,776,431**	7.4	1,226

X-DNA matches between Elsa Schmaus and Marilyn Schmitt

Chr	Start location	End location	Centimorgans (cM)	SNPs
X	43,541,328	47,341,897	8.0	546
X	108,904,776	111,961,783	4.1	295
X	112,322,741	114,942,982	4.3	275
X	118,428,476	119,801,480	3.7	242
X	**147,692,466**	**150,082,478**	6.3	341
X	**150,089,755**	**151,568,664**	4.8	273

X-DNA matches between Elizabeth Noyes and Elsa Schmaus

Chr	Start location	End location	Centimorgans (cM)	SNPs
X	10,013,642	13,044,765	4.3	530
X	13,479,258	20,135,114	8.3	788
X	50,404,527	67,990,048	5.9	751
X	**146,500,671**	**149,344,611**	5.7	342

Table 23.4 (*cont.*)

X-DNA matches between Elizabeth Noyes and Marilyn Schmitt

Chr	Start location	End location	Centimorgans (cM)	SNPs
X	54,471,131	68,305,672	4.1	539
X	96,888,041	100,022,144	4.0	326
X	119,105,738	120,855,809	3.5	252
X	142,016,182	143,415,278	3.4	222
X	**147,692,466**	**149,874,189**	**5.6**	282

X-DNA matches between Elizabeth Noyes and Mary Ellen Desmond

Chr	Start location	End location	Centimorgans (cM)	SNPs
X	31,151,660	32,325,295	4.3	381
X	34,930,981	37,946,057	3.4	275
X	45,437,167	47,289,190	3.5	246
X	50,626,354	58,276,219	3.7	453
X	133,191,565	136,274,223	3.2	388
X	141,244,479	143,866,262	6.4	450
X	**147,692,466**	**149,876,606**	**5.7**	283

X-DNA matches between Mary Ellen Desmond and Elsa Schmaus

Chr	Start location	End location	Centimorgans (cM)	SNPs
X	9,503,470	12,366,236	4.8	460
X	49,348,271	53,888,348	3.1	320
X	96,726,313	99,630,571	3.5	292
X	109,151,543	113,282,415	6.3	396
X	**144,754,823**	**146,455,809**	3.6	278
X	**151,805,387**	**153,378,750**	3.7	293

X-DNA matches between Mary Ellen Desmond and Marilyn Schmitt

Chr	Start location	End location	Centimorgans (cM)	SNPs
X	108,583,637	112,115,059	4.7	353
X	112,322,741	114,580,118	3.8	226
X	118,601,015	119,800,355	3.3	203
X	142,249,687	143,712,720	3.7	251
X	**144,787,952**	**146,978,728**	4.2	371
X	**147,660,329**	**149,519,155**	4.5	237

X-DNA matches between Maryana Panyarskaya & Elizabeth Noyes

Chr	Start location	End location	Centimorgans (cM)	SNPs
X	3,022,405	4,499,980	6.0	284
X	6,144,767	8,458,794	3.1	471
X	18,709,806	21,921,357	3.3	490
X	32,425,038	32,902,397	3.2	205
X	41,709,887	44,315,214	**3.7**	545
X	44,942,961	48,631,670	**6.5**	618
X	53,718,534	67,985,390	**3.5**	929

Table 23.4 (*cont.*)

Chr	Start location	End location	Centimorgans (cM)	SNPs
X	109,476,475	112,372,126	4.4	396
X	118,583,348	119,775,096	3.3	268
X	131,875,879	135,251,995	4.0	504
X	141,439,008	143,945,948	6.0	572
X	**146,259,065**	**149,398,024**	6.2	587
X	**150,824,704**	**152,249,383**	4.9	283

X-DNA matches between Anna Rumianteeva (Maryana's mother) & Elizabeth Noyes

Chr	Start location	End location	Centimorgans (cM)	SNPs
X	5,750,117	8,451,028	3.4	563
X	22,941,185	23,698,072	3.5	248
X	32,392,711	32,902,397	3.4	219
X	41,223,411	44,122,488	3.9	560
X	44,942,961	46,837,342	3.5	299
X	51,206,885	68,300,850	**5.7**	1,179
X	96,222,232	99,603,685	4.2	469
X	107,281,221	112,372,126	5.4	643
X	118,073,617	119,285,790	3.1	224
X	122,143,150	123,894,481	3.8	378
X	138,461,021	139,771,669	3.9	277
X	**146,495,898**	**149,293,064**	**5.5**	472
X	**150,685,174**	**151,922,021**	4.5	276

X-DNA matches Maryana Panyarskaya & Mary Ellen Desmond

Chr	Start location	End location	Centimorgans (cM)	SNPs
X	9,644,738	11,799,025	3.5	306
X	45,435,256	62,140,538	10.7	1,092
X	109,353,801	113,380,578	6.1	376
X	142,249,687	143,944,970	4.2	283
X	**147,692,466**	**149,433,547**	4.1	207

X-DNA matches between Maryana Panyarskaya & Elsa Schmaus

Chr	Start location	End location	Centimorgans (cM)	SNPs
X	18,311,035	20,443,627	3.1	225
X	55,099,743	68,124,714	3.3	438
X	109,353,801	111,961,783	3.6	238
X	138,261,388	139,773,727	4.3	206
X	141,779,863	143,453,049	4.0	275
X	**146,480,705**	**148,149,284**	**3.3**	235
X	**150,817,675**	**152,249,383**	5.0	205

X-DNA matches between Maryana Panyarskaya & Marilyn Schmitt

Chr	Start location	End location	Centimorgans (cM)	SNPs
X	41,859,746	46,828,482	8.3	671

Table 23.4 (*cont.*)

X	112,841,080	114,942,982	3.3	226
X	118,573,983	119,774,905	3.3	202
X	**147,884,018**	**149,683,999**	**4.3**	226
X	**150,722,881**	**152,702,933**	6.3	317

GENEALOGICAL BACKGROUND OF PROBANDS

Kitty Munson Cooper is fortunate to have a substantial paper trail showing families on her father's side who came from Norway to the United States. Her paternal grandmother's family has been traced for many generations claiming descent from Charlemagne and King Harald I (Harald Harfagre or Fairhair), who united Norway and founded a dynasty (*c.* 890–930), and further ancestral royal lines have been identified. On her mother's side, Kitty descends from Bavarian Jewish and Catholic lines. Her father Lawrence S. Munson has no record of any Jewish ancestry.

Elizabeth Noyes claims that her paternal line goes back to the Norman brothers William and Robert de Noyers, who were recorded in the Domesday Book as estate owners and managed land for the king. She has also traced her mother's line back for the best part of 500 years. Her mother was a Peabody whose tenth- to twelfth-generation ancestors are given as Pabodye, which I would take as being eponymous with a Norman locality. However, Elizabeth suggests her Viking connections are firstly on her father's side through a great-grandmother who was a Crewdson from the north-west of England, to where they may have come from Ireland. She backs this up with some DNA tests of a cousin of that name showing an X-DNA match in the region of 146–153. Secondly, on her mother's side, mitochondrial DNA tests indicate that Elizabeth's mother's grandmother, Janet Emma Giles, belonged to haplogroup I 4 and may have been from a line of Viking origin. There is no record of any Jewish ancestry.

Mary Ellen Desmond's Irish ancestry includes a putative Desmond (of Munster) descent from Norman nobility. Her family came to America from 'the Black water', which they believe to be near the ancient estate of the Desmond Earls on the Blackwater river in county Cork. There is a family tradition of connection to the Geraldine Desmonds and the 'White Knights'. Maternal ancestors include Cotter (Mac Oitir) and Dillon, respectively of Norse-Gaelic and Norman origins, while more recent Scandinavian cousins are indicated by autosomal DNA matches. There is no record of any Jewish ancestry.

Maryana Panyarskaya has a half-Jewish father and a Russian mother. I and my cousin Elsa show MRCA of 4.2 and 3.6 from autosomal matches with Viktor Panyarskij, who on his father's side has ancient Jewish ancestry. He has the longest shared autosomal DNA segment of 14.4 cM and total shared DNA of 92.0 cM with my paternal first cousin Elsa and is thus a not so distant cousin of ours. Maryana's Russian mother's paternal grandmother was from Karelia and there are numerous distant Swedish and Norwegian cousins from this source. However, Maryana's father's Ukrainian (partly Jewish) mother also shows rather similar X-DNA matches with my close cousins and with Elizabeth Noyes and Mary Ellen Desmond.

Maryana has an autosomal DNA match with the latter, indicating a common ancestor say two to three hundred years ago. But there is no sign of autosomal matches between Maryana, her mother, and her paternal grandmother and Elizabeth Noyes. And yet their X-DNA matches are substantial.

As for the author's background, ancestral lines go back to the ancient Kalonymos of Narbonne and descendants of Davidic Exilarchs linked with the Carolingian and subsequent dynasties.

CONCLUSION

The autosomal DNA data and genetic admixtures for four non-Jewish Europeans are shown in Table 23.1, The autosomal DNA data of these Norwegian, English, Irish, and Russian probands were subjected to the new Eurogenes (Davidski) **J test**, which is particularly suitable for showing up small Ashkenazi Jewish admixtures, and the results confirmed such admixture to be less than the margin of error (about 2 per cent).

In Carolingian times an admixture of Jews, Franks, and Norsemen (Danes) may have been propagated in the west while in the east Norse cousins left their lasting mark on Rus from the Baltic to the Black Sea. But some common ancestors of the probands date from more recent times than others. Since the time of the Renaissance, there has been much movement and intermarriage across the continent of Europe, adding to the genetic imprint left by the grand migrations of the ancient Norsemen.

While not all X-DNA matches on a particular segment might be on the segment inherited from the same ancestor, it does appear that the X-DNA matches between these 'Jewish' and 'non-Jewish' probands indicate some common ancestry, and that this common ancestry may include a Norse contribution.

SOURCES

[1] The websites of Family Tree DNA, 23andme, and Gedmatch, as well as *Leon Kull's Half-Identical Regions (HIR)* website
[2] Edward Gelles 'Autosomal DNA matches between close cousins', *The Galitzianer*, Vol.10. No.1 March 2012.
[3] *Idem*, 'Autosomal DNA and genetic origins of some Ashkenazi cousins', www.jewishgen.org/galicia/assets/images/AutosomalAshkenazi.pdf.
[4] *Idem, An Ancient Lineage*. (London: Vallentine Mitchell 2006), Chapter 37, 'Historical Impact of Ancient Myth'.

ACKNOWLEDGEMENTS

I am indebted to Kitty Munson Cooper, Kathleen Dubin, Elizabeth Noyes, and Maryana Panyarskaya for information about their family backgrounds.

Chapter 24

Genetic admixture of Ashkenazi Jews

Relating to their millennial migrations

The website GEDmatch.com provides a valuable facility for arriving at a rough idea of the genetic admixture of individual probands by comparing their autosomal DNA data obtained from one or other of several commercial test providers, currently Family Tree DNA, 23andme, and Ancestry.com. Several models have been developed which allow these DNA data of individuals to be compared with different sets of bio-geographical reference groups.

Using several of the models in this pilot study, a small group of Ashkenazi Jews is compared with some selected West and East European non-Jews. The qualitative results are that for each of these models the genetic mixtures of the Jews, and non-Jewish West and East European probands are patently distinct. The Ashkenazi Jews reflect their complex millennial journey in a well-defined genetic admixture.

GENETIC GENEALOGY AND DNA TESTS

Genetic studies of the Jewish people have made great strides in the past decade, and the supporting role of genetics in genealogy and anthropology is becoming increasingly important.

The methodology of genealogical research is being extended by use of commercially available DNA tests. One of the leading companies in this field is Family Tree DNA of Houston, Texas, who offer tests for matching individual Y-DNA, mitochondrial DNA, and autosomal DNA on their substantial database.

I have recently carried out a comparison of autosomal DNA data with several close cousins and a select handful of more distant relatives. I used the above-mentioned company's *Family Finder* test, which discovers matches with significant DNA segments among the 22 out of 23 chromosome pairs that are not related to sex and can thus show up common ancestry, both male and female, on both sides of a family. This *Family Finder* test is still in the process of development and its present shortcomings make it much more useful for my purpose of comparing related groups of substantially known pedigree than in testing an isolated individual. I understand that the testing company's algorithms are being developed to make more allowance for the particularity of Jewish endogamy (inbreeding). The test's calculations of 'genetic distance' to a most recent common ancestor will improve and the size of its database will surely expand to make it a useful tool in genealogical research. The autosomal DNA matches on the *Family Finder* database can be compared with those obtained from similar tests offered by other companies such as 23andme and Ancestry.com when their respective data are uploaded on to the most innovative website, GEDmatch.com.

OUR MILLENNIAL JOURNEY

Most Jewish people searching for their roots find it difficult enough to work back for more than half a dozen generations, particularly when their more recent roots are in eastern Europe where so many records have been lost. However, some of our ancient rabbinic families can trace their pedigrees back to Rabbi Solomon ben Isaac of Troyes, known as Rashi, who lived in the eleventh century, and to the Kalonymos who flourished from the time of the Carolingians in the eighth century. Going back further to biblical times and to the time of King David three thousand years ago one is largely in the realms of myth and legend, which I believe to have great value for our culture but is not amenable to the kind of proof we can expect to have for our later family genealogies.

We have been brought up on the chapters in Genesis that relate our tribal origins. We were told that our patriarch Abraham came from 'Ur in the Chaldees'. Ancient writers quote a tale that Aristotle had spoken to a learned Jew who believed his people were descended from Indian philosophers. Such legends might be revisited in the context of recent genetic studies indicating that many thousands of years ago some of our forebears moved from India and Persia to Mesopotamia – present-day northern Iraq and Iran – and that genetic markers of the mixture with the people encountered in these migrations have come down to us. We are all familiar with the biblical account of our forebears in the old Persian Empire, deliverance from slavery in Egypt, settlement in the promised land, King David and his successors. When the kingdom of Israel fell to the Assyrians, its so-called ten 'lost tribes of Israel' were widely dispersed to Anatolia and the Caucasus, whence some went eastwards to the Persian Empire and India. Some Jewish presence in the Arabian peninsula may also date from this period.

Over a century later, the kingdom of Judea suffered a similar fate. Jerusalem was captured by the Babylonians, the first temple was destroyed, and the majority of its inhabitants were deported. After two generations had passed, many Jews finally returned and resurrected their state, but the descendants of those who did not return formed a large Jewish community that continued in Baghdad until recent times. Contemporaneous with these historic events, Jewish settlements were established all round the Mediterranean littoral. With Alexander the Great, Macedonian Greek influence and genetic admixture reached into India.

There was substantial Greek influence in Judea during the following Seleucid rule, and an important Hellenised Jewish community in Egypt. They were drawn to the hub of the Roman Empire before the great Diaspora that followed the destruction of the second temple, when large numbers of Jews were brought to Italy. Later came the rise of Islam and its outward spread from the Arabian peninsula. The Moorish invasion of Spain and the centuries-long process of conquest and reconquest led to conversions and intermarriage with Moors and Christians. At the same time, more Italian Jews crossed the Alps and some mixed with Visigoths and Franks.

The era of the Crusades from the end of the eleventh century saw the beginning of a millennial persecution that led not only to waves of Jewish migration from western to eastern Europe but also to the segregation of Jewish communities that became increasingly endogamous. From France and the Rhineland and from Italy via Austria and Bohemia our ancestors came to Poland and beyond, where they met eastern Jews who reached these lands from Anatolia, coming up the river valleys through present-day Rumania. These eastern Jews may also have included some from Khazaria north of the Black Sea.

There were persecutions in Spain at the end of the fourteenth century. A hundred years later, the Inquisition put an end to an ancient and brilliant culture on the Iberian peninsula and drove many Sephardi Jews to Holland and then to England, while others found refuge in the Ottoman Empire, in Salonica, and the Greek Islands, as well as in Constantinople, and some were in due course found in the distant corners of that empire. From the eighteenth century Age of Enlightenment the millennial eastern movement was gradually reversed and many Ashkenazi Jews moved back to the western lands where they had lived in the Middle Ages.

OUR GENETIC ORIGINS

This history is reflected in our genetic inheritance. Without having to delve too deeply into modern advances in genetics as applied to anthropology, such as bottlenecks, founder effects, and genetic drift, one can now obtain a rough idea of ancient genetic background by uploading autosomal data from the *Family Finder* test to the aforementioned GEDmatch. A number of models have been developed in which DNA data of probands are compared with different bio-geographical reference groups.

In the present essay I do not concern myself with a quantitative assessment of individual admixtures. My more modest purpose is to study some Ashkenazi Jews from my wider family circle and then to compare these with some West and East European probands of relatively well-known pedigree who appear not to have any noticeable Jewish admixture.

The first table (24.1) shows data for my close cousins and a few distant cousins who belong to the Halpern DNA study group with whom we share ancestral links to the ancient rabbinic family that took their name from Heilbronn in Germany. They appear to share a genetic background, which is in line with the general conclusions from numerous and much more extensive studies of Ashkenazi origins using mainly Y-DNA and mitochondrial DNA comparisons.

This model, called Dodecad v3, compares DNA of probands with that of select groups characterised as 'West Asian', 'South-West Asian', 'North-West African', 'Mediterranean', 'West European', 'East European', and so on. Jews in the Caucasus may be included under 'West Asian', while the very substantial 'Mediterranean' admixture for Ashkenazi Jews would be more 'European' in the western and more 'Jewish' in its eastern parts. The table shows about 5 per cent for East European and generally less than 5 per cent for North-West African. North-West African DNA may hark back to the time of the Moorish invasion of Spain and relate to an admixture which my families share to some extent with Sephardi Jews.

The low East European percentage might at first sight seem surprising, considering that many of our ancestors were in Galicia, Poland, Lithuania, and the Russian Pale for several hundred years. However, we know that during this period they lived in endogamous inward-looking communities. Our history and known genealogy clearly shows that several family lines came from Western Europe, including Portugal and Spain, France, Italy, and the Rhineland. Some Khazars may have got to Spain, but it seems that, at least as far as my Ashkenazi family circle is concerned, the genetic contribution from Khazar or East European DNA was not very significant. In a small number of instances, where known relatives showed higher East European percentages and other deviations from the 'norm' for my group of cousins, further enquiry established the presence of a non-Jewish or part-Jewish parent or grandparent.

Table 24.1 Genetic admixtures of some Ashkenazi cousins
from autosomal DNA data (after Dienekes Pontikos, Dodecad v3) (GEDmatch)

Ashkenazi Jews	W Asian	SW Asian	Mediterranean	NW African	West European	East European	NE Asian	Other
	Middle Eastern		Italian, Greek, etc.	Moorish				
Edward Gelles	22.5	13.1	31.1	4.3	20.2	5.7	0.5	2.6
Elsa Schmaus	23.2	13.8	32.9	3.4	18.8	5.1	0.5	2.3
Thaddeus Taube	22.7	12.4	32.7	3.2	20.7	3.4	0.4	4.5
Carmel Halperin	23.8	12.6	34.3	2.9	19.0	3.1	1.3	3.0
Leibish Halpern	25.2	13.9	30.9	6.6	15.5	3.9	0.9	3.1
Steven D. Bloom	23.9	13.8	31.3	2.9	17.8	6.0	1.2	3.1
Jeff Meyerson	21.3	12.2	32.8	1.9	20.8	7.0	0.4	3.6

In the preceding chapter these Ashkenazi Jews and a small group of Europeans were shown to have significant X-DNA matches. The European group comprised English, Irish, Norwegian, and Russian probands, whose genealogical past was fairly well known. A newly available test for the presence of a significant Ashkenazi Jewish admixture, the Eurogenes Davidski J model, confirmed that these Europeans appeared to have very little Jewish admixture.

The extent to which the admixtures shown for my Ashkenazi Jews in Table 24.1 represent a well-defined genetic profile shared by a wider range of Ashkenazim emerges from comparisons of Jewish and non-Jewish Europeans.

Tables 24.2 and 24.3 show the results of this comparison using the above-mentioned Dodecad v3 model and the Davidski Eurogenes EU models. There are now a considerable number of models with the Eurogenes Davidski approach using different bio-geographical reference groups.

No quantitative comparison of admixture percentages is made between the tables. The object of presenting them is to show that my probands fall into well-defined groups of Ashkenazi Jews, West Europeans, and East Europeans for each of the several models used in the comparisons. The data indicate that there is a significant amount of shared DNA between Ashkenazi Jews and European non-Jews and indeed between Europeans of different nationality and geographical origins, as a consequence of millennial pan-European migrations. Many Ashkenazi Jews do have a well-defined genetic profile which appears to have been the result of a genetic 'bottleneck' in the high Middle Ages, whence descent came from a relatively small group of forebears. Within this Ashkenazi profile there are most interesting second-order variations which reflect the short- and longer-term genetic histories of individuals.

GEDmatch has further facilities for studying individual genetic admixture proportions from their autosomal DNA data. Some of the more recently offered models such as the 'four population sharing' analyses are still very much in the process of development. However, some results of applying earlier models to a comparison of the autosomal DNA data for myself and three non-Jewish European probands are presented below. In the genetic admixtures shown in the following tables the term 'Ashkenazi' refers to the fairly well-defined mixture of European and Eastern DNA.

Table 24.2 Genetic admixture proportions of Jewish and Gentile probands from GEDmatch (after Dienekes Pontikos – Dodecad v3 model)

Name	1	2	3	4	5	6	7	8	9	10	11	12	13
	ASHKENAZI JEWS					MIXED		W EUROPEAN			MIXED	E EUROPEAN	
W European	20.2	18.8	21.3	16.1	17.9	33.6	44.8	54.8	52.9	56.0	35.9	37.1	37.5
E European	5.7	5.1	2.8	3.2	5.4	8.7	9.2	11.3	12.3	14.4	27.8	31.3	36.0
Mediterranean	31.1	32.9	33.3	32.7	32.9	29.1	27.3	24.4	24.7	20.5	17.5	18.2	12.6
W Asian	22.5	23.2	23.4	25.3	24.1	17.2	10.0	5.7	6.3	5.6	7.7	7.2	3.2
SW Asian	13.1	13.8	12.5	14.7	12.6	6.3	5.6	1.4	1.3	–	3.3	2.8	0.9
NW African	4.3	3.4	3.2	4.4	3.3	2.7	–	0.6	1.0	0.5	1.8	1.4	0.7

ASHKENAZI: 1 **Edward Gelles** *close cousins* 2 **Elsa Schmaus** 3 **Tad Taube** *distant cousins* 4 **Jeffrey D. Wexler** 5 **Larry Horowitz**

MIXED: 6 **Marilyn Schmitt** (½ Ashkenazi + ½ Norwegian) 7 **Kitty Munson Cooper** (¼ Ashkenazi + ¼ German + ½ Norwegian)

W EUROPEAN: 8 **Mary Ellen Desmond** (Irish) 9 **Elizabeth Noyes** (English) 10 **Lawrence Munson** (Norwegian) *father of Kitty*

MIXED: 11 **Maryana Panyarskaya** (½ Russian + ¼ Ashkenazi + some Scandinavian)

E. EUROPEAN: 12 **Neonila Ruddenko** (Ukrainian + some mixed Slav and Jewish) 13 **Anna Rumianteeva** (Russian + some mixed Slav and Karelian) *12 and 13 being grandmother and mother of Maryana*

313

Table 24.3 Genetic admixture proportions from GEDmatch (after Davidski Eurogenes EU model)

NAME	1	2	3	4	5	6	7	8	9	10	11	12	13
	ASHKENAZI JEWS					MIXED		W EUROPEAN			MIXED	E EUROPEAN	
South Baltic	3.7	7.6	6.7	2.5	4.7	9.5	10.5	13.2	14.8	16.0	25.0	29.6	31.9
East European	6.0	1.7	0.6	5.1	5.2	5.7	9.3	10.1	11.0	13.8	21.4	20.2	26.2
North-Central Euro	11.1	9.9	10.1	9.8	8.7	20.1	26.4	27.9	27.5	30.1	14.7	17.4	17.5
Atlantic	10.9	11.8	11.9	8.3	10.6	15.4	20.6	30.4	26.2	25.1	12.6	12.5	12.6
West Mediter'n	14.3	12.3	15.2	15.3	13.7	14.3	11.6	11.9	12.9	8.6	8.6	8.2	3.0
East Mediter'n	25.7	30.5	27.7	30.4	31.7	17.6	10.0	-	4.0	-	6.1	4.0	2.6
West Asian	14.0	10.7	10.5	10.7	12.2	9.9	4.6	4.9	2.5	4.0	5.9	5.1	-
Middle Eastern	13.2	14.9	15.0	15.6	11.2	7.0	4.4	-	-	-	1.4	2.6	-
South Asian	-	-	-	0.6	0.3	-	1.9	1.6	1.1	1.1	1.0	0.1	1.8
East African	0.7	-	0.6	0.4	0.7	0.2	-	-	-	-	0.7	0.1	-
East Asian	-	-	1.4	-	0.2	-	0.2	-	-	-	-	-	-
Siberian	0.4	0.4	0.1	1.3	0.8	-	-	-	1.2	2.4	0.1	4.4	-

ASHKENAZI: 1 **Edward Gelles** *close cousins* 2 **Elsa Schmaus** 3 **Tad Taube** *distant cousins* 4 **Jeffrey D. Wexler** 5 **Larry Horowitz**
MIXED: 6 **Marilyn Schmitt** (½ Ashkenazi + ½ Norwegian), 7 **Kitty Munson Cooper** (¼ Ashkenazi + ¼ German + ½ Norwegian)
ATLANTIC: 8 **Mary Ellen Desmond** (Irish) 9 **Elizabeth Noyes** (English) 10 **Lawrence Munson** (Norwegian) *father of Kitty*
MIXED: 11 **Maryana Panyarskaya** (½ Russian + ¼ Ashkenazi + Scandinavian)
EAST EURO: 12 **Neonila Rudenko** (Ukrainian + some mixed Slav and Jewish)
13 **Anna Rumianteeva** (Russian + some mixed Slav and Karelian) *12 and 13 being grandmother and mother of Maryana*

Table 24.4 Single population sharing from autosomal DNA tests (distance in generations)

Ashkenazi		Irish	Norwegian	Russian
Edward Gelles Dodecad v3 Oracle	Edward Gelles Eurogenes EU Oracle	Mary Ellen Desmond Eurogenes EU Oracle	Lawrence Munson Eurogenes EU Oracle	Anna Rumianteeva Eurogenes EU Oracle
Ashkenazi Jews 3.01	Ashkenazi Jews 3.69	Irish 2.85	Norwegian 2.11	NW-Russian 5.82
Ashkenazi Jews 4.43	S-Italian 7.28	Orcadian 3.21	S&C Swedish 2.50	Belorussian 5.97
Morocco Jews 9.12	Greek 9.27	Scottish 3.82	Danish 3.98	East European 7.01
Tuscan 11.88	Tuscan 13.95	Cornish 3.93	Dutch 5.90	W-Russian 7.01
Tuscan 12.64	N-Italian 17.70	English 5.26	Orcadian 6.14	Ukrainian 7.35
TSI 13.05	Turkish 18.51	Dutch 6.18	English 6.53	N-Russian 7.58
O-Italian 13.85	Romanian 19.18	Danish 7,21	W&C-German 6.67	Lithuanian 8.49
Sicilian 13.99	Serbian 20.29	W&C-German 7.60	N-Swedish 6.70	East Russian 8.50
C-Italian 14.02	Iraqi 22.11	Norwegian 8.37	Irish 7.10	Ukrainian 8.67
Sephardic Jews 16.09	Assyrian 22.85	S&C-Swedish 9.24	Scottish 7.98	Polish 9.05
Sicilian 16.21	Portuguese 23.04	French 12.19	Cornish 8.08	East Finnish 9.31
Greek 16.59	Armenian 23.49	N-Swedish 13.20	Austrian 13.11	Erzya 10.39
S-Italian 17.17	Mandean 24.27	Austrian 14.50	South Finnish 15.74	South Finnish 11.26
Tuscan 19.75	Kurdish 24.41	Spanish 19.49	French 15.86	Udmurt 18.52
Romanian 20.30	Iranian 24.61	Hungarian 19.51	Hungarian 17.34	Komi 18.70
Uzbek Jews 20.55	Spanish 25.10	Portuguese 19.68	Polish 19.55	Hungarian 19.09
Turkish 21.09	Samaritan 25.21	South Finnish 21.82	East Finnish 20.80	North Swedish 19.34
N-Italian 21.56	Austrian 26.37	French Basque 22.35	Serbian 20.80	Austrian 22.29
Palestinian 22.07	Hungarian 26.54	Serbian 22.47	East European 21.07	S&C-Swedish 23.22
Lebanese 22.14	French 26.83	N-Italian 23.66	W-Russian 21.52	Serbian 23.48

315

Table 24.5 Mixed-mode population sharing for Ashkenazi –
Edward Gelles (Eurogenes EU Oracle test)

#	Primary population			Secondary population	Distance
1	93.9%	AJ	6.1%	Lezgin	3.03
2	95.2%	AJ	4.8%	German	3.24
3	95.3%	AJ	4.7%	Irish	3.26
4	95.6%	AJ	4.4%	Scottish	3.3
5	95.5%	AJ	4.5%	Orcadian	3.31
6	95.4%	AJ	4.6%	English	3.33
7	95.4%	AJ	4.6%	Cornish	3.34
8	95.8%	AJ	4.2%	Danish	3.36
9	95.4%	AJ	4.6%	Dutch	3.36
10	96.0%	AJ	4.0%	Norwegian	3.37
11	95.4%	AJ	4.6%	West & Central German	3.38
12	95.0%	AJ	5.0%	French	3.41
13	96.3%	AJ	3.7%	South & Central Swedish	3.41
14	96.6%	AJ	3.4%	North Swedish	3.45
15	96.7%	AJ	3.3%	French Basque	3.45
16	97.5%	AJ	2.5%	Kalash	3.47
17	91.9%	AJ	8.1%	Tuscan	3.49
18	95.8%	AJ	4.2%	Spanish	3.52
19	95.6%	AJ	4.4%	Portuguese	3.53
20	96.2%	AJ	3.8%	Austrian	3.54

Note:
AJ: Ashkenazi Jewish

Table 24.4 has a comparison via the Eurogenes EU Oracle test for single population sharing of the ancestral backgrounds of an Ashkenazi and of non-Jewish Irish, Norwegian, and Russian probands. All share some West and North European DNA but the strong Mediterranean and particularly the Italian admixture of the Ashkenazi is absent or muted in the other probands.

Tables 24.5–8 show results of a 'two population' approach for Edward Gelles, Mary Ellen Desmond (Irish), Lawrence Munson (Norwegian), and Anna Rumianteeva (Russian) using Eurogenes EU Oracle test. The listed secondary populations include affinities with some ethnic groups mainly in the Caucasus and on the Indian subcontinent whose basic details are to be found on Wikipedia. The genealogical background of the probands is to be found in the preceding Chapter 23 entitled 'X-DNA matches and European Roots'.

Tables 24.5a to 24.8a show the results of applying the more recent Eurogenes K36 model, which gives an overview of genetic admixture derived from relating the DNA data for individual probands to 36

Table 24.5a Edward Gelles: genetic admixture (Eurogenes K36)

Population	
Amerindian	–
Arabian	6.21%
Armenian	6.42%
Basque	1.28%
Central African	–
Central Euro	2.80%
East African	–
East Asian	–
East Balkan	2.99%
East Central Asian	–
East Central Euro	0.84%
East Med	10.00%
Eastern Euro	–
Fennoscandian	2.91%
French	0.73%
Iberian	10.59%
Indo-Chinese	–
Italian	13.73%
Malayan	–
Near Eastern	15.76%
North African	2.55%
North Atlantic	5.99%
North Caucasian	4.31%
North Sea	3.85%
Northeast African	–
Oceanian	0.26%
Omotic	–
Pygmy	–
Siberian	–
South Asian	–
South Central Asian	–
South Chinese	–
Volga-Ural	0.53%
West African	–
West Caucasian	3.42%
West Med	4.84%

Table 24.6 Mixed-mode population sharing for Irish –
Mary Ellen Desmond (Eurogenes EU Oracle test)

#	Primary population		Secondary population		Distance
1	98.1%	Irish	1.9%	Sardinian	2.68
2	96.3%	Irish	3.7%	French Basque	2.72
3	77.9%	Irish	22.1%	Cornish	2.73
4	93.8%	Irish	6.2%	French	2.74
5	96.6%	Irish	3.4%	Spanish	2.77
6	96.9%	Irish	3.1%	Portuguese	2.78
7	87.8%	Irish	12.2%	English	2.78
8	99.4%	Irish	0.6%	South Indian	2.79
9	93.5%	Orcadian	6.5%	French Basque	2.82
10	95.0%	Irish	5.0%	Dutch	2.83
11	99.5%	Irish	0.5%	Mozabite Berber	2.83
12	99.6%	Irish	0.4%	Bangladeshi	2.84
13	99.5%	Irish	0.5%	Moroccan	2.84
14	99.0%	Irish	1.0%	North Italian	2.84
15	99.7%	Irish	0.3%	Gujarati	2.84
16	99.7%	Irish	0.3%	Indian	2.84
17	99.9%	Irish	0.1%	Tuscan	2.85
18	97.6%	Irish	2.4%	Orcadian	2.85
19	100%	Irish	0%	Algerian	2.85
20	100%	Irish	0%	Ashkenazi Jew	2.85

bio-geographical reference groups. While bearing in mind that the results from the K36 model are not to be taken as more than a rough and ready indicator, it is interesting to compare them with those from the Eurogenes EU Oracle.

To take, for example, the genetic admixture of Edward Gelles shown in Tables 24.5 and 24.5a. In the first, the mixed-mode population sharing Eurogenes EU Oracle model, we see Edward Gelles as largely 'Ashkenazi' with traces of affinity to secondary populations including Lezgin (west of the Caspian Sea) and Kalash (north-west India), perhaps recalling influences of the ancient dispersion of the ten lost tribes of Israel by the Assyrians and of later migrations from the Caucasus and from the time of Alexander the Great. A similar chart for my mixed-mode population sharing using the Dodecad v3 model also suggests some small Arabian and Moorish affinities.

Table 24.6a Mary Ellen Desmond: genetic admixture (Eurogenes K36)

Population	
Amerindian	0.27%
Arabian	–
Armenian	–
Basque	6.14%
Central African	–
Central Euro	8.77%
East African	–
East Asian	–
East Balkan	2.11%
East Central Asian	–
East Central Euro	6.57%
East Med	–
Eastern Euro	4.25%
Fennoscandian	7.49%
French	6.90%
Iberian	14.54%
Indo-Chinese	–
Italian	0.57%
Malayan	–
Near Eastern	–
North African	–
North Atlantic	20.54%
North Caucasian	0.61%
North Sea	18.68%
Northeast African	–
Oceanian	–
Omotic	–
Pygmy	–
Siberian	–
South Asian	–
South Central Asian	2.44%
South Chinese	–
Volga-Ural	–
West African	–
West Caucasian	0.11%
West Med	–

In Table 24.5a the K36 model breaks down 'Ashkenazi' into contributory European and Eastern DNA. The overall picture is a genetic admixture with roughly half European and half Eastern affinities.

The largest constituents of my admixture according to Table 24.5a are Near Eastern, Italian, Iberian, and East Mediterranean. The

Table 24.7 Mixed-mode population sharing for Norwegian –
Lawrence Munson (Eurogenes EU Oracle test)

#	Primary population		Secondary population		Distance
1	78.8%	South & Central Swedish	21.2%	Irish	1.67
2	76.9%	South & Central Swedish	23.1%	Orcadian	1.76
3	81.8%	South & Central Swedish	18.2%	Scottish	1.79
4	99.0%	Norwegian	1.0%	South Indian	1.91
5	98.8%	Norwegian	1.2%	Gujarati	1.93
6	98.8%	Norwegian	1.2%	Indian	1.93
7	87.3%	Norwegian	12.7%	Orcadian	1.94
8	98.8%	Norwegian	1.2%	Bangladeshi	1.94
9	89.0%	Norwegian	11.0%	Irish	1.94
10	90.3%	Norwegian	9.7%	Scottish	1.94
11	98.7%	Norwegian	1.3%	Sindhi	1.96
12	83.5%	South & Central Swedish	16.5%	Cornish	1.96
13	98.7%	Norwegian	1.3%	Burusho	1.97
14	98.8%	Norwegian	1.2%	Kalash	2
15	80.7%	South & Central Swedish	19.3%	English	2
16	99.4%	Norwegian	0.6%	Nganassan	2.01
17	99.3%	Norwegian	0.7%	Koryak	2.01
18	98.9%	Norwegian	1.1%	Balochi	2.02
19	92.5%	Norwegian	7.5%	Cornish	2.02
20	98.9%	Norwegian	1.1%	Brahui	2.02

small but significant contributions designated as North Sea (UK,
Ireland etc.), North Atlantic, and Fennoscandian (Scandinavia and
Baltic) are of particular interest to me as drawing attention to clues
from unfinished genealogical work.

SUMMARY AND CONCLUSION

The pilot study described in this and the preceding chapter sets
out to determine whether some commercially available DNA tests
and computations based on their results can provide a simple and
convenient way of obtaining some insight into genetic admixture
proportions of Ashkenazi Jews.

Table 24.7a Lawrence Munson: genetic admixture (Eurogenes K36)

Population	
Amerindian	–
Arabian	–
Armenian	–
Basque	2.83%
Central African	–
Central Euro	6.72%
East African	–
East Asian	–
East Balkan	3.09%
East Central Asian	–
East Central Euro	8.58%
East Med	–
Eastern Euro	5.77%
Fennoscandian	14.06%
French	4.77%
Iberian	4.96%
Indo-Chinese	–
Italian	3.83%
Malayan	–
Near Eastern	–
North African	–
North Atlantic	18.16%
North Caucasian	0.26%
North Sea	23.80%
Northeast African	–
Oceanian	0.58%
Omotic	–
Pygmy	–
Siberian	–
South Asian	–
South Central Asian	1.47%
South Chinese	–
Volga-Ural	0.64%
West African	–
West Caucasian	–
West Med	0.42%

I found that some close cousins of mine and others who could be described as of Ashkenazi Jewish descent unexpectedly showed X-DNA matches with a number of non-Jewish West and East Europeans. From the known genealogical background of these probands I tentatively concluded that the matches might be attributed to fairly distant connections, perhaps going back to the time of the great Norse migrations. The X-DNA study (outlined in Chapter 23) has brief notes on the family backgrounds of some of these probands, who are also involved in the comparison of genetic admixture proportions of European Jews and Gentiles that is presented in Tables 24.2–8 of the present chapter.

GEDmatch website facilities include several models for deriving genetic mixture proportions, namely Dienekes Pontikos Dodecad v3 and several Davidski models, such as Eurogenes EU and Eurogenes

Table 24.8 Mixed-mode population sharing for Russian – Anna Rumianteeva (Eurogenes EU Oracle test)

#	Primary population		Secondary population		Distance
1	93.0%	Belorussian	7.0%	Selkup	3.11
2	93.4%	Northwest Russian	6.6%	Selkup	3.24
3	64.4%	Northwest Russian	35.6%	East Finnish	3.27
4	95.9%	Northwest Russian	4.1%	Nganassan	3.49
5	53.5%	North Russian	46.5%	Lithuanian	3.5
6	95.1%	Northwest Russian	4.9%	Chukchi	3.52
7	95.3%	Northwest Russian	4.7%	Koryak	3.53
8	80.0%	Northwest Russian	20.0%	Komi	3.58
9	58.3%	Belorussian	41.7%	North Russian	3.6
10	79.5%	Belorussian	20.5%	Komi	3.64
11	95.9%	Belorussian	4.1%	Nganassan	3.69
12	79.6%	Belorussian	20.4%	Udmurt	3.76
13	95.2%	Belorussian	4.8%	Chukchi	3.8
14	95.3%	Belorussian	4.7%	Koryak	3.82
15	52.8%	Lithuanian	47.2%	East Finnish	3.87
16	50.0%	Lithuanian	50.0%	East Russian	3.87
17	80.8%	Northwest Russian	19.2%	Udmurt	3.95
18	70.9%	Lithuanian	29.1%	Komi	3.95
19	60.2%	Northwest Russian	39.8%	North Russian	3.96
20	70.7%	Lithuanian	29.3%	Udmurt	3.96

Table 24.8a Anna Rumianteeva: genetic admixture (Eurogenes K36)

Population	
Amerindian	–
Arabian	–
Armenian	–
Basque	–
Central African	0.13%
Central Euro	7.64%
East African	–
East Asian	–
East Balkan	2.68%
East Central Asian	–
East Central Euro	24.13%
East Med	0.88%
Eastern Euro	22.71%
Fennoscandian	23.26%
French	1.44%
Iberian	–
Indo-Chinese	–
Italian	2.13%
Malayan	–
Near Eastern	–
North African	–
North Atlantic	5.54%
North Caucasian	–
North Sea	4.52%
Northeast African	–
Oceanian	–
Omotic	–
Pygmy	–
Siberian	1.73%
South Asian	0.83%
South Central Asian	–
South Chinese	–
Volga-Ural	2.37%
West African	–
West Caucasian	–
West Med	–

K36. These take the autosomal DNA data of probands and relate them to differing sets of bio-geographical reference populations. For the purposes of my initial pilot study, I have been concerned with a broad comparison of Ashkenazi Jews with non-Jewish West and East Europeans, and in each of the several models I used for these comparisons the three groups of probands stood out clearly from each other. The Ashkenazi probands included my close cousins, whose Jewish ancestry I knew from my traditional methodology, and distant cousins who certainly had at least four fully Jewish grandparents. The family background of non-Jewish probands was kindly provided by the families concerned and their belief in the absence of Jewish ancestry was supported by the Eurogenes J test that is specifically designed to show up any significant Ashkenazi admixture.

My tables show a well-defined profile for some Ashkenazi Jews in a pattern that is repeated in my tests of many other Jewish probands. A comparison with the numerous non-Jewish probands suggests that Ashkenazi Jews typically have a mixed European and Eastern genetic make-up, as indeed many earlier comparative Y-DNA and mtDNA studies have also indicated. This is broadly consistent with the history of their millennial migrations. The typical Ashkenazi European–Eastern mixture seems to be about 40:60, with a fair degree of regional and individual variation. Generally, higher Mediterranean and North-West African, and lower East European admixture levels are distinguishing Ashkenazi indicators as compared with the typical non-Jewish West and East Europeans. Probands who are known to have a recent mixed genetic background are immediately identifiable. Indeed, I have frequently spotted a non-Jewish grandparent from a proband's genetic admixture proportions as thrown up by GEDmatch.

Smaller variations from the typical Ashkenazi admixture reflect the extent to which they carry DNA from their ancestral connections with Sephardi, Moroccan, and Mizrachi Jews, from earlier times in the Middle East, Anatolia, the Caucasus, the Persian Empire, and the Mediterranean littoral. Ashkenazi Jews are considered to be primarily of German medieval origin, but their European background is made up from many strands dictated by a history in Europe that stretches across the continent from the Atlantic to the Urals and from the Baltic to the Black Sea. Romans, Visigoths, Franks, and Normans, and many others crossed paths with Jews in the West before later migrations brought some of our forebears to eastern Europe.

My background is predominantly Ashkenazi, the European–Eastern mixture of which the preceding tables have illustrated. The affinity of my DNA to that of secondary populations suggests interesting traces of early forebears from the Caucasus and India. The test shows Scandinavian and British traces that are also seen with the West European probands.

The Irish and Norwegian probands have substantial admixtures of sundry European origin, including Cornish and English, and Irish, Orcadian, Scottish, English, and Cornish respectively. Both probands also relate to traces of Indian secondary populations. The Russian proband has substantial Finnish admixture. Her paternal grandmother was from Karelia and there are numerous Scandinavian cousins from this source. There are also a variety of traces from small ethnic groups in various parts of Russia and Siberia.

The genetic admixture data go well with the results of X-DNA matches presented in the preceding chapter. The overall conclusion is that these test facilities on the GEDmatch website can provide a useful accessory tool for the genealogist and family historian and an introduction to deeper enquiries in the field of genetic anthropology.

ONLINE RESOURCES

Aristotle in Jewish Legend (Jewish Encyclopedia – online)
Jews and Alexander the Great (Jewish Encyclopedia, etc.)
Ten Lost Tribes of Israel (Wikipedia – with references)
History of the Jews in India (Wikipedia – with references)
Jews in the Caucasus (Wikipedia, Jewish Encyclopedia, etc.)
Persian Jews (Wikipedia and many other websites)
History of the Jews in the Arabian Peninsula (Wikipedia – with references)
Khazaria (Wikipedia and many other websites) www.khazaria.com/genetics/abstracts.html (a useful summary of recent work in Jewish genetic genealogy)
Genetic Genealogy
Genealogical DNA test
Family Tree DNA
23andme
Ancestry.com
GEDmatch
Dienekes Pontikos

Eurogenes Davidski

DNA, Ancestry, and Human Migration

'Using Genome-Wide SNP scans to explore your genetic heritage', *The Genetic Genealogist*, August 2010.

Top 10 things to do with your FTDNA raw data (June 16, 2011)

Ellen Levy-Coffman, 'A Mosaic of People: The Jewish Story and a Reassessment of the DNA Evidence', *Journal of Genetic Genealogy* (2007): www.jogg.info/11/coffman.htm.

J.W. Holliday, 'The Mystery of Ashkenazic Origins', http://majorityrights.com/weblog/comments/the_mystery_of_ashkenazic_origins/ – critique of the above article.

Marta D. Costa *et al.*, 'A Substantial Prehistoric European Ancestry Amongst Ashkenazi Maternal Lineages', *Nature Communications*, Vol. 4, 2543 (8 October 2013).

Garret Hellenthal *et al.*, 'A Genetic Atlas of Human Admixture History', *Science*, 14 February 2014, Vol. 343, No. 6172, pp. 747–51, www.sciencemag.org.

Shai Carmi *et al.*, 'Sequencing an Ashkenazi Reference Panel Supports Population-Targeted Personal Genomics and Illuminates Jewish and European Origins', *Nature Communications* Vol. 5, 4835 doi:10.1038/ncomms5835 (published 9 September 2014) (DNA study of large group of Ashkenazi probands and group of non-Jewish Europeans – supports Ashkenazi descent from a few hundred people at the time of a genetic bottleneck about 600 to 800 years ago).

Jeffrey D. Wexler, web master of the LeviteDNA website that has up-to-date references to current work on a variety of Jewish DNA topics.

Epilogue

Who am I and where did I come from?

This volume describes my personal odyssey in search for answers to the above questions and the bearing these have on the history of European Jewry.

Incursions from Asia and North Africa and millennial migrations within the continent led to the admixture of peoples in the Europe we know today, with its legacies of Greece, Rome, and Israel, of classical culture and Judeo-Christian ethics, as well as reminders of other occasionally potent influences.

From earliest childhood in Vienna I took my cultural heritage to have European and Jewish strands. The *Anschluss* of Austria to Hitler's *Third Reich* in 1938 brought home to me the pernicious pseudo-scientific theories of race which had their origins in the nineteenth-century rise of nationalism and were enthusiastically developed by the Nazi regime, with catastrophic consequences for the Jews and lasting damage to European culture. We now know that the idea of a superior Aryan race and inferior races is absurd and that Europeans, of whatever origin and religious affiliation, are the result of millennial genetic admixture. Recent studies of Ashkenazi Jews show that they have a distinct genetic profile. Their roughly similar proportions of Eastern and European DNA is thought to be the result of genetic bottlenecks that occurred in Europe hundreds of years ago. Their admixture has particular affinities to that of both European and Eastern peoples of the Mediterranean littoral.

My parents told me very little about our family background. I was not very interested at the time and in retrospect I believe that they were merely passing on oral traditions. Nevertheless, these are worth recording here because they became relevant 60 years later when I finally embarked on a deep genealogical study of my ancestry.

My father, who was expected to become a rabbi following in his paternal line, spent some time studying at the Munkacz Yeshiva in Hungary before breaking away from his ultra-orthodox parents in his quest for a secular education. He studied economics at Czernowitz under Professor Joseph Schumpeter and continued his law studies at the University of Vienna where he obtained his degree of Dr Juris. He mentioned that our rabbinic line came from Brody in Galicia and he quite often quoted sayings from the Talmud, Rabbi Akiva of old being the name I most vividly recall. He talked more frequently about Moses Mendelssohn. At the time I attributed this to the enthusiasm of Jewish students of his day for the great emancipator of the Age of Enlightenment. But there may be more to that, as emerged much later.

My mother also came from an ultra-orthodox Galician family, but by the time of her marriage in Vienna in 1921, she and my father were equally assimilated to liberal Viennese standards. My maternal grandmother was of a family which was generally acknowledged to be descended from Saul Wahl, the sixteenth-century Jewish community leader who, according to legend, was supposed to have been *Rex pro tempore* during the Polish interregnum of 1587. My mother told me occasionally that we were of royal descent, but she was rather diffident about the details. At the time I thought she was referring to Saul Wahl. I think she was rather hurt that I did not take the story very seriously. But again, more than half a century later, it has assumed a rather different complexion.

These tenuous recollections and my reading of standard Jewish histories (Graetz and Dubnow) were the starting points for studies presented in this volume and in my previous books. I was particularly intrigued by the comments of Simon Dubnow, who called the alleged election of Saul Wahl to be king for a day a bizarre whim of the Polish Szlachta (the noble electors).

My first published article on Saul Wahl described how his rise to eminence in sixteenth-century Poland was not due to a 'bizarre whim'. It had more to do with his descent from an ancient family who became Chief Rabbis of Padua and Venice and to his education at the University of Padua, which was the *alma mater* of influential Polish noblemen, including the Chancellor Jan Zamoyski. Saul's biblical learning may have impressed them in this Age of Faith, and the patronage of the great Lithuanian nobleman Prince Radziwill is believed to have furthered his career as a major entrepreneur and contributor to the Polish–Lithuanian economy.

Among sources for my continuing researches was the hagiographical work on Saul Wahl and his family written in the early eighteenth century by his direct descendant, Rabbi Pinchas Katzenellenbogen, passages of which I have subjected to critical review. It casts an interesting light on the traditions current in my mother's family. The most important source which opened up research on my paternal Brody line was a fragment of the Records of the Rabbinical Court of Brody. My published work describes archival and other searches across Europe and the very great variety of sources that have come to be drawn upon in these studies.

My family tree has connections to many ancient rabbinic lines – Gelles, Jaffe, Horowitz, Chajes, Halpern, Shapiro, Katzenellenbogen, Wahl, Loew, Margolioth, HaKohen, and many others. Several of these lines go back to the Treivish rabbis of medieval France, to the eleventh-century Rabbi of Troyes known as Rashi, who is widely believed to be of royal Davidic descent, and then to the Kalonymos, Princes of Narbonne, with their putative connections to the Carolingian dynasty and to their Iberian cousins, the Shem Tov Halevi and Benveniste.

Some parts of this grand tapestry are well documented, like the descent from my direct paternal ancestor, the early eighteenth-century scholar of the Brody Klaus, Moses Menachem Mendel Levush, known as Moses Gelles after his marriage to a daughter of Rabbi Samuel Gelles. Other connections, such as my links to the sixteenth-century Chief Rabbis of Prague, are based on less specific genealogical evidence.

My undoubted connections to the Rhineland, the heartland of medieval Ashkenaz, still await archival documentation, but are strikingly shown by strong DNA matches with a nexus of well-documented families including latter-day Guggenheim, Oppenheim, Wertheimer, Salomon, Stern, Rothschild, and others. Moses Mendelssohn and I have a common ancestor in Saul Wahl, while the philosopher's grandson, the composer Felix Mendelssohn-Bartholdy also shares with me several other notable ancestors, including Rabbi Mordecai Jaffe of Prague and Pinchas Halevi Ish Horowitz, the one-time President of the Council of the Four Lands, which acted as the semi-autonomous governing body of Polish Jewry.

In summary, my genealogical research, including pilot studies in genetic genealogy and anthropology using commercial DNA tests, is largely supportive of historical accounts. My wider family roots go back to the Middle East, Anatolia, and the Caucasus, and to Italy, Spain and Portugal, south-western and northern France, the Rhineland and the Low Countries. Later we were in Bohemia and other parts of the Austro-Hungarian Empire and in eastern Europe extending to Silesia, Poland, and Lithuania, Galicia, Bukowina, Ukraine, and beyond. There are affinities relating to the Moorish invasion of Spain and there are also traces of Scandinavian and British connections. A truly pan-European journey stretching over more than two millennia.

There were long periods of Jewish endogamy, but at other times there was widespread admixture, particularly in the Mediterranean littoral. The fourteenth- and fifteenth-century persecutions in Spain and Portugal gave rise to much conversion and subsequent intermarriage, as well as to the migration of Sephardic Jews to Holland and then to England, and also to the Ottoman Empire, where many settled in Salonica and the Greek Islands.

An instance of later mass conversion was that of the Polish Frankists in the mid eighteenth century. These followers of Jacob Frank, who were excommunicated for heresy by the orthodox rabbis, were welcomed by the Catholic Church in their thousands and many later intermarried with the Polish nobility.

The story of the families in my extended family circle could be taken as a paradigm for the millennial history of European Jews. My emphasis has been on Ashkenazi families, but many of these could look back to some ancient Sephardic and Mizrachi connections. During this history, which saw long periods of segregation, persecutions, and expulsions in different parts of our continent, Jews and Christians co-existed with a greater or lesser degree of economic and cultural interaction and also intermittently continued a process of genetic admixture.

Since the Age of Emancipation in the eighteenth century, an increasing number of people with Jewish backgrounds have made major contributions to the secular culture of our continent – pre-eminently in philosophy, sociology, economics, medicine, jurisprudence, mathematics, natural science, literature, and music. Some of these distinguished Europeans have been introduced in this volume in the context of setting the results of modern genealogical enquiry against the background of our continent's social and cultural history.

Jews flourished in western and central Europe a long time ago. Indeed, they have been called 'the first Europeans' in a cultural sense. My present inter-disciplinary study could contribute to a discussion of that proposition.

Published work on genealogy and history by Edward Gelles 2000–13

BOOKS

1   *An Ancient Lineage: European Roots of a Jewish Family: Gelles – Griffel – Wahl – Chajes – Safier – Loew – Taube.* London: Vallentine Mitchell, July 2006 (**ISBN** 0 85 303 680 2).

2   *Family Connections: Gelles – Horowitz – Chajes: A Genealogical Study.* The Netherlands: Shaker Publishing, February 2008 (**ISBN** 978 90 423 0338 6).

3   *Family Connections: Gelles – Shapiro – Friedman.* The Netherlands: Shaker Publishing, June 2009 (**ISBN** 978 90 423 0370 6).

4   *Ephemeral and Eternal: Josef Gelles – A Brief Life.* The Netherlands: Shaker Publishing, June 2010 (**ISBN** 978 90 423 0392 8).

5   *Meeting my Ancestors: Genealogy, Genes, and Heritage.* The Netherlands: Shaker Publishing, March 2011 (**ISBN** 978 90 423 0403 1).

6   *The Jewish Journey: A Passage Through European History.* London: I.B. Tauris, 2016 (**ISBN** 978 1 78453 453 0).

ARTICLES

2000

1   Saul Wahl: A Jewish Legend, *Judaism Today*, No. 14, Winter 1999–2000.

2   In Search of My Pedigree, *Shemot*, Vol. 8, No. 2, June 2000.

3   The Wahls of Nadworna, *Shemot*, Vol. 8, No. 3, September 2000.

4   Chief Rabbis in the Genes, *Manna*, No. 69, Autumn 2000.

5   All Quiet on the Eastern Front, *Avotaynu*, Vol. 16, No. 4, Winter 2000.

2001

6   Searching for Eve: A Methodological Lesson, *Avotaynu*, Vol. 17, No. 2, Summer 2001.

7   Galician Roots, *The Galitzianer*, Vol. 9, No. 1, November 2001.

2002

8   Capitalists and Rabbis, *The Galitzianer*, Vol. 9, No. 2, February 2002.

9   Economic Background to some Family Links, *The Galitzianer*, Vol. 9, No. 3, May 2002.

10 Finding Rabbi Moses Gelles, *Avotaynu*, Vol. 18, No. 1, Spring 2002.

11 Abraham Low's Ship's Manifest, *Shemot*, Vol. 10, No. 2, June 2002.

12 Genealogy for Moral Support, *The Galitzianer*, Vol. 9, No. 4, August 2002.

13 The Safiers of Tarnobrzeg, *Shemot*, Vol. 10, No. 3, September 2002.

14 My Mother's People, *Sharsheret Hadorot*, Vol. 16, No. 4, October 2002.

15 A Tale of Two Cities, *The Galitzianer*, Vol. 10, No. 1, November 2002.

2003

16 My Father's People, *Sharsheret Hadorot*, Vol. 17, No. 1, February 2003.

17 The Wohls of Krakow, *The Galitzianer*, Vol. 10, No. 2, February 2003.

18 Davidic Descent, *Sharsheret Hadorot*, Vol. 17, No. 2, June 2003.

19 A Nineteenth Century Pictorial Record of Brody, *The Galitzianer*, Vol. 10, No. 4, August 2003.

2004

20 David and Chaim Gans of Prague, *Shemot*, Vol. 12, No. 1, March 2004.

21 Rabbi Shmuel Hillman of Metz and his Family Connections, *Sharsheret Hadorot*, Vol. 18, No. 2, May 2004.

22 Chayes Family Connections, *Shemot*, Vol. 12, No. 2, June 2004.

23 Jewish Community Life in Brody, *Sharsheret Hadorot*, Vol. 18, No. 4, November 2004.

2005

24 Genealogical Background of some Hasidic Sages, *Sharsheret Hadorot*, Vol. 19, No. 1, February 2005.

25 Rabbis of Solotwina near Stanislau, *Sharsheret Hadorot*, Vol. 19, No. 4, November 2005.

2006

26 Gelles of Brody and some Fraenkel-Horowitz Connections, *Sharsheret Hadorot*, Vol. 20, No. 1, February 2006.

27 Marriages between some Rabbinic Families in Galicia, *The Galitzianer*, Vol. 14, No. 1, November 2006.

2007

28 They Met in Trieste, *Everton's Genealogical Helper*, Sept/Oct 2007.

2008

29 From the Baltic to the Black Sea, *Sharsheret Hadorot*, Vol. 22, No. 2, May 2008.

30 Die Familie Chajes und ihre genealogischen Verbindunge, *'Adler' Zeitschrift für Genealogie und Heraldik*, Vol. 25, No. 4, 2008.

31 End of the Gelles Rabbinic Line, *The Galitzianer*, Vol. 16, No. 1, November 2008.

2010

Postcards and other ephemera in genealogical research

32 Josef and Giza Gelles of Boryslaw, *The Galitzianer*, Vol. 17, No. 2, February 2010.
33 Josef Gelles and the Solotwina Rabbinate, *The Galitzianer*, Vol. 17, No. 3, May 2010.
34 DNA Tests in the Search for Common Ancestors Genes and Genealogy of the Gelles and Polonsky Families (with Jeffrey Mark Paull), *The Galitzianer*, Vol. 18, No. 1, November 2010.

2011–12

35 DNA tests and common ancestors, *The Galitzianer*, Vol. 18, No. 2, February 2011.
36 Mes liens ancestraux avec la France, *GEN AMI*, No. 57, September 2011.
37 Autosomal DNA Matches Between Close Cousins: The Genetic Heritage of Some Galician Families. A précis is in *The Galitzianer*, Vol. 19, No. 1, March 2012. The full article is on the JewishGen website: www.jewishgen.org/galicia/assets/images/AutosomalDNAmatches.pdf.
38 Autosomal DNA and Genetic Origins of Some Ashkenazi Cousins. The article is on the JewishGen website: www.jewishgen.org/galicia/assets/images/AutosomalAshkenazi.pdf.
39 Jewish Community Life in Brody, *The Galitzianer*, Vol. 19, No. 3, September 2012.

2013

40 Capitalists and Rabbis, *The Galitzianer*, Vol. 20, No. 1, March 2013.

Glossary

Admor	Chasidic rabbi/community leader
Agudas	Society or party, e.g. Agudas Israel
Amoraim	Talmudic sages
Ashkenazi	Jew of German extraction/pertaining to central and East European Jewry
Arendar	Purchaser of a licence to run an estate with the benefit of specified monopoly rights
Av Beth Din	Rabbinical head of the religious court of a community – abbreviated ABD
Avot	Forefathers
Beit Hamidrash	House of study
bat	daughter of
ben	son of
Besht	Israel ben Eliezer, known as the Baal Shem Tov, founder of the eighteenth-century Chasidic movement
Chabad	Lubavich branch of Chasidic movement
Chacham	Title of Sephardic Rabbi/a wise man
Charif	Sharp-witted, cf. Witteles, Spitzkopf, Chacham
Chasidim	Members of the Chasidic movement
Chazan	Synagogue overseer/cantor
Chevra Kadisha	Burial society
Chidushei	Novellae

Court Jews	Jews accorded special privileges and sometimes titles of nobility by various European rulers for financial and other services (mainly in the seventeenth and eighteenth centuries)
Dayan	Judge, a member of the Rabbinical Court
Diaspora	Greek word for dispersion – the worldwide dispersion of the Jews
Dönmeh	Followers of the false messiah Shabbatai Zvi in the Ottoman Empire
Emunah	Belief
Frankists	Members of the Jewish sect led by Jacob Frank (1726–91). Also called Zoharists after the mystical work that inspired them. Most became Catholic converts c.1760.
Gabbai	Elected head of a synagogue
Gaon	Ancient title given to heads of academies/ rabbinical eminence
Gedulat	Greatness of
Gemarrah	Later scholarly dictums of the oral law
Ghetto	Quarter of a city to which Jews were restricted
Golah	Exile/emigration
Haggada	Legend, anecdote, or parable of rabbinic literature
Halakha	Jewish religious law
Haskalah	Jewish enlightenment of eighteenth and early nineteenth centuries
Herem	Excommunication
Kabbalah	Tradition/an ancient corpus of Jewish mysticism and esoteric knowledge
Kahal/Kehillot	Jewish community/communities
Keneset	Gatherings
Khazaria	Tribal kingdom north of the Black Sea that flourished in the seventh–tenth century. Some of its Turkic ruling class converted to Judaism in the ninth century
Kinnui	Nickname or secular given name
Klaus	Collegiate house of study
Kohen/Kohanim	Of the priestly caste – descendants of Aaron, the High Priest
Levi/Levites	Members of the tribe of Levi that included the priests Kohanim (called HaKohen, Katz, Kahane) and their assistants (called Halevi, Halevi Segal, or Segal)

Maggid	Preacher
Manhig	Community leader, see Parnas
Marranos	Iberian converts to Christianity who remained hidden Jews
Maskilim	Members of the Halakha
Mechutan	Relationship of the parents of a married couple
Megilla	Scroll
Melamed	Teacher
Meorei	Luminaries
Midrash	Expositions of the written law/commentary
Mishna	The first section of the Talmud – oral law
Mitnagim	Jewish opponents of Chasidism
Mishpachot	Families
Mizrachi	Jew of Middle Eastern extraction
Moreh	Religious teacher
Nasi	Prince or president/also a rabbinical title more honorific than ABD
Ne'eman	Treasurer/secretary of community
Nefesh	Soul
Parnas	Warden of community
Parochet	Curtain covering the Holy Ark in synagogue
Pilpul	Dialectic used in the exposition of the Talmud
Pinkas	Community record
Pogrom	Russian word for destruction or devastation
Rabbi	Religious teacher/also title for religious leader of community
Reb	Courtesy title of a gentleman
Rebbe	Title of Chasidic Rabbi
Rebetzin	Title of Rabbi's wife
Romaniot	Jew of Byzantine extraction
Rosh	Head, e.g. Rosh Yeshivah – Head of the Yeshiva
Ruach	Spirit – ancient Israelites described the soul as composed of three parts, Ruach, Nefesh, and Neshamah
Sanhedrin	Jewish High Court of 71 elders in ancient times
Schul	Yiddish colloquial for Synagogue
Sefardi	Jew of Iberian extraction
Sefer	Book
Sefiroth	Ten emanations or divine attributes of the Kabbalah
Sha'ar	Gate
Shabbataians	Followers of Shabbatai Zevi (1626–76), who influenced the later Frankists

Shamash	Synagogue beadle
Shechinah	The divine presence
She'er	Remnant
Shem	Name
Shtadlan	Negotiator with authorities on behalf of a Jewish community
Shtetl	Little town
Talmud	Body of Jewish oral law comprising the Mishna and Gamarrah
Tannaim	Sages of the Mishna
Targum	Aramaic exposition of the written law
Tikkun	Restoration of harmony in the universe – a concept of the Lurianic Kabbalah
Torah	Instruction or Divine Law/the Pentateuch
Vaad arba arazot	Council of the Four Lands – the semi-autonomous governing body of Polish Jewry for two centuries
Yahrzeit	Anniversary of death
Yeshiva	Talmudic academy of higher learning
Yichus	Pedigree or lineage
Yizkor	Memorial prayer
Yochasin	Genealogical tree
Zaddik	Saint/title of Chasidic master
Zikaron	Memorial
Zimzum	Contraction of the Infinite (En Sof) – a concept of the Lurianic Kabbalah

SOME WELL-KNOWN RABBINICAL TEXTS AND THEIR AUTHORS

Ahavat Zion	*Love of Zion* (Moses Ashkenazi Halpern)
Bayis Chadash	*New House* (Joel Sirkes)
Chelkas Mekokek	*Staff of the Lawgiver* (Moses Lima)
Da'at Kedoshim	*Knowledge of the Holy Ones* (I.T. Eisenstadt)
Levushim	*Garments or Robes of Learning* (Mordecai Yaffe)
Ma'alot Hayochasin	*Steps of Pedigree* (Ephraim Zalman Margolis)
Megaleh Amukot	*Revealed Depths* (Nathan Nata Shapiro)
Meginei Shlomo	*Shields of Solomon* (Yehoshua Heschel of Krakow)
Ohalei Shem	*Tents of Names*, i.e. notables or men of learning (Shmuel Nach Gottlieb)
Otzar Harabbanim	*Treasury of Rabbis* (Nathan Zvi Friedman)
Pnei Yehoshua	*Face of Yoshua* (Jacob Joshua of Frankfurt)

Seder Hadoroth	*Order of Generations* (Jechiel Heilprin)
Shem Hagedolim	*Names of the Great Ones* (Chaim Joseph David Azulai)
Siftei Kohen	*(From) the Lips of a Priest* (Shabbatai Katz)
Toldot Anshei Shem	*Generations of men of note* (David Tebele Efrati)
Letoldot Hakehillot	*Generations of Polish communities*
Bepolin	(Zvi Hirsch Horowitz)
Tevuot Shor	*Produce of the Ox* (Alexander Sender Shor)
Tosafot Yomtov	*Additions of Yomtov* (Yomtov Lipmann Heller)
Turei Zahav	*Rows of Gold* (David Halevi Segal)
Yesh Manhilin	*Some Bequeath* (Phineas Katzenellenbogen)
Zemach David	*Sprig of David* (David Gans)
Zohar	*Splendour* – work of Jewish mysticism (attributed to Moses de Leon of Granada (d. *c.*1305))

GENETIC GENEALOGY

cM	Centimorgan is a unit which is used to measure genetic distance
DNA	Deoxyribonucleic acid encodes genetic instructions used in the development and functioning of all living organisms (see Chapters 21–23 for the applications of different types of DNA tests to genetic genealogy)
proband	A person serving as the starting point for the genetic study of a family
SNP	Single Nucleotide Polymorphism, a change in DNA code at a specific point or locus
STR	Short Tandem Repeat short sequences of DNA that are repeated numerous times in a head-to-tail manner. With STRs the polymorphisms are due to the different number of copies of the repeat element that can occur in a group of individuals.
allele	A genetic variant at a specific point (locus) in the genetic code
ROH	Runs of homozygosity. Identical alleles relating to a trait – as in dominant alleles from each parent – are said to be homozygous. ROH are contiguous lengths of homozygous genotypes that are present in an individual due to parents transmitting identical haplotypes to their offspring. (See Chapter 21 for estimates of the degree of relationship between an individual's parents based on ROH analysis.)

Index

Page numbers in *italics* refer to photographs or charts.

Spelling of some family names sometimes vary for different reasons, for example Gelles / Gellis / Gelis, Jaffe / Yoffe / Yofe, and Chajes / Chayes / Chayut.